DESPERATE VALOUR

DESPERATE VALOUR

TRIUMPH AT ANZIO

FLINT WHITLOCK
Author of *The Rock of Anzio*

DA CAPO PRESS

Da Capo Press
Hachette Book Group
1290 Avenue of the Americas, New York, NY 10104
dacapopress.com
@DaCapoPress, @DaCapoPR

Printed in the United States of America

First Edition: October 2018

Published by Da Capo Press, an imprint of Perseus Books, LLC, a subsidiary of Hachette Book Group, Inc. The Da Capo Press name and logo is a trademark of the Hachette Book Group.

The Hachette Speakers Bureau provides a wide range of authors for speaking events. To find out more, go to www.hachettespeakersbureau.com or call (866) 376-6591.

The publisher is not responsible for websites (or their content) that are not owned by the publisher.

The publishers have generously given permission to use extended quotations from the following copyrighted works: From *James Arness: An Autobiography* by James Arness with James E. Wise Jr. (MacFarland, 2001); *Gli uomini della sbarco* by Silvano Casaldi (Herald Editore, 2006); *Calculated Risk* by Mark W. Clark (Harper & Brothers, 1950); *Closing the Ring*, volume 5 of *The Second World War* by Winston S. Churchill (Houghton Mifflin, US/Cassell, UK, 1951); *The Perilous Road to Rome and Beyond* by Edward Grace (Pen & Sword, 1993); *Aprilia: I giorni della guerra—e gli occhi di un bambino* by Pasqualino Nuti (2014); *Brave Men* by Ernie Pyle (Henry Holt, 1944).

Print book interior design by Trish Wilkinson

Library of Congress Cataloging-in-Publication Data has been applied for.

ISBNs: 978-0-306-82572-9 (hardcover), 978-0-306-82573-6 (ebook)

LSC-C

10 9 8 7 6 5 4 3 2 1

*Dedicated to the memory of all
who served at Anzio*

CONTENTS

Contents

MAPS

PREFACE

A S TODAY SPRINTS FURTHER AWAY from yesterday, the events that held the world's attention so firmly from January to May 1944 are receding in memory nearly to the point of invisibility. The name Anzio that figured so prominently in newspaper and magazine accounts of the day is now barely recognized by today's generation, seven decades removed from the war. Ask the average casual tourist who has been to Italy recently if they had included Anzio in their itinerary, and one is likely to get a blank stare and the question, "Where is that?"

But if one does make the forty-mile drive from Rome to Anzio, one is struck by the ancient, serene beauty of the place. A little imagination is all it takes to conjure images of Roman legions marching down the roads beneath the spreading branches of the magnificent umbrella pines—the *Pinus pinea* that Italian composer Ottorino Respighi captured so evocatively in his tone poem *Pines of Rome.*

On the coastline just south of the bathers' beaches at Anzio, the ruins of Nero's once-fabulous seaside retreat still exist, but the twenty-first century now intrudes. Cars—Fiats, Lancias, Alfa Romeos, Maseratis, Ferraris—clog the streets, and mopeds buzz past like noisy hornets. (In fact, in Italian, *Vespa* means "wasp.") Once the visitor arrives in the heart of Anzio, shops and seafood restaurants that line the enclosed harbor, their facades clad in soft pastel colors, beckon seductively, and the harrowing drive is quickly forgotten. Music can be heard, and sunburned people relax at the outdoor tables, enjoying the vino and calamari and

the brilliant red ball of the sun diving in its nightly ritual into the Tyrrhenian Sea.

It is hard to envision that this place—so redolent today of *la dolce
vita*—was a scene of war so terrible and violent that the residents of Anzio, neighboring Nettuno, and the nearby towns of Aprilia, Carroceto,
Campoleone, and Cisterna seem to want to forget all about it. Virtually
no signs of the once-widespread death and destruction are visible. The
wrecked buildings have all been repaired or replaced. It is not until one
drives north on SR 207 (Via Nettunese—formerly the Via Anziate, or
the Albano Highway, along which much of the hard fighting took place)
that leads out of town that one is suddenly reminded of a titanic battle
that was once fought here.

Unfortunately, given all the commercial, industrial, and residential
development that has taken place here in the past seven decades—on
what was once a bloody battlefield—one may find on buildings in the
port of Anzio only a few small plaques that commemorate the battle
and the ships that were sunk and the men who were lost here. Another
reminder of the horrific and heroic events is the well-tended British War
Cemetery along SR 207 (its American counterpart lies a few miles to the
east in Nettuno). A small sign, obscured by foliage, on the abutment
walls of the infamous "Overpass" (or "Flyover," as the British called it) a
few miles north of Anzio, where the Via Genio Civile (SP 12A) crosses
SR 207, declares in Italian, German, and English: "Campo di Carne—On
this site thousands of men fought and died." To say that the pitiful, poi-
gnant sign on the Overpass or Flyover is an understatement is, in itself,
an understatement.

Thousands of men did, in fact, fight and die within six miles of this
site. The battle devoured thousands of raw recruits and grizzled veterans
alike, on both sides, as if the armies were making a human sacrifice to
Mars, the Roman god of war, in order to curry his favor. It is therefore
important—even imperative—that we take a moment and step back in
time to study, through the use of the words of the men (and women,
too) who were there and who demonstrated such "desperate valour," as
Churchill put it, one of the longest, bloodiest, and most pivotal battles of
the Second World War.

For much too long, the Anzio operation, code-named Operation Shingle, has been regarded merely as a needless, costly, and failed invasion. I believe that viewpoint is shortsighted and that it should be seen instead as one of the most successful defenses in military history—one that eclipses the British 24th of Foot Regiment's stand at Rorke's Drift during the Zulu Wars in 1879, the 101st U.S. Airborne Division's Anthony McAuliffe saying "Nuts" to German demands for surrender at Bastogne, the Soviets' ironfisted grip on besieged Stalingrad and Leningrad, the unyielding American defense of Pork Chop Hill in Korea in 1953, and the U.S. Marines' valiant stand at Khe Sanh during the Vietnam War in 1968.

At Anzio, as in all of the above battles, because of the sheer courage and determination of the defenders—the "desperate valour"—the enemy was thwarted in his desire to wipe out the defenders and realize victory.

What they accomplished must not be forgotten.

Flint Whitlock

But fortune, hitherto baffling, rewarded the desperate valour of the British and American armies. . . . The fighting was intense, losses on both sides were heavy, but the deadly battle was won.

WINSTON S. CHURCHILL

How can a man die better than facing fearful odds . . .

THOMAS BABBINGTON MACAULEY

Cowards die many times before their deaths;
the valiant never taste of death but once.

WILLIAM SHAKESPEARE
JULIUS CAESAR

Prologue

FROM THE VERY BEGINNING, THE Allies' Italian campaign had not gone well.

After the British and Americans had defeated German and Italian forces in North Africa in May 1943, there was disagreement as to what to do next. The Americans wanted to go all out in preparation for an invasion of the European continent and attack Germany directly—an operation that would be code-named Overlord.

British Prime Minister Winston Spencer Churchill was cool to the concept of a cross-Channel invasion and its possibly high casualties. He felt the best way to defeat Germany, since the Allies already had a huge military presence in the Mediterranean, was to strike at what he called "the soft underbelly of Europe" by taking Sicily, moving up through Italy and then the Balkan countries, and attacking across Germany's southern border.

But such a maneuver was unacceptable to Soviet Premier Joseph Stalin, whose nation had been suffering terribly since the summer of 1941 and was barely holding off the Nazi hordes. He was pleading with Churchill and American President Franklin D. Roosevelt for a "second front" against Hitler's Nazi Germany to relieve the pressure on the USSR. He needed help, and he needed it *now*.

Adding impetus to this idea was the fact that, after Sicily fell, the Italian king, Victor Emmanuel III, wishing to prevent the conflict from reaching and devastating the Italian mainland, had ousted Fascist leader

Benito Mussolini as head of government and declared Italy neutral. Churchill felt certain that now it would be possible to move through Italy (in addition to invading Greece and the Balkan countries), cross the Alps and Austria, and penetrate Germany. Stalin did not care about the tactics; all he wanted was for the British and Americans to get on with it, to do *something* that would open the needed second front so that he could save his Soviet Union.

Therefore, Operation Avalanche—Lieutenant General Mark Wayne Clark's Fifth U.S. Army's invasion at Salerno—was launched in September 1943; it was nearly stopped on the beaches. The Eighth British Army's twin invasions on the "toe" (at Reggio di Calabria) of the Italian "boot" (Operation Baytown) and the "heel" (Operation Slapstick) had met less resistance, but the Eighth's commander, General Bernard Law Montgomery, had not proceeded with any sense of urgency (at least to the American mind), thus allowing the Germans who were occupying Italy to respond and resist with unusual determination.

Having gained their footing after their invasions of southern Italy, the British and Americans began marching up the peninsula; Rome is only 145 straight-line miles from Salerno. But it was a very slow march, with treacherous mountains, a tenacious German army under Field Marshal Albert Kesselring, and Old Man Winter standing in their way. By the time Clark and Montgomery reached the Germans' main defensive line (named Gustav) that stretched across the width of Italy and was anchored by Monte Cassino, the Allied armies were exhausted and depleted; Rome might as well have been on the moon.

Adding to the Allies' agony was the fact that the pre-Overlord buildup in Britain was draining resources (men, machines, and shipping) from the Mediterranean Theater. If Rome was to be taken, it would have to be taken quickly, before the Italian campaign withered away into an irrelevant sideshow.

To make matters more uncertain, American General Dwight David Eisenhower, who had successfully engineered the invasions of North Africa, Sicily, and Italy while supreme commander of the Allied Expeditionary Force, North African Theater, was being transferred to England to take command of the Supreme Headquarters Allied Expeditionary Force in Britain and Operation Overlord.

INVASION OF ITALY

After landing in southern Italy in September 1943, the Allied armies fought their way northward through Italy's Apennine Mountains until being stopped by stout German defenses in the Gustav Line that ran through Cassino.

With the Allied armies in Italy stuck at the Gustav Line in the autumn of 1943, Field Marshal Harold Alexander, head of Fifteenth Army Group, was seeking ways to overcome the German defenses. Clark thought that an amphibious maneuver around the western end of the line would do the trick; the Germans, he felt, were sure to panic at this threat to their rear and would abandon the Gustav Line and head toward the more defensible Alps. The planners pored over maps of Italy and determined that the twin coastal towns of Anzio and Nettuno, ninety miles from Naples and forty miles from Rome, would be the ideal place for the landing.

Because of the impending transfer of the bulk of Allied shipping in the Mediterranean to Britain, if such an end run was to be implemented, time was of the essence. But dissension in the ranks broke out, and the idea of the flanking maneuver was alternately killed, resurrected, and killed again, only to be resurrected once more.[1]

Of this proposed amphibious flanking maneuver, Churchill said that the "stubborn German resistance" across the width of Italy "had already led General Eisenhower to . . . land with one division south of the Tiber and make a dart for Rome, in conjunction with an attack by the main armies. . . . I had of course always been a partisan of the 'end run,' as the Americans called it, or 'cat-claw,' which was my term."[2]

Churchill was a man of action, a human dynamo, never someone who quietly accepted the status quo. While some may be content to lie about and await their fate, Churchill never would. Even after being taken prisoner by the Boers in South Africa in November 1899, he was constantly thinking up schemes to escape. The same was true now about his attitude toward the Italian campaign. Clark may have been the person who had first conceived the idea of the end run, but it was Churchill whose force of will would put the concept into motion. The stalemate along the Gustav Line must not be allowed to stand—something had to be done to break it, even if the Allies possessed insufficient time and resources, given the pressure of Overlord, in which to do it.

Around November 12, 1943, Alexander directed Clark to solidify planning for the end run. It was initially thought that the operation could be accomplished by only one division: Major General Lucian K. Truscott Jr.'s 3rd U.S. Infantry Division, augmented by the 6615th U.S. Ranger Force. The operation would be launched as soon as the rest of Fifth Army, breaking through the Gustav Line, had reached and taken Frosinone, the mythical home of Romulus and Remus—the legendary founders of Rome—less than fifty miles from Rome. This was expected to be accomplished by December 20.

But when Truscott learned on November 13 about the operation and that his 3rd Division was to be the sole division involved, he reacted to

the news with incredulity, especially at all the optimistic assumptions being made by the Pollyannas who had devised the scheme: "There would
be [landing] craft available to lift only one division with seven days' ammunition and supply," he wrote in his memoirs, "and there would be no
craft available for resupply and reinforcement. . . . Within seven days,
the main forces [along the Gustav Line] would fight their way up the
Liri and Sacco Valleys to join up with the 3rd Infantry Division. General
Clark remarked to me that if the Division merely held a beachhead at
Anzio, he believed that it would cause the Germans so much concern
that they would withdraw from the southern front. My reaction was
rather pessimistic." Truscott was not only pessimistic but realistic.[3]

Nevertheless, the end run began to take on a life of its own. When
Churchill ran the idea past Roosevelt, the American president saw no
problem as long as the operation did not negatively impact Overlord.
Planning for the maneuver, which was given the code name Operation
Shingle, went ahead full steam. A force was selected to make the invasion: American Major General John Porter Lucas's VI Corps.* Lucas had
been in charge of VI Corps during the Salerno invasion, and his calm,
steady leadership had been instrumental in preventing an Allied disaster.

The Allies had two experienced commanders at the helm. In command of the Fifth U.S. Army was Lieutenant General Mark Wayne
Clark. Born in the exclusive Chicago suburb of Highland Park, Clark
attended West Point at the same time that Dwight D. Eisenhower (two
years ahead of him) and other future and prominent World War II generals (Omar N. Bradley, "Lightning Joe" Collins, Joseph T. McNarney,
Matthew B. Ridgway, and many others) were there; Clark graduated in
1917.[4] With America's entry into World War I, Clark served in France,
where he was wounded. After recuperating, he was assigned to a job
in logistics—a job he disliked but performed with his usual dedication,
even if his enthusiasm was a bit forced. In the postwar world of the army,
when the pay was low and promotions slow, he toiled anonymously
in a variety of staff jobs, yet his superiors regarded him favorably: "a

---

*VI Corps consisted of the 3rd U.S. Infantry Division, 1st U.S. Armored Division,
6615th U.S. Ranger Force, 504th Parachute Infantry Regiment, 36th U.S. Engineer Combat Regiment, British 1st Division, and other supporting units.

promising young officer," "enterprising," "industrious," "efficient," "dependable," "active," and "very presentable."

During the interwar years, a variety of assignments brought him into contact with his friend "Ike" Eisenhower and future Army Chief of Staff George C. Marshall, among others. After the outbreak of World War II, his star rose swiftly, and he was assigned to be Ike's deputy for Operation Torch, the November 1943 invasion of North Africa. Once the Allies declared victory there, and again in Sicily, Clark was given command of the Fifth U.S. Army, then forming in the States, and led it during Operation Avalanche—the Salerno invasion—which had been a close-run thing. Only with extraordinary heroism was the Fifth Army able to prevail.[5]

Clark's only obvious failing, according to Truscott, was his need for personal publicity: "Few men had greater personal charm than Clark, and no superior commander ever made greater efforts to support subordinates in their tasks," Truscott said. "I cannot recall that Clark ever disapproved of any request I made, and he was always untiring in his efforts to immediately expedite any logistical or tactical problem." But "when Clark visited my command post, he usually arrived with an entourage including correspondents and photographers. His public relations officer required all press dispatches, even from Anzio, to include the phrase 'Lieutenant General Mark W. Clark's Fifth Army.'"[6]

Clark's superior, Field Marshal Sir Harold Rupert Leofric Alexander, too, had risen through the ranks to achieve his high level of command. Born on December 10, 1891, in the tony Mayfair section of London as the third son of the Fourth Earl and Countess of Caledon, he was educated at Harrow and at the Royal Military College at Sandhurst. Commissioned a second lieutenant in 1911, he was just in time for World War I, distinguishing himself in battle with the Irish Guards Regiment at Ypres (where he was seriously wounded). He recuperated and returned to the front, was promoted to major, and earned both the Distinguished Service Order and the French Legion of Honor for his actions at the Somme. Writer Rudyard Kipling, in his history of the Irish Guards, extolled Alexander, saying, "His subordinates loved him, even when he fell upon them blisteringly for their shortcomings."[7]

In May 1940, as commanding general of the 1st British Division, Alexander returned to France with the British Expeditionary Force to fight the Germans. During the pullback to the Channel coast, he was given command of the I British Corps and directed the evacuation of 300,000 British and French forces from Dunkirk; he was reportedly the last man to leave France during that rescue. Sir Harold (he was knighted in January 1942) was then posted the next month to Burma, where he was named commander of all British forces and placed in charge of extricating British and Indian troops in the face of an unstoppable Japanese advance; he barely avoided capture himself.[8]

From the steamy jungles of Burma, Sir Harold, now a full general, was posted in August 1942 to become commander in chief of British forces in the Middle East Command that was fighting Germany's Afrika Korps in the deserts of North Africa, where he brought hope and confidence to his troops.[9] Along with his field commander, Bernard Law Montgomery, head of the Eighth British Army, Alexander devised a strategy that eventually resulted in driving the Afrika Korps forces (first under Erwin Rommel and then Hans-Jürgen von Arnem) out of Egypt and into Tunis, where, with American forces also now engaged, they were forced to surrender in May 1943.[10] Sir Harold then was named commander of the newly formed Eighteenth Army Group (which controlled both George Patton Jr.'s Seventh U.S. Army and Montgomery's Eighth; Eighteenth Army Group later became Fifteenth Army Group) in the Mediterranean, where he served under Eisenhower for the invasion of Sicily.[11]

Truscott said of Sir Harold, whom he had first met in Tunisia, "His quiet, unassuming, and dignified manner always put the staff completely at ease. His instant comprehension of complicated and difficult situations always surprised them. . . . Alexander was, in my opinion, outstanding among the Allied leaders."[12]

Alexander, too, saw the end-run operation in very positive terms: "[Shingle] had been designed as a pincer movement, to force Kesselring to draw off his strength from the Cassino front to protect his threatened rear, thereby weakening his main front and giving us a good opportunity to break through his winter line [that is, the Gustav Line]." He added that the Anzio operation gave him "the means to employ a double-handed punch—from the beachhead and from Cassino. . . . Without this double-handed punch I do not believe we should ever have been able to break through the German defences at Cassino."[13]

Unfortunately, Alexander and Clark detested each other, although the Britisher's animosity was concealed beneath a well-polished veneer. Clark, however, let his negative feelings be known, once even privately dismissing his superior as "a peanut and a feather duster."[14]

But in Shingle they were united. Alexander and Clark saw two scenarios, both of which were favorable to the Allies. The first was the best-case result: By landing a major Allied force behind the Gustav Line, Kesselring would panic and immediately withdraw Colonel General Heinrich von Vietinghoff's Tenth Army from the defenses and retreat northward. The Allies would then be able to swiftly capture Rome and chase the Germans all the way to the Alps—and perhaps beyond.

The second scenario posited that if Shingle failed to immediately cause Kesselring to abandon the Gustav Line, then the Allied Fifth and Eighth Armies along that line would make a major assault, crack through it, push into the Liri Valley on the road to Rome, and be in Frosinone within forty-eight hours. That would be the moment for VI Corps to come bursting out of the Anzio beachhead, link up with the other forces at Frosinone, and march together into Rome, driving the fleeing Germans ahead of them.

Not much thought was given to a possible third scenario: Kesselring would hold fast on the Gustav Line while scraping up enough units to encircle the Anzio area and bottle up the invasion forces on the beachhead, thus creating twin stalemates. Wrongly believing that the Germans had few other major forces that could be called on to contain the Anzio invasion force, Alexander and Clark deemed this third scenario extremely unlikely. Further, aside from a few submarines, the German navy was practically nonexistent, and the Luftwaffe—the air force—was so ineffective as to be practically worthless.

But soon—very soon—more than 100,000 Allied soldiers, sailors, and airmen would be battling for their lives because of Churchill's, Alexander's, and Clark's overoptimism, false assumptions, and miscalculations.

CHAPTER 1

"We have every confidence in you"

JANUARY 1944

I T WAS THE FRIGID PREDAWN of January 22, 1944, and death hung heavily in the air. An armada of 374 British and American ships, landing craft, and an assortment of other vessels, filled with 36,000 nervous, determined men, was roaring hell-bent for the darkened Italian coastline.

In one of the landing craft, a twenty-eight-year-old U.S. Army major from upstate New York named Alvah Miller, commander of the 3rd Battalion of the U.S. Ranger Force, was peering over the gunwale of his landing craft at the darkness ahead in the Anzio-Nettuno harbor. His mind was a jumbled squirrel's nest of thoughts. When would the Germans open fire? Surely, the Germans couldn't be asleep, so why was there no artillery or machine-gun fire to greet their arrival? Didn't the same thing happen to the Rangers just four months earlier when they had landed at Maiori, a fishing village at the base of the Sorrento Peninsula, as part of Operation Avalanche—the invasion of mainland Italy? The Germans let the Rangers come ashore and climb to the top of Chiunzi Pass over the mountain separating Salerno from Naples, and then all hell broke loose. When was hell going to break loose now? Major Alvah Miller didn't know—nor did he have any idea that he had only one week left to live.

Thirty-year-old Major Peter Henry "Skipper" Mornement, commanding C Company of the 2nd Battalion, North Staffordshire Regiment, was aboard another landing craft, this one heading toward "Peter"

Beach in the British sector north of Anzio. He may have given some thought to his mother, wife, and son back in London, but his mind was probably more focused on his company's mission once they reached land—*if* they reached land. He did not suspect that he would soon be wounded, taken prisoner, and die in an Italian hospital.

On another landing craft, this one on its way to "X-Ray" Beach, south of Anzio, a fresh-faced nineteen-year-old private first class named John C. Squires of Louisville, Kentucky, a member of the 3rd U.S. Infantry Division, was understandably nervous about going into combat for the first time. Although he gripped his M-1 Garand rifle tightly, he hoped he wouldn't have to use it because he was his company's messenger, not a frontline infantryman. He did not believe that he was capable of performing acts so heroic that he would be awarded the Medal of Honor, but he would. Unfortunately, it would be a posthumous award, for he would not live to receive it.

Aboard the command ship USS *Biscayne*, fifty-four-year-old Major General John Porter Lucas felt as helpless as a spectator at a sporting event. This operation, which had been given the code name Shingle, was his baby, and all these men in all these ships about to hit their respective beaches were his responsibility. "I mustn't stick my neck out and do anything foolish," he probably thought, recalling the words of his boss, Lieutenant General Mark Clark, Fifth U.S. Army commander. He knew that Salerno had almost been a disaster; the same thing must not happen here. He would take his time, move cautiously, risk nothing. He could not foresee that his cautious, slow-and-steady performance during this operation would cost him his job, his career, and his reputation.

OPERATION SHINGLE HAD BEEN BORN out of necessity, and although such a maneuver—landing behind German lines—had been discussed since October, it gave the appearance of having been cobbled together at the last minute. The unexpectedly stubborn German resistance along the Gustav Line had dashed all hope of capturing and liberating Rome by the end of 1943, thereby necessitating the end run up the coast. An adequate number of landing craft had to be assembled from all over the Mediterranean, warships formed into a task force, air assets reassigned, units added to VI Corps, sufficient supplies gathered, and a rehearsal scheduled.

Adding to the headaches was the fact that Clark and British Field Marshal Harold Alexander had a contentious working relationship, with the gentlemanly Alexander complaining privately that the egocentric Clark was a vain prima donna who also had a habit of speaking sharply and nastily to him.[1]

Events were moving ahead at a rapid pace—too rapid for Lucas's taste—and were threatening to spin out of his control. Decisions, too, were being made without his knowledge, advice, or consent. On January 7, 1944, some of his VI Corps staff officers attended (without him) a meeting with Churchill in Marrakech, Morocco, in which Lucas's officers "maintained that past experiences had shown that a rehearsal was absolutely necessary, but Mr. Churchill argued that all these troops were trained and therefore needed no rehearsal." What Mr. Churchill failed to appreciate, or was not told, was that not "all" of the troops were trained or combat experienced; a good many of them were raw replacements who had had only minimal training and had not taken part in the previous amphibious landings or the ground combat that followed the invasions of Sicily and Salerno.

Three days later, another conference was held from which Lucas was again inexplicably excluded. Lucas noted, "Apparently Shingle has become the most important operation in the present scheme of things. Sir Harold [Alexander] started the conference by stating that the operation would take place on January 22 [1944] with the troops as scheduled, and that there would be no more discussion of these two points. He quoted Mr. Churchill as saying, 'It will astonish the world,' and added, 'It will certainly frighten Kesselring.'" Lucas had his doubts; the one who was frightened was Lucas.

Because everything about Shingle was being imposed on him and there would be "no more discussion," Lucas said that he "felt like a lamb being led to the slaughter, but I thought that I was entitled to one last bleat, so I registered a protest against the target date, as it gave me too little time for rehearsal. . . . I was ruled down, as I knew I would be. . . . When I said this to General Alexander yesterday, he said, 'We have every confidence in you; that's why you were picked.'"[2]

Sir Harold's verbal pat on the head was reassuring, but Lucas still wasn't certain what the objective of his mission was. It was clear that his

VI Corps was supposed to grab the beachhead and the port of Anzio, push several miles inland, but then what? Make a mad dash for Rome, just forty miles away, and capture the entire city with just a small force? Or was the operation supposed to throw Field Marshal Albert Kesselring, commanding Army Group C, into such a panic that he would pull the Tenth German Army out of the Gustav Line and flee for the Alps?*

Or was Lucas merely supposed to hang on to the Anzio beaches and wait for more troops and supplies to arrive so that a proper advance in strength could be mounted that would take the Allied Fifth and Eighth Armies all the way through Rome and to the Alps—and into Austria and ultimately into southern Germany? Seeking clarification, Lucas asked Clark, "Just what the hell am I supposed to do?" Clark replied, "Don't stick your neck out, Johnny. I did at Salerno and got into trouble. You can forget this goddam Rome business." Lucas took the comment to be an inviolable order that meant "Don't be aggressive or do anything foolish."[3]

This cautionary view was reinforced by Fifth Army operations officer Brigadier General Donald W. Brann, who met with Lucas on January 12, 1944, and told him that his primary task was to seize and secure a beachhead. Clark did not want him galloping off to the Alban Hills and run the risk of the Germans possibly destroying his VI Corps. But—and this was a big *but*—if he saw an opportunity to capture the Alban Hills, he should take it. The most important thing, however, was to establish and hold a beachhead.[4] It was no wonder that Lucas confided to his diary on January 10, "This whole affair had a strong odor of Gallipoli† and apparently the same amateur was still on the coach's bench."[5]

---

*Alexander admitted years later, "I think we may well have underestimated the remarkable resistance and toughness of the Germans, expecting them to be frightened by such a threat to their rear." Many men paid with their lives because of that "underestimation." Field Marshal Earl (Harold R. L. G.) Alexander, *The Alexander Memoirs, 1940–1945*, 125.

†When Churchill, as First Lord of the Admiralty, sent in the ANZAC Force (Australians and New Zealanders, along with French and British troops) to Gallipoli on April 25, 1915, he was convinced that the Turks, holding the peninsula and fighting on Germany's side, would run for the hills the first time they set eyes on some "real" soldiers. It did not turn out that way, and the ANZAC forces suffered

PRIOR TO LAUNCHING SHINGLE, A major push by Fifth Army against the western end of the Gustav Line was set in motion in order to keep the German forces pinned there. The American operation kicked off on January 15, 1944, but immediately came up short, with the 36th U.S. Infantry Division suffering horrendous casualties trying to cross the Rapido River.

On the same day that the offensive began, the voluminous Fifth Army order for Operation Shingle was published, and Lucas was anything but pleased. "Instead of advancing *to* seize Colli Laziali [another name for the Alban Hills]," he wrote, "I was to 'advance *on*' that terrain feature, and no mention of Rome was made whatsoever." Don Brann had already made it clear three days earlier that "my primary mission was to seize and secure a beachhead." Lucas understood that he was *not* to "push on at the risk of sacrificing my Corps. Should conditions warrant, however, I was free to move to and seize Colli Laziali."⁶ A more ambiguous order has probably never been issued.

ON JANUARY 18, VI CORPS held a full-scale dress rehearsal for Shingle—a rehearsal that confirmed Murphy's Law: "Anything that *can* go wrong *will* go wrong." Although the British rehearsal, conducted by the Royal Navy about six miles south of Salerno, went off with only a few minor hitches, the practice landings of Lucian Truscott's 3rd Infantry Division at the same place—code-named Operation Webfoot—were a disaster.⁷ Truscott noted:

[The battalions] had been disembarked so far at sea that few had landed on their proper beaches, and all had landed late. No artillery, tanks, or tank destroyers [TDs] were yet on shore at 0800 [8:00 A.M.], although all should have been ashore by daylight with the infantry battalions. Then in fragments came the appalling news. Through some error in navigation, the transport area had been many miles farther from the shore than it should have been. In darkness, the LSTs [Landing Ship, Tank—sometimes mordantly called a "large, slow target"] had opened their

---

a bloody beating, losing thousands of men and failing to establish more than a toehold on the western coast of Turkey. Lyn MacDonald, *Somme*, 158–160.

doors, lowered their ramps, discharged the DUKWs* which carried the artillery into rough seas, where twenty or more had swamped and sunk. Incomplete reports indicated that the artillery pieces and communication equipment of perhaps two battalions had been dumped into the sea. . . . Beaches were in a chaotic condition, and the whole landing plan was completely disrupted.[8]

Forty-three of the amphibious vehicles were lost during the debacle, which was blamed squarely on the navy. Also lost were nineteen 105mm howitzers and nine antitank guns—guns that had to be taken from divisions scheduled to come in later.[9] Peter Geoffrey Bate, a driver for a British artillery unit landing nearby, recalled that he saw "about thirty DUKWs go straight to the bottom."[10]

Truscott requested from Clark permission to conduct a second rehearsal in hopes of correcting the errors, but Clark shook his head. "Lucian, I've got your report here and it's bad. But you won't get another rehearsal. The date has been set at the very highest level. There is no possibility of delaying it even for a day. You have got to do it." Truscott protested that he wasn't requesting that Shingle be delayed—only that another rehearsal be scheduled. No dice. Disastrous rehearsal or not, one was all that the 3rd Division and VI Corps were going to get.[11]

Lucas, too, was beyond upset at the fouled-up rehearsal. "Everything went wrong," he complained in his diary. The 3rd Division's part was the worst—"the most mixed-up affair I have ever seen. . . . Not a single unit landed on the proper beach, not a single unit landed in the proper order, not a single unit was less than an hour and a half late."[12]

It was true. The U.S. Navy's VIII Amphibious Force, under the command of Rear Admiral Frank Lowry, had released the DUKWs too far from shore and dropped infantry units at the wrong places, in the wrong order, and at the wrong times. An officer in the 3rd Division called the rehearsal "a complete fiasco."[13] Clark was also furious at the navy, claiming

---

*Pronounced "duck." The DUKW was a two-and-a-half-ton amphibious truck manufactured by General Motors and was designed to operate both on land and in the water. Bernard Fitzsimons, ed., *The Illustrated Encyclopedia of 20th Century Weapons and Warfare*, 44.

that "overwhelming mismanagement by the Navy" had resulted in the foul-ups and loss of equipment that Fifth Army would be hard-pressed to replace. Admiral Lowry, red-faced and thoroughly chastised by Clark, reacted by lambasting the ships' commanders, telling them the actual landings had better be letter perfect. Any ship not within three and a half miles of Anzio at H-hour on the D-day* morning of January 22, he warned them, would get "a kick in a soft spot by a cruiser."[14]

In the world of the theater, it is said that if the dress rehearsal goes badly, opening night is destined to go perfectly. The planners and participants of Operation Shingle fervently hoped that the hoary maxim would hold true for a military operation as well.

Patton was no help. He flew from Sicily to visit his friend Lucas in Naples and tell him good-bye. "He seemed much disturbed and preoccupied," Lucas wrote, "but finally blurted out, 'John, there is no one in the Army I hate to see killed as much as you, but you can't get out of this alive. Of course, you might be only badly wounded. No one ever blames a wounded general for anything.' The following morning, he buttonholed one of my aides . . . and told him 'Look here, if things get too bad, shoot the old man in the "back end," but don't you dare kill the old bastard.'"[15]

The rehearsals were now, for better or for worse, finished, and there was no use crying over spilled howitzers and drowned DUKWs; it was now time for the real thing.

ALBERT KONRAD KESSELRING, HEAD OF German forces in Italy, was an old hand at war and did not frighten easily. Born the son of a schoolteacher on November 30, 1885, in Marksteft, Bavaria, he began his military career in 1904 as an officer cadet and was posted to an artillery regiment. When the Great War broke out, he was transferred to the German Air Service and trained as a balloon observer. In 1921, at the age of thirty-six, he obtained his pilot's license and was eventually promoted to major general in the reconstituted Luftwaffe. In 1939, as commander

---

*The day that any military operation begins is designated "D day." Over time, however, the term *D-Day* has become synonymous with Operation Overlord, the Normandy invasion, on June 6, 1944.

of the First Air Fleet, Kesselring had his aviators provide air support for the invasion of Poland. The following year he was transferred to head up the Second Air Fleet during the German invasions of France, Holland, and Belgium. His pilots also attacked British and Allied troops trying to escape to Britain from Dunkirk. During the battle of Britain in the summer and fall of 1940, his Second Air Fleet bombed London and the next summer supported Operation Barbarossa, the German invasion of the Soviet Union.

Kesselring was then transferred to North Africa to become commander of all air and ground forces in the Mediterranean area. After the Allies had beaten the Germans and Italians, secured North Africa, and then taken Sicily in the summer of 1943, Kesselring and his troops nearly destroyed Mark Clark's attempts to gain a foothold at Salerno during Operation Avalanche. At this time, he was subordinate to Field Marshal Erwin Rommel, the famed "Desert Fox," who had managed to hold North Africa against the Allies longer than anyone could have foreseen. When, in November 1943, Hitler ordered Rommel transferred to France to take charge of improving the German "Atlantic Wall" defenses there in order to stop the Allies' expected cross-Channel invasion, the Führer installed Kesselring, a wily fox in his own right, as commander of the German army in Italy—Army Group C.[16]

Because of the increased Allied activity around the Garigliano River in early and mid-January 1944, Kesselring sensed that the Allies were about to spring something big; his spies in Naples and Pozzuoli confirmed it when they spotted Allied troops and landing craft being brought into the port cities. "On the three nights preceding the [Anzio] landing," Kesselring later wrote, "I had ordered an emergency alert throughout the whole of Italy."[17]

Kesselring had read the tea leaves correctly. To keep Colonel General Heinrich von Vietinghoff's Tenth Army units pinned down all along the Gustav Line, Clark, beginning on January 12, had launched strong ground, air, and naval attacks against the line that would, with any luck, propel Major General Geoffrey Keyes's II U.S. Corps through the German defenses and into the Liri Valley, where it might push quickly northward and link up with Lucas's VI Corps driving inland from the Anzio beachhead. Clark had already told Alexander on January 2 that "I intend to attack in greatest possible strength in [the] Liri Valley several days in advance of Shingle with the object of drawing maximum number of enemy reserves to that front and fixing them there. In that way and that way only can the Shingle force exercise a decisive influence in the operation to capture Rome."[18]

At least that was the plan. The reality would be something altogether different.

BACK IN THE NAPLES PORT of Pozzuoli, the armada was getting ready to depart for Anzio. George Avery (Company B, 84th Chemical Mortar Battalion) said that his battalion was attached to the 3rd Infantry Division, "and that fact alone let us know that wherever we were going it would not be pleasant. The 3rd were veterans of North Africa, Sicily and Salerno and had been involved in every major engagement."[19]

Truscott's 3rd Division was scheduled to hit its assigned beach at 2:00 A.M. on January 22 with three battalions abreast, supported by a 105mm self-propelled field artillery battalion, a battery of 155mm guns, a medium tank battalion, a tank-destroyer battalion, an antiaircraft automatic weapons battalion, and the 84th Chemical Mortar Battalion that could fire either smoke or high-explosive shells. Added to this force to take the towns of Anzio and Nettuno were the 504th Parachute Infantry Regiment and the American Ranger Force.[20]

Avery was trucked from the battalion's staging area in Pozzuoli, where the unit headed directly to the docks, and he saw

a massive group of ships was gathered at the piers as well as anchored offshore. Ships dockside were being loaded at a steady rate and it was apparent that we were some of the last to arrive. We were driven to an LST and immediately boarded. Dozens of little kids were at dockside chanting "Anzio," "Anzio, Joe," and begging for cigarettes and candy. Adults were roaming the docks selling oranges, walnuts, "cherry brandy" and "cognac." Old women were begging for food with outstretched arms.

A troop transport direct from New York was moored close to us, and had been there for days. These troops were going unassigned to Anzio, having not yet set foot on Italian soil, and were destined to supply the replacement depots—"repple depple" in infantry talk. Our hearts went

out to them. And, for the very first time, we crossed paths with the 83rd
Chemical Mortar Battalion. It had joined the war somewhere in Sicily,
but had skipped action in Italy for reasons unknown, and was being
loaded aboard a LST of its own.

Avery continued:

Aboard ship we were invited to make ourselves at home. . . . Having no
sleeping quarters, we were fed hot Navy food on deck in mess gear with
unlimited coffee served in galvanized cans heated over gas burners and
left on deck all night. I have never forgotten that thoughtfulness. I chose
to sleep under a truck carrying who-knows-what on the open deck. We
were issued bandoliers of rifle ammo, hand grenades, and three chocolate bars. Now we really knew. These chocolate bars were given to us
almost always when there was to be a prolonged battle and food might be
short. The chocolate is as hard as a rock, has to be cut to be eaten, never
melts, can be carried in your pocket for days and substituted for food.*

"The following dawn the entire convoy . . . set sail in a calm sea, on
a beautiful, cloudless, sunny day," said Avery. "None of us knew where
our destination (Anzio) was. Toward late afternoon there was friendly
air traffic high above us that every once in a while made its appearance
until night fell. Late that night, the sergeants were called by our officers
and returned with maps and instructions." The grand effort to surprise
the Germans at Anzio and perhaps break their firm grip on Italy had
begun.[21]

---

*Before the war, the Hershey Chocolate Company of Pennsylvania was tasked
by the U.S. Army to develop a four-ounce ration bar that would not melt, would
be high in nutritional value, and would taste only slightly better than "a boiled
potato" (the latter quality to make the bar basically unpalatable so that it would be
eaten only as a last resort to prevent starvation). The end product was called the
"Field Ration D Bar" and provided 600 calories. In 1943 the formula was changed
to improve the taste slightly; the two-ounce product was called the "Hershey's
Tropical Chocolate Bar." By war's end, the company would produce almost 400
million D Ration and Tropical bars. www.hersheyarchives.org.

On D-day eve, January 21, Major General John Lucas began to feel a bit more positive. The weather was predicted to remain good, and there were no signs that the Germans suspected anything. "I think we have a good chance to make a killing," he noted, but he could not shake the feeling that disaster lurked in his future. "I have many misgivings but I am also optimistic." He was then overcome with gloom:

> I struggle to be calm and collected. . . . I wish the higher levels were not so over-optimistic. The Fifth Army is attacking violently towards the Cassino Line and has sucked many German troops to the south* and the high command seems to think they will stay there. I don't see why. They can still slow us up there and move against me at the same time. . . . The strain of a thing like this is a terrible burden. Who the hell wants to be a general?[22]

FULL OF HOPE AND MISGIVINGS, the men of the Allied armada, known as Task Force 81, left Naples before dawn on January 21. The 374-ship flotilla—bigger than anything anyone had seen since Fifth Army hit the beaches at Salerno the previous September—was loaded with 36,000 British and American soldiers and 3,200 vehicles, plus artillery pieces, ammunition, food, medical supplies, and everything an invading force would need to sustain itself for a period of several days. Small naval parties were to precede the ground-force assault waves to locate the beaches and mark them with colored lights. These resources were divided into two task forces—one carrying and supporting the American troops, the other the British. Fifty-two ships of Task Force Peter, commanded by Rear Admiral Thomas H. Troubridge, Royal Navy, would deliver the British contingent to Peter Beach, while Rear Admiral Frank Lowry was in command of the 74 vessels of Task Force X-Ray that would carry the American forces to its landing beaches, dubbed X-Ray, south of Nettuno. Rather than pound the coast with a lengthy naval bombardment

---

*In actuality, given the Italian peninsula's shape and forty-five-degree angle, Cassino is almost exactly due *east* of Anzio (Anzio: latitude 41° 35′ N; Cassino: 41° 30′ N). Cassino has been so often referred to as being "south" of Anzio that we will continue to use that terminology.

that would spoil the "surprise," the two navies decided to fire a short but intense ten-minute barrage by a pair of British assault vessels equipped with 1,500 5-inch rockets. It was not all a strictly naval show; supporting the operation were hundreds of planes of the British Desert Air Force and the U.S. VII Air Support Command.[23]

In London, once he was informed that the first wave of the invasion force had shoved off from their docks in the Naples area, Winston Churchill sent a cable to beleaguered Soviet leader Joseph Stalin: "We have launched the big attack against the German armies defending Rome which I told you about at Teheran. The weather conditions seem favorable. I hope to have good news for you before long."[24]

After leaving Naples, the convoy swung south around Capri to avoid German sea mines and to deceive any German agents who might be observing, then headed north. After nightfall on January 21, the vessels made a sharp turn to starboard toward Anzio and at five minutes after midnight dropped anchor off the Anzio-Nettuno shore. Assault craft were lowered into the water and patrol vessels herded them into formation. There was no reply from the Germans. "The shoreline," as the U.S. Army's official history said, "was dark and silent."[25]

Despite Lucas's earlier pessimism, Operation Shingle had started out brilliantly. It would not remain so for long.

CHAPTER 2

"One of the most complete surprises in history"

JANUARY 22 (MORNING)

A S THE ALLIED ARMADA APPROACHED the darkened shoreline, the men in the first wave of Operation Shingle repeatedly fingered the safeties on their rifles and wondered what they were about to experience: A full-fledged enemy attempt to destroy them at the water's edge? Or would the Germans wait until they were all congregated ashore before pounding them into oblivion? Or would the Germans, being caught totally by surprise, make no response at all? Of all the possibilities, the latter seemed to be the least likely.

After all, as many of the men in the scores of landing craft remembered, the Germans and Italians just a half year earlier during Operation Husky had met them at the shoreline of southeastern Sicily with such voluminous volleys of artillery, mortar, and machine-gun fire that the invasion had nearly stopped before it could get started. And then, during Operation Avalanche—the invasion of Italy along the beaches north and south of Salerno on September 9, 1943—the landings were hit with such a massive wall of enemy fire that the troops barely managed to claw their way ashore. No doubt visions of bloody U.S. Army and Marine Corps landings in the Pacific also spun through many American heads that chilly morning, while more than a few British soldiers likely flashed on the failed 1942 landings at the French coastal town of Dieppe and the

Turkish coast at Gallipoli in the previous world war. Churchill, too, may have been thinking that the anticipated success of his Anzio plan would do much to erase the bitter taste of the disaster at Gallipoli—a disastrous invasion that he had conceived and for which he was blamed twenty-nine years earlier while in his role of First Lord of the Admiralty.

What awaited them now on this darkened shore? They could see nothing, and no enemy shells reached out to hit them in their vulnerable vessels. As the boats bounced forever onward, and the cold spray from the wakes being kicked up by the prows sloshed over the gunwales and soaked the men, the butterflies in thousands of stomachs turned into pterodactyls, clawing at the guts of soldiers who would, in just a few more minutes, find out what was in store for them. All that the men in the boats knew was that they were heading for two towns that most of them had never heard of—Anzio and Nettuno. And almost none of them had ever heard of Aprilia—a tiny speck on a map where, in the coming days, weeks, and months, much of the "battle of Anzio" would really take place and where hundreds of them would either meet a gruesome end or cover themselves in glory.

HEADING FOR PETER BEACH, ABOUT five miles north of Anzio proper, were the soldiers of the king—the men of Major General William Ronald Campbell Penney's 1st British Infantry Division, the vanguard of the entire amphibious assault landing at Anzio, wet and cold in the bellies of their vessels, bouncing toward the black predawn shore, fully expecting that at any moment, the awful crash of artillery and machine guns would erupt and they would be under fire once more, just as they had been in 1940 while trying to save France and in 1943 at the Kasserine Pass, Tunisia, and elsewhere.[1]

The 15,000 men of the 1st British Infantry Division, whose lineage can be traced back to the Napoleonic Wars, stood tensely at the gunwales, waiting for the inevitable munitions to be hurled at them. Penney himself was sure that the opening salvos would occur at any moment, and he was surprised that the Germans were taking so long to respond to an invasion they surely must have known was coming.

The mustachioed Penney (to his associates he was "Ronald," and to his closest friends he was "Bunny"), born in Berwick-on-Tweed on

May 16, 1896, was an experienced career officer. He had attended the Royal Military Academy at Woolwich and, in November 1914, was commissioned into the Royal Engineers. During the Great War, he received the Military Cross and both the French and the Belgian Croix de Guerre. For the next twenty-two years, he was a signals officer before being appointed commander of the 1st British Infantry Division on October 14, 1943.[2]

Penney's division was composed of three brigades: the 2nd Infantry Brigade (commanded by Brigadier Eric Edward James Moore and made up of the 1st Battalion, Loyal Regiment; 2nd Battalion of the North Staffordshire Regiment; and 6th Battalion, Gordon Highlanders Regiment), the 3rd Infantry Brigade (commanded by Brigadier J. G. James, consisting of the 1st Battalion, Duke of Wellington's Regiment [West Riding]; 2nd Battalion, Sherwood Foresters; and the 1st Battalion, King's Shropshire Light Infantry Regiment [KSLI]), and the 24th Guards Brigade (commanded by Brigadier A. S. P. "Glaxo" Murray, for all composed of the 1st Battalion of the Scots Guards; 1st Battalion of the Irish Guards; and the 5th Battalion, Grenadier Guards).* Another unit in the British force that morning included Colonel Ronnie Tod's 2nd Special Service Brigade, made up of two battalion-size units: Numbers 9 and 43 Commandos.[3]

Peter Beach ran from Tor Caldara to Tor San Lorenzo, five miles north of Anzio. On Peter Beach the sand is narrow, and thirty-foot bluffs rise abruptly. A few steep paths lead from the beach to the flat terrain above, where a profuse forest of stately umbrella pines grew.[4] But it was too quiet. The Germans were either totally asleep or else very much awake and lying in wait to blow the armada out of the water. No one knew which. Yet there was nothing. No bombs, bullets, or even parachute flares illuminated the flotilla for German gunners on the beach.

---

* A word about regiments. In modern times, the United States, Germany, and other nations designate their regiments with numbers. The British, however, have traditionally identified their regiments by names—either the names of their colonels (as in the 1600s) or, from the mid-1800s onward, by the town, county, or region from which the troops were recruited (for example, Sherwood Foresters). That tradition continues to this day, although British soldiers today do not always come from the region that bears the name of their regiment. www.britishmilitaryhistory.co.uk.

While this formidable armada was approaching Anzio, some seventy-five miles to the northwest another operation was taking place. Eric Alley, a British sailor aboard the destroyer HMS *Inglefield*, said that his ship and three others were carrying out a diversionary bombardment of the port of Civitavecchia, just north of the mouth of the River Tiber. "Using dummy landing craft, our task was to divert attention from the actual landings on the beaches of Anzio to the south."[5]

As the landing craft neared Peter Beach, the rockets were let loose and saturated the beaches with fiery explosions. One of the British soldiers in the landing craft recalled, "The immensity of what was about to happen struck [my mates] speechless. The jokes and the conversation of a few minutes ago . . . were now forgotten." The British warships now trained their guns in the direction of land and opened fire. "Suddenly the shoreline rose to convulsion," the soldier said. "Men, trees, houses, earth, stones were flung skywards. An intense rocket barrage had begun. . . . The sky was rent by an insane howling shrieking madness. A giant thunder filled all men with fear. The land erupted into great orange flames. . . . As the preliminary bombardment ended, there was an ominous silence from the land."[6]

Silence indeed. On January 22 only one German battalion—from Lieutenant General Walter Fries's 29th Panzer-Grenadier Division—was present in the immediate area; it had been moved out of the fighting at the Gustav Line shortly before the invasion and was at Anzio for rest and recuperation. How could 1,000 men stand up to 30,000?[7]

But soon a few German guns near Peter Beach began to fire back. The return fire wasn't much—a few halfhearted shells—but it was almost a relief, as the lack of enemy response was worrying in its silence. The ships carrying the British suddenly ran into an unexpected obstacle: a sandbar that inadequate preinvasion intelligence reports had failed to discover. Unable to progress any farther, the landing craft were forced to discharge their troops some 300 feet from the shoreline; fortunately, the water was relatively shallow, and the men began splashing ashore, holding their weapons above their heads.[8]

Trevor Bray, a soldier with the 6th Battalion, Gordon Highlanders Regiment—an element of the 2nd Infantry Brigade, 1st Division—was on an LCT (Landing Craft, Tank) along with a number of American-built and British-operated Sherman tanks. He recalled that his ship ran aground at Peter Beach at Anzio. "A crunch and a jolt then a great roar as the tank engines came to life. The bows of our ship opened up like a pelican's bill and they trundled off. My concern was that they were within inches of my toes, these 52-ton monsters! They then raced up the beach and we followed."*9

Peter Geoffrey Bate, with a British artillery unit, recalled that the rocket barrage from two British landing craft lit up the night sky as the DUKW in which he was riding continued its slow approach toward the beach. Suddenly, return artillery began splashing around the amphibious vehicle—the Germans, rousing themselves from their sleep, began to fight back. "Shells start bursting around us." Bate recalled that 88mm shells began bursting in the water, which terrified the American driving the DUKW. He said, "'I didn't sign up for this,' and starts heading back out to sea. Our lieutenant draws his Smith and Wesson .38—'Turn this bloody thing around or I'll blow your head off.'"10

As the steel hulls of the landing craft scraped the shallow sand just off Peter Beach and the ramps either opened like pelican bills or slammed down with a tremendous *whoosh*, the men charged out, screaming, into the surf, waiting for the inevitable moment when enemy munitions would begin to tear through their woolen uniforms and make bloody hash out of their flesh. The men somehow reached the shore unscathed and flopped onto the cold sand, their eyes straining to see something—anything—in the dark.

"Bloody 'ell," more than one of the soldiers probably muttered on that morning. "Where's the bleedin' Jerries?"†

---

* The British soon discovered that the tracked and wheeled vehicles that disembarked at Peter Beach had difficulty trying to cross the loose sand. Subsequent arrivals of British vehicles were diverted to the Anzio port itself. Alexander, *Alexander Memoirs*, 124.

† The Germans were given several derogatory nicknames by their British and American foes, including "Jerries," "Huns," "Krauts," "Fritzes," "Boches," and "Squareheads." American war correspondent Ernie Pyle commented, "Another name was '*Tedeschi*,' the Italian word for Germans. The 'ch' is hard, like the 'k' in Kansas. About a third of the time our soldiers spoke of the Germans as 'the *Tedeschi*.'" Ernie Pyle, *Brave Men*, 242.

"We must've landed on the wrong beach," another puzzled soldier no doubt growled. "Just *like* the bloody navy."

William Woodruff, a captain in the 1st British Division's 24th Guards Brigade, was as surprised by this lack of enemy response as his men. Here he and the rest of the brigade were on the far-left flank of the entire invasion area—a place that should have been swarming with alert German guards, land mines, barbed wire, stout concrete bunkers, and a profusion of guns of all calibers blasting away to repel the invasion.[11] But there had been no opposition to the British landing; it was almost like an exercise back in Britain. Except for a few desultory rounds from an 88mm gun firing aimlessly from shore, there was nothing. The coastal defenses were all but unmanned by a handful of German and Italian soldiers; the only injuries came from beach mines. One unit of British troops captured a few startled Germans who said they were in the area only because they had been sent to shoot cattle to feed their regiment. Another group—a few German soldiers in pajamas, convalescing from the Cassino front—was rousted out of a beach hut.

The 24th Guards Brigade's commander, Glaxo Murray, drove in his jeep down the coast road to Anzio, meeting along the way a few startled Germans who fled as he drove by. Even Field Marshal Alexander, wearing his red-banded hat, was able to tour the beachhead by jeep that morning, look about, and seem pleased by what he saw. A member of the 5th Grenadier Guards said, "We were again reminded of the likeness of the operation to an exercise—the Chief Umpire visiting the forward positions and finding things to his satisfaction."

Within the 2nd Brigade, the 1st Loyals, under Lieutenant Colonel E. Fulbrook, headed along the coast road in a northwesterly direction to a stream seven miles from Anzio without encountering any opposition. On the right flank, the Scots Guards of the Guards Brigade advanced down the road toward Anzio. In the center the 1st North Staffordshires and the 6th Gordons traveled north toward Aprilia: no enemy contact.

The 1st Irish Guards Battalion, with no one to fight, took the moment to relax under the bushes to wait, chat, and smoke, while Brigadier Murray and Lieutenant Colonel C. G. Gordon-Lennox of the 5th Grenadiers took a jeep to locate Lieutenant Colonel D. Wedderburn and his

1st Scots Guards. "It was a great relief," said Brigadier Murray, "to find that it had all been so easy. We realised that we had gained complete surprise and felt that this was the moment to go forward. But it was not to be, and we had to obey orders and remain in our concentration area."[12]

Yet despite the anticlimactic landing, Captain William Woodruff couldn't help but think that the operation—Operation Shingle, which was employing tens of thousands of troops, hundreds of naval craft of all sorts, and 2,700 aircraft—was an operation that should never have been conducted, for it seemed to have no focus, no compelling purpose, no good reason to do or die.[13]

A FEW MILES TO THE south, in the dark, hundreds more landing craft carrying Major General Lucian Truscott's 14,000-man-strong 3rd U.S. Division were plunging ahead toward X-Ray Beach, a deserted stretch of sand and grass between Nettuno and Torre Astura.

As the Allied armada approached, the commanders of the ships, and the men on them, breathed a sign of relief that they had not been detected by the Germans. Aboard the small and overcrowded USS *Biscayne*, a former seaplane tender converted into VI Corps' flagship, lying three and a half miles offshore, Lucas and his staff, along with dozens of others, had been up early to observe the preinvasion "softening up" of the coastline. Lucas reflected, "The hours on shipboard preceding the landing were quiet and peaceful and were the only ones I had had for many months with no burden of responsibility on my shoulders. My work is done and all of us were in the hands of our naval friends."

Then the rockets opened up. The use of ship-mounted rocket launchers was a new development for Lucas, who noted, "It was perfectly terrific. . . . Each rocket contains thirty pounds of TNT and 780 [rockets] per ship [an LST] are discharged in about two minutes, covering a large expanse of beach. Wire is cut by their detonation, land mines exploded, and those defenders in the vicinity who are not killed are stunned and completely helpless."[14]

Aboard one of the LCIs (Landing Craft, Infantry), Stanley R. Smith (Company I, 30th Infantry Regiment, 3rd U.S. Infantry Division) from Brunswick, Maine, recalled:

The time arrived for the start of the landing. At 0200 [2:00 A.M.] we heard the sound of the guns as they started shelling the beaches. The time came for us to go. We were told to "saddle up" and we started to get our equipment on and check our rifles—making sure that they were loaded and the safety was on. We started up the stairs through the blackout curtains and onto the deck. When we arrived on deck it was very dark and we were surprised to realize that although the guns were still firing, there was no "answering" fire from shore![15]

The display of firepower was truly awe-inspiring, and all those aboard the ships watching the rockets lighting up the night held a common belief—or at least a fervent hope—that nothing would be left alive after the munitions were finished converting the dark landscape into a flaming cauldron.

Another soldier in the arriving 3rd Infantry Division was twenty-year-old Private James Aurness of Minneapolis. A lantern-jawed, six-foot-seven-inch-tall "drink of water," Aurness was selected by his section leader in Company E, 7th Infantry Regiment, to be the first off the landing craft in order to test the depth of the water. "If you go under," his section leader told him, "we know we have to move the boat closer to shore." Aurness carried with him two large burlap sacks full of TNT that he was supposed to hand off to an engineer unit on shore. "Any second I expected to hear heavy gunfire open up on us," Aurness said.

The troops from the other landing craft were scrambling ashore, and soon there were 15,000 of us stretched out on the beach for maybe a mile. Within seconds after getting ashore, we realized that we weren't going to die. Not a shot was fired. It was an incredible moment. I've never forgotten it—first a feeling of sheer terror, fearing you were going to die as you stepped from the boat. Then there were 15,000 soldiers standing on the beach, all with the same sense of relief. The landing had been completely unopposed. There was a kind of a noise, a roar, something indescribable, as 15,000 men realized they were still alive. Then we silently moved inland toward our objectives without meeting enemy opposition.[16]

Stanley Smith, on another LCI, glanced at the helmets of the men around him, looking at the blue-and-white-striped 3rd Division insignia painted on the sides of the steel pots and a four-inch vertical white stripe painted on the back. "That was a good idea," he noted, so that each soldier could see the helmet of the man in front of him. "The only thing was, it was so dark you couldn't see a damned thing!"

The LCI had two staircase ramps along each side of the bow down which the men disembarked. "We formed two lines, one on the right and one on the left," Smith said.

I was on the right side and started my on-the-job training. As I said, it was very, very dark and I sure couldn't see the guy in front of me. We were supposed to keep a five-yard distance between each man, but that was next to impossible. We kept moving down the ramp and it wasn't too long [before] I felt my feet in water. Just kept walking and, when there were no more steps, into the water you went! Just before I reached the last step, the thought flashed through my mind: "I wonder how deep the water is?" It was very soon that I was to find out. As I went into the water, I thought my feet would never touch bottom. After what seemed like forever, they finally touched bottom, the water was up to my neck and very, very cold. We all had our arms over our heads, carrying our rifles to keep them dry. I am six feet tall and. . . . I have often thought how the fellows that were shorter than I made out.

Smith started making his way to shore and finally reached the beach.

I have no idea how far I had to wade to get there. It seemed like a long way; maybe it seemed that way because of the cold water, the pitch-black night, and nerves on edge. When I arrived on the beach there was a bit of confusion trying to get the companies together. I heard someone say, "I Company! Get the hell over here!" I went over and joined the rest of the company and found the platoon and squad I belonged to. It was a bit later that I realized again that there was no enemy fire directed toward us. They told us to move toward the north and, just as dawn was breaking, we halted and were told to dig in. In the daylight we could see what

kind of terrain we were on. The ground was flat, just like a table, and to
the north—to our front and right—was the Alban Hills. Beyond those
hills was a flat plain that led to Rome. The place where we landed had at
one time been a marshland; the Italians had dug canals to drain off the
water. When we started to dig foxholes, about a foot down we struck water. The day was sunny and we got a chance to get our clothes dried out.[17]

Frank Pistone, a radioman with Company L, 7th Infantry Regiment,
3rd Infantry Division, had with him a rifle, an ammunition belt, several
bandoliers of ammunition, six grenades, and three days' supply of food,
and, as platoon runner, he also carried the platoon's battery-operated
radio. He recalled that at 2:00 A.M., his company jumped from the transport ship into a landing craft that would take them to shore. After going
a short distance, the sailor who was driving the landing craft stopped it,
lowered the front ramp, and ordered the men to disembark and wade in,
for the water was too shallow for him to go any farther.

We obeyed and began walking to the beach in about four feet of very
cold water. It was a strange event, for we did not hear a single rifle shot.
    We then assembled on the beach with our lieutenant, who then or-
dered us to advance inland in a combat mode and to not make any noise.
As ordered, we began walking inland, very surprised and happy that we
had not met any resistance on the beach. It was now about 3:00 AM of
a very cold and dark night. Many of the farmers owned dogs on their
farms and they must have sensed our presence, for they began barking.
We all wished that they would shut up and go to sleep, for if German
soldiers were nearby, they certainly would check on why the dogs were
all barking. Some power must have been watching over us, for the enemy
did not respond and we continued our advance for about six miles, until
daybreak, without any opposition.[18]

At the same time, the 1st, 3rd, and 4th Battalions of the elite U.S.
Army Rangers (formally known as the 6615th Ranger Force), being led by their founder and commander, Colonel William O. Darby,
were planting boots on the concrete dock inside Anzio harbor. These
men with blackened faces were arguably the toughest soldiers in the

American Army. They had already seen plenty of combat in North Africa, Sicily, and Salerno and had recently come down from fighting in the frigid hills near Monte Cassino. As always, they were itching for a fight and couldn't wait to "mix it up" with the Germans.[19]

Of course, not everyone was fond of the Rangers, or the British Commandos, for that matter. As one historian observed, "The high brass was dubious of the Rangers. It was the same all over. The British brass didn't like [Colonel Sir Archibald David] Stirling's Commandos, either. The professionals always distrusted anybody who didn't fight by the book. . . . Nobody really liked elite or special troops. The generals distrusted them, and the dogfaces [i.e., ordinary infantrymen] hated anybody who thought they were hot stuff."[20]

The thirty-two-year-old Darby didn't care what anyone thought of his men, just as long as they gave them a role in the fighting. He described his unit's mission: "The Rangers were to land directly in front of Anzio, burst into the town, and sweep out to occupy a half-moon of beachhead territory limited in extent by a 'phase line.'"

Accompanying the Rangers were additional boats filled with members of the 504th Parachute Infantry Regiment, Company H of the 36th Engineer Combat Regiment, and the 83rd and 84th Chemical Mortar Battalions. Darby added, "The Rangers were given the difficult assignment of landing in the harbor and fanning out to occupy both Anzio and Nettuno. Then, after putting roadblocks on the coastal road to the north and south, we expected to contact the 1st British Division and the 3rd American Division which were landing simultaneously north of Anzio and south of Nettuno, respectively."

As at the Brits' Peter Beach, everything was going like clockwork at X-Ray Beach. The landings could not have been more perfect. No enemy fire raked the vulnerable landing craft, and no enemy ships, submarines, torpedo boats, or aircraft showed up to challenge the invaders. Darby said, "I had laughingly [told the navy] that when I got out of my boat in the center of the flotilla, I wanted to be at the front door of the [Nettuno] casino [the Paradiso sul Mare]. The Navy put me down on the exact spot."

The Rangers continued to make progress and secure their gains as D-day skies grew light. Darby sent Major Alvah Miller's 3rd Battalion to silence a battery of four 100mm guns on the north side of Anzio (they

eventually made contact that day with elements of Penney's 1st Division)
and Lieutenant Colonel Roy Murray's 4th Ranger Battalion to take control
of an area north of the railroad station. While these actions were taking
place, more landing craft arrived with additional stocks of ammunition
and the remainder of the 83rd and 84th Chemical Mortar Battalions.[21]
The Rangers would not be in Anzio or Nettuno for long; soon they would
be headed to another place in the line, a place called Cisterna di Littoria, a
name that brings chills to students of military history even today.

EARLIER, AN HOUR AFTER THE first salvo of Allied rockets splattered the
beaches around Anzio, frantic messages began flying into German
Army Group C's mountain-bunker headquarters inside Monte Soratte
at Sant'Oreste, some thirty-five miles north of Rome. General Siegfried
Westphal, General Field Marshal Albert Kesseling's forty-two-year-old
chief of staff, was awakened, and, after receiving preliminary reports
about the landings, he woke his boss with the not-unexpected news.

The fifty-eight-year-old Kesselring was soon at his desk, making calls
and issuing orders, along with invoking the code words "*Case Richard.*"
He had long felt that the Allies might try to outflank his forces along
the Gustav Line to the south, and, like any experienced commander, he
and his staff had already developed a number of contingency plans to
counter the variety of perceived threats. In case of a landing on the Tyrrhenian coast, a Kesselring plan called *Marder I* would go into effect;
Marder II would be declared for a landing on the Adriatic side. For an
invasion at or near Livorno, Case *Ludwig* (the first letter of the "case"
corresponded with the first letter of the geographic area) would be ini-
tiated; for Genoa, it was Case *Gustav*; for the Venice-Rimini area, it was
Viktor; for Istria, it was *Ida*; and for anything threatening Rome—and
that was what Anzio represented—it was Case *Richard*.[22] But getting
troops to the Anzio bridgehead would take time—time that Kesselring
thought he had precious little of.

The genial Kesselring was well known as an excellent piano player
and a master of parlor magic, and he would demonstrate every bit of
that latter skill as he seemed to pull whole regiments and divisions out of
thin air like rabbits out of a showman's hat.[23] He had always believed the
Allies would eventually make a play for Rome, and now they had done

OPERATION SHINGLE LANDINGS

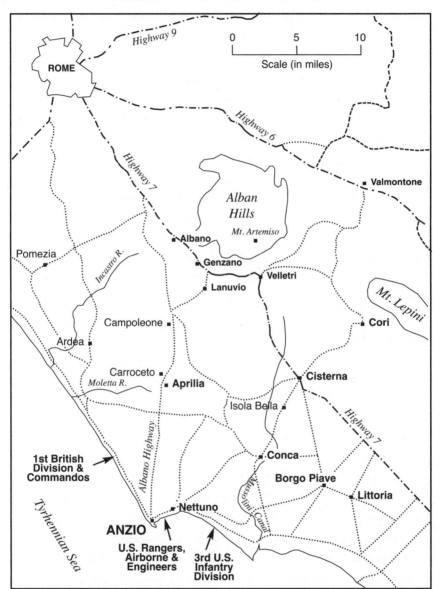

January 22, 1944: Successfully landing in and around the twin coastal towns of Anzio and Nettuno, the U.S. VI Corps was less than forty miles from Rome but soon found itself stuck at the beachhead.

so. He checked to see which units he might be able to rush to the area in order to choke off the danger. From Heinrich von Vietinghoff's Tenth Army at the Gustav Line, Kesselring pulled out a battle group from the 29th Panzer-Grenadier Division. The 29th, under Major General Walter Fries (whom Kesselring called "one of my best division commanders" and who had done much to hinder Fifth Army's advance at San Pietro Infine in December), had fought in Poland and France before being nearly destroyed at Stalingrad. Re-formed in southwestern France in the spring of 1943, it then fought in the Sicily campaign before being evacuated to mainland Italy.[24]

Another panzer-grenadier division alerted for Anzio was Lieutenant General Ernst-Günther Baade's 90th, which had begun life in August 1941 in the deserts of North Africa as the Division z.b.V. Afrika (which translates to a "special use" division). After surrendering in Tunisia in May 1943, it was reborn with troops from the Division Sardinien in Sardinia in July 1943 and was brought to Italy three months later, where it was again badly mauled but once more reconstituted.[25] Despite Vietinghoff's howls of protest, it was requisitioned by Kesselring just as the Gustav Line had come under renewed assault. Against his better judgment, Kesselring had returned the 90th to the Tenth Army. Westphal remarked:

> Looking back, this was clearly a mistake, for the attack and landing on the Tenth Army's front were only diversionary manoeuvres, designed to tie down our forces and, if possible, to lay bare the defences of Rome. The enemy's stratagem succeeded completely. There now occurred the very thing that should have been avoided at all costs. At the moment of the [Anzio] landing, the only troops available south of Rome for the initial defence, apart from a few auxiliary coastal batteries, were two battalions. That was all! Otherwise, there was absolutely nothing on hand to oppose the enemy on the same day.[26]

He ordered a *Kampfgruppe* (combat group) from Major General Heinrich Trettner's newly formed 4th Parachute Division, located in Terni, to head for Anzio; on the evening of the twenty-second, elements of this division were already taking up positions near the Alban Hills north of Anzio. Kesselring then grabbed a reconnaissance battalion sitting in reserve near Terracina.

Other units ordered to rush to Anzio included Lieutenant General Hans-Hellmuth Pfeiffer's Genoa-based 65th Infantry (minus one regiment) and Major General Wilhelm Raapke's 71st Infantry Divisions. Formed in 1942 and previously stationed in Holland, the 65th had not seen much action before being transferred to Italy in August 1943. The 71st, on the other hand, had been heavily engaged ever since the invasion of France, after which it was transferred to the Russian front, where it took heavy casualties at Stalingrad. After the remnants were reinforced with an infusion of fresh troops in Denmark, it was sent to Slovenia in August 1943 before being transferred to Italy.[27] The 71st had been on its way to join Vietinghoff's forces at the Gustav Line when it was diverted to Anzio.[28]

Another division—Lieutenant General Fritz-Hubert Gräser's 3rd Panzer-Grenadier (minus a regiment)—had also been ordered to the Gustav Line at the time of the Shingle landings. The 3rd Panzer-Grenadiers, originally formed as the 3rd Infantry Division, had fought in the Polish and French campaigns and then on the Eastern Front, before being virtually destroyed at Stalingrad. After being merged with the 386th Panzer-Grenadier Division, it came to Italy in June 1943 and fought against the Allies moving up from Salerno.[29] Also joining the march to Anzio was Heinz Greiner's 362nd Division, stationed in Rimini. A combat group from SS Brigadier General Max Simon's newly formed 16th SS Panzer-Grenadier (*Reichsführer SS*) Division in Livorno was also ordered to mount up and get to Anzio as quickly as possible.[30]

During the morning's rush to react to the crisis, Kesselring, knowing he needed a staff organization to control his counterattack, ordered the staffs of I Parachute Corps, under the estimable General of Paratroops Alfred Schlemm, and the LXXVI Panzer Corps, commanded by General of Panzer Troops Traugott Herr, from the Adriatic side to decamp to the Anzio area "in order to create a solid operational frame."[31] He then directed Vietinghoff to pull Major General Smilo Freiherr von Lüttwitz's 26th Panzer Division—which had been formed in France in the autumn of 1942 and had seen little combat until the following fall, when it was transferred to Italy[32]—out of the Gustav Line and put it in reserve in the event that it was needed to reinforce the Anzio defenses.[33]

As soon as he had set the pieces into motion, Kesselring notified Hitler's forward headquarters at Rastenburg in East Prussia about the invasion. Hitler, in turn, looked at a situation map and told Kesselring simply to "lance the abscess south of Rome," giving permission for his field marshal to bolster his defenses—something Kesselring was already doing.[34] Hitler wanted the Allied landing force not merely defeated but so badly mauled that the shock waves would reach all the way to London and Washington—shock waves that would tell Roosevelt and Churchill that if they thought the German army was on its last legs and ready to fold, they had another thought coming. Given a severe-enough beating, Hitler believed, Churchill and Roosevelt might even be forced to reconsider the wisdom of invading the Continent, an invasion Hitler knew was in the late planning stages. If he had anything to say about it, Anzio would be another Dunkirk, another Dieppe, another Gallipoli, for the Allies.

After the heady years of 1940, 1941, and 1942, when Hitler's war machine ran virtually unchecked, Nazi Germany had suffered a devastating series of defeats and reversals, and he desperately need a major victory; Anzio presented just such an opportunity. No matter what it cost in blood and treasure, national honor and even national survival depended on crushing the Allies at Anzio. With Hitler on his side, and appreciating the importance of stopping the invading forces before they could advance inland, Kesselring was moving whole regiments and divisions around like chess pieces, preparing for the moment when he could unleash a heavy counteroffensive that would block this new threat and turn this impertinent invasion into an unmitigated Allied disaster.

Virtually alone among the panoply of dour, scowling German generals and field marshals, the genial, ever-optimistic Albert Kesselring bore the nickname "Smiling Albert" for his trademark toothy grin.[35] Although he was a Luftwaffe officer, he had an uncanny grasp of infantry tactics and the innate ability to quickly assess a problem or situation and devise a solid solution.[36] Over the next few days, Kesselring would show the type of excellent generalship that demonstrated his cool head and sound decision making. He would shift enough troops, tanks, and artillery pieces (as well as the air force) to the Anzio-Nettuno area to prevent any breakout that would seriously threaten either Rome or German positions along the Gustav Line. With his opponents inexplicably adhering close to the shoreline, Kesselring realized that he had the opportunity to destroy the invaders with counterattacks and artillery fire.

To take overall command of the units he was pushing into the Anzio area, Kesselring ordered the commander of the Fourteenth German Army,* Colonel General Friedrich August "Eberhard" Mackensen, to fly from Verona, in northern Italy, and set up his headquarters in Rome in a complex of buildings located at the top of the Via Veneto. Mackensen and his Fourteenth Army staff would be responsible for keeping the Allies bottled up at the beachhead and for the eventual counterattack that would wipe them out.[37]

Mackensen was one of Kesselring's most competent field commanders, and his bloodline was an esteemed, thoroughly Prussian one. He was the monocled son of Field Marshal August von Mackensen, one of Germany's heroes of the Great War; his older brother Hans Georg von Mackensen was Germany's ambassador to Italy from 1938 to 1943.[†] Eberhard had been wounded during World War I, remained in the army, and eventually was elevated to chief of staff of the Fourteenth Army during the 1939 invasion of Poland. Then, during Germany's 1940 invasion of France, he became chief of staff of General Wilhelm List's

---

* The Fourteenth Army had taken part in the 1939 Polish campaign and then was deactivated until being reactivated in Italy in late 1943 with Mackensen at its head. Its chief responsibility at that time was the defense of Rome, but it was also used as a training command where depleted units fighting on the Gustav Line would be rotated off the line to rest and refit (that is, receive personnel replacements, ammunition, and weapons that had been lost) before being returned to combat. Field Marshal Lord Carter, *The Imperial War Museum Book of the War in Italy, 1943–1945*, 92; Carlo D'Este, *Fatal Decision: Anzio and the Battle for Rome*, 130.

† Italian forces had long performed so ineptly on the battlefield that, although nominally a full partner with Germany and Japan in the Tripartite Axis, Italy had, in actuality, become an occupied country run as a German puppet state. A secret agent working in Italy for the Allies noted that "the anti-Fascist sympathies of the Italian people are growing today because they hate Mussolini for having sold out their country to Hitler. Italy is no longer ruled by *Il Duce*, but by Hans Georg von Mackensen, the German Ambassador in Rome." *Life*, February 9, 1942, 95.

Twelfth Army. In January 1941 he assumed command of the III Army
Corps in Army Group South during the campaign in southern Russia
and the Caucasus. His star continued to rise when, in November 1942,
after General Paul Ewald von Kleist took command of Army Group A,
Mackensen was appointed commander of the First Panzer Army, which
he led in the Third Battle of Kharkov in March 1943. After that battle,
Mackensen was promoted to colonel general and given command of the
Fourteenth Army in Italy.[38]

Now constituting Fourteenth Army were two battle-hardened corps:
the LXXVI Panzer Corps and the I Parachute Corps. The LXXVI Panzer
Corps was composed of four divisions: Gräser's 3rd Panzer-Grenadier
Division, Lüttwitz's 26th Panzer Division (from Tenth Army), Raapke's
71st Infantry Division, and Greiner's 362nd Infantry Division. Additionally, Major General Paul Conrath's Hermann Göring Parachute-
Panzer Division,* which was scheduled to be transferred out of Italy,
had its orders canceled and was now available. (Other units that would
arrive before the end of the month included the 1027th and 1028th
Panzer-Grenadier Regiments, the 309th Panzer-Grenadier Regiment—
also known as the Infantry Lehr Demonstration Regiment—the Artillery Demonstration Regiment, the Tiger Battalion, and bits and pieces
of additional units.)[39]

Schlemm's I Parachute Corps was made up of Trettner's 4th Parachute Division; General of Panzer Troops Walter Fries's 29th Panzer-
Grenadier Division; Major General Hans-Georg Hildebrandt's 715th
Motorized Infantry Division, coming from Avignon, France; and the
114th Jäger Division (formerly the 714th Motorized Infantry Division),
under Lieutenant General Alexander Bouquin, stationed in northern
Yugoslavia. Also available to Kesselring were the considerable resources
of the Luftwaffe, especially the Second Air Fleet under General Field
Marshal Wolfram Freiherr von Richthofen, cousin of the World War I
aviator Manfred von Richthofen—the famed "Red Baron."[40] Kesselring

---

* An odd appellation, meaning that it was a combination tank and parachute division under the aegis of the Luftwaffe, that is, the German air force, but was
deployed as an armored division within the framework of the army. Alfred Otte,
The HG Panzer Division, 113.

ordered Maximilian Ritter von Pohl, who commanded the Luftwaffe in central Italy, to surround the beachhead with his 88mm dual-purpose antiaircraft batteries in order to keep Allied tanks at bay.[41]

Marshal Rodolfo Graziani, the minister of war in the deposed Mussolini's "Italian Social Republic" puppet state, made available to Kesselring two Italian units still loyal to Il Duce and the Germans: the "Barbarigo" Battalion of the naval unit Decima Flottiglia MAS and the "Nembo" Parachute Battalion from the RSI Parachute Regiment "Folgore."* These were attached to Schlemm's 1st Parachute Corps.[42] Two other Italian units that would fight hard and well on the side of the Germans at Anzio were the 2nd SS "Vendetta" Battalion and the 29th Italian SS Rifle Battalion, which reached the beachhead in March.[43] The beachhead was about to become a very crowded place.

All of the Fourteenth Army's division and corps commanders were seasoned and battle wise, each of them, except for Trettner, veterans of the Great War. Most were also veterans of the Eastern Front, so the difficulties of combat in a harsh climate were not new to them. They were among the most competent, experienced, and highly decorated officers in the German army. For example, the thirty-seven-year-old Trettner had served with the Luftwaffe during the Spanish incursion in 1937 and was the recipient of the Knight's Cross of the Iron Cross with Oak Leaves; Pfeiffer held the same award, while Gräser, commander of the 3rd Panzer-Grenadier Division, was a veteran of the fighting on the Eastern Front as well as in North Africa and also was a holder of the Knight's Cross of the Iron Cross.[44]

Kesselring later admitted that gathering disparate units from various other areas "was a higgledy-piggledy jumble," yet somehow he pulled it off. He acknowledged that the "first hours of 22 January . . . were full of anxiety," but he came to quickly feel that "the worst danger had been staved off."[45] Westphal felt the same: "The enemy remained astonishingly passive. Apparently his hands were kept quite full by the task of

---

* The Barbarigo Battalion would be cut to pieces during the Anzio fighting and withdrawn; the Nembo fought well and continued to hold its positions until the Allied breakout in May. Richard Lamb, *War in Italy, 1943–1945: A Brutal Story*, 94.

consolidating his bridgehead. It was therefore possible to build up a new front to oppose him."[46]

ALSO COMING ASHORE ON THE twenty-second was the 36th Engineer Combat Regiment. Lieutenant Colonel George W. Gardes (who would lead the regiment after its commander, Colonel Thomas H. Stanley, was killed in June 1944) reflected on his unit's assignment:

> This was quite a sizeable job in view of the bombing, plus the fact that the port area was heavily mined. When the Germans evacuated the port of Anzio, they detonated some of the mines but they were only partially successful, with the result that most of the buildings that were still standing contained the explosives that were all prepared for the demolitions. Also, part of the regimental headquarters arrived in the afternoon and set up headquarters directly across from the railway station. That night the shelling became quite heavy and in the early part of the evening a number of casualties occurred, including that of Colonel Barabee, who commanded the 1st Battalion.

Company H of the 36th Engineers landed along with the Rangers at Nettuno, while the rest of the regiment came ashore within Anzio's harbor; the 1st Battalion marched up to Anzio and began clearing the port of mines and booby traps.[47]

THE FIRST SIGN TO THE Allies that the enemy was reacting to the invasion came around noon on D day, when waves of German fighter-bombers began roaring over the beachhead, attacking ships and men on the ground. They were met by fighters of Major General John K. Cannon's Twelfth U.S. Air Force, and aerial dogfights took place over the heads of the infantry, who watched in amazement at the spectacle above them.

As his landing craft approached the beach, George Avery (Company A, 84th Chemical Mortar Battalion) observed:

> The naval guns were bombarding the Nettuno-Anzio area, producing fires, black smoke, and dense dust. . . . The German air force made an appearance with a bombing run that ended somewhere between our line

of ships. The sky now was full of exploding shells and we all were in our helmets (what goes up, must come down). Guns from all the ships were firing at German planes, and we came under a shower of falling hot-metal fragments. The noise was awful. Just ahead of us, a British transport had run into a sea mine, was overturned and burning, with the sea full of equipment and men.

The battle had shifted to the sky, with American, British, and German warplanes circling, diving, spinning, and firing away at each other.

Avery was in the second wave, riding in waterproofed jeeps that carried the mortars and mortar ammo. "We had grounded on the beach, as intended," he said.

> The ramps were down, and off we drove, expecting to run into German fire. In the sea behind us, the 83rd Chemical Mortar Battalion was caught in an attack bombing run, their LST aflame and sinking miles from shore. No German artillery fire raked the beach and there was no rifle fire. The only Germans we saw were dead. We raced through the shambles that were Anzio, with no Italian in sight, no barking dogs, no pleading children. The battalion moved to a wooded area and waited for orders from the 3rd Division. In a very short time we were in our wooded assembly area. We dug deep holes and twice that day we were subjected to bombing and strafing runs. We had not yet fired a mortar round or used our rifles. As we were required to wait, and nothing seemed to be happening, we posted guards and went to sleep.[48]

WHILE KESSELRING WAS STILL RUSHING his forces to Anzio, British General Penney, wanting to see what sort of enemy opposition was in front of him, sent a reconnaissance patrol up the Via Anziate (also known as the Albano Road and Albano Highway) to scout the area. Lieutenant John Michael Hargreaves,* commanding the Grenadier Guards' Carrier Platoon, took a reconnaissance unit made up of Bren

---

* Hargreaves would be killed three days later, on January 25, 1944, during the fight for Carroceto. William Dugdale, *Settling the Bill: The Memoirs of Bill Dugdale*, 106; Lloyd Clark, *Anzio: Italy and the Battle for Rome—1944*, 125.

gun carriers* to scout the highway toward Rome. The patrol went past
Aprilia and Campoleone and the Alban Hills, past Lake Albano and the
pope's summer residence at Castel Gandolfo, past the Cinecittà movie
studios and the Basilica of Saint John Lateran and as far as the gate of the
Appian Way along the Aurelian Walls, and then turned around and beat
it back to Anzio—all without incident. He reported that the patrol had
encountered no enemy anywhere along the route, but his report was not
acted upon. As one of the Grenadier Guards officers wrote, "It was the
first and only British military visit to Rome until the following June."[49]

If the report of Hargreaves's mission reached Lucas (and there is
no indication that it did), it would have presented a further quandary
for the corps commander. Did the lack of an enemy presence between
Anzio and Rome mean that he should obey the part of his orders that
said he *could advance* on the Alban Hills "if the opportunity presented
itself"? Or should he obey Clark's command to not "stick his neck out"
and "forget this goddam Rome business"? Were the Germans hiding,
simply lying in wait and observing through powerful glasses the pouring of troops and vehicles and supplies into Anzio's harbor? If he began
moving his corps across open ground toward Rome, would the enemy
come swooping down from the hills and blast his force into oblivion?
Without concrete information, it's better to do nothing foolish, Lucas
decided, than to do something rash and lose everything.†

---

* The Bren gun carrier (formally known as a Universal Carrier) was a small, lightly
armored tracked vehicle developed by the British in the 1930s and used for a variety of purposes. The gun it carried was a .303-caliber machine gun that weighed
around twenty-two pounds, was fed by a curved box magazine, had a rate of fire
of 500 rounds per minute, and could be carried by an infantryman as well as being
vehicle mounted. Its name derives from Brno, Czechoslovakia, where the original
model was developed, and Enfield, home of the British Royal Small Arms Factory.
Ian V. Hogg and John Weeks, *The Illustrated Encyclopedia of Military Vehicles*,
195; John Quick, *Dictionary of Weapons and Military Terms*, 74–75.

† Another officer, an American lieutenant named John T. Cummings (36th Engineer Regiment), said that he and his driver traveled up the Albano Highway by
jeep on the morning of January 22 all the way to Rome without encountering hostile forces. Upon his return, Cummings submitted a report that the route to Rome
was, for all intents and purposes, free of enemy troops. If Lucas saw his report, no
action was taken. D'Este, *Fatal Decision*, 124.

EVERYTHING WAS GOING AS WELL as the planners of Operation Shingle could have hoped for; Lucas certainly thought so. He wrote with pride in his diary, "We achieved what is certainly one of the most complete surprises in history." This positive thought was confirmed when Clark and Alexander visited the beachhead area later on D day to confer with Lucas; his superiors, too, seemed pleased with the landings. Alexander was especially happy that things had gone so well. Buoyantly, he told Lucas, "You have certainly given the folks at home something to talk about."[50]

But what was the next step? Lucas did not know, and neither Clark nor Alexander saw fit to advise him. After Alexander and Clark departed and headed back to their headquarters at the Versailles-like palace at Caserta, leaving Lucas in limbo, the corps commander decided to do the prudent thing: stay close to shore and build up his resources until the day he was ordered to advance farther inland.[51]

Once Clark and Alexander had departed, Lucas met with his division commanders and gave them his directives: "Stay where you are and fortify your positions. Be ready for counter-attacks as had happened at Salerno." The division commanders then passed that information on to their subordinates. The 24th Guards Brigade commander, Brigadier Glaxo Murray, returned to the 24th's bivouac area from his meeting with Penney and told his battalion commanders, "There are no orders for us, but we have been given some rather vague counter-attack roles."[52]

Like every other unit on the beachhead, Penney's division did not have orders to move quickly inland and seize territory; barring incident, the outskirts of Rome could have been reached in less than two hours. But Penney received no instructions except to stay where he was and await further instructions. His men dug in and waited.

A member of the Guards Brigade grumbled, "What were we messing about at? Rome was only thirty miles up the road; we could have been drinking vino with the Pope by now."[53]

Much to their dismay, the troops on the beach felt that the surprise landing, and the opportunities that accrued to it, were quickly being frittered away.

CHAPTER 3

"The whole world seemed to be marching"
JANUARY 22 (AFTERNOON)

ORIGINALLY, IT WAS PLANNED THAT the 504th Parachute Infantry Regiment would be dropped around Rome, but this was canceled when the planners feared not only that it would alert the Germans to the fact that an amphibious invasion was coming but that, if the landing forces did not quickly take Rome, the paratroopers would also all be killed or captured.[1]

The initial mission of another airborne force, the 509th Parachute Infantry Battalion* (an independent battalion not a part of the 504th PIR that had already seen heavy fighting at the mountain town of San Pietro Infine a month earlier, as well as the fierce fighting across Sicily and during the drive on Naples), was to move to the Mussolini Canal, running north–south a couple of miles west of Littoria, and secure a line 3,300 yards long, along with three bridges over the canal, which represented the easternmost boundary of the invasion area.[2] Lieutenant Colonel

---

* On December 10, 1943, the 2nd Battalion of the 509th Parachute Infantry Regiment was officially redesignated the 509th Parachute Infantry Battalion. The 509th PIB would be an independent battalion (that is, not an element of a regiment or a division). After Anzio the battalion would continue to fight, taking part in the invasion of southern France, Operation Market Garden, and the battle of the Bulge. Jim T. Broumley, *The Boldest Plan Is the Best: The Combat History of the 509th Parachute Infantry Battalion During WWII.*

William P. Yarborough, the thirty-two-year-old commanding officer of
the 509th PIB, said that his unit was not disappointed to arrive in Anzio
by landing craft rather than via a parachute drop, "because we felt confident and we wanted to fight and wanted to be part of the scene." Despite
his airborne battalion's seaborne delivery to Anzio, Yarborough said:

> We were especially happy to have been assigned with Darby because I
> had known Darby before and had a high regard for him. But mixing
> paratroops and Rangers was like mixing oil and water. I just can't tell
> you what the differences were between our two units. . . . Every [para-
> trooper] shaved every day no matter what. . . . Our people looked sharp.
> I required it and they took pride in the paratrooper uniform. . . . Darby's
> guys looked like cutthroats. They looked like the sweepings of the
> barrooms. And they wore stubble beards, and any kind of a uniform;
> some of them had tanker uniforms on, some had just anything they
> wanted. . . . [Eventually our two units] became staunch friends. So, when
> we went into Anzio, we were a force working together.[3]

One of the airborne officers, Second Lieutenant Edward Reuter
(Company A, 509th PIB), recalled that Nettuno was deserted, "but I did
see one dead German on the street the Rangers had killed. We marched
inland about a mile and were told to dig in. Everyone carried a small antitank mine, just enough to blow the tread off a tank, and we placed these
on the roads. A German fighter plane came in for a strafing run; the
noise was tremendous. I lay in my shallow slit trench and had uncon-
trollable shakes. I was determined that I could never allow fear to take
over like that again, and it never did. This was my baptism to combat."

The following day the paratroopers moved farther inland and came
across other members of the 504th PIR, also moving forward. Reuter
said, "There was Frank Belfoy and we waved at each other." Earlier,
in Naples, Belfoy had given Reuter the name and address of a girl in
St. Paul, Minnesota, to whom he had been writing and asked Reuter to
write her "if anything happened to him. The next day Frank was killed
going to the aid of his company commander who had just been shot by
a sniper. Later, I corresponded with his girlfriend for about a year, until
she married a serviceman."[4]

SOME UNITS ARRIVED AT ANZIO and Nettuno that were not infantry outfits and had no direct combat role, but their jobs were important none-
theless. One such unsung support unit was the 51st Signal Battalion.
As the troops reached shore and fanned out, the 51st Signal Battalion
headed for the fortresslike Villa Borghese, built by Cardinal Vincenzo
Costaguti in 1648 and located in a large forested park just to the north
of Nettuno. Sergeant Sal Chiefari, a member of the unit, said that his
battalion had the job of setting up communications in the villa, which
would become the forward headquarters of Fifth Army and given the
code name Lightning Advance.[5]

Another support unit was the 53rd DUKW Battalion, which used the
amphibious General Motors trucks to ferry troops and supplies to shore.
The DUKW was an ingenious invention—a veritable swimming truck.
A member of the battalion, Joe F. Dickerson, explained:

> A DUKW was a motorboat on wheels. . . . Our invasion job was to carry
> men and guns and deposit them safely on shore. Then we settled down
> to the routine, yet all-important task of transporting the ammo and ra-
> tions that are the lifeblood of the beachhead. The insignia of our unit was
> Donald Duck clasping a shell under his wing, symbolizing the work of
> bringing in the ammo.
>
>   The DUKWs got off pretty easy during the Anzio-Nettuno landing—
> two were destroyed by land mines, one was hit by a bomb, and a fourth
> sank off and never came up. But that's just when the going got tougher—
> shells and bombs followed us around throughout the day. We had a ca-
> sualty list of nine men killed and about thirty injured. The only danger
> from shelling and bombing while on the job was when the DUKWs drew
> alongside a Liberty ship,[*] the target for enemy artillery and planes.[6]

---

* "Liberty ship" was the name given to the EC2-type ship designed for "emergency" construction by the U.S. Maritime Commission in World War II. From
September 1941 until the war's end, 2,711 of these cargo ships were built. It took
an average of seventy days and $2 million to build one Liberty ship. "American
Merchant Marine at War," www.usmm.org.

VI CORPS MOVES INLAND

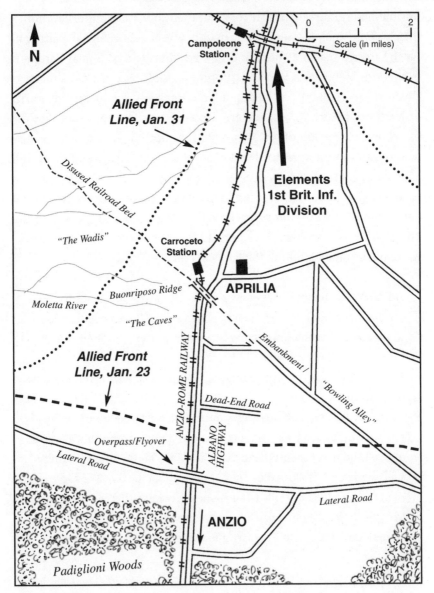

Elements of the U.S. VI Corps were able to move inland about ten miles, but it took four months for them to get beyond Campoleone Station.

NO CITY HAS EVER CONSENTED to becoming the scene of a battle. War too often just happens to crash like a runaway freight train into whatever towns, cities, and villages that have the misfortune of lying in its path. Battles, too, have a way of developing geographical misnomers—a sort of historical shorthand that distorts the truth for the sake of brevity. The battle of Bunker Hill, in the American Revolution, was actually fought at Boston's Breed's Hill. The battle of Waterloo in 1815 really took place at Braine-l'Alleud and Lasne, Belgium. The huge 1943 German-Soviet tank engagement known as the battle of Kursk occurred closer to the Soviet village of Prokhorovka than to Kursk. The Belgian village of Baugnez rather than Malmédy was where the December 1944 massacre of American prisoners of war (POWs) by the SS took place. And a goodly portion of what is called the battle of Anzio was actually fought ten miles to the north—in, at, and around the small town of Aprilia.

Even Aprilia itself has been the victim of misidentification. When British and American troops first laid eyes on the town during Operation Shingle, they immediately dubbed it "the Factory"—a misnomer that has stuck. Their error is understandable. From a distance—across vast stretches of treeless farmland—the town *did* resemble an industrial complex. The tight cluster of low, squarish buildings, with their evenly spaced windows, did look very much like a factory—an impression made even more striking given the tall church bell tower and an even taller square tower attached to the House of Fascism that were apparently mistaken for industrial chimneys.

Before 1935 Aprilia did not exist. It was one of a series of starkly modern towns that Mussolini had commissioned to be built in sparsely populated areas. After Littoria, Sabaudia, and Pontina, Aprilia was the fourth town created in the former Pontine wetlands along the coast south of Rome—an area known as the Roman Agro. After a year and a half of furious construction, the new town was ready for its formal inauguration. On October 29, 1937, with a specially built grandstand erected in the main town square, Aprilia had its coming-out party.

Attending the event were a number of local, national, and international dignitaries, including Mussolini and a German delegation led by Hitler's Deputy Führer Rudolf Hess. The whole scene was made festive with the addition of a profusion of Italian flags, Fascist banners, and the red-white-black swastika flags of Nazi Germany. In front of the church was installed a bronze statue of Saint Michael the Archangel, the city's patron saint, created by a twenty-three-year-old sculptor named Venanzo Crocetti. Ringing this central piazza were a few small, newly built homes and apartment buildings—enough to house an initial population of about 2,000 residents.

The new town was gleaming in its simple modernity—flat and unadorned facades, repetitive arcade arches, rigidly aligned rectangular windows—a major departure from the traditional ancient-Roman style common throughout much of the rest of Italy. Fascist architecture, by contrast, tended to emphasize the power of the state and minimize the importance of the individual.[7] Soon Aprilia would become a prime focal point in the upcoming battle because of its strategic location that controlled the network of roads in the area; anyone wanting to advance upon Rome—or keep the other side from advancing—would first need to control Aprilia.[8]

Luckily, when the British and American forces splashed ashore from their landing craft at Anzio and Nettuno, the Germans had evacuated most of the residents of Aprilia, sparing the civilians from witnessing the desperate battle for, and ultimate destruction of, their homes. They would not immediately know that their pristine eight-year-old town would become the focal point of a savage months-long battle between the German and Allied armies, or that it would change hands several times, or that it would be completely demolished during the course of the fighting.

The fighting that swirled around and through Aprilia would see an unusual occurrence. Despite the fact that the British and Americans were allies, throughout the war they almost never fought side by side; overlapping units would cause too many command, control, and supply issues (British ammunition, for example, could not be used in American weapons and vice versa). During the Italian campaign, which lasted from September 9, 1943, until May 2, 1945, the British Eighth Army (with its Commonwealth components such as Indians, South Africans, and Canadians, plus the French and Poles) almost always confined its operations to the eastern half of the Italian peninsula, while the American Fifth Army fought primarily in the western half. Only at such places as Monte Cassino as well as Anzio and Aprilia were British and American units fighting in close proximity to one another—even, at times, intermingled.

SHORTLY AFTER THE INITIAL LANDINGS, American war correspondent Ernie Pyle of the Scripps-Howard newspaper chain arrived by LST and created a landscape painting out of words:

> Anzio and Nettuno run together along the coast, forming practically one city. There is really only one main street, which runs along the low blocks just back of the first row of waterfront buildings. The two cities stretch for about three miles, but extend only a few blocks back from the waterfront. A low hill covered with tall cedar trees rises just back of them, and along some of the streets there are palm trees. . . . At one point, the towns extend two hundred yards from the water's edge, forming a solid flank of fine stone buildings four and five stories high. Most of these are apartment houses, business offices, and rich people's villas.
>
> When we landed, there was no civilian life in Anzio-Nettuno. The Germans had evacuated everybody before we arrived, and we found the place deserted.[9]

IN APRILIA, TOO, MOST OF the civilian population had been evacuated from the town prior to the invasion. An exception was the Nuti family. The patriarch, Assunto Nuti, had arrived in Aprilia in February 1940 to take over as chief of the town's Guardia Municipale, or city police force, and he knew that his services would be needed even if the town was vacant. Yet he faced his own crisis—the safety of his young family: his wife, Rina, and their two sons, nine-year-old son Pasqualino and sixteen-month-old Franco.

Pasqualino had been more or less aware of the German presence in his town shortly before the invasion. One day, as a way of amusing himself, he put a line of stones across the road leading to Carroceto when a German Army staff car approached and then came to a screeching halt at the "barrier." A German officer got out of the car and began kicking the offending stones out of the way and spotted Pasqualino standing nervously nearby. Likely assuming that the child was a very young partisan, the officer proceeded to try to kick him. "Returning home," the boy noted, "I said nothing to my parents, not wanting other reproaches."

On the D-day morning of January 22, the skies above Aprilia thundered with the new and frightening sounds of war. Pasqualino recalled, "That morning, I sensed something different in the air. An indefinable mood had accompanied me through the night, leaving me at the mercy of the drowsiness caused by the constant rumble of gunfire coming from the Anzio seafront and a bustle of low-flying aircraft that flew over Aprilia and Nettuno. Worried, I turned to my dad; he whispered in a faint voice, 'The Americans have landed at Anzio. Help your mother to collect the necessary things; we are going to take refuge at the slaughterhouse,'" which was located on the northeast perimeter of town, not far from the cemetery.

Within minutes the Nuti family put food into a small bundle and left town. "Fear did not give us time to turn and take one last look at Aprilia that had always seemed pleasant. Along the way, we came across other *Apriliani* also in search of a safe haven. We began to scatter into the surrounding countryside to search for refuge outside the town. Our retreat outside Aprilia was the slaughterhouse, which was completely isolated from the urban center." On their way to the slaughterhouse, the Nuti family ran into lines of the few other remaining Aprilia citizens, all abandoning the town in hopes of finding safety. "The only hope we carried was that, after the passage of the Allies, we could return to our homes. Unfortunately, we did not."[10]

WHILE THE SMALL BANDS OF citizens were scrambling to get out of harm's way, the 509th PIB that had landed at Anzio by ship instead of by silk was moving toward Nettuno, where they rooted out German defenders hiding in some of the buildings, all the while keeping their heads low against flying shrapnel from enemy artillery rounds that were beginning to fall.

LATE IN THE AFTERNOON OF January 22, Stanley Smith (3rd Infantry Division), resting with his unit and drying out his clothing that had been soaked during the wade in, recalled that his platoon sergeant suddenly yelled out, "Saddle up and move out!" "Oh, how I would come to hate that order," Smith said. "So move out we did. Now on the march, we had two single-file columns, one on each side of the road. They told us to keep a five-yard interval between each man. That was in case, if a shell landed close by, there was a very good chance that not too many would get hurt. Still, there wasn't any enemy fire coming from up ahead of us—very strange."

Smith's unit had been on the move for about three-quarters of an hour when they heard a burst of fire from a Thompson sub-machine gun.

What had happened was there was a German *kubelwagen* (like our jeep) that came down the road and, as they approached the column, someone opened up and the German "jeep" went into a ditch. There were two Germans in the "jeep" and they were both killed by the sub-machine gun. They were carrying a couple of "jerry cans" [five-gallon cans] of German coffee. The coffee was still warm and somebody told us that anyone that wanted coffee could help themselves. We didn't want it to go to waste, so we broke out our canteen cups and started to pour. It didn't taste too bad—not as good as American coffee, but for German coffee it was okay.

The absence of German defenders explained to Smith why, at that time, the Americans were not running into major opposition: "The Germans were using Anzio as kind of a 'rest area,' so the German troops that were there, which were just a few, were just resting. A couple of days later that was to change for sure! We kept moving long after dark and, after a while, we stopped on the side of what turned out to be a canal. We were told to dig in, and we did."[11]

ALEXANDER'S FIRST REPORT THAT THE initial landings had achieved surprise was telegraphed to his prime minister's underground command post (CP) in London: "We appear to have got almost complete surprise," Alexander wrote. "I have stressed the importance of strong-hitting mobile patrols being boldly pushed out to gain contact with the enemy, but so far have not received reports of their activities."

Churchill cabled back, "Am very glad you are pegging out claims rather than digging in beach-heads." Churchill's happiness would be short-lived. He was soon growing livid at the reported lack of forward progress: "But now came disaster, and the ruin in its prime purpose of the enterprise. General Lucas confined himself to occupying his beach-head and having equipment and vehicles brought ashore. . . . The defences of the beach-head were growing, but the opportunity for which great exertions had been made was gone."[12]

Churchill's frustrations with Lucas knew no bounds, and, while he could not sack an American general, he could apply pressure on those who could.

AS THE DAYS WENT BY, more ground units would be added to the German side. However, all this buildup came at a cost; Kesselring knew that if the bottom of the barrel had not exactly been reached, the scrapings were indeed paltry. If these forces were unable to defeat, or at least halt, the Allies at Anzio and along the Cassino front, there were no more reserves upon which he could call.[13] As units were piecemealed into the area, Kesselring pushed them into position, not wanting to surrender a single foot of ground.

But something had gone seriously amiss. Someone—Kesselring never knew whom—had arbitrarily changed his orders, thus preventing the immediate German counterattacks from being launched. Despite this, Kesselring, as he toured the makeshift defensive posture around the beachhead, realized that the Allies had failed to capitalize on their surprise landings. Any worry that he may have had about Rome falling swiftly or the Gustav Line being threatened from behind quickly dissipated. He was certain that time was on the German side.[14]

IF THE NEWS ABOUT SHINGLE did not immediately panic Kesselring, it also did not unduly frighten Hitler or throw him into one of his usual tirades; he had many more worries on his mind—such as the ongoing problems on the Eastern Front. Three days earlier, on the nineteenth, Stalin had launched a massive attempt to liberate the key industrial city of Novgorod, some 100 miles south of Leningrad. It was part of a major counteroffensive against Hitler's forces on what has been called the Dnieper Front that would eventually lead to the Red Army's retaking of the Crimea and the Ukraine. But Hitler had complete faith and confidence in Albert Kesselring, one of his most capable commanders; he need not worry about Italy.

By the evening of January 22, all roads leading to Anzio were crowded with German vehicles packed with soldiers. The roads, however, were very dangerous places for German units to be, primarily because of the Allies' air superiority. Whenever a line of trucks and tanks showed itself, Allied planes swooped down to make short work of them, as well as destroy the bridges, rail lines, and marshaling yards. Mechanical problems also plagued the panzers.

One example is the story of the 508th Heavy Tank Battalion. The battalion's forty-five Tiger I tanks had been shipped by rail from Metz, France, to Ficulle, a railhead 120 miles from Anzio. Because of Allied aircraft prowling the skies, further rail transport was difficult; the battalion took to the roads for the remaining distance, going through Rome. This long-distance drive put a heavy strain on the Tigers' mechanical components, causing about 60 percent of the tanks to suffer breakdowns along the narrow, winding mountain roads.[15]

Wilhelm Ernst Terheggen (Hermann Göring Parachute-Panzer Division) recalled that his unit had been in Arce, between Frosinone and Cassino, on January 22 when they received the news of the Allied landing. Since they were alerted to move to the Anzio area the next morning, Terheggen and a few fellow officers decided to get drunk at a farewell party that night; it might the beginning of the end for all of them. Once on the road the next day, with bleary eyes Terheggen marveled at the sight of so many tanks, trucks, self-propelled guns, staff cars, and towed artillery pieces rolling westward to the coast: "The whole world seemed to be marching toward Nettuno," he said.[16]

WITH THE DUSK OF D day falling over the western half of the invasion area, the Loyals had pushed up to the Fosso del Diavolo (the "Devil's Ditch"), while the 1st British Division's 1st Reconnaissance Regiment was two miles north of them, feeling in the growing darkness for a German front line that seemed not to be there. With field glasses, the officers scanned the bleak horizon and, due east of Carroceto, saw a collection of buildings that, according to their maps, was named "Aprilia." They could also see movement: members of the 3rd Panzer-Grenadier Division had taken up residence and were well armed.

The 2nd Battalion of the North Staffordshire Regiment, which had seen heavy action in Tunisia in 1943, was in possession of the low ridge at Campo di Carne (soon to earn its name, Field of Meat) south of the town, with the 6th Battalion, Gordon Highlanders, to their southeast. Between Aprilia and Anzio, the Commandos of Ronnie Tod's 2nd Special Service Brigade had pushed eastward from the Via Anziate—the main highway that led directly through Aprilia on its way to Rome—and had made contact with elements of the U.S. Rangers that had advanced on their right flank. And yet—there was still no sign of serious enemy opposition. Was it possible that the invasion had caught the Germans completely by surprise? Was Rome within VI Corps' grasp, ripe for the plucking?

As the first day came to a close, a nervous Churchill, in his underground headquarters beneath the New Public Offices Building in London's Whitehall government complex, was following developments in faraway Italy. "It was with tense, but I trust suppressed, excitement," he wrote, "that I awaited the outcome of this considerable stroke."[17]

Churchill would have a long wait for the outcome.

CHAPTER 4

"A whale wallowing on the beaches!"

JANUARY 23-24

AS DAWN OF D-PLUS-ONE ARRIVED, the brigades of General Penney's 1st British Division continued inching northward, still wondering where the Germans were and why, except for some scattered artillery rounds and a few aerial strafing runs, they had made no serious effort to strike back.

In the Guards Brigade's sector on the left flank, Major R. H. "Tim" Bull claimed first contact with the Germans. Seeing a motorcycle with a passenger in the sidecar speeding down the coast road from the direction of Anzio, he took a well-aimed shot and killed the passenger; the driver roared off, never to be seen again.[1]

Edward "Ted" Grace, a young officer serving with Lieutenant Colonel James Peddie's 6th Battalion, Gordon Highlanders, recalled that the morning of January 23 opened with his unit occupying a stretch of the Albano Highway between Anzio and Aprilia. The men were supremely unhappy that they were not being let off the leash, that they had been thrust into the strategic beachhead to do nothing but "sit on their ruddy arses."

Soon he heard the sound of a vehicle coming rapidly down the road toward them. As only the Germans were to their front, he knew that it had to belong to the enemy, and so his men all took up positions and readied their weapons in anticipation. Within seconds the vehicle, an armored car, rounded a corner and came into view. "As it raced through our line,"

Grace said, "we let off a hail of small-arms fire. The bullets ricocheted off its metal plating while its machine gun fired harmlessly over our heads. It roared past us like an armadillo swarmed by wasps. We all cheered and waved our defiance. It was a musical comedy that helped to restore our confidence." (Grace later learned that the armored car continued barreling down the road into Anzio, where it was captured by the Americans.)

The front grew quiet again. One of Grace's men, a Sergeant Maclaren, growled in his best Scottish burr while eating lunch under a tree: "By now we could have cut the main road to Rome and been halfway there. Nothing could stop us today. But tomorrow—who knows?"[2]

ANOTHER UNIT ABOUT TO BE thrust into action was the 45th U.S. Infantry Division, which, like the 1st Armored, had already had a belly full of war. After landing on Sicily's Gela beachhead on July 9–10, 1943, the 45th had fought in a month-long battle for every foot of rocky, dusty ground on its way northward across the island and then was selected for the Operation Avalanche landings at Salerno on September 9. They arrived just in time to take the full brunt of the Germans' counterattack designed to split the Allied beachhead; it was the 45th, fighting with a desperate fury, that deserves the credit for saving the beachhead.[3]

The 45th then took part in Fifth Army's long and costly march up the shin of the Italian boot, over rivers and mountains and finally into position at a town called Venafro, just southeast of Cassino. There the division spent a cold and deadly winter in the mountains before being called upon for its third amphibious assault landing—on the shores of Anzio and Nettuno. "We made so many landings," said James R. Bird, a member of the 45th's Battery A, 160th Field Artillery Battalion, "we began to think we had joined the Marines."[4]

The 45th's nickname, "the Thunderbirds," had been chosen to reflect the division's southwestern American heritage. An amalgamation of the Colorado and Oklahoma National Guard regiments,* the division at one

---

*The Colorado regiment was the 157th, commanded by Colonel Walter P. O'Brien, while the Oklahoma contingent was made up of the 179th and 180th Infantry Regiments, commanded by Colonels Malcolm R. Kammerer and James O. Smith, respectively. Flint Whitlock, *The Rock of Anzio: A History of the US 45th Infantry Division—from Sicily to Dachau.*

time had some 3,000 American Indians in its ranks. It was brought to federal active-duty status in September 1940, along with three other National Guard divisions: the 30th, the 41st, and the 44th. Its divisional sleeve insignia was a golden thunderbird on a red diamond, thought by Native peoples to be a sacred bearer of unlimited happiness; the thunderbird replaced the 45th's prewar insignia: a golden swastika on a red background.[5]

A once-tough, swaggering outfit weaned during the hardscrabble Dust Bowl Depression days in America's Southwest, the 45th had been reduced to a shadow of its former self, with its blood, like most of the other units at Anzio, spilled during a half year of almost constant combat. The Thunderbirds' wings were tattered and frayed, and its swagger had turned into a limp, but its official marching song—the clanging, raucous, minstrel-hall favorite, "There'll Be a Hot Time in the Old Town Tonight," written in 1896—could still bring a smile and stir the soul of an old, proud, bedraggled Thunderbird.

Oddly enough, the Thunderbirds' commander was an eagle—Major General William Willis Eagles. Born in Indiana in 1895 and graduated from West Point in 1917, he began his World War II career as the assistant division commander of the 3rd Infantry Division during Operations Torch, Husky, and Avalanche. A calm and steady officer (Lucas had called him a "quiet, determined soldier, with broad experience" and "one of our most accomplished division commanders")[6] who would have looked perfectly at home as the president of a bank or major corporation, Eagles was assigned to command the 45th in November 1943 when he took over from the successful Major General Troy Middleton, who departed Italy for England to command VIII Corps—a corps that would be part of the Normandy invasion and the campaign across Europe.[7]

After being selected as part of the "second wave" at Anzio, the 45th was transported from the frigid, snowy heights of Venafro to the Naples area, and, on the night of January 20–21, the division's 179th Infantry Regiment was moved to a staging area between Pozzuoli and the Bay of Naples and placed under the control of the 1st U.S. Armored Division. The staging area was most unpleasant, as it was deep inside Monte Nuovo, an ancient volcanic crater (formed by its last eruption in AD 1538) whose floor was 700 feet below sea level and was immersed in an impenetrable fog so thick that, according to the regimental historian, "men were lost ten feet from their pup tents. . . . The cold was biting, intense. And, as a staging area, the place was sealed. No one could get out."[8]

The Thunderbirds would soon find themselves at Anzio—another place where no one could get out.

ALSO ABOUT TO BE CAUGHT up in the fighting was the Nuti family, taking refuge in the slaughterhouse at the northeast corner of Aprilia and waiting for news about the advance of the Americans and British. The night of D day passed with both sides trying to feel each other out; dawn on January 23 was cold and gray, with the leaden skies still spitting rain. Pasqualino recalled, "My mother was busy feeding a bowl of soup to little Franco, who was only sixteen months old, when suddenly we heard a loud explosion very close to the building and the window panes shattered. The first instinctive gesture of my father was to pick up little Franco and shout, 'Everyone out!' I will never forget the scene of my mother, who ran with the pot of soup—and me—in tow."

Dashing eastward down the Via Carroceto in the direction of Cisterna, the Nuti family was nearly killed by another exploding shell and was forced to jump into a ditch along the roadway. Pasqualino said:

We realized that the explosion was caused by a shot fired by the Allies, who were at Campo di Carne. . . . Meanwhile, other people began to join us; the only sound was the reassuring voice of my father who told everyone to lie down with their bellies flat on the ground as soon as we heard the whistle of a shell, which was followed by the explosion, which happened more and more closely.

The continuous shelling followed us for a kilometer or so, until we reached a farm. Almost by magic, there was a great quiet. We found ourselves on the threshing floor of the farmhouse with my heart in my throat, trembling with fear, and my mother still holding the pot of soup. Papa threw himself to the ground, covering Franco with his body, until he felt safe under his body. There was fear for many hard hours, but at dusk my family decided to return to the slaughterhouse. It was at this point that Mom and Dad, for fear of being again within range of the deadly shooting of the guns, decided to take refuge for the night in a nearby cemetery [located just north of the slaughterhouse].

Before long, we were camped in a corner of the morgue along with some other families who had chosen the same solution. There was no bed to lie down on, but a few chairs had been recovered for the more elderly and some blankets to cover up and lie down on the floor. After a long, cold, and painful night, we watched to see the dawn again. The thought of my father was to bring his family back to the slaughterhouse, despite the risk that would entail. To think about spending another night in the cemetery would have been disheartening—a scenario that no child in the world would ever want to see.[9]

ONE OF THE GERMAN SOLDIERS motoring toward Anzio was Wilhelm Ernst Terheggen, a member of the Hermann Göring Parachute-Panzer Division. His unit had been in Arce, located about fourteen miles southeast of Frosinone in the Liri Valley, when the order came to head for Anzio; by 2:00 A.M. on January 23, his unit was on the road. He recalled, "Just before Castel Liri, the vehicle with Lieutenant Klingmann and I went down into a ditch—the driver had fallen asleep. Without damage we continued the drive. However, since I knew the way, I climbed on a motorcycle and went in front to serve as a guide. The march continued expeditiously, the tanks advancing with good speed."[10]

With the village of Aprilia virtually empty of civilians, Gräser's men of the 3rd Panzer-Grenadier Division, many of whom were veterans of the Eastern Front and Stalingrad, moved in, occupied the buildings, and prepared to defend it against all comers. The Allies would give them three uninterrupted days to complete their tasks.

MACKENSEN ROLLED UP TO KESSELRING'S Monte Soratte headquarters on the twenty-third to find the Anzio situation well in hand. "I regarded our defence as consolidated and that we no longer had to reckon with any major reverses," said Kesselring with satisfaction. He then gave Mackensen two major objectives: strengthen the defensive ring around the beachhead, and begin attacks that would reduce and ultimately eliminate the bridgehead.

But Kesselring knew that the topography around Anzio precluded flanking maneuvers; trying to launch a major attack along the coast north of Anzio was ruled out because the Moletta River and its deeply furrowed tributaries—as well as the thickly forested terrain and profusion of mines the British were sowing—would not permit the effective employment of armored forces. And an attack along the coast would bring his assaulting forces within range of Allied warships. Nor would an attack against the right, or eastern, flank of the invasion area likely be successful; the Mussolini Canal, with its steep concrete banks, formed an effective tank barrier. No, Kesselring concluded, the only possible way to destroy the Allies would be through costly, head-on frontal attacks supported by as much tank and artillery power as he could muster.[11]

ON JANUARY 23, WHILE THE initial wave of the invasion force was still digging in around Anzio and Nettuno, the Thunderbirds of the 179th Infantry Regiment left their frigid, foggy staging area and marched down to the docks at Pozzuoli and boarded a British LST, the HMS *Thruster*, which departed for Anzio the next day. The journey by sea was uneventful, save for an attack by German torpedo bombers whose aerial torpedoes skimmed past the ship, missing it by a few feet.[12]

Twenty-four-year-old James R. Safrit, of North Carolina (Company F, 2nd Battalion, 179th), had been transferred into the 45th Division after serving with Company E of the 41st Armored Infantry Regiment, 2nd Armored Division, in North Africa. He was an old veteran by now, having fought in Sicily, at Salerno, and in Fifth Army's drive up to Venafro. He recalled arriving at Anzio:

We moved in toward the harbor without any trouble. The Jerries seemed to be taken completely by surprise. We figured, "Hell, maybe we're finally getting a break." An invasion without any opposition—that would really be something for the old 45th. But we should have known better, because from out of the sun came a flight of FW-190s.

Those big bombs straddled our LST with near misses. One bomb landed on one side of the boat and another on the other side and it rocked violently like a cork, and a few of us on deck went flying into the water. The next thing I knew, I was bobbing up and down in my "Mae West" [life jacket], swallowing gobs of salt water. There were three Kraut planes, but luckily for us, they made only one pass at our convoy and sped back to their lines. Almost immediately, a torpedo boat fished us out of the water, scared, but unhurt. As far as I know, we didn't lose a man. We moved along the Mussolini Canal and dug in. The Germans brought in reinforcements and things started getting rough.[13]

Another of the Thunderbirds landing at Anzio was twenty-year-old buck sergeant Lee Anderson (Company F, 179th). He had been a student at the University of Minnesota before enlisting and being assigned to the 45th Infantry Division. He had made the invasion at Salerno and was wounded at Venafro in December 1943 when a piece of an artillery round struck him in the arm. After recuperating in the 300th General Hospital in Naples, he shipped out to Anzio. Anderson said, "I was very seasick on the voyage and was glad to land. The landing was uneventful. Anzio was easy compared to Salerno."[14] It would not, however, remain "easy."

IN LONDON, CHURCHILL WAS FUMING at VI Corps' inaction and angrily cabled Alexander, "I expected to see a wild cat roaring into the mountains, and what do I find? A whale wallowing on the beaches!"[15]

Clark, too, was unhappy with the inertia. His diary entry of the twenty-third contradicts his previous instructions to Lucas to be cautious and not stick his neck out: "Lucas must be aggressive. He must take some chances. He must use the 3rd Division to push out."[16]

After the war, Alexander noted, "The commander of the assault troops, the American General John Lucas, missed his opportunity [to take Rome] by being too slow, too cautious. He failed to realize the great advantage that surprise had given him. He allowed time to beat him."[17]

Evidently, all the commanders were playing CYA—cover your ass—with their writings in order for the stalled invasion not to be blamed on them. No one wanted to be held responsible for the shambles that Shingle was on the verge of becoming, least of all the VI Corps commander himself. Lucas, however, was deaf to any entreaties to rush his forces into all-out battle before he thought they were ready.*[18]

---

* At the end of D day, there would be 36,034 British and American troops at Anzio and some 3,069 vehicles. Samuel Eliot Morison, *History of United States Naval Operations in World War II*, 343.

HERALDING THE LANDINGS AT ANZIO and Nettuno to American readers was the January 23 edition of the *New York Times*, whose six-column front-page headline crowed, "Allied Units Land Behind Nazis in Italy, 16 Miles from Rome; Little Opposition." The accompanying article, by Milton Bracker, said, "In the most stunning and potentially hazardous operation of the Italian campaign so far, British and American troops of the Fifth Army waded ashore on the west coast of Italy south of Rome at 2 AM today." The names Anzio and Nettuno were not mentioned in this initial report.

Bracker, apparently reporting what he had been told at an official press briefing, noted, "Only two enemy fighters ventured out against the ships and met a storm of fire. Our fighters, in layers, ruled the skies. Far below, the pilots distinguished a few jeeps and Allied troops moving as far inland as four miles. . . . The towns in the vicinity of the landing seemed virtually deserted. Plane after plane reported only the continuing disembarkation on the flat coast."

Louis Raffenelli, one of the American pilots who had taken part in the momentous operation, was quoted in the article as saying, "I believe the Germans were caught unawares. They must have been looking for us up the line somewhere. I scoured all over the area and couldn't find anything worth shooting at."[19]

It would not be long, however, before Raffenelli and his fellow pilots would find plenty worth shooting at.

LIKE THE PREVIOUS DAWN, JANUARY 24 came up cold, wet, and gray. For the troops cooling their heels on the beachhead, or, rather, trying to find warmth and shelter from the pelting rainstorm, it was time to move—or at least time for the Allies to send out more patrols to find out what was to their front.

Anxious to get the fight started, a strong reconnaissance patrol of Bren gun carriers and a few antitank guns from Penney's 1st British Division rattled northward up the Albano Highway, past cultivated fields and whitewashed farm buildings known as *podere*. A few cows, ignorant of the impending danger, grazed placidly at haystacks and food troughs.

At Campo di Carne, three miles north of the "Flyover," as the British called it (or the "Overpass," as the Americans had dubbed it), the recce patrol passed beneath the elevated bed of a disused railway that ran diagonally across the landscape—a route the British called "the Embankment" and the Yanks called "the Bowling Alley" because it was so flat, level, and straight.* Immediately north of the intersection of the Albano Highway and the Embankment or Bowling Alley lay the town of Aprilia.[20]

No sooner had a British recon patrol reached the outskirts of tiny Carroceto than it came under fire from the direction of Aprilia. Moving east toward Aprilia to investigate further, the patrol was hit by 88mm fire from self-propelled guns, and then a panzer and some infantry appeared, seemingly to cut off the Brits' escape route back down the Albano Highway. Discretion being the better part of valor, the recon group hastily wheeled about and departed. No men had been hurt, but somehow five of them had gone missing.[21]

Lieutenant Horst Heinrich (3rd Battalion, 29th Panzer-Grenadier Regiment, 3rd Panzer-Grenadier Division) recalled that his unit had been rushed to the Anzio-Nettuno area the previous day. He was in a building known as the Villa Crocetta, near Campoleone Station, where his duty had been to "install four companies of our battalion in positions 800 meters south of Campoleone Station on both sides of the road in the direction of Aprilia. There we received the first fire of artillery. During the assignment of the companies, we had many wounded because of a strong volley of artillery batteries. The battle raged around Aprilia."[22]

ON THAT DAY, ELEMENTS OF the 1st U.S. Armored Division began arriving at the Anzio harbor. Machine gunner Private first class James Luzzi (Company C, 6th Armored Infantry Regiment) was disembarking from an LST when a wave of German planes came streaking over. "My squad was on top near the bow when we were attacked by Stuka dive bombers," he recalled. "We manned our .30- and .50-caliber guns and fired at the Stukas. One Stuka dived down and dropped its bomb. As we watched

---

*After the war, this railroad bed was converted into a highway that connects Rome and Littoria (today Latina) and today carries the route designation "Strada Statale 148—Via Pontina."

it fall toward our deck, we were ready for it to hit us. But, thankfully, it missed the bow and hit the water without doing any damage."[23]

Stukas weren't the only worry. After rolling off their LSTs and reaching shore, the men of the 1st Armored Division endured a few tense moments as long-range German artillery crashed around them. Once the smoke and dust had cleared, they then moved into their bivouac area in the Padiglione Woods, an area of dense umbrella pines and undergrowth situated halfway between Anzio and Aprilia where, according to the division's history, it was so quiet "the men could hear owls hooting in the woods."

The 1st Armored Division's leader, Major General Ernest Nason Harmon, West Point class of 1917, was an old-fashioned type of military leader—a brusque, no-nonsense individual whom both his troops and his enemy feared. As commander of the division, he had led his men during the desperate battles in North Africa following Operation Torch and again during the bloody month-long slugfest for Sicily, followed by the invasion of mainland Italy and the slow, agonizing slog up "the boot" to Cassino.

The division had been molded in his carved-from-granite image. Like him, they were itching for another fight.[24] Ernie Harmon was an old-school disciplinarian like George S. Patton Jr. "Old Gravel Voice," as he was called by his troops, was born in Lowell, Massachusetts, on February 26, 1894, grew up in Vermont, and attended Norwich University for a year before earning an appointment to West Point, where he was the middleweight boxing champion; he graduated and was commissioned in 1917, the year the United States entered World War I. As a cavalry officer in the Great War, he led a horse-mounted cavalry troop in the battles of the Meuse-Argonne. After the war, Harmon, a superb athlete, competed in the modern pentathlon during the 1920 Paris Olympics, but war, not games, loomed in his future.

During the Operation Torch landings in North Africa, Harmon commanded a task force that combined the 9th Infantry and the 2nd Armored Divisions that landed at Safi, 140 miles south of Casablanca. In February 1943, Lieutenant General Dwight D. Eisenhower sent the blunt-spoken Harmon to II Corps commander Major General Lloyd Fredendall's headquarters to investigate complaints that Fredendall was

less than effective as a commander, especially after the Germans defeated II Corps at Sidi Bou Zid and Kasserine Pass, Tunisia—the first
major battles of the ground war between the Americans and Germans.
Discovering that Fredendall was out of touch with his command and
arrogantly refused to cooperate with his British allies, Harmon told Eisenhower that Fredendall was a moral and physical coward for rarely
visiting the front lines. Harmon became II Corps' unofficial commander
pro tem while Fredendall fretted in his safe dugout. Upon Harmon's rec-
ommendation, Ike relieved Fredendall and replaced him with George S.
Patton Jr.[25]

Harmon went back to commanding 2nd Armored but not for long; in
April 1943, he took command of the dispirited 1st Armored Division in
Tunisia after its commander, Orlando Ward, had faltered badly during
the defeat at Kasserine Pass.[26] Personally fearless, Harmon was driven
to lead by example. During one battle in Tunisia, the general was in his
usual place—in his jeep at the front—when he saw a group of Allied
tanks pinned down by heavy German fire, unable to advance. Disdain-
ing the enemy fire, Harmon drove over to the tank force commander
and yelled, "All right, you follow my jeep forward!" The embarrassed
officer did as he was ordered, and the breakthrough was made.[27]

The division could not have had a finer, more aggressive commander,
but not everyone in the 1st Armored felt a fondness for him.[28] An officer
who once served under Harmon noted:

> Legend has it that when he reached the 1st Armored Division he imme-
> diately called a meeting of all the officers. He held the meeting on the
> slope of the highest ground in the area and just chewed them out right in
> front of God and the enemy over their performance [at Kasserine Pass].
> After that the 1st Armored was never defeated again. They went back
> into combat and won back all the territory they had lost. . . . The 1st
> Armored officers hated his guts, and to this day you won't find anybody
> from the 1st Armored Division who has anything good to say about
> General Harmon. . . . I always felt he [Harmon] was a better commander
> than Patton because he was not interested in personal glory or making
> the front page of a newspaper. His only goal was to get the job done as
> efficiently and effectively as possible.[29]

After a period of retraining, Harmon commanded the division during the Allied invasion of Italy at Salerno in September 1943 and the fight northward.

Patton's obscenity-laced speeches are well known, but Harmon's were not far behind. Lieutenant General Omar N. Bradley once commented that Harmon "had a pretty good vocabulary of his own, but it didn't equal George's. They used to call him the 'poor man's George Patton.'"[30] And, like Patton, Harmon also had a penchant for ivory-handled revolvers, wearing a pair of them in shoulder holsters, along with his trademark riding breeches and knee-high horse-cavalry boots.[31]

Harmon described his first meeting at Anzio with Lucas "in his map-hung office; [he] laid down his inevitable corn-cob pipe, and [we] shook hands. There was the sound of firing in the distance. 'Glad to see you,' Lucas said briefly. 'You're needed here.'"[32]

After the war Harmon wrote, "I am not a sentimentalist but a Regular Army disciplinarian. War is hard and I believe in hard, rigorous training. Disciplined, tough, well-trained troops live the longest. But there was something about Anzio which touched even my supposed granite heart. There were no malingerers there, no gold bricks. . . . It is true that all of us were in the same boat: we were there to stay or die."[33]

ALEXANDER AND CLARK HAD HOPED—EVEN assumed—that Kesselring would panic at the amphibious thrust at Anzio-Nettuno and would weaken his Gustav Line in preparation for a withdrawal northward, but such was not the case. So, on January 24, certain that another major attack against the Cassino front would help to dislodge the enemy forces there, Clark ordered Major General Charles W. Ryder's 34th "Red Bull" U.S. Infantry Division to begin an assault up the impossibly steep slopes of the 1,700-foot Monte Cassino. Everyone thought—wrongly, as it turned out—that the Germans were inside the evacuated monastery and were using the building as an observation post. But a week's brutal fighting would leave the 34th Division decimated almost beyond repair—and the sixth-century Benedictine abbey atop the mountain still intact within German lines. (On February 11, what was left of the 34th would be withdrawn; a terrible fate awaited the historic abbey.)[34]

MORE ELEMENTS OF THE 179TH Infantry Regiment of the 45th U.S. Division reached Anzio on the morning of the twenty-fourth and immediately began piling out of their landing craft and moving inland. With the 179th was Corporal Ray Sherman, a machine gunner with Company K, 3rd Battalion. He recalled that his LST's arrival was greeted by the Luftwaffe. "All the larger ships, which were in the harbor, had barrage balloons or small dirigibles flying overhead," he remembered. "The enemy made numerous attempts to inflict damage. Our planes usually drove them off, sometimes with dogfights with losses to both sides. We disembarked and made our way through the city to the north. The machine-gun section which I was in set up and covered various crossroads and routes of infiltration."

Once in place, the 179th came under heavy shelling. A weapon that Ray Sherman especially hated was the six-barreled *Nebelwerfer*, multi-barrel rocket launchers that GIs had dubbed the "Screaming Meemies" and "Moaning Minnies." Sherman said this rocket launcher "would encircle an area and completely cover us with devastating shrapnel. During one particularly heavy concentration, I was lying near another soldier who had an entrenching shovel lying nearby. I hollered and told him, 'If you are not going to use it, throw it over here!' I lay on my belly and dug a little trench real fast for myself. When those shells came in, they made a screeching noise. The trees in the area were only stubs and stumps due to the heavy shelling."[35]

Often overlooked in combat histories, the lowly entrenching tools, which hung like miniature shovels from the packs of the GIs, performed yeoman service, enabling the vulnerable infantry to scratch a potentially lifesaving hole in the earth. On occasion, soldiers might be given the loan of a more substantial shovel strapped to the side of a jeep, truck, or halftrack or borrow one from a combat engineer outfit. And, in a last desperate measure, when the ammunition had run out and the enemy was overrunning one's position, the little shovels could be employed as cudgels to slash and bludgeon the enemy to death.

WITH CLARK, ALEXANDER, AND EVEN Churchill all breathing down his neck and demanding that he do *something*, Lucas felt that he finally had enough troops and supplies ashore to enable Penney's 1st British Division to make a modest advance all the way to Campoleone Station, fourteen miles north of Anzio. At the same time, Lucas ordered Truscott's 3rd Division, with the 504th Parachute Infantry Regiment guarding its flank, to capture Cisterna, twelve miles inland on the right flank of the Allied beachhead. Lucas also made a rare foray to the front to visit some of the British units. "They are splendid soldiers," he wrote in his diary. "No braver men in the world."[36]

The 3rd Division's crusty, outspoken forty-eight-year-old commander, Lucian King Truscott Jr., looking every inch the prototypical American fighting man with his iron jaw, steely eyes, and raspy voice (he had caught a cold, which turned into laryngitis), appeared to have been chiseled out of a block of solid granite. Unlike dozens of other officers who became generals during the war, Truscott, born in Texas and raised in Arizona, did not attend West Point but earned an army commission through other channels. But, like Lucas, he had served in a cavalry unit seeking to punish Mexican bandito Pancho Villa after his 1916 raid into Columbus, New Mexico. (Even as a two-star general in command of the 3rd Infantry Division, he continued to wear jodhpurs and knee-high cavalry boots, topped off by a leather aviator's flight jacket.)

Like Patton, Harmon, and Lucas, Truscott excelled at polo, a game he played with a passion, once telling his son, Lucian III (who would also make the army his career),

> Let me tell you something, and don't ever forget it. You play games to win, not to lose. And you fight wars to win! That's spelled W-I-N! And every good player in the game and every good commander in a war—and I mean every really *good* player or *good* commander—every damn one of them has to have some sonofabitch in him. If he doesn't, he isn't a good commander. And he never *will* be a good commander. Polo games and wars aren't won by gentlemen. They're won by men who can be first-class sonsofbitches when they have to be. It's as simple as that. No sonofabitch, no commander.[37]

Quite possibly, of all the American commanders at Anzio, it was Truscott who best understood what it was going to take to *win* at Anzio.

During the 3rd's advance toward Cisterna on January 24, Truscott narrowly escaped death. A German airplane bombed Truscott's headquarters, and the general was slightly wounded in the leg; his leather cavalry boots saved him from a more serious injury. "I took a Purple Heart [medal] up and pinned it on him," Lucas wrote in his diary.[38]

STANLEY SMITH, ONE OF TRUSCOTT'S men, recalled that during the advance toward Cisterna, his squad was pinned down by some Germans in a farmhouse, but the enemy was persuaded by some intense fire to give up.

> Me and the fellow I was with wandered over to the house. They had about a dozen Krauts in the front yard with their hands up. Have no idea what happened to the rest of the Germans; guess when the barrage started they took off. I joined the rest of the fellows guarding them.
>
> One of them dropped his gas-mask container. He pointed to it and said the Italian word for "food." They used their gas-mask containers as we did—to keep our rations in. I told him to pick it up, in English, which I'm sure he couldn't understand. I also told him that if he made a false move, he was one dead Kraut. I don't think my rifle was loaded and if he did [make a move], there wasn't a damned thing I could do about it. We gathered the Kraut prisoners and moved them toward our side of the lines.
>
> That night in our platoon, we lost the BAR* man killed and his assistant badly wounded. That was the first men we had lost, as far as I know, since the first day we landed. From that night on, it was all "downhill!" The only thing I remember about the BAR man is he was a Southerner and he was always singing the song *Brown's Ferry Blues*. After he was killed, I never heard that song again.[39]

---

*Browning Automatic Rifle. Invented by John Browning for World War I, the model used in World War II was the M1918A2. It weighed 18.3 pounds, fired from a 20-round box magazine the same .30-06-caliber round as the M-1 Garand rifle, could be fired from the shoulder in a standing position or in a prone position with its bipod, and had a maximum range of about 3,500 yards. Its full-automatic rate of fire of 500–650 rounds per minute was half the rate of the Germans' MG-42. Quick, *Dictionary of Weapons and Military Terms*, 82.

GENERAL PENNEY ORDERED AN ELEMENT of his division, Glaxo Murray's 24th Guards Brigade with its three battalions—the 5th Grenadier Guards, 1st Scots Guards, and 1st Irish Guards, augmented by one squadron of the 46th Royal Tank Regiment and one medium and two field regiments of artillery—to act as the "point unit" and capture Aprilia as a stepping-stone to Campoleone Station, four miles north of Aprilia. Both towns would need to be in Allied hands before a full-scale advance on Rome could begin. Aprilia's importance was that it controlled a network of roads—roads that were essential to vehicles because the rains turned the fields into nothing more than a swamp.[40] However, the Germans had already beaten the Allies to Aprilia; Lieutenant General Fritz-Hubert Gräser, commander of the 3rd Panzer-Grenadier Division, had already sent a force of men into the town—the 3rd Battalion of the 29th Panzer-Grenadier Regiment—where they laid mines and set up machine-gun and mortar positions to prepare for the Allies' arrival.[41]

Number 1 Company of the 5th Grenadier Guards acted as the point for the rest of the brigade, advancing from the brigade's assembly area just south of the Embankment and up the Albano Highway. Observing the advance of the Guards from two and a half miles away were Penney and his staff, using binoculars atop the only other high ground in the area: the Flyover/Overpass that carried the road that ran from the west coast to Padiglione. Two companies of the 5th Battalion were mounted in vehicles, while the third was on foot.

Onward they rode and marched, some men carrying the "manpack" No. 18 radios (which the British called "wireless sets") that had a maximum range of five miles, while some of the vehicles were equipped with the No. 62 wireless set. Reliable communications were essential on the modern battlefield. The radios allowed forward units to communicate with battalion or regimental headquarters behind them. The radios were also a way of bringing some semblance of order out of chaotic situations, a way for commanders on every level to hear what individuals and individual units were doing at any given moment, a way to transmit orders and instructions, a way to see the big picture made up of many small, disparate pieces. The radios gave a comforting sense, too, that the men on the front lines were not alone, that they were a part of a fraternity, that—as long as they could hear a human voice speaking their language

on the other end—everything would be all right, even if such naive op-
timism was misplaced.

Standing outside their *podere* in the morning light, a few Italian
farmers and their families who still remained applauded as the troops
and vehicles went by, seemingly glad to see that their land, given to them
by Mussolini, would soon be free of German domination. Most of the
men of Number 1 Company were in good spirits, too, filled with the
pride that came with the knowledge that they were spearheading the entire VI Corps advance that would soon—they hoped and believed—take
them into Rome.

Behind them, on the Albano Highway, a traffic jam extending almost all the way back to the Flyover/Overpass consisted of a variety of
vehicles—scout cars, Bren carriers, ambulances, and trucks full of food,
bullets, mortar bombs, land mines, spools of communications wire, and
coils of barbed wire—set to follow and support the ground troops.[42]

Not far behind the advancing Guards was a civilian unit known as the
American Field Service, a group of volunteers who drove ambulances in
combat zones in North Africa, France, the Middle East, India, Burma, and
Italy. A historian of the American Field Service wrote, "The immediate objective of the assault was [Aprilia] . . . the dominant topographic position
and compact structure of which rendered it the principal strategic point on
the beachhead. The 137 Field Ambulance . . . served the Guards Brigade."[43]

As the 24th Guards Brigade came within range, the 3rd Battalion, 29th
Panzer-Grenadier Regiment, 3rd Panzer-Grenadier Division, opened up
with their deadly MG-42s. Mortars coughed and artillery tubes barked,
and within seconds sections of the roadway were hurled into the air by
a heavy barrage of shells, the bursts blasting geysers of mud and water
skyward, a line of geysers marching toward the British troops like a series
of volcanoes coming to life, each detonation jolting the ground as though
some mighty behemoth were advancing across the landscape with thundering footsteps. With the deadly hailstorm of shells and white-hot flying
shards of steel ripping through their ranks, the British troops quickly
fanned out to assault Aprilia and Carroceto, where at least some cover
might be available.[44]

At one point, Sergeant Joe Dunne (Number 3 Company, Number 13 Platoon, 1st Irish Guards—commonly known as "the Micks")

distinguished himself when he charged through the front door of a farmhouse filled with German soldiers and sent them running for their lives out the back door. It was not the last time that Dunne would demonstrate his courage.[45]

Some distance behind the advancing Guards, an officer in the Duke of Wellington's Regiment recalled watching the long line of Guardsmen "still marching steadily in extended formation down each side [of the Albano Highway], but from Carroceto itself could be heard the rattle of small-arms fire. Looking at the dark bulk of the Alban Hills, which formed a backcloth for the whole scene, we could now see flashes of the two 88mm guns which were firing air bursts [over the troops]. The General told me they were out of range of our guns, but had asked for fighter-bombers to engage them. It was maddening to see the exact position of the guns but yet be impotent."[46]

AS NIGHT ON JANUARY 24 fell, Colonel Peddie's 6th Gordons were still outposting the front. Lieutenant Ted Grace was ordered by Major Lindsay Bridgman, his company commander, to take a platoon-size recce patrol out into the darkness. They had gone but a short distance when they heard what sounded like enemy movement on the other side of a stone wall.

Deploying his men for an ambush from behind the wall, Grace noted:

> Then exactly as planned, Corporal Boyes' section opened fire, shattering the silence as though a far larger force was attacking. The Germans, caught by surprise, evidently decided to retreat. We heard them shouting and running towards us along the ridge of the hill. They were rushing straight into our ambush! I heard myself shouting "Fire!" Their shapes were hardly visible against the blackness of the wood behind. Our platoon fired a volley into the dark. Then followed total confusion. The Germans were on top of us, firing blindly as they ran. Then they stampeded headlong beyond us, without realizing where we were, and finally disappearing along the valley.

The ambush was not terribly costly to the Gordons: one Scotsman had been wounded in the arm, while a German had also been wounded and taken prisoner; others no doubt escaped. Told by Major Bridgman to report to Colonel Peddie, Grace hightailed it over to the command post. After he gave his report about the patrol's actions, he was told by the battalion commander, "Get back to your platoon quickly, Ted. Stand by all night in case the enemy break through."

"Do we know what's happening up there?" Grace asked.

"All we know is that the Guards Brigade are making an attack to capture Campoleone, but we don't yet know the strength of the enemy. It sounds as though the Guards are running into more than they had bargained for. We may be called upon to follow through."

As Grace hurried back to his unit, it began to rain—a downpour accompanied by thunder and lightning. With raindrops clinking heavily on their steel helmets, the ground turned into a quagmire and nearly sucked the boots off their feet. In what would prove to be a futile attempt to keep dry, the soldiers began to pull out from their packs their rubberized canvas rain sheets, but the trenches quickly began to turn slimy with mud and fill with water as the rain continued to beat down. Then the boom of thunder was followed by the roar of artillery. First, the northern horizon in the direction of the Alban Hills began sparkling with lights—the muzzle flashes of scores of Krupp guns.

Then came the shriek of shells and the awful, shuddering BOOMs, the concussions of the explosions that pounded on eardrums and chests, followed by the blazing spouts of mud and dirt, the whine of shell fragments spinning through the air, and then the smells of burned powder and torn-up earth. The ripping sound of the Germans' MG-34s and MG-42s punctuated the darkness, accompanied by the snap, whiz, and crack of bullets zipping past or thwacking into the mud. The men gripped their Lee-Enfield rifles tightly and checked their ammunition pouches, expecting an infantry and tank assault at any moment. It would be a long, sleepless night.

Grace said, "As we were later to learn, the Guards' nightmare was far worse than ours." The Guards had reached Aprilia.[47] There, Murray's 24th Guards Brigade ran into a hornet's nest. Members of Gräser's 3rd Panzer-Grenadier Division had taken up positions in and around the town, turning it into a fortress, a fortress soon to be under months of siege.

AT 2:30 P.M. THAT AFTERNOON, Glaxo Murray's 24th Guards Brigade launched a full-out assault against the Germans occupying Aprilia. Number 2 Company ran off across an open field to penetrate the east side of the town, while Number 4 Company hit the west side. But the going was slow, with the streets choked with rubble and each building being a stout miniature fortress.[48]

The Germans holed up in the town, although outnumbered, proved to be tough opponents. With superior numbers, however, it did not take long for the 24th Guards Brigade, supported by tanks, to push through a hastily laid minefield, and, with the Scots Guards and Irish Guards battalions laying down covering fire, the 5th Battalion, Grenadier Guards, then drove the enemy from Aprilia, taking 111 prisoners in the process.[49]

Sydney Arthur Wright was one of the Grenadier Guards who took charge of the group of prisoners from the 3rd Battalion, 29th Panzer-Grenadier Regiment. After he and a mate, Bill Taylor, had spent an hour digging a slit trench in anticipation of a counterattack, he was ordered to escort those 111 German prisoners of war back to the Anzio port. He was accompanied by an officer, a sergeant, a corporal, and two more guardsmen. Once the prisoners were delivered, Wright and the others returned to Aprilia. On the way back, however, the group was heavily shelled and was forced to take shelter for a half hour in some farm buildings off the road. Wright learned later this half-hour delay saved his life. As the patrol returned to Aprilia, the shelling began once more. By the time Wright returned to his slit trench, he discovered that a huge shell had exploded nearby and killed another soldier who had taken his place and also badly wounded his mate Bill Taylor.[50]

A number of the prisoners were not German at all but rather from the French province of Alsace-Lorraine* and were only too happy to provide information to intelligence officers during interrogation. One prisoner was a young officer who expressed astonishment when he saw his first Sherman tank, belonging to the 46th Royal Tank Regiment,

---

*Following its victory in the Franco-Prussian War, Prussia/Germany annexed this territory, but it was returned to France through the provisions of the Treaty of Versailles in 1919. It was taken back by the Germans following the fall of France in 1940. William L. Shirer, *The Rise and Fall of the Third Reich*, 1278n.

rolling toward him. "If *I* had that," he pointed and told his captors, "I would be in Rome by now."[51]

BUT THE AMERICANS AND BRITISH were not in Rome; they were arrayed around Anzio, having lost the chance to swiftly advance farther. Lucas was beset by well-grounded fears and was reluctant to risk his landing force, which he considered still too small and fragile for any sort of adventurous expedition. "I must keep my feet on the ground," he confided to his diary on the twenty-fifth, "and my forces in hand and do nothing foolish. This is the most important thing I have ever tried to do and will not be stampeded."[52]

No one, with the possible exception of Churchill, was expecting a stampede, but it was clear that slow, incremental movements out of the beachhead were beginning to rankle officers and enlisted men alike. Alexander was especially miffed with Lucas and told Clark, "I am very much dissatisfied with General Lucas. I have no confidence in him and in his ability to control the situation. I very much fear that there might be a disaster at Anzio with Lucas in command—and you know what will happen to you and me if there is a disaster at Anzio." Alexander believed that Lucas was worn out physically and under great mental strain and began hinting that perhaps Truscott was in better physical and mental condition to undertake the role of VI Corps' commanding general.[53]

Not long afterward, Lieutenant Grace was wounded and evacuated, and he did not learn what had happened that night until he was recovering in the hospital. A young 5th Grenadier Guards officer in a nearby bed recounted his unit's expensive assault on Aprilia: "That afternoon we were ordered to attack [Aprilia]," the officer told him.

First the artillery put down a barrage on the buildings—should have knocked the stuffing out of them. Then a smoke screen was laid down. Our company, with B Company, charged down from the Embankment [the elevated roadway over the Albano Highway a few hundred yards south of Carroceto]. But the wind blew the smoke away and we were sitting—or rather, running—ducks. Before we got to the first building, a rain of machine-gun fire swept into us. I saw Major Anthony and Major Miller fall, and many of the men. My platoon was to attack a small building on the right. I saw a machine gun firing from an upper window. There was an old cattle shed nearby, so we all dived behind that. Our Bren gunner from behind a stone wall fired up on the window while Private Andrews ran out and hurled a grenade through the broken glass. End of machine gun!

The Grenadier officer continued:

More firing was coming from what looked like a schoolhouse nearby. This was the next for our platoon to capture. It was an ugly situation. I could see the other company was in deep trouble. Many of the men were still lying in the open, killed or wounded. We could do nothing but move on, one section at a time, trying to give covering fire at every step. I somehow knew that something was waiting for me inside that school. We reached the door. I kicked it down. I saw a sudden movement inside, so I threw in a grenade. The explosion inside the hall was deafening. I jumped over two Jerries who had been knocked out, but a burst of fire from a Spandau[*] ripped through my arm and side. That's about all I can remember.

Grace said that it wasn't until after the war that he learned what else had happened during the Guards' assault on Aprilia:

By the time that darkness fell [on January 24], the battalion of Grenadier Guards had successfully overcome all resistance at the cinema, school-house, block of flats, and the main tower, but at great cost. The commanding officer, Lieutenant Colonel C. G. Gordon-Lennox, made sure that all the wounded had been evacuated, and then organized all-round

---

[*] "Spandau" was the name given by British troops to the Germans' 7.92mm x 57mm general-purpose machine gun, more commonly known as the MG-42. The devastating weapon was second only to the 88mm dual-purpose artillery piece that was feared most by the Allies, for it could spit out 1,200 to 1,500 rounds per minute—twice the cyclic rate of the British Vickers and American Browning M-2 machine guns—accompanied by a distinctive, blood-chilling sound that made some Allied troops refer to the gun as "Hitler's buzz saw." Fitzsimons, *Illustrated Encyclopedia of 20th Century Weapons and Warfare*, 73.

defence, while patrols were sent out to clear the immediate area. For some hours there was silence. Then shortly before midnight, the German artillery opened up with a shattering barrage. Tracer bullets flashed across the sky, to be answered by fierce machine-gun fire from the [24th] Guards Brigade. This was the beginning of the battle that we had heard as we waited in our water-logged slit trenches. Then came the violent thunderstorm. It seemed like a fierce war between gods and men.[54]

THE WAR WAS ALSO TAKING place on the Tyrrhenian Sea on the night of January 24–25—a night that would prove fateful for men and ships in Anzio harbor. While evacuating casualties from the beachhead, three well-lighted and clearly marked British hospital ships—HMS *St. David*, *St. Andrew*, and *Leinster*—were attacked by the Luftwaffe. The *St. David*, with 226 medical personnel and patients on board, received a direct hit and quickly sank. Two army nurses on board were among 130 survivors rescued by the damaged *Leinster*, but 96 perished. Of the two German planes that attacked the *St. David*, one was shot down by gunners on the nearby Liberty ship *Bret Harte*. An American doctor recalled that the plane that sank the *St. David* did so with Hs-293 glider bombs.*[55]

MEANWHILE, AT APRILIA, THE 6TH Gordons, who had entered the town after the 5th Grenadier Guards and helped push out the Germans, were enduring both the thunderstorm and the waves of German artillery falling all around their position.

"Following the artillery," Lieutenant Ted Grace said, working from official reports and what he subsequently learned from his fellow soldiers, "the Germans launched the expected counter-attack upon the area of [Aprilia]. The Guards were ready and poured forth a hail of fire into the darkness. During the torrential storm it was impossible to see the

---

* The Hs-293 glider bomb—the forerunner of today's cruise missiles—was a revolutionary new weapon in the German arsenal. Developed by the Henschel aircraft company in 1940 as an antishipping weapon, the Hs-293 was radio controlled from its launch aircraft. It had a powerful rocket motor that enabled it to travel at an average speed of 750 feet per second. The range, depending on the altitude, varied between four and eight and a half kilometers. About a thousand of these missiles were produced. John Christopher, *The Race for Hitler's X-Planes*, 134.

enemy. The German infantry stumbled on, firing wildly but unable to reach their objectives. Far into the night the battle continued."[56]

WHILE THE STRUGGLE FOR APRILIA was growing, Pasqualino Nuti recalled the day the soldiers of the British 1st Division arrived at his town. "My father learned this news with all the family when we reached the coveted slaughterhouse. He then decided to go to the Commune to meet with the *Podesta*, the Secretary Communale, and other colleagues and welcome the liberators. . . . After advising the other families not to leave until he returned, he walked with two other acquaintances on the Carroceto Way towards Aprilia."

The Nuti family reached the intersection of Carroceto Way and Via Grande (today known as the Via Verdi-Carducci), where they were stopped by British troops who were in control of the crossroads. Lying nearby in the adjacent ditches, other soldiers were preparing for an attack.

> The patrol leader told my father to halt and, in perfect Italian, asked, "*Dove andate? Non si puo passare!*" ("Where are you going? You cannot pass!") My father started to explain his motives to "the liberators" but the patrol leader interrupted him, saying, "The Germans are coming—turn around and look!" There were German soldiers, armed to the teeth, who were approaching from Aprilia. They were part of the German divisions which had come from France, Yugoslavia, and Germany to counter the beachhead allies.
>
> In a flash my father was back at the slaughterhouse, closed the door with the latch, barred the windows, and ordered everyone there to take shelter in some corner of the building, as long as it was safe. Then I hid under the table while dad and mom, with little Franco, crouched in a corner of the room. It was about 9:30 AM when we heard the first shots of gunfire from the Germans settled around the slaughterhouse and the British facing them in the ditches of Via Grande. It was just the beginning of a violent fight, which will become the first battle of the landing at Anzio.
>
> Lightning was unleashed in the uproar, and the battle was becoming more brutal with machine guns, mortars, grenades, and loud noises repeating endlessly. The German soldiers were continually moving around

the slaughterhouse, moving back and forth and shouting out. The door of the slaughterhouse had been hit several times, but fortunately it had never been opened, while the windows were shattered. I crouched under the table, trembling, frightened, and with bated breath, and then suddenly a loud bang echoed in the room. "Now the war had also entered our house," I thought. It was a shot fired from outside; the bullet went through the front door and stuck with force in the central pedestal that held the table under which I huddled. I found myself right on the trajectory of the bullet, there was a slight itching to my knees, and I scratched my hand and found myself covered in blood; frightened and worried, without making any complaint, I went to my parents, who promptly medicated the injury. The bullet had just grazed my knees—two centimeters more would have been enough to make the wound more disturbing.

After a moment of consolation from my parents, I lay under the bed while, outside, the furious battle between the Germans and English continued unabated. It had been about two hours since the conflict had begun and no sign of truce appeared to calm my fast-beating heart. Other bullets hit our room through the windows and the front door; holes, rubble, and dust were and remain an indelible memory. Around 4:00 PM, suddenly the battle stopped. Silence and quiet finally returned.

The elder Nuti removed the bar from the door, opened it, and carefully looked outside. "There was presented a catastrophic vision," said his son. "It seemed like an apocalypse! All around us everything was destroyed, the air was imbued with smoke with a pungent smell that enveloped the whole area, arms and ammunition lay abandoned, the dead were scattered on the ground, maybe someone still breathing. There was no time to lose; we had to hurry and get out of this hell. The only salvation was the Americans. By the Germans, never!"

A group of women, children, and the elderly came to Assunti Nuti seeking help. "My father took the responsibility to save them from the pit of hell," said Pasqualino. And the scene on Carroceto Street was indeed hellish, with masses of dead and

dismembered bodies of German soldiers, some on the embankment, others laying on machine guns. The whole area was a mass of scrap.

Without delay and without fear, my father started to move forward, trying not to dwell on what the eyes saw, and covered his mouth and nose
so as not to breathe the air that emanated from the putrid corpses. The
group managed to get out of the area walking in single file along the edge
of the canals, accompanied by the voice of an old woman, carrying a picture of the Madonna and asking everyone to pray the rosary aloud. . . .

We walked without stopping until we arrived at the Via Grande Cir-
convallazione (today the Via Botticelli), where we finally met the Allies.
British troops were stationed along the ditches and in a friendly manner
urged us to hurry along so as not to hinder the defense. We also stopped
reciting the Rosary; it was no longer the time.[57]

It was time, instead, for the next phase of the battle for Aprilia to
begin.

CHAPTER 5

"That one night has haunted me ever since"

JANUARY 25-29

T HE SITUATION AT APRILIA WAS in great flux, with possession of the village still being contested. Lieutenant Ted Grace said, "By first light [on the twenty-fifth], the Germans had managed to infiltrate back into a cluster of huts about two hundred yards beyond the town. As these huts were in a commanding position on high ground, it was essential to drive the enemy out. Colonel C. G. Gordon-Lennox could see from the top of the tower that the German infantry were forming up for attack. He ordered Number 3 Company to seize the initiative and attack first."

And so it did. Grace recounted that Lieutenant D. Wedderburn's assault platoon "charged across the open ground while the other platoons gave intensive covering fire. Several of his men fell before reaching their objective, but the Germans were quickly overwhelmed after fierce hand-to-hand fighting. With only eight men left standing, Wedderburn arranged the defence of the huts area, while a team of stretcher bearers ran up to rescue the wounded on both sides."[1]

The 5th Grenadier Guards, too, had sprinted across the open ground under fire to reach Aprilia but paid a heavy price. Once he had reached the relative safety of the town's rubble, Lieutenant Bill Dugdale (Number 1 Company, 5th Grenadier Guards) discovered that three of the company's officers were dead; he was appointed commander of both

the Carrier and the Anti-Tank Platoons. The 5th Battalion was then ordered to continue the attack through the Scots Guards, who were barely
clinging to the ground northwest of Aprilia. The situation did not look
promising. He said, "The Germans had now got a very tight grip around
the northwest and north sides of the salient, and every inch of ground
gained had to be fought for."

Dugdale was greatly impressed by "the extremely gallant efforts of
the London Scottish and the [Irish Guards] attacking and attempting
to capture Campoleone, across a marsh, where they could not have ar-
moured support. They got to within half a mile of the village before they
were finally pinned down." The fire coming from the German side was
simply too intense for anyone to continue advancing, and so the attackers went to ground and stayed there, wondering whether they would be
able to continue or be called back, or if that piece of muddy earth they
were hugging would be their final resting place.[2]

ON THE GERMAN SIDE OF the battlefield, the situation wasn't much better.
Lieutenant Horst Heinrich (29th Regiment, 3rd Panzer-Grenadier Division) recalled:

> Our 3rd Battalion didn't succeed in rejecting the English or stopping
> them on the high ground one kilometer from [Aprilia]. First battalion
> was sent ahead to the high ground north of Buonriposo [Ridge]. In the
> early morning of 25 January, we were struck by the artillery for over one
> hour. That put upside-down literally every square meter of our position.
> We attacked Aprilia that day with two battle groups. From the north
> attacked Kampfgruppe Schonfeld, 29th Regiment's commander, and the
> 3rd Battalion; and from the west the Kampfgruppe Haen, 103rd Panzer
> Abteilung's commander, with his unit and 1st Company, with the water
> tower of Aprilia as its [objective].
>
> Lieutenant Semrau had to take possession of the water tower from
> which was coming accurate machine-gun fire, while the battle group
> with its Tiger VI tanks had to break toward Aprilia. We fired on the
> water-tank with one panzer and one anti-tank gun but we didn't suc-
> ceed in striking it. The occupants of the water-tank bravely defended
> themselves. Semrau attacked with his platoon, but he was jammed by

the defenders' fire. The attack to Aprilia, however, failed because of the strong defense in the center of town. Thus the groups were forced to return to their former positions.[3]

AS THE DAY WORE ON and combat slackened somewhat, Sydney Arthur Wright (5th Grenadier Guards) in Aprilia was told to grab a mine detector and accompany a chaplain named Browning and several other men to drive an ambulance into the churned-up, blood-soaked fields around the town. Their mission was to retrieve the body of Wright's company commander, Captain Christopher Ford, and other Guards who had earlier gone out on a reconnaissance patrol with four jeeps and had not returned. Somehow Captain Ford's patrol had taken a wrong turn on the way back and ended up in no-man's-land, where a German machine gunner had killed everyone in the party.

Wright recalled that, as he and the chaplain and the others went out with the ambulance, they came across "dozens of Irish Guardsmen, dead. They were face down, as if asleep (as indeed they were, with God), complete with all their equipment. They couldn't have stood a chance, nor could the company commander." Wright noticed that one of the dead jeep drivers was pinned halfway under his destroyed vehicle. "Two of us pulled him out, but unfortunately the bottom half of his body stayed in the jeep."

Wright searched for Captain Ford, eventually finding his bullet-stitched body about 250 yards away. A member of the recovery party was Captain Ford's brother, George. Wright called out that he had found the captain's body and asked if there was anything he wanted from it before it was placed in the ambulance. His brother said yes, his cuff links and tiepin; they had been a Christmas present from their mother.

The recovery party returned to Aprilia with their grim cargo, and Wright took up a firing position in the basement of a building. He noted that the basement windows were half above and half below ground. Outside the windows that faced toward the enemy, someone had left dozens of jerry cans full of petrol. As luck would have it, a shell exploded and split open some of the cans; the fuel poured into the basement and caught fire, forcing Wright and his mates to quickly evacuate the building. He said that a German sniper in the bell tower began firing on them as they streamed out of the building, but the guardsmen made quick work of the sniper.[4]

AS FLAT AND FEATURELESS AS the space between the Embankment and Aprilia was, just the opposite was the case to the west of the Albano Highway—an area the British troops referred to as the Wadis or Wadi Country. (A member of the Royal Engineers explained: "'Wadi' is a word we brought with us from our North Africa campaign, being the Arabic word for a dried-up watercourse; this area of the front became known as 'Wadi Country.'")[5]

Burrowed into this eroded, convoluted landscape west of the 24th Guards Brigade's positions at Aprilia and Carroceto were the units of the 2nd British Infantry Brigade—the 1st Battalion, Loyal (Lancashire) Regiment; Lieutenant Colonel A. J. Snodgrass's 2nd Battalion of the North Staffordshire Regiment; and the 6th Battalion, Gordon Highlanders Regiment. The 2nd Brigade was under the command of forty-nine-year-old Brigadier Eric Edward James Moore, who had led the unit since 1941.

In this wild area, dominated by the Moletta River and its numerous tributaries, the officers and men of the 2nd Brigade were wondering if they could possibly hang on, for the terrain was more suited for small, stealthy patrols than large-unit action and certainly unsuitable for any sort of armored or wheeled-vehicle maneuvering. The ground—a mass of deep, bramble-choked, and water-filled gullies—prompted one soldier to say, "What had seemed to the eye to be good 'tank country' proved to be anything but, thus denying vital tank support during previous battles. Just one of those unknowns which can influence the outcome of a battle."

As is often the case during battles, terrain features were given names by troops on the ground for ready identification. "Our Wadis were named after their shapes," said the soldier. "So there were 'North Lobster Claw,' 'South Lobster Claw,' 'Starfish,' 'The Boot,' 'The Fortress,' and others. The systems were quite extensive and, at places, close to the other; the German positions were only sixty yards from 'The Fortress,' so there was constant skirmishing with positions changing hands and, at times, both sides being in the same Wadi. Close-range mortar fire was a constant threat. This supposedly static warfare was in fact very active and the mounting casualties always a worry."[6]

If there was to be a general pushing of the front northward, it would not be Wadi Country through which the push would occur. However, just because the ground was unsuitable for the 2nd Brigade participating in any major northward attack did not prevent the Germans from harassing the British with snipers, probing patrols, and artillery fire.

AT ANOTHER LOCATION WITHIN THE ruins of Aprilia, the men of Captain Thomas S. Hohler's Number 3 Company, 5th Grenadier Guards, were holding positions in the rubble. The scene was awful: houses broken open, spilling their guts—furniture, sinks, bathtubs, piping and electrical wiring, pots and pans, iron radiators, jagged shards of crockery, radios, telephones, a colored print of a saint here, a crucifix there, family photos behind shattered glass, books, albums, twisted bicycles, shredded papers, a birdless birdcage, a dog stiff with rigor mortis being dined on by flies. The buildings had gaping holes in them, and roofs were open to the sky; the two square towers that had fooled soldiers into thinking they were industrial chimneys were pockmarked and considerably worse for the wear, and the streets were filled with splintered beams and collapsed walls. Here and there an abandoned family pet scurried for cover. The church of Saint Michael was a ruin; the bronze statue of the saint in front of the building was still on its pedestal but was punctured with scores of holes made by flying bullets and shell fragments.

Captain Hohler could see a group of German infantry and tanks assembling near the wooden huts outside of town and correctly assumed they were about to charge his position again; he decided that his company must hit them before they hit him. Gripping their Lee-Enfields and their Sten guns, Hohler's men charged across the exposed ground between the town and the huts, the shock of their assault managing to drive the tanks and infantry back a short distance. But then the panzers halted and opened up with their machine guns, wounding or killing a number of the soldiers and shattering Hohler's forearm. Hohler managed to stumble into one of the huts and evade capture by playing dead. Hours later, in pain and weak from loss of blood, he somehow made it back to his company command post, only to find that all the men there had been killed by a German artillery round.[7]

During Hohler's assault on the huts, the remaining platoon of his company was occupying the upper story of a farmhouse southeast of Aprilia, lying flat on the floor and hoping not to be destroyed by panzers blasting away at their hiding place. Miraculously finding themselves still alive at nightfall, the men pulled out and made their way back to friendly lines. Hohler also returned to safety.[8]

THE MISERABLE ITALIAN WINTER WEATHER was on full display. John Kenneally, a Bren gunner in Number 1 Company, 5th Battalion, Grenadier Guards, holed up in Aprilia, recalled, "It had rained incessantly for two days and we were chilled with inactivity. The battalion was well established by dusk on 25th February and, apart from occasional shelling and sniping, things were comparatively quiet. As darkness came on, so did the rain and we spent another cold, soggy night. Dawn came with a heavy hailstorm and we had a wet breakfast."

Added to the hailstorm and interrupting the breakfast was a panzer attack against Kenneally's company, accompanied by a tremendous shelling. He said, "The Germans poured a huge concentration of fire on all the battalion's positions. Guns of all types and calibres opened up on us; there were 150 and 220mm and, for good measure, a monster railway gun which fired a shell that looked like a mini submarine, the only beauty of which was that you could see it coming. I saw one such shell land on a large farmhouse and it completely disintegrated."[9]

In actuality, there were two monster 280mm Krupp railway guns in the Alban Hills—guns that the Germans called "Robert" and "Leopold" but that the Allies had dubbed "Anzio Annie" and the "Anzio Express." Both had barrels seventy-one feet long and could fire a 562-pound shell forty miles. The guns were kept in tunnels in the hills, rolled out, fired, and then rolled back in, making them virtually undetectable and impervious to Allied air attacks.[10] Bert Reed, a British gunner and driver with the 22nd Battery, 24th Field Regiment, Royal Artillery, recalled the day that one of the massive shells exploded near his position: "The shell crater was so big we made good use of it because it was almost like a Roman amphitheatre. Sometimes an American band would [later] perform at the base of the crater while we sat all around inside on the slopes. This was a lot safer as the enemy shells just whizzed overhead."[11]

COMING ASHORE AFTER DARK ON the twenty-fifth was Headquarters Company, 11th Armored Infantry Battalion (AIB), 1st U.S. Armored Division. According to Staff Sergeant Joe D. Craver, "When we got ashore and into position that night, the Luftwaffe came over and dropped anti-personnel bombs on us continuously. We had eighteen casualties and several deaths."[12]

The men of the 11th AIB settled in for a cold, wet, uncomfortable, sleepless night. In addition to the air raids, the boom and thud of artillery seemed ceaseless, each explosion jarring the ground as though hit by a giant sledgehammer. Countless parachute flares and star shells lit up the darkness with an eerie, colorless glow, and spiderwebs of tracers crisscrossed the sky. Men in their dugouts and foxholes shivered, their teeth chattered as much with terror as with the cold, and they briskly rubbed their arms and wiggled their toes to keep the blood circulating. It was a long and fear-filled night, with each man wondering what he had gotten himself into.

General Alexander reported to the prime minister that, although the beachhead was secure for the time being, neither he nor Clark was especially pleased with Lucas's reluctance to push his forces out. To get a better handle on the situation, he told Churchill that he and Clark planned to visit Lucas personally again and assess the situation for themselves. Churchill cabled back, "I am glad to learn that Clark is going to visit the beachhead. It would be unpleasant if your troops were sealed off there and the main army [fighting at the Gustav Line] could not advance up from the south." Unpleasant, indeed—and prophetic as well.[13]

THE *THRUSTER*, CARRYING MORE MEN of the 45th Division's 179th Regiment, returned to Nettuno at 11:00 P.M. on January 25 and received an unfriendly greeting by the Luftwaffe, whose planes daringly dodged barrage-balloon cables and flew through a screen of antiaircraft fire thrown up by shore batteries and the guns of various craft docked in the harbor. Four times that night the enemy aircraft attacked, and four times they were repelled, with one dive-bomber crashing in flames into the sea and another retreating with smoke pouring from its engines.[14]

As January 25 came to a close, Aprilia was still under the control of the 24th Guards Brigade, strung out in a thin line among what were once buildings, but it was a tenuous tenancy. In an attempt to provide some defense in depth, the 1st Battalion, Irish Guards, was moved to the area of the Embankment, while the 1st Scots Guards took up positions about a mile to the south. That night, however, the Germans, members of Gräser's 3rd Panzer-Grenadier Division, returned to Aprilia, using their well-practiced tactic of stealth to infiltrate between the widely spaced Guards. Their movements were aided by a drenching rain and hailstorm that kept visibility poor and British heads low. Having crept to within 200 yards of the northern perimeter of the town and the group of wooden farmers' huts just beyond the northeastern perimeter, the Germans opened up with heavy machine guns and fire from several Tiger tanks and five self-propelled howitzers.

The attackers gave the defenders a rude pounding. The 5th Grenadier Guards and, to their left, the 2nd North Staffs took the brunt of the attack, with grenades being flung back and forth and much hand-to-hand fighting taking place into the rubble-choked village streets. Before long, the North Staffs gave way, and their position was overrun, with many prisoners taken. The rest of the British line held fast and fought back with equal brutality; three German guns were knocked out in the first few minutes of the battle by the antitank guns of the Grenadiers and the Scots Guards, who had just arrived. The Germans pulled back temporarily to regroup beyond a slight rise in the ground and then launched another assault; Number 3 Company of the Grenadiers was waiting for them and left the ground littered with dead and wounded Germans. Except for the mournful cries and moans of the wounded, calling out *Hilfe!* (Help!) and *Mutti!* (Mother!), the night went quiet again.

Before the Brits could cheer their victory, however, the Germans came at them once more in the dark, this time accompanied by two Tiger tanks; in the melee that followed, one platoon of Grenadiers was reduced to seven men. After the brief but violent skirmish in which more British soldiers were taken prisoner, the Germans retreated, with their captives forced to ride atop the panzers, thus preventing the Grenadiers from firing on them.[15]

DAWN ON JANUARY 26 BROUGHT a renewed aerial attack—but by the Luftwaffe, not the Allies. Although the ceiling was low, and the skies were laced with wind, rain, and sleet, German aircraft pounded the Anzio docks and ships in the harbor, while the American and British warplanes sheltered at their bases. Lucas noted that at 8:45 that morning the beachhead endured "the biggest air raid yet. The Hun is determined to ruin me and knows that if I lost Anzio harbor, I am in a hell of a fix. I went to look at the mess. Trucks are burning and the town is a shambles, but ships are being unloaded. Casualties have been heavy."

Three hours and fifteen minutes later, Lucas noted, "A bomb just fell outside my window. There goes the rest of the glass." He would soon move VI Corps headquarters from a vulnerable Italian army barracks at 39 Via Santa Maria in Nettuno to a vast complex of caves a quarter mile long, formerly used to store wine under the streets of the city.[16]

THE HARBOR WASN'T THE ONLY place visited by German warplanes. Four times on January 26 Luftwaffe planes streaked low over the 45th Division's positions north of town and bombed and shot up everything in sight. The antiaircraft batteries on ship and shore replied and drove off the enemy with a stunning display of expert gunnery. The Thunderbirds were then reminded about Newton's law of gravity: what goes up must come down. A number of casualties were caused by pieces of exploding antiaircraft shells raining down on the men in their unprotected holes; before long, foxholes were sporting roofs made from logs or whatever lumber could be scrounged from the debris piles of destroyed buildings.[17]

Things were a bit sticky for the British, too. Twenty-eight-year-old Major Henry L. S. Young was the commanding officer of the Support Company (that is, Heavy Weapons), 1st Battalion, Irish Guards. As such, it was his responsibility to deploy the antitank guns and medium machine guns into the right positions and keep them there. Young was no stranger to combat, having served with the 24th Guards Brigade in the Norwegian campaign at Narvik and again in North Africa. Young also had a special dislike for the Germans; his father had been killed fighting the Boche in France during the First World War.

On the morning of January 26, Young saw that the Germans were strongly counterattacking the Guards' position and had knocked out four of the battalion's antitank guns at Carroceto Station, west of Aprilia; an enemy breakthrough seemed imminent. While being heavily shelled himself, Young chose new positions for the remaining available antitank guns and got them into position, thus closing the gap in the antitank defenses in the nick of time. But Young was not yet done; three days later he would perform another act of remarkable heroism.[18]

THE LUFTWAFFE KEPT UP ITS aerial attacks. A dozen bombers showed up; seven were shot down. As each flaming plane plunged to earth, the men on the ground cheered as though they were spectators at a football game.[19] One of those cheering was Lieutenant Robert LaDu, executive officer of Company F, 2nd Battalion, 179th: "The Germans sent twelve aircraft in. It was just beginning to turn a little dark and they came in and strafed and used anti-personnel bombs. Seven got shot down by our small-arms fire—rifles and machine guns and pistols—anything that could fire. That was really amazing."[20]

Medic Ray McAllister, 45th Infantry Division, said:

Periodically there were dogfights over the beachhead. I understood that the black pilots—Tuskegee airmen—were the ones covering us for a time. They never seemed to hesitate to tangle with the Focke-Wulfs and Messerschmitts that strafed us, or the Dorniers that bombed us. On one occasion a plane, ours or theirs, got its tail shot off and we watched it spiral down so gently that I have no doubt everyone still alive walked away from the crash. One night a German bomber flew over and dropped a cluster bomb which opened as it fell and sprayed the area with tiny mortar shell-like bomblets. Each was deadly if it hit in your hole or close to you. As it came over, I was face down in the foxhole and, when the bombing was over, I had tightly clenched fists and was singing, over and over, "I've got spurs that jingle jangle jingle; I've got spurs that jingle jangle jingle; I've got . . . " Several bomblets hit within ten feet of me but none hit my hole. One guy had a dud hit right alongside his body, in his hole. If it had hit him, the impact would probably have killed him without it going off.[21]

Private Paul Brown, whose unit, the 179th's Service Company and Graves Registration Service (GRS), would have the grim task of scouring the battlefield nightly to retrieve the bodies of those killed in action, wrote in his diary, "We are sitting here like clay pidgins [sic]. Waves of enemy fighters and bombers come over regularly. We shot down between 10 & 12 of their planes & they got at least 6 of ours. German anti-aircraft is heavy all around us. . . . Several of our boys are getting hit by falling flak. Our Regiment is not in action yet. . . . Still sitting here."[22]

They wouldn't be "still sitting here" for much longer.

BRITISH CASUALTIES WERE MOUNTING. To treat the growing number of wounded, a casualty clearing station was established in a yellow stucco house between Aprilia and the Overpass. Most of the wounded stoically endured their pain, telling the medics to tend to those who were in worse shape than they were. An Irish Guards chaplain named Brookes spent much of the twenty-sixth comforting and doing whatever else he could for the badly hurt and dying. In many cases, he could do nothing but pray for them.[23]

That day, another company of Brits, aided by some American tanks, attacked and pushed the Germans out of the area of the huts on the northeastern outskirts of Aprilia, thus securing—at least temporarily—the northeastern flank.[24] Like the cavalry arriving in the nick of time in an old Hollywood western, the American Sherman tanks[*] were a most welcome sight to the beleaguered British. They were the vanguard of the

---

[*] At thirty tons, the M4 Sherman tank was considered a "medium" tank. It replaced the ungainly, M3 Lee (with its U.S. turret) and M3 Grant (British turret). Its main armament was a 75mm gun that proved to be ineffective when compared to the armament of the German Tiger tank. But the Sherman, powered by a 400 hp Continental gasoline engine, was produced in huge numbers (nearly 50,000 of all variants), and so it made up in quantity what it lacked in quality. However, its high profile—nearly ten feet tall—and relatively thin frontal glacis and side armor made it an easy target for enemy gunners. Hogg and Weeks, *Illustrated Encyclopedia of Military Vehicles*, 122–123.

1st U.S. Armored Division—a unit that had already seen plenty of action in North Africa, Sicily, and southern Italy.

TO PROVIDE A PLACE WHERE a combination supply depot/maintenance and rest area could be established, the British set up "B Echelon," located astride the Albano Highway about halfway between Anzio and the southern edge of the Padiglione Woods, where the Americans had their own rest and assembly area. There, the British units built up stocks of ammunition and other supplies to prepare for the heavy enemy attacks that were expected to resume at any moment. Because the Albano Highway was constantly being shelled, supplies had to be sent forward mostly at night. Also at B Echelon were a number of services, especially for the rest and relaxation of the frontline troops, who were being given a brief respite.

A soldier recalled, "One such was the 'Anzio Ritz'—a small, underground movie theater just large enough to hold sixteen men. Here, men out of the line could relax for an hour and see films, shown by the Army Kinematograph Service, to take their minds off what was going on above. What with the heat of the projector, sweaty bodies, and fag smoking, the atmosphere became somewhat ripe!"[25]

Another British soldier, nineteen-year-old Fred Mason of the 2nd North Staffs, remembered B Echelon: British troops would be rotated off the front lines after a few days and sent to B Echelon. "It was a place of supposed rest. Some of our artillery guns were fired from there. We still lived in holes in the ground, but at least we could walk around." Mason also recalled the cinema: "It was a hole in the ground and big enough to be covered by a medium-sized tent."[26]

JOHN P. LUCAS NOTED IN his diary on January 26 his growing anxiety about his job security. But he was firmly convinced that "slow and steady" was his watchword and that he must resist all attempts by higher authority to push him into doing something rash that would result in the destruction of his VI Corps. "Apparently some of the higher levels think I have not advanced with maximum speed," he jotted down, and added, "I think more has been accomplished than anyone has a right to expect. This venture was always a desperate one and I could never see much chance for it to succeed, if success means driving the Germans north of Rome."[27]

Few military operations have taken place in which the officer charged with its conduct was as pessimistic about its chances of success as was Operation Shingle.

BY JANUARY 27, FIVE DAYS after the initial landings, the port of Anzio was a bustling harbor full of LCIs, LCTs, DUKWs, and various and sundry other naval craft, most of which were delivering men, guns, ammunition, rations, vehicles, medicines, and other supplies to the burgeoning beachhead. Antiaircraft guns were positioned around the harbor, and barrage balloons, designed to keep marauding enemy aircraft at bay, floated above the cargo ships. Near Nettuno a small airfield was established for the 307th Fighter Squadron.[28]

On the beach about three miles east of Nettuno stood a forest of large olive-drab canvas tents covered with large white panels sporting bright-red crosses. It was the U.S. Army's 56th Evacuation Hospital, and it was well within range of just about every piece of German artillery ringing the beachhead. The place where the hospital was located would soon ruefully be known as "Hell's Half Acre."

On this day, a young army nurse lieutenant from Iowa named Avis Dagit had come into the port of Anzio with twenty-five other nurses aboard a British LCT in the midst of a German air raid. No sooner had they disembarked and were trucked to the hospital area to settle down for the night when "a loud, chilling scream pierced the stillness. It grew louder and louder when it passed overhead," wrote Dagit. "The ground shook when the missile landed with a thunderous thud beyond us."

"My God, what was that?" whispered someone, as if she was afraid the sound of her voice would attract the enemy.

"Sounds like shells to me," Dagit offered, her voice choked with fear.

The shelling—what the British called "getting stonked"—continued intermittently throughout the night, and the unpleasant welcome extended into the next morning. A dogfight broke out above the beachhead. "German planes appeared overhead," Dagit recalled, "with American planes in pursuit. The planes dived and swooped with guns blazing. Puffs of black smoke filled the sky and the rat-a-tat-tat of antiaircraft guns sent up a deafening roar.

"'Get him! Get him!' we shouted, even though the gunners could not hear us."

The group of nurses saw an American plane spiral downward, leaving a trail of smoke. "'Oh, that Jerry got our plane!' we cried in anguish. The pilot ejected and slowly drifted to earth. We ducked the dirt and flames that shot skyward when the plane plummeted to earth two hundred yards away. A German plane fell across the road from where we were standing at about the same time. The other German planes disappeared into the morning sunshine."

On the beach about three miles east of Nettuno, the doctors, nurses, and orderlies spent that day and the next setting up their canvas hospital: tents that would house the operating rooms, the pre-op tent, the laboratory, the X-ray facilities, the recovery wards, the pharmacy, the showers, the supply rooms, the living quarters. Occasionally, their construction activities had to be halted when trucks and jeeps and ambulances arrived bearing wounded men in need of immediate medical care—men with sucking chest wounds, gaping head injuries, jaws and faces missing, abdomens torn open by bullet and shell, arms and legs and genitals blown away, men burned beyond recognition.

Avis felt alone and frightened by the horrible scenes all around her. "What was going to happen to us?" she wondered. "Death, doom, and disaster surrounded us. I wanted to run, but there was no place to go. . . . Fear paralyzed me. . . . I hadn't eaten for twenty-four hours, but I wasn't thinking of food. My legs were heavy and the sight of the endless number of wounded seared my mind. I was neither emotionally nor physically prepared for the shock and horror that greeted me. I opened the tent flap and a scream stuck in my throat. The smell of blood and flesh hit me. I saw litter after litter filled with men wounded beyond description."

During the 56th Evac Hospital's first thirty-six hours, more than 1,100 patients were admitted. "The 750-bed hospital expanded to 1,200 by adding more tents," she said. But the carnage at Anzio and its environs had become so great that the 56th was incapable of handling it all;

soon the 56th was joined by the 33rd Field Hospital and then the 93rd and 95th Evac Hospitals.[29]

Another of those working at the 56th was nurse Lieutenant Mary Louise Roberts. She recalled, "Fighting was fierce and the medical staff worked twelve- to fifteen-hour shifts tending to wounded soldiers. At one point I was asked if I and my fifty nurses wanted to be evacuated. I said 'No'—even though my life was endangered."[30]

NIGHTFALL BROUGHT NO RESPITE FROM the aerial assaults by Richthofen's daring Luftwaffe pilots. On the twenty-seventh, during several more raids, falling shrapnel and antiaircraft shells landed in the 179th Regiment's area, causing casualties. Paul Brown (179th Service Company and Graves Registration Service) wrote in his diary, "Dive bombers were busy all night. Came low over us after dropping bombs on beach 1½ miles away. Several planes have been shot down. Ours also. Pilots don't get out every time. Capt. Bloom, medics, Capt. Strickler, Service Co., along with two D. Co., got hit by flak. Our tanks have been firing point blank most of morning at enemy. We are expected to counterattack most any time. Bombs are getting closer each time."[31]

Eventually, though, the Germans realized that they were losing more planes and pilots than they could afford and drastically cut back on the frequency of their attacks. The aerial assaults, however, would not completely end.

THE U.S. RANGERS WERE NOW right where they wanted to be: in the thick of the action. Colonel Darby said that his 3rd and 4th Ranger Battalions, along with the 509th Parachute Infantry Battalion, "moved forward in a skirmish line to a road running from Carroceto eastward. The enemy was in foxholes and was using every house as a center of defense," while the British, holed up in Aprilia, were being heavily stonked. The Rangers, too, were trading mortar fire with the Germans' heavier artillery.

One of Darby's men, a Sergeant Campbell, recalled, "There was one time we saw a German come out of his foxhole for a minute, and as the mortars were zeroed in, we gave him concentration Number 3. He must have had some ammo in that hole because the next thing we saw of that Jerry, he was about twenty feet in the air, turning end over end."[32]

NO DOUBT INFLUENCED BY CHURCHILL'S demands for more progress at Anzio, Alexander's impatience with Lucas was growing. The chain of command made it impossible for him to directly order Lucas to do anything, so he prodded Clark into building a fire under his subordinate.[33] Clark had suggested to Lucas back on January 25 that he consider using the 3rd Division and Rangers to make a strong push to capture Cisterna, as that would extend the beachhead line even farther inland and provide a solid anchor for defense; the suggestions turned into orders.[34]

It was clear that VI Corps, despite having caught the Germans by surprise on the twenty-second, had failed to capitalize on the gift and remained rooted close to the shoreline on which it had landed. Although Lucas was reluctant to push his troops all the way to Rome, or even to the Alban Hills, and thus create a salient that could be chopped to pieces by any serious German counterattack, many experts without the weight of responsibility on their shoulders agree that he could have—and should have—made a more aggressive move to capture Cisterna. But, fearful of the consequences of overextending himself, Lucas instead chose to be prudent and continue to build up his beachhead. The delay enabled Kesselring to take the initiative.[35]

IN THE APRILIA AREA, THE 29th Panzer-Grenadier Regiment was still trying to oust the 24th Guards Brigade from the town. During the effort, Lieutenant Horst Heinrich suddenly became commander of the 3rd Company when its leader was killed by a mortar burst. "I took command of the company," he said, "which formed the left wing of the regiment to about two kilometers south of the Campoleone-Cisterna railway line. In the position of the battalion there was, in the direction of the front, a one-meter-deep ditch. The shelter hole of my tank was in a cross ditch. About 300 meters behind my company there was Lieutenant Steingruber's 2nd Company, and 800 meters back Captain Rossmann's battalion positions. Our positions could be watched by the British, who were only 200 meters from us."[36]

TRUSCOTT WROTE IN HIS MEMOIRS, "During our effort to capture Cisterna . . . General Alexander came to my Command Post at Conca. After

we had explained the situation, he wished to see the terrain about Cisterna. I was almost immobilized from a wound in my left leg which I had
received a few days earlier. Accordingly, I sent [assistant division commander Brigadier General John "Iron Mike"] O'Daniel to escort General
Alexander, having first endeavored unsuccessfully to persuade General
Alexander to exchange his red-banded cap for my helmet."

A frontline American company commander later angrily complained
to a colonel who had accompanied the Alexander-O'Daniel party, "By
God, colonel, you tell General O'Daniel and that guy with the red hat-
band that if they want to prove how brave they are, please do it some-
place else. They walked over my front line, and as soon as they left, the
Boche shelled the hell out of us!"[37]

Elsewhere within the 3rd Division sector, Stanley R. Smith (Company I, 30th Regiment) had his first shock during his division's advance
toward Cisterna. "I was filling my canteen with water from a five-gallon
jerrycan," he later wrote.

> Happened to glance up and saw about four or five fellows lying in a row
> like they were asleep. When I looked closer, I realized that they were
> dead! That was the first time I ever saw an American soldier that had
> been killed. It was sure a strange feeling, stranger still because I never got
> the chance to know them. Maybe that was just as well. I tried to get close
> to some of the fellows, but after a while I would keep my distance. The
> only reason for this was that one day they would be there and the next
> they may be gone—killed, wounded, or missing. I would feel very sad,
> so, if I didn't get too close to anyone, I wouldn't get hurt.[38]

Smith's desire to distance himself emotionally from his fellow soldiers was a common one in wartime. It may seem callous, but new replacements arriving at a unit that had suffered casualties were usually
ignored by the soldiers they were joining. Some soldiers have said they
that didn't even bother to learn the names of the men who had come
to take the place of departed buddies, and the new arrivals were almost
always given the most dangerous and unpleasant jobs—digging latrine
holes, walking point during a combat patrol, being in the forefront of an

attack, and so on. It was emotionally distressing to make a new friend, only to have him get killed; therefore, it was easier not to get to know the replacements.[39]

WITH PRESSURE GROWING ON HIM to do *something* to break the tightening ring around the beachhead, on Friday, January 28, Lucas decided that he would send Penney's 1st Division, augmented by the tanks of Harmon's Combat Command A, all the way to Albano. At the same time, Truscott's 3rd Division, with Darby's Rangers and the 82nd Airborne Division's 504th PIR attached, would make a thrust to take Cisterna and be ready to drive on Albano and Valmontone, the latter twenty-three straight-line miles inland, but sixty-two miles by road. If successful, the attack would effectively cut the two main highways between Rome and the Cassino front, thus isolating the German Tenth Army. But Lucas, without knowledge of how many German troops were in front of him, still agonized that such a thrust ran the risk of his force being torn to shreds. And hadn't Clark warned him not to take any risks or do anything foolish?

But action was required. To protect Penney during the northward advance, Lucas reluctantly decided to commit the 45th Division's 179th Infantry Regiment to cover the salient's right flank. As this area—mostly farmers' flat fields—was then lightly held by the Germans, there had been little in the way of serious fighting except for the occasional patrol or exchange of artillery fire between the German gunners and the 179th Regiment's 160th Field Artillery Battalion. But serious fighting would soon envelop this area—fighting that has been described as some of the bloodiest of the entire war.[40]

THE 45TH INFANTRY DIVISION'S MEDICAL personnel came ashore on January 28. Dr. Peter C. Graffagnino, a surgeon in the 157th Regiment, recalled being surprised by an idyllic setting:

> The Navy landed us on the beaches north of Anzio on the afternoon of January 28, six days after the initial invasion, and the beachhead was still quiet. The weather was chilly but pleasant, and the sun was shining. The gently rolling, fertile reclaimed farmlands stretched inland for fifteen or

twenty miles, where, in the distance, the Alban Hills rising to three thousand feet were obscured in a purple gray haze. Crops were growing and
the forests of pine and cork in the Padiglione Woods . . . were fresh and
green. The sea, beneath the colorful sunset to our west, was smooth and
peaceful. There was nothing forbidding about any of it, and, after the
cold and rain and snow of the mountains [at Venafro, near Cassino], it
seemed like a Garden of Eden.

Graffagnino noted, "Lieutenant Colonel [Lawrence] Brown, our
brand-new battalion commander, had joined us in the staging area at
Pozzuoli north of Naples just before sailing. He was young, 'Regular
Army,' fresh from the States, and had never been in combat before. His
inexperience and his personality conflicts with some of his staff officers
soon set off a chain of events that turned us all into reluctant heroes and
eventually denied Hitler the satisfaction of another Dunkirk."[41]
Many other 45th soldiers were also not terribly fond of Colonel
Brown. One of them, Louis V. "Cody" Wims, said, "Our Colonel . . . was a
most abrasive personality, never had a kind word for anybody. . . . Hon-
est, never heard him have a kind word for anybody."[42]
More replacements were piling onto Anzio's shores. Private Murray
Levine, one such newbie in the 45th's 157th Infantry Regiment, nervously reported to his assigned unit, Company G. "I jokingly went over
to the lieutenant and I said, 'You know, my eyes aren't too good.' He
said, 'Don't worry about it. We'll put you up front, and you'll see everything.' I thought that was funny as hell. We all laughed. 'We'll put you
up front,' he says. 'Oh, good—I was worried.'"[43]

ON FEBRUARY 28, A REMARKABLE soldier performed a remarkable deed.
Twenty-five-year-old Technician Fifth Grade Eric Gunnar Gibson, a
Sweden-born, Chicago-raised cook (Company I, 30th Infantry Regiment, 3rd Infantry Division), earned the first of twenty-six Medals of
Honor that would be awarded to American servicemen during the battle
of Anzio and the breakout that followed.
In the vicinity of the tiny village of Isola Bella, German troops launched
a ground attack that threatened to overrun Company I. Although not a
trained frontline infantryman, Gibson nevertheless saw the danger that

the German assault posed to his unit's right flank, swiftly organized a small group of green replacements who had not been in combat before, grabbed a Thompson sub-machine gun, and rushed toward the danger. During his ad hoc squad's assault, Gibson personally killed five Germans and took two others prisoner. Not yet finished, he then went running, leaping, and dodging through machine-gun fire to single-handedly wipe out another position. Although more familiar with a frying pan than a Tommy gun, the cook continued his assault, moving toward other German positions even though enemy artillery shells were falling all about him. Like a man possessed, he kept advancing through a rain of bullets and exploding shells, spraying each enemy position as he came to it until, ultimately, he was cut down while storming an outpost.[*44]

ON THE MORNING OF JANUARY 28, determined to personally light a fire under Lucas, Mark Clark decided to make a trip by PT[†] (patrol torpedo) boat from the mouth of the Volturno River near Cassino to Anzio. It was almost the last trip he ever took.

The general and his entourage climbed aboard *PT-201* for a run up the coast. It was a trip fraught with danger, as the Luftwaffe was active in attacking ships approaching Anzio harbor, and there were rumors that the Germans had submarines and torpedo boats in the area, ready to pounce. About seven miles south of Anzio, in the predawn darkness, an American minesweeper, thinking perhaps that *PT-201* was a German torpedo boat, challenged it with her blinker light.

The PT boat skipper signaled back, but, as Clark said, "The captain of the minesweeper apparently misread our signal, or perhaps it was just that everybody along the coast that dark and windy morning was trigger-happy. Anyway, the minesweeper fired on us, cutting loose with 40mm and 5-inch shells. Their marksmanship, unfortunately, was pretty

---

[*] Gibson was inducted into the Quartermaster Hall of Fame in 1999. The NCO Academy Dining Facility at Fort Lee, Virginia, is named Gibson Hall in honor of him. www.qmfound.com.

[†] Small, fast torpedo-armed boats developed for the U.S. Navy to attack enemy ships.

good. A number of shells struck our PT boat and the second one went right through the stool on which I had been sitting."

The boat's skipper was wounded in both legs and collapsed, and the other three officers on board were also hit and no one was at the controls. While Clark held the wounded skipper in his arms, another injured officer took the wheel and gunned the engines, trying to outrun the "friendly" shells. Clark said, "By the time we were clear, our deck seemed to be littered with casualties and running in blood." Luckily, *PT-201* came across a British minesweeper that had a doctor aboard, and the dead and wounded were transferred to the larger ship.

Still, getting into Anzio harbor was no cakewalk, as the Germans that morning were staging one of their usual air raids on the port; it was quite some time before *PT-210* was able to dock and then for Clark to drive to Lucas's command post, where the corps commander briefed his superior on the situation, which Clark saw as becoming more precarious with each passing day.[45]

PT-201'S CLOSE CALL WAS NOT the only action at sea. On January 29, the British light cruiser HMS *Spartan* was part of a task force that was providing antiaircraft support to ships in Anzio harbor. Just before 6:00 P.M., eighteen Dornier Do-217 bombers appeared out of the dusk to launch a glide-bomb attack on the Allied fleet. *Spartan* was at anchor when an Hs-293 dive-bomb slammed into her port side and exploded in the aft boiler room, causing a fire, secondary explosions, and severe flooding that soon saw the ship heeling to port.[46]

One of the surviving crewmen, Derek Evans, said that his battle station was at an Oerlikon gun* on the starboard side aft. He was knocked unconscious by the explosions but was later told that someone lashed him to a Carley float and put him over the side. "I have a very hazy memory of being in the water, wondering how, and why, I was in this predicament. My legs wouldn't work and my fingers on my right hand

---

*The Oerlikon gun was a German-designed, Swiss-improved, and U.S.-manufactured 20mm automatic cannon used by Allied navies during the war. Primarily an antiaircraft weapon, the Oerlikon could also be used against floating or shore targets. Quick, *Dictionary of Weapons and Military Terms*, 333.

were bent backwards at right angles to the back of my hand. No proper recall then until I came round in a sick bay or something similar."

Efforts to extinguish *Spartan*'s blaze were futile, and so, about an hour after being hit, the order was given to abandon ship; 503 men were picked up by several ships before she finally sank in some thirty feet of water, but 66 men died.[47]

Milton Briggs, a radioman aboard the American light cruiser USS *Brooklyn*, saw *Spartan* go down and wondered if *Brooklyn* was next:

> We held our breath, prayed, and waited for an end that didn't come. . . .
> The beachhead was in flames and the sky was alight with fire and smoke.
> The scene numbed us on the bridge as we lay there, and our tongues were
> silent as death. One ensign, on his knees, gave out with "God save us!"
> and I guess God answered. . . . That one night has haunted me ever since.
> It will chill my dreams until the day I die. That night, I knew that I would
> not die in battle. I never felt fear again, though we faced death many
> times in the days that followed.[48]

THE MEN OF THE SERVICES of supply were doing their best to keep up with the demand for ammunition, food, fuel, medical supplies, clothing, tentage, spare parts, and all the other accoutrements of war. Someone had come up with the idea of loading fifty cargo trucks with 1,500 tons of vital supplies every day, backing the trucks onto six LSTs, and sailing the ships from Naples to Anzio. Once they arrived, the trucks were immediately driven off and headed for the supply dumps for distribution to the units. The empty trucks that had hauled the supplies the previous day were then loaded onto the LSTs for the return trip. Additionally, each week fifteen smaller ships loaded with supplies reached the port, supplemented every ten days by Liberty ships bringing in heavy equipment. The navy was bringing in an average of almost 4,000 tons of supplies per day—an amazing feat.[49]

IT HAD BEEN A WEEK since the American and British troops had landed in Anzio and Nettuno, setting the German response into motion. On the twenty-ninth of January, two massive forces were on the same track and were about to smash headfirst into each other. Mackensen had given his Fourteenth Army its mission: "Annihilate the beachhead which the enemy is reinforcing. The attack is to be made as soon as possible, depending on the arrival of the necessary forces, which is being delayed, as the railroad system in Italy has been crippled by enemy [air] raids."[50]

From Radio Vittoria, the Allies' secret transmitter operated by spies in Rome, came word that the Germans were planning a major counterattack at Anzio on January 29, and this alert was passed on to all units on the beachhead. As events turned out, however, the German attack was postponed to February 3 because not all the units were in place.[51]

But there was still plenty the Germans could throw at the Allies until they were ready for the big counterattack, aircraft being one. Anti-aircraft gunners did their best to beat off the swarms of enemy aircraft that were making life difficult for the boys in the ships. On January 29 sixty German planes—Junkers 88s, Dornier 217s, and Heinkel 177s—came swooping down, only to be met by the massed fire of 90mm guns. Five planes were shot down, but countless more got through the screen to hit the ships.[52]

ALSO ON THE TWENTY-NINTH, MARK Clark, in an effort to get Alexander off his back, stormed into Lucas's headquarters. Clark, who had just escaped being killed aboard *PT-201*, was obviously in a foul mood when he saw that the grease-pencil lines on the acetate-covered situation maps in the headquarters had hardly changed since his previous visit.

"Clark is up here," Lucas groused in his diary,

> and I am afraid he intends to stay for several days. His gloomy attitude is certainly bad for me. He thinks I should have been more aggressive on D-day and should have gotten tanks and things out to the front. I think he realizes the serious nature of the whole operation. His forces are divided in the face of a superior enemy on interior lines and now neither of the parts is capable of inflicting a real defeat on those facing it. There has been no chance, with [the lack of] available shipping, to build "Shingle" up to a decisive strength and anyone with any knowledge of logistics could have seen that from the start. I have done what I was ordered to do, desperate though it was. I can win if I am let alone but I don't know whether I can stand the strain of having so many people looking over my shoulder.[53]

The next day, with his commanding general still in town and looking over his shoulder, Lucas wrote, "I don't blame [Clark] for being terribly disappointed. He and those above him thought this landing would shake the Cassino line loose at once but they had no right to think that, because the German is strong in Italy and will give up no ground if he can help it."[54]

STANLEY SMITH, 3RD INFANTRY DIVISION, recalled that he and a buddy needed water for their canteens, "so we stopped [at a stream] and filled up. We had water-purifying tablets and we threw a couple into each canteen. The only problem was that were two dead German soldiers laying in the water and they had been there more than a couple of days! When we saw that, our guts almost made a flip-flop, but thank God nothing happened."[55]

Another 3rd Infantry Division soldier, Private James Aurness, was out on a patrol with other members of his platoon when he came across three bodies lying in a farmer's field. "They were Americans," Aurness said,

and one of them was still alive. He was terribly wounded by shrapnel, and just lay there moaning. I yelled for a medic and he raced over and tended to the guy. As we moved on, we found more bodies and assumed they'd been killed during the night. Then we sighted some of our Sherman tanks up ahead, arranged in a skirmish line. We were ordered to stay behind them: troops usually follow tanks into a skirmish. For an hour or so nothing moved, until we heard a creaking noise a short distance ahead. Over a hill toward us lumbered several "Tigers." . . .

The Shermans and Tigers started firing at each other. We stayed behind our tanks, ready to fight any German infantry that might appear. A couple of ours were hit and caught fire; luckily, the crews were able to escape before being trapped. The tanks exploded into fireballs as the Germans continued to target them. The battle went on for an hour or so before both sides disengaged. No enemy were sighted, so we continued our patrol up the Nettuno-Cisterna road. It was frustrating, because when we made these patrols, we could see Cisterna in the distance. But German fire always stopped us from advancing too far, and it seemed to increase by the day.[56]

MEANWHILE, FARTHER TO THE WEST, with German artillery falling accurately and almost without pause, more 1st U.S. Armored Division tanks advanced during the afternoon of the twenty-ninth and began blasting every building within sight near Aprilia, hoping that the enemy artillery observers were in one or more of them. But whenever a tank departed from the paved roadway, it sank into the mud. The tanks that came to the rescue of the first found themselves mired as well in the muck; it would take all night to winch them to higher, drier ground.

Also that night, the rest of Combat Command A (minus the 2nd Battalion of the 6th Armored Infantry Regiment) and the 27th Armored Field Artillery Battalion were brought forward to prepare for the main attack scheduled for the following morning. Lucas decided that the British would attack Campoleone Station, located on the Anzio-Rome railroad line, without a preliminary artillery bombardment that would alert the enemy to the fact that an attack was coming. Furthermore, through the spreading of false information, Fifth Army hoped to fool the Germans into thinking that another amphibious landing was about to take place at the port city of Civitavecchia, forty miles farther up the coast from Anzio. Such a threat, Clark hoped, might cause Kesselring to weaken his grip on Anzio-Nettuno and send units northward to deal with this new possibility.[57]

Indeed, so worried was Hitler about this possibility that he ordered Kesselring to postpone Mackensen's counterattack that had been rescheduled for February 1. Realizing that one of his best units, Conrath's Hermann Göring Parachute-Panzer Division, was worn out and in serious need of rest and refitting, Kesselring sent the division to the Civitavecchia-Lucca-Pisa-Livorno area to rest but remain on alert in case of an Allied landing there.[58]

Ernie Harmon, meanwhile, pushed some of his 1st Armored Division tanks up to Aprilia to help the British hold on to their tenuous gains. But, for the life of him, Harmon could not understand "why all the 1st Armored Division strength was assigned to the British sector. As I told Colonel Darby subsequently, fifty of my tanks in daylight support of the Rangers would have made this sacrifice [during the Cisterna assault] of crack troops unnecessary. We could have gone in and got 'em." But the fighting around Aprilia meant that the tanks were rendered ineffective because of wadis that were fifty feet deep and the thick mud that im-mobilized the Shermans like they were insects stuck on a giant sheet of flypaper.

Harmon remembered one incident in particular: "Four tanks were stuck in the mud and I ordered an armored wrecker to pull them out. The wrecker was ambushed by the Germans. I sent four more tanks to rescue the wrecker. Then I sent more tanks in after them. . . . Because I was stubborn, I lost twenty-four tanks while I was trying to succor four."

Harmon decided to make a personal visit to an embattled British position.

> It was on the day of my armor's farthest advance that I had the privilege of relieving a group of British soldiers who had held a position under the most punishing circumstances. They belonged to the Sherwood Forest-ers. My tank climbed the hill and then I called a halt and got out to walk. There were dead bodies everywhere. I had never seen so many dead men in one place. They lay so close together that I had to step with care.
>
> I shouted for the commanding officer. From a foxhole there arose a mud-covered corporal with a handlebar moustache. He was the highest-ranking officer still alive. He stood stiffly at attention.
>
> "How is it going?" I asked. The answer was all around us.
>
> "Well, sir," the corporal said, "there were 116 of us when we first came up and there are now sixteen of us left. We're ordered to hold out until sundown, and I think, with a little good fortune, we can manage to do so."

Looking at the handful of mud-and-blood-caked Tommies smiling at him, Harmon noted, "I think my great respect for the stubbornness and fighting ability of the British enlisted man was born that afternoon."[59]

MAJOR HENRY L. S. YOUNG, commanding officer of the Support Com-pany, 1st Battalion, Irish Guards, who had distinguished himself three days earlier near Aprilia, again demonstrated the mettle of British sol-diers. On the night of January 29–30, he went forward with the rifle com-panies to reconnoiter positions for siting his antitank weapons, mortars, and heavy machine guns. His recon mission turned into a full-fledged combat action, with Young narrowly avoiding being hit while killing several Germans and taking others prisoner.

In recommending him for the Military Cross, Young's battalion commander wrote that he went about his duties "with an aloof calmness that had an immense steadying and encouraging effect on all who saw him and all those under his command." So impressed with Young's courage was 1st Division commander Penney that he upgraded the request to an immediate Distinguished Service Order, second only to the Victoria Cross in importance.

Such was the indomitability of the men who fought at Anzio. Although twenty-six Americans would be awarded the Medal of Honor during the fighting and the breakout, ten of them posthumously, the British would award only two Victoria Crosses during that same period of time. Yet the courage they displayed was no less deserving of their nation's highest award.[60]

The 5th Grenadier Guards, too, were having a rough go that required all the courage they could muster. Lucas wrote in his diary, "The Grenadier Guards had hard luck last night. The CO, second in command, and all the company commanders [were] either killed, wounded, or captured. This will immobilize them for a time, certainly." Lucas also noted that the Germans outnumbered his forces, "71,500 to my 61,000. . . . The situation is crowded with doubt and uncertainty."[61]

ON THE COLD, GRAY, AND drizzly afternoon of February 29, a reconnaissance-in-force was made by elements of Harmon's 1st Armored Division. By studying maps and aerial photos, the division's planners saw that there was the straight and flat raised bed of a narrow, unused railroad line variously called (by the Americans) the Bowling Alley and the Embankment (by the British) that diagonally bisected the area between Carroceto and Littoria; it would give the Shermans' tracks some solid footing. The decision was made to utilize this feature to allow the tanks and their armored infantry battalions to quickly strike to the northwest, where elements of Penney's 1st British Division were struggling to hold the line. Because of the soft, muddy ground as well as the rivers, streams, and deep wadis that ran through the terrain like giant claw marks west of the highway, keeping to the highway was essential for the armor.

Harmon gave this assignment to 1st Armored's Combat Command A—a regiment-size unit—under Colonel Kent Lambert. The point unit headed northwest, left the Bowling Alley, and crossed a small stream, where immediately a tank and a halftrack became stuck in the mud. German artillery observers saw the immobilized armor and called in a barrage by 88s that killed nine men, wounded several others, and caused the whole enterprise to come to a halt and turn back.[62]

Lieutenant Horst Heinrich (29th Panzer-Grenadier Regiment) recalled, "On 29 January we heard the sounds of tanks but we didn't see them. I strengthened our position in anticipation of a new attack. Suddenly, in front of our company appeared one patrol tank. One of our non-commissioned officers threw a hand grenade and the tank stopped without being damaged. . . . That night a pioneer [engineer] platoon was sent ahead to plant mines on the left flank, but hell broke out."[63]

FARTHER TO THE EAST, THE American attack against Cisterna was kicking off, and Private first class George Avery (84th Chemical Mortar Battalion) was a part of it:

> We had taken some mortars and were walking at night to reinforce an already occupied mortar position manned by Company B. This location had earned the name, "The Rabbit Farm," but I don't know why.
>
> A large group of Rangers were passing through us and we were instructed to get off the road until the unit had passed. A ship exploded in Anzio harbor and lit up our area, just about turning night into day. A desperate firefight broke out just a few hundred yards in front of us. Germans were approaching the same point on the road ahead that the Rangers were going to fortify. All of us were exposed by the ship burning at Anzio, and the firefight turned into a battle before a battle. We mortar men could not move because we had no cover to protect us.[64]

The fateful night of January 29–30 was moonless and still. One hour before the 3rd Infantry Division was scheduled to begin its attack on Cisterna, the 1st, 3rd, and 4th Ranger Battalions moved out from their assembly area and crossed the line of departure. They were scheduled to make the initial contact at Cisterna, shock the Germans with the violence of their assault, and allow the 3rd to move through them and seize the town.

Colonel Darby said that his troops

> were accompanied by a tank-destroyer company and a cannon [antitank] company as well as our friendly companions of the 83rd Chemical Mortar Battalion. The riflemen carried two bandoliers of ammunition strung over their shoulders and grenades stuffed in their pockets. The mortar crews carried three rounds for each weapon. Machine guns were left behind. Other than our rifles and automatic weapons, there was a plentiful supply of sticky grenades* and many antitank rocket launchers scattered throughout the Ranger force. . . . The men were in good spirits as they swung out for their seven-mile march from the assembly area to the line of departure.[65]

What none of these men in good spirits knew is that, the previous day, Mackensen had brought up the 26th Panzer-Grenadier Division to take over that portion of the line that had been held by the Hermann Göring Parachute-Panzer Division. A Ranger officer, Lieutenant William L. Newnan, of Company B, explained why Cisterna di Littoria, a community said to have been founded by Saint Peter in the first century AD, was important: "Cisterna was a natural point for us to attack for this reason: it was astride the Appian Way [Highway 7], one of the three main roads south to Cassino, and, had the Allies controlled the Appian Way to Cassino, the Jerries would have been very embarrassed, because it would have been very difficult to bring in food and ammunition, and also reinforcements. That is why the Rangers were pushed into Cisterna."[66]

---

* The sticky grenade, or "sticky bomb," as it was sometimes called, was a British invention. Looking like a softball on a stick or a giant's lollipop, the 2.25-pound device with an adhesive outer coating could be stuck against the hull of an armored vehicle before it exploded. Fitzsimons, *Illustrated Encyclopedia of 20th Century Weapons and Warfare*, 101.

There was another, larger, reason. If Cisterna could be taken by the Yanks, VI Corps would control Highway 7 and be in position to take Velletri, north of Cisterna at the base of the Alban Hills. Highway 6, the only other main route through the Liri Valley, could then be blocked. With the main escape routes of the German Tenth Army fleeing from the Gustav Line thus in Allied hands, escape would be nearly impossible, annihilation of the Tenth Army would be certain to follow, and a swift victory in Italy would be assured.[67]

To get to Cisterna from their line of departure, the Rangers had to pass through Isola Bella, a tiny farming community two miles from Cisterna. There they slipped into the deep irrigation ditches that flanked the roadway and silently bypassed two batteries of German *Nebelwerfer*. Darby said, "There was no hint of disaster as we plodded ahead, passing enemy machine-gun and mortar nests. . . . The Germans showed no hostile intent and gave no signs that they knew we were sifting through their defenses."

Near Isola Bella, Major Jack Dobson's 1st and Major Alvah Miller's 3rd Ranger Battalions suddenly found themselves part of a salient, became separated in the dark, and lost contact with each other. Then Dobson's Rangers stumbled into a German bivouac where more than a hundred enemy soldiers were sleeping on the ground about a hundred yards from the outskirts of Cisterna, and the Germans received a deadly wake-up call when the Americans opened up on them. In some places men with knives and bayonets grappled in mortal combat until the hundred-man German unit had been all but wiped out.

Meanwhile, Lieutenant Colonel Roy Murray's 4th Battalion ran into a stronger concentration of enemy troops than they had been led to expect; the darkness suddenly lit up with tracers, flares, and explosions. "All night the 4th Battalion had a running fight," with Germans in their way, recalled Darby, and were seriously behind schedule.[68]

THE INVASION THAT HAD STARTED so promisingly a week earlier was quickly devolving into the kind of stalemate that had destroyed Allied morale at the Gustav Line, frustrated Alexander and Clark, worried Lucas, and infuriated Churchill. Through excellent leadership, the parlor magician Kesselring continued to conjure enough troops, tanks, and artillery pieces (as well as the Luftwaffe) to prevent any breakout that would seriously threaten either Rome or German positions along the Gustav Line. The forward elements of Lucas's VI Corps had not advanced much more than ten miles beyond Anzio and, without room to maneuver, remained vulnerable to enemy ground attacks as well as artillery fire and aerial assault.

The situation was about to get even worse.

CHAPTER 6

"They . . . had fought to the limit of human endurance"

JANUARY 30–31

A S DAWN ON THE THIRTIETH broke, the battle for Cisterna raged on while Dobson's and Miller's men fought desperately against the German 715th Motorized Infantry Division. Confusion and fear ran through the Rangers' ranks like heat lightning as more German infantry, tanks, self-propelled artillery, and 20mm antiaircraft guns—nasty four-barreled, truck-mounted weapons that could be depressed horizontally to provide direct fire—were rushed into the area. Rangers armed with bazookas—60mm rocket launchers—managed to knock out a few of the panzers and other vehicles, but it was an uneven fight.[1]

Courage was in abundance. One of the Rangers, Carl H. Lehman (Company C) ran through the Germans' bivouac area, firing from the hip at anything that moved. "I continued my run up the hedgerow until my attention was caught by the clatter of a flak wagon which pulled into view on a low ridge perhaps 100 yards to the left," he said. With the flak wagon silhouetted against the dawn sky, Lehman saw the Germans preparing the gun for firing. He raised his rifle and began unloading on the enemy in the truck and then was joined by a few more Rangers. He recalled that, after the Germans had been killed or chased off, "All the metal of the M-1 was hot and the wood was smoking." Lehman then dashed across a field and headed for a two-story building, where he climbed the stairs to the second floor. Directly beneath one of the windows was a German armored vehicle—a self-propelled howitzer and a crew of four. He dropped a grenade into it and took off running before it exploded. "I did not inspect the results," he said.[2]

During the approach to Isola Bella, Major Alvah Miller, 3rd Battalion CO, was standing hip deep in the muddy water of the Pantano ditch, trying to raise Darby's headquarters on the radio when a German Tiger tank suddenly appeared on a small bridge over the ditch, only a few yards away. The tank's turret turned directly toward Miller and fired, decapitating the officer. The Tiger was then knocked out by a Ranger wielding a sticky grenade.[3]

The advantage quickly shifted to the Germans. In the middle of a field, knowing that retreat was impossible, the 1st Battalion's commander, Major Jack Dobson, rallied his men to rush forward, toward Cisterna. In his memoirs, Dobson wrote that seventeen panzers and self-propelled guns overran his battalion's position, "but we knocked out fifteen of them with bazookas, grenades, and about everything else we could lay our hands on."[4]

Another Ranger, Private "Lacey" Smith, saw a tank with its commander's hatch open, sprinted toward it, jumped aboard, and threw a grenade in but then was sent flying when an American bazooka round exploded against the hull. Lying stunned on the ground, Smith saw the panzer rolling toward him, about to crush him with its steel tracks. "As I looked up," Smith remembered, "the beast was moving towards me and the commander's head was sticking out of the top. Frank Steele shot him straight between the eyes, and I attached a sticky bomb to its track and ran for cover." That tank was hors de combat, but there were more to take its place.[5]

Another Ranger, Sergeant Tom Fergen, encountered another panzer: "One tank came out of a driveway behind a house ahead of us. One of my squad climbed aboard it while it was moving and dropped an incendiary grenade into the open turret. At the same time a bazooka gunner hit it head on, and I was up beside it with a sticky grenade. The grenade exploded while I was getting away. I ducked in time to see the tank blow up and start burning. One of the crew got out and tried to get under the tank, but I shot him."[6]

ADVANCE ON CISTERNA

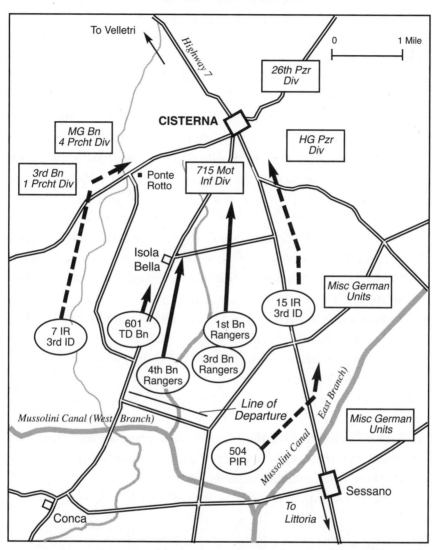

On the eastern flank of the beachhead, the Germans repeatedly stymied the 3rd U.S. Infantry Division and the Ranger Force's efforts to capture Cisterna di Littoria, a key town in the area. (Positions approximate)

Fergen may have been describing an action involving Major Jack Dobson, who shot a panzer commander with his pistol, leaped onto the tank, and dropped a white phosphorus grenade into the open turret hatch, destroying the tank and burning to death all those inside it. But Dobson was hit in the hip by a flying metal splinter. Immobilized, he was quickly taken prisoner.[7]

Meanwhile, Darby was doing the best he could to maintain radio contact with the three battalions, encouraging them to hold on as long as possible and giving them hope with news that tanks and elements of the 3rd Infantry Division were on their way to support them. The Rangers' valor and Darby's words of encouragement, however, were insufficient, as the 1st and 3rd Battalions were soon surrounded but continued to fight on for five more hours against impossible odds. At last, unable to escape, and with no hope of reinforcements coming to their rescue, the survivors eventually succumbed to the inevitable and were forced to surrender.

Murray's 4th Ranger Battalion, too, reaching Isola Bella, had its hands full with enemy attacks, including salvos of artillery fire. Soon they would be forced to pull back to avoid annihilation. Murray later said that, after German prisoners were interrogated, "our attack was expected by the enemy and that a parachute regiment [the Parachute Lehr Regiment, a demonstration unit] newly arrived in the area had been moved to defensive positions south of the town. . . . The prisoners claimed . . . that the destruction of the two [Ranger] units was accomplished by closing in from all sides of the triangle of roads south of Cisterna."[8]

Ranger Lieutenant William Newnan concurred:

What happened in Cisterna, in brief, can perhaps best be described in football terms—the old mousetrap play. We had the feeling that we had, perhaps, been allowed to penetrate the lines as a rushing tackle or guard is allowed to penetrate the lines in football and then mousetrapped on either side when we had got through. That was a very dark day for us. The Jerries had a great deal more strength than we thought they had there. As a result, elements of the 3rd Division, who were to support us by moving up on our right, were stopped entirely and the armored support that was supposed to have come up to us was stopped also. The net result was that we were pretty much on our own and, after a day's fighting, roughly from a quarter of six in the morning until four in the afternoon, we were entirely out of ammunition and the game was finished.[9]

Survivors later told Sergeant Milton Lehman, a correspondent for the GI newspaper *Stars and Stripes*, about their experiences. Piecing their accounts together, Lehman wrote, "When the sun came up, the Rangers were surrounded. Between sunrise and 0700 hours when radio silence was broken, the Rangers knew that the battle was lost. Sunrise doomed them and marked the beginning of the hopeless, heroic fight. . . . Slowly and bitterly the last orders were given by the company commanders . . . the tall, bespectacled, thin-faced West Pointer telling his men to go. 'I hate to do this,' the captain said, 'but it's too late now. That direction is south. Take out, and God bless you.'"[10]

Sergeant John Nowak, a member of the 601st Tank Destroyer Battalion that was accompanying the 4th Ranger Battalion, noted:

We were machine-gunned and sniped at. We saw twenty Rangers [4th Battalion] in a ditch who were trying to get back, so we covered their retreat with 3-inch [cannon] fire. I spotted many Krauts dug in on both sides of the road. At one I fired the .50-caliber and knocked his automatic rifle from his possession. At another I fired a Tommy gun. There were many dead U.S. and Kraut soldiers lying around the fields and on the roads. An advancing infantryman on our left was hit and we could hear him yell, "They got me!" We put him on the rear of our TD and brought him to an aid station. . . . We fired 200 rounds of the 3-inch that day and my TD was credited with knocking out several machine-gun nests, an observation post, and six Krauts.[11]

Surrounded and out of ammo and options, Lieutenant William Newnan, along with the surviving members of his platoon, were forced to throw down their weapons and throw up their hands. He recalled:

Being captured was quite a shock to all of us. We had been able to visualize very graphically the idea of being badly hurt, or perhaps even being killed, but the idea of being taken prisoner was something that none of us had considered at all. . . . We were moved immediately on trucks from the Cisterna area to a town about fifteen kilometers [nine miles] away and put in a large warehouse. We were taken care of at that time very well, I thought, by the Germans. I believe, from talking to other men, that is the usual experience. Front-line troops (because they are faced with the same things that you are, and tomorrow may be in the same position you are in) treat you better than rear-echelon troops do.

Newnan said that he and the other Ranger prisoners were interrogated by German officers who spoke perfect English, but no one offered any information other than their names, ranks, and serial numbers. The next day the captives were again loaded into trucks and hauled off in the direction of Rome. Before getting there, however, the whole lot (now including British prisoners) was housed for a few days in a barbed-wire enclosure at a town called Laterina, near Arezzo. Determined not to remain a captive of the German army, Newnan made his escape and hid out in Rome until its liberation.[12]

Carl Lehman was not so lucky. He was captured later in the afternoon after the Rangers' assault had fallen apart. He was nearly shot by his captors when they found a pocketful of embroidered Nazi insignia that Lehman had torn off of German uniforms. A German *Feldwebel* (sergeant) refused the request of "a little bastard" who begged for permission to shoot Lehman. As Lehman was being led away with other Ranger prisoners, the sergeant came over and said, "'You haff a Churman name, Carl!' I was blessing the Feldwebel's obviously sainted mother for having birthed him."[13]

With considerable understatement, Bill Darby wrote later, "It was evident that the Rangers in Cisterna were not going to be relieved that day. Later intelligence showed that the enemy had some 12,000 men at the town of Velletri, twelve miles from Cisterna." Kesselring and Mackensen had foreseen the possibility of an attack on Cisterna and had brought up sufficient forces to deal with it.[14]

For the Cisterna assault, Darby, uncharacteristically, had been in his rear command post instead of up front with his men, where he preferred to be. When the reports were coming in by radio from his forward battalions, punctuated by the sounds of gunshots and explosions, informing him that his troops were surrounded and unable to infiltrate back, Darby put his head down on his arm and wept. The colonel's driver recalled, "Darby had always put the safety of his men first, and he couldn't stand the thought of what was happening to them."[15]

When the roll call was taken later, it was learned that, of the 760 men in the 1st and 3rd Battalions at the start of the battle, only six escaped; the rest were either killed or captured. With solemn pride, Darby said, "Of the group who returned, one said, 'We're Rangers. You can never wipe out all the Rangers; we've been through too much for that.'" Nevertheless, as a combat organization, the 6615th Ranger Force was finished.[16]

Never one to shy away from exploiting an Allied tragedy, the American-born Mildred Gillars, better known as the Nazi radio propagandist "Axis Sally," broadcast to her listeners at Anzio such humorous gems as "Join the Rangers and see Berlin" and "Colonel Darby—the Lone Ranger."[17]

Months after the disaster, Darby wrote, "There was something to be proud of in the grim story—something that welled up in the heart of every soldier who heard the Rangers' story: They had done their duty, had fought to the limit of human endurance, and almost inevitably—as with other groups of soldiers in history who had taken the long chance by raiding into enemy-held territory—they had met their fate."[18]

Later, as George Avery noted, "A second attempt was made by the 3rd Infantry Division to reach Cisterna, and had penetrated its outskirts, but met such resistance that no progress whatever was made. . . . After the loss of [almost] 800 men dead, a retreat was called and the 3rd returned to their jumping-off line."[19]

ELSEWHERE ON THE FRONT, THE British staged another attack against Campoleone Station. Lieutenant Horst Heinrich (3rd Battalion, 29th Panzer-Grenadier Regiment, 3rd Panzer-Grenadier Division) said that at 1:00 A.M. on January 30, an artillery barrage that lasted two hours deluged his unit's position. "Since I was expecting an attack by the infantry, I destroyed all the secret orders that I had received before they started to fire toward my hole. Radio communication was destroyed. The engineers that were planting the mines were without protection and found themselves under the fire of the artillery and they suffered terrible losses.

The English tried to penetrate into our lines and I shouted 'Achtung, Angriff!' ('Attention, attack!'). We succeeded in holding some positions but the English broke the line." The break in the line, however, was only temporary. The first of several major counterattacks to drive the Allies back into the sea was coming.[20]

"THE SOUTHERN FRONT [AT CASSINO] is like two boxers in the ring, both about to collapse," noted Mark Clark in his diary on January 30. "I have committed my last reserve and I am sure the Boche has done the same. . . . I have been disappointed by the lack of aggressiveness on the part of VI Corps [at Anzio], although it would have been wrong in my opinion to attack to capture our final objective [the Alban Hills] on this front. [But] reconnaissance in force with tanks should have been more aggressive to capture Cisterna and Campoleone."[21]

It seems clear that, even a week after the Shingle landings, Clark remained conflicted and confused about the mission's objectives and about his own role in defining them and ensuring that Lucas knew what he was supposed to do. One thing he knew for certain was, with a German counterattack due at any moment, that the Anzio beachhead needed strengthening. Lucas, with the higher echelons demanding him to perform miracles with a depleted force against a superior enemy, had sent out a plea for additional units. His request went up the chain of command to Clark and then to Alexander. The latter agreed that VI Corps needed strengthening if the operation was to be salvaged, and so he ordered the tall, slim Lieutenant General Richard L. McCreery, commanding X Corps, battling on the Garigliano River near the western end of the Gustav Line, to cannibalize his front and send whatever units that could be spared to Anzio.

As a consequence, Brigadier K. C. Davidson's 168th (2nd London) Brigade (composed of the 1st Battalion, London Irish Rifles [LIR]; 1st Battalion, London Scottish Regiment; 10th Battalion, Royal Berkshire Regiment; and 46th Royal Tank Regiment) was packed up and pulled out of Major General Gerald Templer's 56th British Division, trucked down to Pozzuoli, put on ships, and transported to Anzio; the rest of the 56th would soon follow.[22]

ON JANUARY 30, THE 2ND and 3rd Battalions of the 36th Engineer Combat Regiment were attached to the 45th Infantry Division to serve not as combat engineers but rather as infantrymen. Their mission was to help establish a defensive line about two miles south of Aprilia that would run from the sea to a point approximately five miles inland. The combat engineers would not be there for long; the next day, a platoon from Company F was sent out as a patrol to suppress German sniper activity but was repelled by mortar fire that killed six engineers and wounded nineteen. That night both battalions were withdrawn and returned to their regiment.[23]

On January 31, Private first class Lloyd C. Hawks, a medic from Park Rapids, Minnesota (Company G, 30th Infantry Regiment, 3rd Infantry Division), had nineteen days earlier celebrated his thirty-third birthday—an "old man" by army standards—when his unit became involved in a fierce firefight near Carano. Seeing two wounded men lying in an exposed position within 30 yards of the enemy, he left his position of relative safety and, heedless of the machine-gun bullets and mortar rounds aimed his way, crawled out to rescue them.

Hawks's helmet, emblazoned with red crosses, was suddenly blown off his head by a bullet, momentarily stunning him. The helmet then started dancing on the ground as at least a dozen more bullets tore through it. Unfazed, Hawks crawled to the casualties, administered first aid to the more seriously wounded man, and dragged him to a covered position 25 yards away. Despite exploding mortar rounds and a continuous stream of machine-gun fire from nearby enemy positions, Hawks returned to administer first aid to the second injured soldier. As he raised himself to obtain bandages from his medical kit, his right hip was shattered by a burst of machine-gun fire; a second burst splintered his left forearm. Despite severe pain and his dangling, useless left arm, Hawks completed the task of bandaging the remaining casualty and, with superhuman effort, dragged him to the same depression to which he had brought the first man. Hawks survived his injuries to receive the Medal of Honor.[24]

ON THE SAME NIGHT AS Hawks's selfless heroics, Sergeant Truman O. Olson (Company B, 7th Infantry Regiment, 3rd Infantry Division) of Christiana, Wisconsin, also earned the Medal of Honor but lost his life in the process. After a savage sixteen-hour assault on German positions near Cisterna, machine gunner Olson and his crew took up an exposed position forward of their lines and awaited the inevitable German counterattack. And launched it was—in determined fury.

Sergeant Olson remained at his gun all night while the enemy continued their probes, picking off members of his crew one by one until he was literally the last man standing. Suffering from exhaustion and an arm wound, Olson manned his gun alone, held off an all-out enemy assault by approximately 200 men supported by mortars and machine guns that the Germans launched at daybreak on January 31. After thirty minutes of fighting, Sergeant Olson was mortally wounded, yet, knowing that only his weapon stood between his company and complete destruction, he refused evacuation.

For an hour and a half after receiving his second, and ultimately fatal, wound, Olson remained swiveling his gun on its tripod, killing at least twenty Germans, wounding many more, and forcing the assaulting enemy elements to withdraw. He had truly performed "above and beyond the call of duty."[25]

TWO BATTALIONS OF BRITISH INFANTRY from Brigadier J. R. James's 3rd Brigade were now burrowed into the ruins of Aprilia as the 29th Panzer-Grenadier Regiment attempted to dislodge them. Lieutenant Horst Heinrich recalled that his company was ordered to attack:

> We assaulted a house occupied by the British. We jumped from the holes next to the house and occupied it. Inside the house we found the baggage of the English, among these a tennis racquet. From the house we watched at 500 meters from us ten English tanks, anti-tank guns, and English infantry. We counted our group. Only eight remained out of forty.
>
> To our right I observed through binoculars German soldiers surrendering with white flags. Shortly after that an English battalion passed directly toward Campoleone; we shot at them from long distance. The English responded to the fire with hits that destroyed the houses around ours, and ours, too; we had to abandon it to find shelter behind the artillery; the battalion took up positions in the slope of the railway.[26]

AT PRECISELY 3:10 ON THE afternoon of January 31, James's men—the 1st Battalion of the Duke of Wellington's Regiment (West Riding) and the 1st Battalion of the King's Shropshire Light Infantry Regiment (which had been one of the last units evacuated at Dunkirk four years earlier)—were supposed to advance from the shattered town and head north, stopping at Campoleone Station to wait for the 2nd Battalion, Sherwood Foresters, to leapfrog through them and continue northward on along the railroad embankment.

But hardly had the 1st DWIR and 1st KSLI left the debris of Aprilia than they received a face full of mortar and artillery fire. Somehow, aided by Sherman tanks from the 46th Royal Tank Battalion, they managed to keep going; behind them came the Sherwood Foresters, under Lieutenant Colonel G. R. G. Bird, also catching hell from the enemy guns. The three battalions finally stumbled and crawled to the railroad embankment near Campoleone, where the Foresters tried to continue on to their objective. But German tanks and a honeycomb of machine-gun nests were waiting for them; the Foresters never stood a chance.

It was not like the battalion had never seen battle before; it had fought, like the 1st KSLI, with the British Expeditionary Force in France in 1940 when the BEF was evacuated from Dunkirk and later battled in the hot sands of Tunisia. But this was something even more horrendous—like trying to walk through a spinning propeller or slip unscathed through a meat grinder. Men were blown apart or cut in two by streams of bullets, while others fell into the mud clutching their wounds and screaming for medics. Seeing his Foresters being ravaged, Bird yelled for his men to pull back while he radioed for artillery support. After receiving a few answering rounds, Bird got his men moving again, but the enemy's position that bristled with tanks and guns had hardly been dented. The British drive again stalled; the men simply could not go on.[27]

Fred Vann (2nd Battalion, Sherwood Foresters) recalled that his battalion, "with A Company led by Major Phillips on the left forward and Major Rubens with C Company, attacked the rail embankment at Campoleone. We failed to penetrate the massed Spandaus and we crossed the road to try a different approach. In a farm overlooking the Campoleone Station, Major Phillips was wounded."[28]

Within a matter of minutes, all the Foresters' company commanders had become casualties, and Colonel Bird had no choice but to withdraw. Bird himself was then hit by shrapnel, and his adjutant and mortar officer were also down; Major Johnnie Hackett took command of what was left of the battalion. The strongest company had only forty men left, while the weakest was down to twenty. When news of the plight of 3rd Brigade reached VI Corps headquarters, Lucas ordered them to cease the attack, pull back, and wait to be relieved by the 168th (2nd London) Brigade. To help stabilize the situation, the 6th Battalion of the Gordons, behind 3rd Brigade, counterattacked and put out a tremendous volume of fire that prevented the Germans from pursuing the Foresters and enabled them, along with DWIR and KSLI, to escape, shaken, back to a position about a mile north of Aprilia. When muster was taken on February 3, it was learned that 3rd Brigade had sustained more than 1,400 casualties.[29]

MARK CLARK WAS GRAVELY WORRIED about developments all along the front. He wrote:

> By nightfall of January 31 the whole front was up against powerful enemy forces and the going was sticky. So many veteran enemy outfits had been identified by then that I began to fear we soon would face a strong counterattack while we were in a more or less disorganized condition. I told Lucas that when Cisterna and Campoleone were captured, we should then take a position in readiness to minimize any enemy counterthrusts. We were still bringing in reinforcements, but we had about reached the point where additional forces would overtax the bridgehead supply system. . . . General Lucas had no choice but to order our forces to dig in all along the front in expectation of a counterattack. There was no question in our minds by this time that the enemy had succeeded in rushing far greater strength than anticipated to the Anzio sector.[30]

"Clark is still here," Lucas grumbled in his diary that same day, but added, "I don't blame him for being disappointed." That evening, after Clark had departed, Lucas recorded, "Clark has gone and, before going, apologized for having harassed me as much as he has. I am glad he did as I really like him very much." Lucas also noted that he had learned that the German combat strength had increased to 95,000 while his own forces numbered only about 76,000.[31]

THE MONTH OF JANUARY 1944 ended with the situation in Italy being little changed. The Germans' Gustav Line was as solid as ever, and the Allied forces at Anzio were going nowhere fast. With the balance tipping in his favor, Kesselring saw February as the perfect time in which his forces would go over to the offensive and eliminate the abscess.

CHAPTER 7

"This is one hell of a place"
FEBRUARY 1–3

T. S. ELIOT ONCE WROTE, "April is the cruellest month," but at Anzio, February 1944 claimed that title, for at no other time would the fighting be as hard, the casualties as heavy, the weather as miserable, and the stakes as high.

As night closed in around the battlefield like a black shroud on February 1, the American and British soldiers got ready, not for rest but for renewed terrors. It was one thing to fight during daylight hours, when one could at least see the enemy, when the enemy had shape and form and could be placed in the sights of one's gun. That was reality. But nighttime was an entirely different equation. Unless flares were burning overhead, hanging from their tiny parachutes, the battlefield at night was a horrorscape of shadows and sounds. That noise ahead—was that an enemy patrol closing in or just a cow stumbling around in search of fodder? Was that whistle a night bird or a coded message from one patrol to another? The rumble of engines—your tanks or theirs? Was that boom off in the distance merely thunder or the start of another artillery barrage?

"The mind plays tricks on you on the battlefield at night," admitted Vere "Tarzan" Williams (Company K, 157th Infantry Regiment, 45th Infantry Division). "The new replacements, they got scared real fast, and us old veterans had a hard time tryin' to calm 'em down. Them kids wanted to up and get out of there at the slightest noise. They was as skit-terish as rabbits."

February also brought more massive artillery duels to the beachhead. The Americans and British marveled, if ruefully, at the German gun-ners' abilities to saturate their positions with high explosives, the long fingers of the artillery reaching out to blast every nook and cranny of the battlefield. "We was packed in there real tight," recalled Williams. "The Germans had the high ground and they could practically look down our throats. It was like shootin' sardines in a can."[1]

REPLACEMENTS FOR THE DEAD AND wounded continued to stream into the beachhead. One new arrival was Private first class Earl A. Reitan (Company F, 7th Infantry Regiment, 3rd Infantry Division), and he had just endured his first artillery barrage. "I had learned a lesson that every infantryman knows," he said. "The main threat is not the enemy soldier facing you, but the death and destruction that come screaming out of the sky."[2]

Another replacement was a teenager, James Tolby Anderson, as-signed to the 3rd Division. He recalled, "As soon as we got off the ship, there on the beachhead we were in combat and could hear the awful sound of war; a railroad gun was shelling us. I guess those first few min-utes in combat are, to say the least, life changing: a lot of us just stood there in terror. I remember plainly a British officer screaming at us, 'What's the matter with you blokes? Do you wanna live always?' as he grabbed me and we jumped in a basement for cover."

Thoroughly frightened, Anderson and two of his buddies from basic training were then transported to the front lines in a mud-smeared jeep and deposited at the headquarters of the 2nd Battalion, 30th Infantry Regiment, where they were assigned to the Ammunition and Pioneer Platoon. "Our main job was to get ammo to the front lines for E, F, and G Companies," Anderson said. He was soon frantically digging a fox-hole under heavy enemy fire, where he "came to the realization that the enemy was real and their objective was to kill me! On the next day, I was in my foxhole and heard a loud noise. As I raised up, I realized the noise was bombers. As the first plane dropped its bombs, it blew my helmet off! I didn't have my chinstrap buckled under my chin and this prevented me from being decapitated. That was the closest one to me; the others, as they exploded, picked me up off the ground!"

Anderson recalled that his unit remained on the beachhead "with enemies all around us for seven to ten days under heavy artillery fire. The Germans were trying to push us into the ocean while we were pushing inland to cut off a German road. Here we lost over half of each company; each company contained approximately 200 men."

One night Anderson was sent along with another soldier to fix a bridge and lay down some sandbags. "This proved to be the worst night I spent in the war. We were shelled all night long. Me and him prayed to get hit so we would be sent back home. We could hear the shells hitting the road and ricocheting off, making an eerie noise. When we got dug in, I couldn't sleep at all. We were on flat ground so we couldn't raise our heads out of the foxhole. The next morning, a U.S. soldier came running by, screaming and yelling that he couldn't take it anymore; the war had driven him crazy."

A couple of days later, an incident occurred that Anderson never forgot.

We had been sleeping in a farmhouse and Wallace Chapman and I drifted off upstairs to write letters home. As we were writing, a shell hit across the road about 150 feet from the farmhouse. Another one followed that one, landing right beside the house. We dropped what we were doing and ran like madmen. As we reached the outside, a shell hit the house and knocked an entire wall out. We went on around to the front and Wallace had made a right turn to try and make it to the nearby stable. Again, with the guidance of the Lord, I ran back toward the house and got behind an old car. A lieutenant was screaming to get the hell out and, one at a time, we ran across the yard. When it came my time, I took off as fast as I could go and tripped over a grape vine. When I hit the ground, a shell hit behind me and covered me with dirt. In a ten-minute span, I was saved twice! The shelling stopped after a little while and we pulled the dead out of the stable. [Eight of his comrades lay dead in it.] We didn't find all of the bodies until the next morning and the stench was terrible. It was shocking to see Wallace dead who I had just been writing a letter with only a few minutes beforehand. I sent home the letter Wallace was writing; he didn't get to finish it.

Anderson and the others in his unit dug defensive positions around the demolished farmhouse and remained there for the next several days. They learned that another farmhouse nearby had been hit by a shell, and many soldiers were dead and some were possibly wounded. "They sent us up there to see what happened," he said.

As we got there, we could hear men still alive in the fallen house. To our surprise, we dug out all of the men and they were all alive. A few nights later, we had to pick up a soldier who had been blown in half by a grenade. The stench was so horrible that we had to carry him close to the ground. As we carried him out, we began to get fired on by American soldiers. They heard us yelling and promptly quit firing. The next night we had to hoist a dead soldier out of a foxhole with a rope because we thought the hole was booby-trapped.

During all of these removals of dead bodies, the enemy was firing on us. There was no fear like the fear of being fired at constantly. One guy named Cohen nearly got sick every time we removed a corpse. It wasn't our job to carry off the dead soldiers but the [Graves Registration teams] were overwhelmed with dead bodies. At one time, both sides called off all fighting for three hours to clear the battlefield of the dead. If they could stop fighting that long, why couldn't they call off *all* fighting?[3]

TO BEEF UP THE BEACHHEAD defenses, an 1,800-man combined American-Canadian Commando unit known as the 1st Special Service Force (SSF) was brought in on February 1 under its commander, Brigadier General Robert T. Frederick. The unit's sleeve insignia was a red spearhead with the letters *USA* written horizontally and the word *CANADA* written vertically. The 1st SSF (consisting of three regiments of two battalions each—about 5,400 men) had already built a fearsome reputation in Italy. It had been trained in parachute and amphibious operations, hand-to-hand combat, and mountain warfare, and the men were some of the toughest barroom brawlers found anywhere. In keeping with their unconventional nature, the Force was armed with a variety of nonstandard or limited-issue weapons such as the M1941 Johnson light machine gun, which greatly increased the unit's firepower. Frederick, too, is credited with developing a fighting knife made exclusively for the Force called the V-42 combat knife, which was a derivative of the Fairbairn-Sykes fighting knife.[4]

After one of its officers was killed by Germans pretending to surrender under a white flag, the 1st SSF became infamous for its ruthless approach to combat, rarely taking prisoners unless specifically ordered to do so. From then on, while silently sneaking up on unsuspecting enemy soldiers in the mountains south of Cassino, some Forcemen even went so far as to leave their calling cards during these nocturnal raids. The men affixed stickers to the bodies of German soldiers whose throats they had slit during their night missions that carried the unit's red spearhead insignia and a warning in German, "*Das Dicke Ende Kommt Noch!*" ("Beware—the worst is yet to come!").

Arriving at Anzio, the 1st SSF took up positions on the right-hand flank of the beachhead, along the Mussolini Canal sector from which they staged their raids; German units pulled back up to a half mile to avoid their aggressive patrols. One night at Anzio the Force was given the nickname the "Devil's Brigade" after some them had found a diary on the body of a dead German soldier in which was written, "The black devils (*Die schwarzen Teufel*) are all around us every time we come into the line." The reference to "black" was because the members of the Force blackened their faces with burned cork before heading out on their nighttime missions. The Forcemen embraced the nickname.[5]

Stars and Stripes cartoonist Bill Mauldin was especially enamored of the 1st SSF, calling them a "swashbuckling unit . . . the kind of men who are likely to volunteer for suicide missions" and who "do not make good spit-and-polish soldiers. They called their officers by their first names if they felt like it, they wore what they pleased, and carried the weapons that suited them best. . . . They had the Germans terrorized."[6]

THE NIGHT OF FEBRUARY 1 was moonless, pitch-black, and as frightening as hell. One of the most nerve-wracking jobs in war is to go out on a night patrol into enemy territory. The 3rd Infantry Division was probing the front near Cisterna that was held by the 26th Panzer Division—not only to learn what enemy units were where, but also to keep the enemy off balance and fearful of an American attack.

Private James Aurness was on just such a patrol and was point man for his platoon, walking carefully and quietly about forty or fifty feet ahead of the man behind him. "I picked my way over the terrain," he recalled.

> Since I couldn't see ahead of me, I never knew whether I'd walk into a big rock or step off into a four-foot ditch. For the first twenty minutes I didn't hear or see anything. I remember looking down and not being able to see my feet step in front of me. Finally, I would just set one foot down slowly, to see if the ground was solid. Then the other. I felt my way along. It was the same for the point men on either side of me, and for the troops following us. We were under strict orders not to speak as we crept along. Except for the night sounds, the air was completely quiet.

Moving as stealthily as he could through a small vineyard in which the vines had been cut low, Aurness froze as he heard voices up ahead of him.

> In what seemed like seconds later, a guttural voice yelled and enemy fire burst out ahead of me. I'd walked right into a German machine-gun nest. I was hit in the right leg but was able to leap over a row of vines anyway, out of the line of fire. Then I fell to the ground in excruciating pain. It felt like the bones in my lower right leg had been all shot to hell. Intense fire started coming at me from both sides. I was almost killed when a "potato masher,"* a German concussion grenade, went off near

---

*The so-called potato-masher grenade looks like a small tin can at the end of a long wooden stick and is known in German as either the Model 24 or Model 39 *Stielhandgranate* (stalk hand grenade). First developed in World War I, the weapon consisted of a grenade body about the size of a small soup can attached to a hollow fourteen-inch-long (365mm) wooden handle through which a friction igniter was inserted. Pulling on a ring at the bottom of the handle would start the timer fuse, and the handle enabled the thrower to toss the device farther than the British Mills bomb or American "pineapple" grenade. *German Hand Grenades,* U.S. Army Bulletin no. 59 (March 7, 1944).

me. The explosion literally lifted me off the ground. The Germans had two machine-gun nests, with infantrymen spread out on either side. The firing was low, about eighteen inches off the ground, so I had to practically hug the earth not to get hit.

There were about fifteen Germans; we had forty riflemen firing and throwing grenades, backed up by a light machine gun. The shooting was intense, but eventually our guys overran them and took them out.

Aurness lay bleeding and in pain in the vineyard for quite some time, struggling to maintain consciousness. After what seemed like hours, members of his platoon, looking for casualties, came across him lying there. A medic was called, and, despite the darkness of the night, he cut Aurness's pants open and inspected the wounds. "He . . . said my leg bones had been severely splintered. Penicillin wasn't used at this point, but sulfa powder did an adequate job of sterilizing wounds. He poured some on and gave me a shot of morphine in the stomach. . . . Many of the others who got hit were in terrible condition, so I was lucky. My wound was not life-threatening, nor would it affect my future, though over the years it's been troublesome, requiring several surgeries."

After a while, the medic returned and said a medical team was on its way to extract him. "While I lay there waiting, I could hear groaning from Germans who were still alive in the machine-gun nest. Our guys had driven through their position, assuming they'd all be killed. It was an eerie thing, lying there in the pitch black listening to one of them call out a name in German that I didn't understand—perhaps a loved one. I had no idea what was going to happen to these soldiers." A litter team then arrived, and Aurness was transported back to a casualty collection point and eventually moved to the 95th Evacuation Hospital at Anzio.[7]

BACK AT THE DOCKS AT Pozzuoli, war correspondent Ernie Pyle stood on the dock, chain-smoking cigarettes while observing a group of young, scared-looking GIs nervously making their way to a landing craft that loomed above them. "Long lines of soldiers, loaded down with gear, marched along the dock to enter adjoining ships. They were replacements to bolster the fighters at Anzio. A person could tell by their faces that they were fresh from America. They carried a new type of barracks

bag, which few of us over there had seen before. The bags were terrifi-
cally heavy, and it was all the boys could do to handle them."[8]

At about this time, a diminutive (five-foot-five), baby-faced staff
sergeant from Texas named Audie Leon Murphy, who would become
America's most highly decorated war hero and be awarded the Medal of
Honor for actions he would perform in France a few months later, arrived at Anzio as one of a boatload of 3rd Infantry Division replacements
(he had just been released from the hospital after suffering a recurring
bout of malaria). He had already seen plenty of action during the battle
for Sicily, the invasion at Salerno, and the drive northward, and now he
was here at this new front, his normally 200-man company reduced to
thirty-four. He wrote, "As we hike inland, jeeps drawing trailerloads of
corpses pass us. The bodies, stacked like wood, are covered with shelter-
halves. But arms and legs bobble grotesquely over the sides of the vehicles. Evidently Graves Registration lacks either time or mattress covers
in which to sack the bodies."[9]

Paul Brown (Graves Registration Unit, 179th Infantry Regiment)
noted in his diary on Tuesday, February 1: "Germans sighted in on CP
[command post], killed two men of Regimental Headquarters Company. These boys sure are jumpy, worst I ever saw. Many are lucky to
be alive. . . . Our cemetery is becoming very large. Rangers are bringing
them in by truckload. This is one hell of a place."[10]

Also on that day, Private first class Alton W. Knappenberger of
Pennsylvania (Company C, 30th Infantry Regiment, 3rd Infantry Division) displayed his marksmanship skills near Cisterna when he single-
handedly killed sixty German soldiers within a two-hour span, despite
being the target of nearly every enemy gun within range. When the small
(five-foot-six and 118-pound) soldier ran out of ammunition, he crawled
over to the dead and wounded, taking enough .30-06 bullet clips to keep
him in the action. When his buddies' ammunition pouches were empty,
he made his way back to his company. After the battle, a general called
him a "one-man army." His Medal of Honor citation noted, "Knappenberger's intrepid action disrupted the enemy attack for over two hours."

Afterward, the shy Knappenberger shunned publicity and was reluctant to talk about the medal and the exploits that brought it to him. "I

was scared all the time I was over there," he later told a newspaper reporter. "I just did what I had to do. You go in there and just try to get
them guys before they get you."[11]

Audie Murphy also had a few words to say about fear: "In the heat
of battle [fear] may go away. Sometimes it vanishes in a blind, red rage
that comes when you see a friend fall. Then again you get so tired that
you become indifferent. But when you are moving into combat, why try
fooling yourself? Fear is right there beside you. . . . I am well acquainted
with fear. It strikes first in the stomach, coming like the disemboweling
hand that is thrust into the carcass of a chicken. I feel now as though icy
fingers have reached into my mid-parts and twisted the intestines into
knots.

"Each of us has his own way of fighting off panic," he continued, recalling a dead friend, Mike Novak, and tried to work himself "into a
rage against the uniformed beings who killed him. But that proves futile.
At this distance the enemy is as impersonal as the gun that blew Little
Mike's pathetic dreams into eternity."[12]

THE BRITISH NUMBER 9 AND 43 Commandos were accustomed to action,
not lying about in damp holes, sweating out another of the constant artillery barrages. But that was exactly what they were doing north of Anzio. Number 9 Commando had earlier been involved in actions that had
demanded courage, dash, and derring-do, such as the famous raid on
the German naval base at St. Nazaire, France, the landings on the Italian
islands of Tremiti and Pianosa, and then the heavy fighting during Operation Partridge at the Garigliano River in December 1943.

During its short stay at Anzio, Number 9 Commando carried out
ten battle patrols, five reconnaissance patrols, and two attacks of troop
strength. On the twenty-fifth of January, the unit was withdrawn and returned to Bacoli, where it was slated to take part in Operation Ornito—a
battle in the rugged mountains north of the Garigliano River.[13]

IT IS THE SOLDIER'S LOT to complain, and the men at Anzio, on both
sides, had a nearly unlimited supply of things to gripe about: the rain, the
cold, the bad food, the ever-present specter of death, and the mud and

subterranean living conditions all reminded more than a few soldiers of the miserable battlefield conditions of the First World War, which had ended only a quarter century before and had been endured by the fathers and uncles of many of the men on both sides at Anzio. Sergeant Lee Anderson (Company F, 179th) recalled, "Italy was cold and wet. We put our extra pair of socks on our shoulders under our shirts to keep them dry. We were so miserable that we hoped we'd get wounded so we could go to the hospital." His hopes would soon be realized.[14]

Nineteen-year-old George Courlas, a BAR man (Company G, 157th), was one of thousands who shared the misery of life at Anzio. "The weather was horrible—rain and cold, and colder at night," he said. "I caught a cold twice that season and ended up at the aid station. On the second occasion, they detained me for two nights. That was a good feeling—I had a cot to sleep on and the food was much better than those K rations in the foxholes."[15]

An officer from a Scottish regiment at Anzio recalled, "Oozing thick mud. Tank hulks. The cold, God, the cold." Harry Shindler, an engineer serving with the Sherwood Foresters, later told a newspaper reporter: "We had a very bad time of it. The Germans could see every inch of the beachhead, so you had to move around very quickly, if you moved at all. We lived underground in foxholes."[16]

An end to the terrible living conditions was nowhere in sight. And just as the men felt it was impossible for the situation to get any worse, it did.

WAR CORRESPONDENT ERNIE PYLE EARNED his living by telling his readers what the boys on the front lines were seeing, feeling, and experiencing. He did it by seeing, feeling, and experiencing the same things they did. A few days after Shingle began, he rode into Anzio harbor on an LST and was almost immediately sorry: "No one could have described Anzio as any haven of peacefulness. In our first day ashore, a bomb exploded so close to the place where I was sitting that a fragment came through the window of the room next to mine. On our second evening a screamer slammed into the hill so suddenly that it almost knocked us down with fright. It smacked into the trees a short distance away. And on the third day ashore, an 88 went off within twenty yards of us. I wished I was in New York."

Pyle grew to hate his encounters with German artillery. One day, while in his room, established for correspondents in an abandoned building in Anzio, it seemed as if the German gunners had specifically targeted his quarters. "I had just reached the window when a terrible blast swirled me around and threw me into the middle of the room. . . . There was debris flying back and forth all over the room. One gigantic explosion came after another. The concussion was terrific. It was like a great blast of air in which my body felt as light and as helpless as a leaf tossed in a whirlwind."[17]

ON FEBRUARY 1, THE 179TH Infantry Regiment, which had been serving temporarily under Penney's command, reverted to 45th Division control, and its former positions in the salient were taken over by the 36th Engineer Combat Regiment; the men of the 179th fell back to their old bivouac area northeast of Nettuno to recover from their ordeal, receive replacements, and await further deployment.[18]

Also on that day, Field Marshal Alexander, wearing his customary sheepskin-lined leather flight jacket and an uncustomary scowl, paid General Lucas a visit. Lucas noted in his diary that the field marshal was "kind enough but I am afraid he is not pleased. My head will probably fall in the basket but I have done my best. There were just too many Germans here for me to lick and they could build up faster than I could. As I told Clark yesterday, I was sent on a desperate mission, one where the odds were greatly against success, and I went without saying anything because I was given an order and my opinion was not asked." Thankful that no major counterattacks had yet been launched against his forces, he added, "The condition in which I find myself [that is, VI Corps] is much better than I ever anticipated or had any right to expect."[19]

But Lucas, after Clark informed him the next day that Intelligence had learned that a heavy German counterattack was imminent, made the decision to call off, for the time being, further attempts to advance. But neither Clark nor Lucas knew how close VI Corps had come to succeeding in their first week on the beachhead or that the Americans and British had inflicted 5,500 casualties on the foe.[20]

And, of course, no one knew at the time that February would see three violent German counterattacks aimed at throwing the invaders 'back into the sea—attacks that, until Hitler's Ardennes Offensive (also known as the battle of the Bulge) in December 1944, would be the largest German counterattacks in the West.

PRIVATE ROBERT E. DODGE WAS a fresh replacement in the 15th Infantry Regiment, 3rd Infantry Division. He arrived at the port of Anzio on February 2 and was welcomed by a serenade of German artillery. Looking at the precariously standing facades of wrecked buildings and a fleet of barrage balloons floating on steel cables over the harbor to discourage German planes from coming too close and shooting up everything, Dodge and the rest of the frightened replacements scurried off their LCI and double-timed inland "for quite a distance when Jerry planes came in strafing and bombing. Our anti-aircraft guns sent up such a cloud of aerial bursts, you wouldn't think anything could fly through it. . . . The noise from the guns was really frightening. This time no one was hurt, but now we realized war was for real."[21]

Real indeed. If a reconnaissance pilot had flown over the beachhead and been able to see the various terrain features and discern what units were spread out across the landscape, this is what he would have seen: two main roads—the Albano Highway heading straight north from Anzio to Aprilia, Campoleone, and Albano beyond, and the highway running northeast from Anzio to Cisterna. These were the only paved roads capable of supporting tanks and other heavy vehicles and thus were the most likely avenues available to both sides for launching attacks and counterattacks. Our hypothetical recon pilot also would have seen the deeply furrowed, brush-covered ravines and gullies of the "wadi area" on the left flank of the Allied line, with the Moletta River being guarded by the 45th Infantry Division's 157th Regiment. To the 157th's right was the 2nd Brigade's 2nd Battalion, North Staffordshire Regiment. To the right of them was the 24th Guards Brigade (echeloned to the southwest, in order of position left to right, the 1st Irish Guards, 1st Scots Guards, and 5th Grenadier Guards).

Barely clinging to the northern point of the salient was Brigadier J. R. James's 3rd Brigade (consisting of the 1st Battalion, Duke of Wellington's Regiment; 2nd Battalion, Sherwood Foresters; and 1st Battalion, King's Shropshire Light Infantry). On the right flank of the salient, and echeloned to the southeast, was the 2nd Brigade (less the 2nd North Staffs), consisting of the 6th Gordons and 1st Loyals, reinforced in the center by the 1st Battalion, Recce Regiment.

On the 1st Loyals' right flank, near Carano, was the 509th U.S. Parachute Infantry Battalion—the "Gingerbread Men."[*] All these units, spread across ten miles of front, were under the command of General Penney and his 1st British Division.[22] They were all aware that a German attack designed to sweep them off the beachhead could come at any moment. But the salient was like a rude gesture aimed at the Germans by the Americans and British, as if to say, "Hey, Hitler—up yours!"

However, as is sometimes the case with rude gestures, the response would turn out to be out of proportion to the original insult. The VI Corps G-2 section could not tell the units precisely when the German counterattack might occur, just that, with signs that the Germans were continuing to truck new units into the area, it was likely to happen very soon. All the Americans and British could do was improve their positions, stock up on food and ammunition, and wait.

ANZIO WAS, BY ALL ACCOUNTS, a meat grinder. As soon as one Allied regiment was reduced to a fraction of its normal strength, it was pulled out of the line and another would take its place; the same fate would then befall the replacement regiment, as though on a never-ending conveyor belt of death and destruction. On February 2, the 45th Division's 157th Regiment moved up to replace one of the battered British units. BAR man Private Murray Levine (Company G, 157th) recalled:

> It was two or three in the morning when we started to move up. The lieutenant said, "Don't make any noise, because the Germans will shell the roads." And, would you believe, they start shelling the roads, anyway. I was so punchy I actually walked into a tree. Banged my head with the

---

[*] The battalion's nickname came from the unit's sleeve patch, which resembled a Native American stick figure that the paratroopers said looked like a gingerbread man; thus, the paratroopers of the 509th dubbed themselves the "Gingerbread Men." Broumley, *Boldest Plan Is the Best*, 152.

helmet—what a noise it made! I was half-asleep. The guys said, "How the heck could you walk into a tree?"

It took us a couple of hours, but we finally got to the front lines. The British outfit was pretty well decimated. Their bodies were lying all over the place. Germans, British, Americans, lying all over.

Even though it was dark, Levine could see the bodies because of all the flares—German and Allied—being fired off. "We got into the foxhole there, and it was muddy. We had mud up beyond our ankles, and we set up our BAR." Now it was a matter of watching and waiting.[23]

ON THE SAME DAY THAT Levine was watching and waiting, Lucas received two visitors he didn't especially want to see—General Alexander, accompanied by Clark. That night Lucas journaled, "I believe he and Clark came up here with the idea that I had failed and should possibly be relieved of command for lack of aggressive action. Neither realized the desperate nature of the fighting, how rapid the German build-up has been, nor how bitterly the enemy has resisted our advance."[24]

Third Infantry Division commander Lucian Truscott wrote, "Early the following morning [February 3] General Lucas called me to say that the Army had just informed him it had secret intelligence that the Germans were in far greater strength than we had thought and were preparing to launch a counterattack to drive the beachhead into the sea. We were to stop all attacks, dig in for defense, and hold the Corps beachhead line at all costs."

SEVERAL DAYS OF DESULTORY SHELLING and sporadic aerial assaults came to an end on the night of February 2–3, and the main combatants, reinforced and relatively refreshed by the brief pause, prepared to step into the ring again. Penney's 1st Division had taken a tremendous pounding and needed to be augmented, if not completely replaced by a fresh formation. Truscott's 3rd Division, too, along with Darby's Ranger Force, had suffered heavy casualties in their costly, abortive attempts to reach Cisterna; Truscott noted that his division alone had lost 3,000 men killed, wounded, and missing since January 22, and the numbers of supporting tanks and tank destroyers had been reduced by about a third.[25]

ATTACKING THE SALIENT

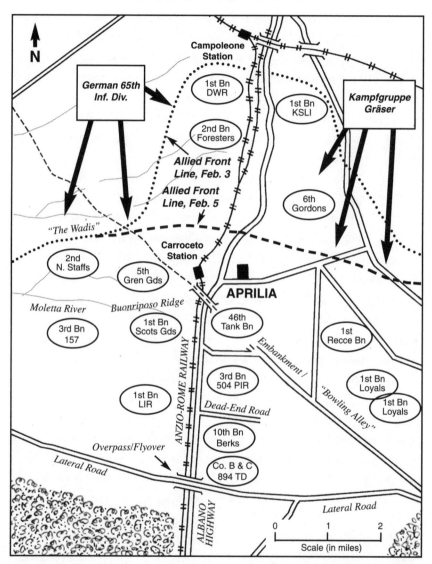

After the British advance toward Campoleone Station created a salient, the Germans fought back and pushed the Allies back to the final defensive line. (Positions approximate)

The 45th Infantry Division had also been hard hit during a very short period of time. "From the start, no one liked Anzio," wrote Jack Hallowell, 157th Regiment. From the high ground farther inland, the Germans could look right down the beachhead's throat, observing almost everything the Allies were doing. "It was like fighting on a stage with the enemy for an audience," Hallowell observed.[26]

The sense of being under constant watch, like a bug under a microscope—and within range of enemy guns—got under everyone's skin. Ernie Pyle noted:

> On the beachhead every inch of our territory was under German artillery fire. There was no rear area that was immune, as in most battle zones. They could reach us with their 88s, and they used everything from that on up. I don't mean to suggest that they kept every foot of our territory drenched with shells all the time, for they certainly didn't. They were short of ammunition, for one thing. But they could reach us, and we never knew where they would shoot next. A man was just as liable to get hit standing in the doorway of the villa where he slept at night as he was in a command post five miles out in the field. . . .
>
> Sometimes we heard them coming, and sometimes we didn't. Sometimes we heard the shell whine after we heard it explode. Sometimes we heard it whine and it never exploded. Sometimes the house trembled and shook and we heard no explosion at all. But one thing I found there was just the same as anywhere else—that same old weakness in the joints when they got to landing close. I had been weak all over Tunisia and Sicily, and in parts of Italy, and I got weaker than ever in Anzio.[27]

DURING A DRIVING RAINSTORM ON February 3, the first elements of Davidson's 168th Brigade began landing in Anzio harbor. The 1st Battalion, London Scottish, was temporarily put under the command of Penney's 1st Division and headed northward to an area called "the Thumb," which represented the tip of the salient near Campoleone. Over boggy ground the two units traveled while being heavily "stonked" until they reached the sector manned by James's battered 3rd Brigade; their arrival would allow the 3rd to begin withdrawing under cover of darkness. The London Scottish made it as far as 400 yards south of the Lateral Road before mud and a heavy barrage forced them to halt. But it was enough to allow the remnants of the 3rd Brigade to escape.

Having left much of its heavy equipment and weapons behind on the front lines, the 3rd Brigade stumbled back through the ranks of the London Scottish, dirty, dispirited, and glad to be relieved, at least temporarily, from their role as Mackensen's punching bag. Now it was the turn of the new arrivals to endure everything the Germans could throw at them. In just a few short hours, the London Scottish would suffer more than a hundred casualties, but they hung on doggedly to their allotted place in the line.[28]

Another of the newly arrived Allied units, just shipped in from Pozzuoli on that cold and gloomy morning, was the 1st Battalion of the London Irish Rifles, an element of the 168th Brigade in Penney's 1st British Division, commanded by ruddy-faced, Dublin-born Lieutenant Colonel I. H. "Rupert" Good.

The London Irish Rifles, a regiment with a long and proud history, was formed in 1859 (when it was then known as the 28th Middlesex Rifle Volunteer Corps). The regiment had engaged in its first combat in South Africa during the Boer Wars of the late 1800s, followed by the Great War. Just two weeks before their arrival at Anzio, the 1st Battalion, wearing their distinctive piper-green headdress called a *caubeen* when not under steel helmets, had taken part in a major river-crossing assault over the Garigliano in the vicinity of Castelforte, San Lorenzo, and Monte Damiano, located south of Cassino, where a large force of heavily armed Germans lay in wait. The assault was a bloody shambles, and numerous members of the battalion were lost; the unit had to be quickly rebuilt.

Lieutenant Colonel Good, a graduate of Sandhurst, had himself already seen considerable fighting in the months preceding Shingle. He had distinguished himself in July 1943 when, as a battalion commander with the Irish Brigade in Sicily, he had performed coolly under heavy enemy fire and was awarded the Distinguished Service Order. But if he thought that the battles in Sicily and at the Garigliano had been bloody—and they most assuredly were—the upcoming fight at Anzio would surpass anything he had known.

His men having disembarked from their transports at Anzio harbor, Good was informed that his unit's mission was to relieve the 1st

Battalion, Reconnaissance Regiment,* holding the front line in and around Aprilia. With this bit of unpleasant news, Good's men strapped their packs to their backs; slung their Lee-Enfields and Sten guns over their shoulders; checked to see that they had sufficient quantities of ammunition, water, and rations; and climbed into olive-green Humber and Leyland lorries and Bren gun carriers to immediately begin making the ten-mile drive north toward Aprilia. They were totally unaware that they were about to become the bull's-eye of the major German attempt to annihilate the invaders.

For miles the battalion rode in silent anxiety, passing beneath one overpass and then another. On either side of the Albano Highway, the barren fields stretched as far as the eye could see, broken only by the occasional two-story stuccoed house or barn. As the men continued on, their eyes caught an incongruous sight up ahead: a collection of modern-looking buildings grouped together with a couple of tall—what?—smokestacks? It looked like an industrial complex of some sort stuck out here in the middle of nowhere. It looked like a—a factory. Soon Aprilia would be known by everyone as "the Factory."[29]

THE FIGHTING WAS ABOUT TO completely swallow Aprilia. Once the 1st London Irish arrived at the ruins of Aprilia, Lieutenant Colonel Good met with Lieutenant Colonel Paddy Brett, commanding the 1st Battalion, Reconnaissance Regiment, and mightily glad were the recce boys to be relieved; after relieving the 24th Guards Brigade, they had had enough of the constant, nerve-rattling shelling and the probes by tanks and infantry. Brett, sporting the recce corps' distinctive khaki beret, briefed Good on the situation: the Jerries were fond of saturating the town with mortar and artillery fire, and German patrols were continually making probing attacks to determine if there were any weak points that could be exploited. It was definitely unhealthy for anyone to show himself during

---

* Darby's Ranger Force, which had moved inland to take a position along the Lateral Road all the way to the Albano Highway, had been relieved at Aprilia by the 1st Reconnaissance Regiment on January 28 so that the Rangers could prepare for their ultimately disastrous assault on Cisterna. Robert W. Black, *The Ranger Force: Darby's Rangers in World War II*, 247.

daylight hours, for to be so incautious was to invite a flurry of ordnance. With that, Brett wished Good the best of luck and told his lads to gather up their equipment and head for the rear in their scout cars, carriers, and lorries.[30]

Good correctly sensed that his battalion was stuck in a vulnerable position. Rumor had it that Intelligence had learned that four enemy divisions—roughly 40,000 men—were expected to attack in the very near future. To Good's west, holding the convoluted ravines of the wadi area, were elements of A. S. P. Murray's 24th Guards Brigade; to the east of Aprilia were elements of William Eagles's 45th Division. Realizing that any German attack against the town—especially a panzer attack— would most likely come down the Albano Highway rather than across the muddy fields, Good instructed his four companies to deploy in a defensive line. D Company would dig in near a road junction about half a mile north of Aprilia, there to link up with a Guards battalion on the left flank. Here, to the left of the Albano Highway, the ground was deeply furrowed by wadis and ditches that "ran almost parallel on either side, and these had constantly to be patrolled day and night." Backing up D Company was Major Jack Cantopher's A Company.

Good sent B Company to the east of Aprilia, where it was spread out "from a road bridge across the Fosso della Ficoccia to a road junction on the fringe of Aprilia" and touched the left shoulder of the 45th Division's 179th Infantry Regiment. C Company was positioned as a reserve company directly south of the town from where it could come to the aid of either A, D, or B Company; battalion headquarters was established in a prominent farmhouse to the rear of C Company. There Captain Alan Mace and his Intelligence Platoon set up an observation post on the second floor of the abandoned building. With no artillery of his own, Good sited his four antitank guns to cover the approaches to B and D Companies from the north, augmented by mortars and machine guns from the Bren Carrier Platoon.

Speaking of the battalion headquarters' position, the regimental history says, "The Germans, of course, were not backward in this respect too, and though they did not at first suspect that the house [that is, Mace's observation post] was being used in day-time, it was unsafe and unwise to appear. For that reason the steps outside the building leading to the upper floors could not be used in daylight, and the intelligence staff sent messages to the Commanding Officer below by telephone."

With the Germans having temporarily abandoned Aprilia, the officers of Good's battalion hastily positioned their men throughout the shattered remains of the town. Bren guns were set up in the ruins of the theater and the school on the town's northern perimeter, while the mortar crews found nests within the piles of fallen brick and timbers that surrounded the Piazza Roma. When the wind was right, the aroma of spilled wine drifted from the demolished wine shop and mingled with the smell of wet plaster and the corpses of men and cattle lying quietly decaying in the surrounding fields. Men carrying radios and reels of communication wire to set up a command post in the bombed-out shell of the church glanced only briefly at the shrapnel-punctured bronze statue of Saint Michael holding his sword and the head of the dragon he had slain. Everywhere there was devastation and the pitiful remnants of a once-vibrant town; battered Saint Michael seemed to be the only symbol of defiance that still stood.

On the battalion's first night in Aprilia, everyone was on the alert; outposts were fully manned, patrols were sent out, minefields and barbed wire were set out, and telephone wires were laid between companies and battalion headquarters. The rain beat down and foxholes filled up. Because the area around Aprilia was flat as a table, the Germans, in their OPs in the Alban Hills, could see everything; consequently, movement was restricted to the nighttime hours. But the quiet became unnerving.[31]

TO THE EAST OF GOOD'S battalion, the 45th Division's 179th Infantry Regiment, under Malcolm R. Kammerer, a well-liked colonel who had commanded the regiment since the previous October, arrived and dug into the sopping, marshy soil as best it could.[32] James R. Safrit (Company F, 2nd Battalion, 179th) recorded in his journal on February 3: "We had been in our new positions in front of the 'Factory'—a real German stronghold. The British 1st Division had been practically wiped out here earlier. . . . We had been penned in our holes all day. We couldn't move because 'Jerry' could see every move we made, and if we raised our heads, a sniper's slug would 'part our wigs.' We were pretty miserable. The holes filled with water. About two feet deep was about as far as we could dig. So we lay there and shivered from our cold and the storm of shells that came in regularly."[33]

The wait for the major German assault to begin ended abruptly on the afternoon of February 3 when hundreds of Krupp guns suddenly opened up and saturated the forward lines with an intense barrage that landed on top of the 1st Battalion, Duke of Wellington's Regiment, near Campoleone, and kept heads low and teeth gritted. This was immediately followed by a company-size ground probe designed to rattle nerves; it was quickly repulsed, but the men knew that the Germans weren't just going to pack up, yell out *auf Wiedersehen*, and go home. Something big was coming, and they sensed it. The third of February would become known as the beginning of the battle for the Campoleone Salient.[34]

On the German side of the line, at Colonel General Mackensen's Fourteenth Army headquarters in Rome, final preparations had been made to switch from a strictly defensive posture to an attacking one. Mackensen wanted to launch a counteroffensive before the Allies could build up their beachhead any further—a counteroffensive that would, if successful, shove the Americans and British back into the sea, thereby obeying Hitler's edict to "lance the abscess below Rome."

With Darby's Rangers having been torn to pieces at Isola Bella, Truscott's 3rd Division stopped cold on their drive toward Cisterna, and the British forced to halt at Aprilia instead of advancing to Campoleone and beyond, now should have been the perfect time for an all-out strike, but the Germans were not yet at full strength. Many of their units were down to just a handful of officers and men; Mackensen decided that he could not attack until he was reinforced, but Kesselring urged him to proceed with what he did have.[35]

To better prepare his Fourteenth Army for its first major strike against the Allied forces, Mackensen requested that Kesselring attach additional troops to his army; Kesselring agreed to the request, and reinforcements were rushed to the area. The staff of Traugott Herr's LXXVI Panzer Corps was transferred from Vietinghoff's Tenth Army along the eastern end of the Gustav Line to Fourteenth Army and given control over the central and eastern sectors of the beachhead perimeter. Herr's corps was composed of five divisions. From the Albano Highway on the western flank to the east, they were the 3rd Panzer-Grenadier, the

715th Infantry (Motorized), the 71st Infantry, and the Hermann Göring Parachute-Panzer Divisions, plus the 26th Panzer Division, most of which was held in corps reserve. Also moving into position along the westernmost portion of the front—from the shore behind the Moletta River to a point west of the Albano Highway—was Schlemm's I Parachute Corps (composed of the 4th Parachute and the 65th Infantry Divisions), which had previously held the entire Anzio front at the time of the Allied landings.[36]

The Germans usually launched their attacks with combat groups that were formed by putting together varying combinations of units. Chosen to be the spearhead of the main German counterattack against the center of the beachhead line was Combat Group Gräser, commanded by the fifty-six-year-old, one-legged Lieutenant General Fritz Hubert Gräser (he had lost his left leg in 1941 while fighting on the Eastern Front), who was also the commander of the 3rd Panzer-Grenadier Division.[37] The components of Combat Group Gräser were the 104th Panzer-Grenadier Regiment reinforced by three additional infantry battalions, two artillery battalions, two companies of combat engineers, and a large number of Mark V Panther tanks.[38]

The assault to amputate the Allies' "Thumb" that jutted in the direction of Rome began late on the night of February 3 when Lieutenant General Hans-Hellmuth Pfeiffer's 65th Infantry Division came out of the deep ravines of the wadi area and punched into Good's 1st Battalion, Irish Rifles, located between Carroceto and Campoleone on the left flank of the salient. The night sky lit up with flares, machine-gun tracers, and the bright flashes of mortar explosions. Confusion reigned in the British ranks, as the Germans seemed to be everywhere—encirclement loomed as an imminent possibility. At 11:00 P.M., Good's battalion radioed that the enemy was trying to infiltrate between their positions and those of 1st Battalion, Scots Guards, on their left; a half hour later the 6th Gordons reported that they, too, were under heavy attack.

The units of Brigadier J. G. James's 3rd Infantry Brigade—the 1st Battalion, King's Shropshire Light Infantry, and the 1st Battalion, Duke of Wellington's Regiment, holding the northernmost bulge of the salient—were also hit by elements of Major General Hans-Georg Hildebrandt's 715th Infantry Division and the three motorized battalions of the 29th Panzer-Grenadier Regiment, an element of Gräser's 3rd Panzer-Grenadier Division. It became obvious that the Germans were attempting to drive deep wedges between the units of the 3rd Brigade in order to lop off the entire salient like a gangrenous appendage.[39]

Lance Corporal George Oliver Jeffs, a stretcher bearer in the 1st Battalion, KSLI, somehow escaped being killed. Having already been concussed several times during the fighting in Tunisia, he was knocked unconscious during the opening minutes of the attack against his unit. Lying in a shell hole with the torn bodies of his mates all around and on top of him, he was ignored by the charging Germans who assumed he was dead. Later found and removed from the human rubble, he was sent back to the hospital. Days later, although still in shock, he came before a medical board to determine his fitness for further combat. Years later his son said, "He was asked what had traumatized him most. It wasn't the fighting or the ill effects of dysentery; it was the constant loss of his mates. What would he do if they ordered him back into the lines? 'Go back sir.' 'Well, you're not going back,' was their reply." Instead, at the end of the war, he was assigned to be a medical orderly in Venice.[40]

David Fraser (who would later become a general, the vice chief of the Imperial General Staff, and knighted as well), then a junior officer serving in the Grenadier Guards, recalled, "On 3rd February the forward positions of 1st Division were attacked, and although the assault was beaten off, the forward brigade was withdrawn."[41] In that forward brigade—the 24th Guards—Major David M. L. Gordon-Watson, commanding the 1st Battalion, Irish Guards, quickly realized that his headquarters position had become untenable, and he was given orders to pull his men out before it was too late. Ambushed while guiding his men to the rear, he personally shot twelve Germans at close range with his Webley revolver and, when that ran out of ammunition, switched to a Sten gun. He and his men even captured a dozen of the enemy. Some of his men were also briefly taken prisoner but, in all the confusion, managed to escape. For his cool display of bravery, Gordon-Watson received the Military Cross.[42]

Another Guardsman, Sergeant Joe Dunne (Number 13 Platoon, 1st Irish Guards), distinguished himself once again when a German ground assault hit his company. Finding the officer in charge of the unit's

4.2-inch mortars, he requested that defensive fires be laid down in order to break up the enemy attack. For unknown reasons, the defensive fire was never delivered, and Dunne and his men faced a swarm of Germans approaching from the far end of a gully in front of them. "My platoon at once engaged the enemy," he reported, "as did 15 Platoon on my left, joined by the attached machine guns. The hayricks in front of Numbers 14 and 15 Platoons were set alight and the Vickers machine guns brought heavy fire to bear in front of our positions. Then, on my platoon front, the enemy seemed to move over both flanks, and only a number of enemy snipers remained."

But Numbers 14 and 15 Platoons were soon overrun, forcing Dunne to pull his unit back to battalion headquarters, under strong attack, and aid in its defense. "We made good progress until we reached the railway," he said, "then we came under heavy fire, which I thought came from our own troops. I shouted to them and found the embankment was strongly held by the enemy, thus making our objective almost impossible to attain. I left two sections of my platoon in the gully, which runs from the road to the railway." Taking eight men with him, Dunne then went forward in an attempt to reach the high ground. Once there, he and his men were pinned down by fire from both flanks and the rear. With their ammunition soon expended and him and most of his men wounded, Dunne had no choice but to surrender to the superior forces. After having been put under guard in a farmhouse, the handful of Irish Guardsmen were encouraged when the house came under fire from a British tank, causing most of the Germans to flee.

Overpowering their two remaining guards, Dunne and his men escaped with their two captors. "We made our way back to the gully," he said, "taking two more prisoners on the way, then passed through the mortar platoon, who were in the gully under the railway line. On reaching the road, we handed over our prisoners, and Guardsman Swift and myself were conveyed by carrier to the dressing station" to have their wounds attended to. Sergeant Joe Dunne would receive the Distinguished Conduct Medal for gallantry in combat.[43]

THE 45TH DIVISION'S 179TH REGIMENT was spared from the onslaught—at least for the moment. James Safrit noted, "When darkness came, we posted guards. One man slept, or tried to, while his buddy pulled guard duty—two hours on and two hours off. I had drifted off to sleep when Burns shook me and whispered, 'Wake up! Krauts!' All he had to say was 'Krauts' and I was wide awake. We sat in our hole trying to see in the pitch-dark night." Safrit noted that he and his buddies soon surmised that the enemy had fortified themselves with booze, and he could hear "German voices singing at the tops of their lungs. As they came closer, we could tell they were as drunk as skunks. By this time, the whole platoon was listening and waiting. Those crazy bastards were really living it up. We were almost ashamed to do what we did when they came in front of our holes. We opened fire and the singing became a rattle. Then everything was quiet. Eventually, after we were sure there were no more coming, the medics came up and carried them off to Graves Registration."

Afterward, Safrit and the others in his platoon discussed what had happened and came to the conclusion that the Germans

> had drunkenly taken the wrong direction and staggered into our lines instead of their own, where they had no doubt intended to go. But, as some guy cracked, "That was high-priced Schnapps they were drinking." We didn't look at the bodies, so I don't know what they looked like—if they were old or young. We were relieved that we couldn't see them because of the dark. We felt bad enough just knowing what had happened, much less having to see what we had done, because no one, no matter how hard or cruel, likes to see death. Strange things like this have happened to many different infantrymen throughout the war on many different fronts. Weird things happen in combat.[44]

JUST BEFORE MIDNIGHT, THE GERMAN artillery batteries let loose another terrific bombardment that fell on the base of the salient to the east of the Albano Highway—right where the 509th Parachute Infantry Battalion was dug in. It started with the booming sounds of guns being fired in the distance, followed seconds later by whistling as Death flew through the air, and ended with tremendous crashing and concussions as the shells hit home and covered the paratroopers with mud. Believing this barrage to be part of the Germans' long-expected counterattack, Clark told Lucas to forget about advancing to Cisterna and Campoleone Station:

"Your beachhead should now be consolidated and disposition should be made suitable for meeting an attack."[45]

Second Lieutenant Edward Reuter (Company A, 509th PIB) was there when the cannonade began. He said:

> German resistance increased, and so did the amount of mortar and artillery coming in. I had been sharing a foxhole with a private who did not know that I was an officer (we did not wear our rank in combat). We were on the reverse side of the hill. . . . Several American tanks pulled up behind us and began to shell enemy positions. They soon drew counterfire, which was going over our heads. We soon became used to this and I got out of my hole and a short round came in. I was in the process of falling to the ground but was hit in the upper right arm, chest, and head by shrapnel; luckily I had my helmet on. There was no pain; I think the hit to the head put me in shock, but I called out that I had been hit and our company medic gave me first aid. On the same day I was wounded, my platoon leader, Lieutenant Lowell Frank was killed. Later in the month, my company commander, [First] Lieutenant [Joseph J.] Winsko and A Company's executive officer were also killed—all by direct hits to their foxholes.

Reuter was helped to the battalion aid station, then taken by jeep to the evacuation hospital on the beachhead, where a doctor plucked out the shrapnel and bandaged his wounds. He was lucky; unlike so many other soldiers who were wounded and then marked "Returned to duty," he did not have to return to the beachhead.[46]

Others were not so fortunate. Dawn on February 4 would bring a renewed assault by the Germans that would require every bit of courage, luck, and fortitude to withstand.

CHAPTER 8

"The British are in serious trouble"

FEBRUARY 4-6

THE CHILLY, DRIZZLY, MISERABLE DAWN of February 4 was a study in gray—gray, shadowy forms moving through a gray mist, accompanied by the gray bulk of panzers rolling across a gray landscape.

The Germans were on a mission: a two-pronged attack to slice off the British salient made up of the 3rd Infantry Brigade, 24th Guards Brigade, and the 168th Brigade that by now bulged more than ten miles north of Anzio. The German plan was simple: surround the Brits in a pocket that could be pounded unmercifully with artillery and tanks.

The attack came with stunning swiftness and violence. First, the 1st Battalion of the 145th Grenadier Regiment of Hans-Hellmuth Pfeiffer's 65th Infantry Division, supported by tanks and SP guns, came rolling out of the fog and rain, screaming and shouting like madmen, and slammed into the left flank of the 1st Irish Guards dug into the mud northwest of Aprilia, slicing through them and advancing all the way to the Campoleone-Nettuno railroad line that paralleled the Albano Highway.

While this fight raged, the second German probe—this one spearheaded by Combat Group Gräser's 104th Panzer-Grenadier Regiment and augmented by six tanks, a battalion each from the 29th and 90th Panzer-Grenadier Divisions,* and elements of the 715th Motorized and

---

* The 90th Panzer-Grenadier Division was commanded by the colorful Major General Ernst Günther Baade, who had been a Rhodes scholar and studied at

3rd Panzer-Grenadier Divisions—was launched against the 6th Gordons of Moore's 2nd Brigade. There was no way that the single battalion could stand against this pressure, and so they buckled and fell back in disarray. With one company of the Gordons overrun, German infantrymen swarmed in, taking over a small ridge to the east of the Albano Highway. Suddenly, three more German infantry battalions, two combat engineer companies, and a number of Mark V (Panther) tanks, supported by two artillery battalions, rushed in to surround James's 3rd Brigade. Penney's 1st Division was effectively isolated.

The Sherman tanks of the 46th Royal Tank Regiment (RTR) trundled forward across the mud, their engines' roaring growl piercing the air, accompanied by the squeaking of the bogey wheels and the clank and rattle of the treads, but their guns did not have the range of the enemy's tanks and artillery; one after another of them were blown apart or completely disabled, forcing the survivors to retreat. The solid overcast and cold downpour meant that no Allied warplanes could come to the aid of the 2nd and 3rd Brigades; the 1st Division was being systematically torn to shreds. No one really expected Penney's division to be able to withstand the overwhelming punishment they were taking from the Germans. In fact, with the situation so critical, Penney requested that Gerald Templer, commanding the 56th British Division, be ready to send Davidson's 168th Infantry Brigade to him for a counterattack; Davidson said that he could spare only one battalion—the 1st Battalion, London Scottish Regiment—for a possible counterattack, but the situation was too uncertain to send more than that.

With disaster looming, something of a miracle seemed to happen that afternoon. The British troops packed into the salient somehow tapped into an unknown reservoir of courage and found the strength and will to resist every German effort to annihilate them. By midafternoon the 1st Irish Guards had escaped the German encirclement, while the 6th Gordons, which, just hours earlier, had been on the verge of breaking

---

Oxford University before the war. An Anglophile who especially loved Scotland, Baade was fond of wearing a kilt and carrying a huge claymore sword into battle. Samuel W. Mitcham, *Rommel's Desert Commanders: The Men Who Served the Desert Fox, North Africa, 1941–42*, 73–81.

and fleeing, refused to give up the ground south of the ridgeline. Part of their newfound tenacity was due to the effective artillery support they received.

In the 3rd Brigade area, the 1st KSLI ambushed a German party escorting a hundred captured British soldiers to the rear and freed them. The 46th RTR returned and began picking off German armor. At that moment, Companies B and C of the 894th U.S. Tank Destroyer Battalion, which had cut its teeth at Kasserine Pass, magically appeared out of the smoke of battle and began knocking off one panzer after another with their M-10's 76.2mm guns.[1]

Bravery was in abundance that wet day. An artillery observation-post officer, a captain named Jupp, of the 67th Field Regiment, Royal Artillery, was acting in support of the 6th Gordon Highlanders. Early on, when the three forward companies of the Gordons were overrun, Jupp and his wireless (radio) operator, a soldier named Cafferey, remained at their post in a Bren carrier for several hours, calling down fire from their battery of 25-pounder howitzers (the equivalent of the American 105mm howitzer) onto the enemy.

At 4:00 P.M., Jupp joined the 6th Gordons as they mounted a counterattack to regain their abandoned positions; Jupp went in with the leading company, but his radio failed and he lost contact with the company. Ignoring the danger, he and Cafferey drove forward in their carrier and, despite intense enemy fire, spotted targets on their own, calling in devastating barrages that tore the German ranks apart. But the enemy would not fall back and eventually surrounded the company of Gordons. There were only fifteen men left in the company, but Jupp and Cafferey joined them to form a defensive position. Suddenly, the wireless set sparked back to life, and Jupp was able to make contact again with the rest of the battalion. Ordered to withdraw to the rear company's position, he remained with them until shortly before midnight, when what was left of the battalion withdrew fully. Jupp's party was one of the last to leave, staying to evacuate six casualties on their carriers.[2]

The 1st Irish Guards also regained their composure, and the 1st Battalion, King's Shropshire Light Infantry, staged a counterattack, hitting the Germans with everything they had in an all-out, do-or-die situation. As dusk was descending over the battlefield, and with the 1st London

Irish and 6th Gordons precariously holding their positions, the just-arrived 1st Battalion, London Scottish Regiment, of Davidson's 168th Brigade, supported by the 46th Royal Tanks, reached the front and almost immediately began dueling with German infantry and panzers, driving them back to north of Campoleone. The gap between the Gordons and the rest of 3rd Brigade was now sealed, at least temporarily. By evening, the German attack had lost much of its steam, allowing the British a brief respite that enabled them to somewhat restore their shattered lines.[3]

That evening, using the cover of darkness, Brigadier J. R. James's battered 3rd Brigade pulled out and returned to B Echelon, where the brigade counted its losses: over 1,400 men had been killed or wounded; more than 900 had been taken prisoner. No one knew what to expect in the coming days, but one thing was certain: the battle was not over. The Germans would be back, and in even greater numbers.[4]

General Lucas was pleased and proud of the stand Penney's forces had made but feared that the salient was dangerously exposed and that a second German attack could spell their doom; he ordered them back to a more defensible line. The 3rd Brigade's 1st KSLI and the 2nd Sherwood Foresters withdrew quickly with only slight losses. The 1st DWIR, under direct fire from enemy tanks, waited until after dark before pulling back; one company had been cut off, and the remainder of the battalion had to abandon most of its antitank guns and heavy equipment.[5]

AS THE SUN SANK INTO the sea on February 4, the American and British soldiers sank into their watery holes and got ready for the night. Some men had tried to install any sort of flooring in their holes in a useless attempt to stay dry—the wooden sides of the ration cases initially worked best, but it was a losing game; the frigid water and mud eventually rose above the crude floors, soaking the soldiers' feet and turning their toes numb.

Audie Murphy (Company B, 15th Infantry Regiment, 3rd Division) recalled: "Rain falls in slanting black streaks, turning our area into a sea of mud. It pulls at our feet like quicksand. We slant the bottoms of our foxholes. Water drains to the lower end, and we dip it out with our helmets. But when the storms really strike, we give up. For hours we crouch in ankle-deep water. . . . When shells hit close, the soft walls of the dugouts crumble. Like turtles we dig ourselves out of the mud and try repairing the damage before another shell arrives or the water rises in our foxholes."[6]

Roofs made of scrounged logs and timbers, covered with earth and parkas and raincapes, were also added during the night in a losing effort to keep out the rain and provide some protection from artillery air bursts. Despite all the home improvements, "we lived like rats in the mud," said Jim Bird, an artilleryman in the 45th.[7]

Sleep was virtually impossible. In one particular "Willie and Joe" cartoon, drawn by *Stars and Stripes* artist Bill Mauldin, his trademark scruffy dogfaces are shown crouching in a water-filled foxhole while shells burst overhead and bullets zip past. One says to the other, "Wisht I could stand up an' git some sleep." It was a perceptive drawing with which virtually every soldier at Anzio could relate.[8]

With their heads below the rims of their foxholes, some soldiers dared to light a cigarette, but the tiny glowing end offered no warmth. Whispers were exchanged between the men, most commenting on how they wished they were home and wondering what their loved ones—parents, wives, girlfriends—were doing at that exact hour. The wet, bone-chilling cold meant that only the most utterly exhausted men would get more than a few moments of sleep—sleep that would be jarringly interrupted all through the night by random and scattered rounds of artillery being lobbed by both sides. Nerves were frayed to the snapping point.

Sentries who were supposed to remain alert for enemy activity for an hour or so before being relieved poked their heads up just far enough so that their bleary eyes could scan the featureless horizon for any signs of movement. Commo checks over the radios and field phones were made frequently. Junior and noncommissioned officers, so tired that they could barely stay awake themselves, moved silently from one outpost to another, whispering the password to the whispered challenges of the sentries, checking to see that their men were alert—or as alert as one could be under the circumstances.

Somewhere to the north beyond Aprilia, invisible to the naked eye, the sentries could almost *feel* the Germans getting ready for their next assault—cleaning their weapons, loading their rifles and sub-machine guns, adding a fine edge to their bayonets, doing some last-minute maintenance on their panzers, writing a final letter home, maybe taking a nip of schnapps to give them some warmth and liquid courage. The rumor about the Rangers being wiped out at Isola Bella had already made the rounds of the Yanks and Tommies and had been confirmed. "We wondered if we would be next," reflected Jim Bird.[9]

Corporal Stanley R. Smith (Company I, 30th Infantry Regiment, 3rd Division) was filled with the tension that covered everyone on the beachhead like a blanket. On the night of February 4, he said:

> We were told to "saddle up and move out." They told us that we were go-ing to move over to our right to relieve one of our companies. We started out and it was very, very dark, and it was drizzling. We were stumbling along across fields and over paths with small rocks strewn around. The ground was slippery and so were the rocks, and we slipped and stumbled over them and sometimes we would fall. There was a lot of cussing under our breaths.
>
> We had no idea where we were. After a while there was an explosion—we had walked down in back of a 105mm artillery battery. They were firing a mission and when that first gun went off—what a hell of a racket! I think I came off the ground about two feet. It scared the living hell out of me, and I don't think I was alone! We continued on our way, still in the rain and cold. It seemed like forever before they told us to halt and dig in. . . . We got dug in and posted the guards and the rest of us settled in for the night.[10]

It would be a long, cold, and sleepless night.

THAT EVENING, FEELING BESIEGED BY both the Germans and his own superiors, John Lucas wrote in his journal:

> News very bad. The British are in serious trouble and I am greatly dis-turbed about them. They have occupied an advance position for days and are now in danger. I ordered General Penney this morning to with-draw but, due to enemy pressure, he has been unable to do so. I hope it is not too late. . . . [Penney] probably never forgave me but I am sure that

another 24 hours would have caused the death of many brave men with nothing gained for us.

I think the old Hun is getting ready to have a go at me. He thinks he can drive me back into the ocean. Maybe so, but it will cost him money. He has more men and guns than I have, but I am buttoning everything up and he is going to get hurt.[11]

THE 168TH BRIGADE HAD YET to feel the full force of the German attack. Lieutenant Colonel Good's 1st Battalion, London Irish Rifles, was ordered to dig in along what was regarded as a VI Corps' "stop line"—a place where the heavy German counterattacks must be stopped. This order was soon changed, and Good received new orders to take his unit to Aprilia and relieve the British troops dug in there. That evening German shells began to fall all across the Aprilia-Carroceto area in ever-increasing ferocity.[12]

Needing to shorten the forward line to make it more defensible, elements of Penney's division had to relinquish two and a half miles of hard-won ground that night and silently withdraw to a line approximately one mile north of Carroceto and Aprilia. The relatively fresh 168th Brigade was moved forward and inserted into the center of the line, while Brigadier J. R. James's battered 3rd Brigade stumbled back into division reserve.

The Germans greeted the new arrivals with an artillery barrage and local ground attacks, causing numerous casualties among the British. For the Germans, there was a fleeting sense of satisfaction: they had eliminated the Campoleone salient, but the success had been purchased at a heavy cost. The attackers, mostly the 104th Panzer-Grenadier Regiment, had suffered nearly 500 dead or wounded and more than 300 captured. Prisoners complained to their British and American captors that they had been hurriedly thrown into the attack without adequate preparation or reconnaissance. Most importantly for the Allies, the German attempt to isolate and destroy the 3rd Brigade had failed. But what lay ahead in the coming days? No one could say.[13]

THE NEXT DAY, FEBRUARY 5, Lucas and his staff were up early, juggling their forces to better prepare for whatever the Germans might have in store for them. On the acetate-covered maps in VI Corps' wine-cellar headquarters, an intermediate line drawn between the forward positions that formed an arc above Carroceto and Aprilia was already irrelevant; below it, centered on the Overpass/Flyover over the Albano Highway, about halfway between Anzio and Aprilia, there was another line with the ominous title "Final Beachhead Defensive Line."

As the Germans continued to bring in more infantry and panzer units, so too did they bring in more artillery. By February 5, the enemy had 372 artillery pieces, 152 of which had calibers exceeding 105mm, concentrated around the beachhead. Directed by observers on the dominating heights of the Alban Hills, the Lepini Mountains, and a water tower at Littoria, the enemy's long-range artillery weapons could drop shells into any part of the limited beachhead area with impunity.

Because the area was so thickly packed with American and British troops and their installations, the Anzio-Nettuno beachhead was a target-rich environment for the German gunners. Guns of all calibers were available—everything from the 105s and long-range 150mm and 170mm pieces to the two monstrous 280mm railcar-mounted K5 (E) Krupp-manufactured guns that the Germans had christened "Leopold" and "Robert" but that the Allies dubbed "Anzio Annie" and the "Anzio Express."* These guns and their carriages were hidden in tunnels running beneath the Alban Hills, rolled out to fire their shells, and then returned to their bombproof homes. Fortunately for those on the receiving end, the guns were wildly inaccurate, but the psychological effect on the Allied troops was inestimable.[14] One 45th Division artilleryman, Bernie L. Stokes, recalled being under a barrage of huge shells: "They'd

_____

*When the Allies finally broke out of the Anzio beachhead in May 1944, the Germans moved the guns to Civitavecchia. There the Germans spiked "Robert" and "Leopold" with explosives to prevent them from falling into Allied hands. On June 7, 1944, the 168th Infantry Regiment of the 34th U.S. Infantry Division found the guns, which were then moved to Naples and then loaded aboard a Liberty ship and shipped to the U.S. Army's Aberdeen Proving Ground in Maryland for testing. As Leopold was the least damaged of the two, it was eventually put on display as a war trophy. In 2010 it was moved to Fort Lee, Virginia, where it remains. J. H. Green, "Anzio," 52; "Historic Enemy Artillery Piece Makes Its Way to Fort Lee," November 24, 2010, www.army.mil/article/48580/historic_enemy_artillery_piece_makes_its_way_to_fort_lee.

come through the air—'*woosh-woosh-woosh.*' Big ol' things really made a lot of noise."[15] Chester Powell, another Thunderbird, said that when one of the big shells flew overhead, "It felt like it was going to suck you out of your foxhole."[16]

To counter the Germans' fire, the Allied navies and air forces, when conditions permitted, went into action. Two P-51 Mustangs of the 111th Reconnaissance Squadron directed the fire of the light cruiser USS *Brooklyn* and three destroyers that sailed close to shore, blasting the enemy guns and positions along the western flank. But the big guns were never hit.[17]

Luckily for the Allies, after the strong attacks of February 4, the Germans temporarily suspended large-scale attacks in order to catch their collective breath and gather more men and ammunition; the pause gave the Americans and British time to improve their defenses. To bolster the front, the 168th Brigade was moved up from VI Corps reserve to strengthen the 1st British Division's line. Because working on the defenses could be deadly during daylight, the preparing of defensive positions was confined to nighttime hours.

The sturdy stone farmhouses, nearly as strong as concrete bunkers, became important parts of the Allies' overall defensive scheme. The ground floors of the houses were fortified with sandbags and timbers and turned into firing positions for machine guns and antitank guns, while the upper stories became ideal observation posts and snipers' perches. The buildings were also perfect for headquarters and medical aid stations. Outside, foxholes and trenches were dug, with telephone wire strung from hole to hole. Mines and barbed wire filled in gaps between positions, and mortars, tanks, and tank destroyers were brought in under cover of darkness and positioned to provide heavier firepower for the infantrymen. Everything that could be done to prepare for the next German onslaught was done. Now it was just a matter of waiting.[18]

THE HEAVY AND GROWING PRESENCE of German artillery was being felt with each passing day.[*] On February 5, German gunners zeroed in on

---

[*] Much has been said and written about the quantity of German artillery fire, but, in reality, the Allies had considerably more. As Eduard Mark points out, in "the

the Allied airstrip at Nettuno and destroyed five British Spitfires, forcing the air base to be abandoned except for emergency landings.[19]

The daylight hours of February 5 passed with the usual exchange of artillery shells, but the Allies couldn't help feeling that they were once again about to become the recipient of something far greater. And so it came to pass that evening when Lucian Truscott's 3rd Division was saturated by a brief bombardment that Truscott, having received a panicky report from one of his battalion commanders, pulled the 30th Regiment back several hundred yards. The Germans had been clever in their attack, using concentrated flares and small-arms fire to simulate a much larger force; there were also reports that the enemy had employed flame-throwing Mark III panzers. Two hours after it had begun, the attack was over, and the Germans fell back to their lines, satisfied that they had inflicted real and psychological damage on the Yanks. Truscott realized that the assault had been a limited one and that he had made a mistake in so hastily withdrawing the two battalions. At daylight the next morning, the two battalions counterattacked and restored their previous lines.[20]

Everywhere across the beachhead, morale was dipping low. Sergeant Audie Murphy (Company B, 15th Infantry Regiment, 3rd Division) certainly felt that way: "A doomlike quality hangs over the beachhead," he wrote.

> Just what it is I cannot say, but it is everywhere. I feel it in the howling of the wind, the falling of the rain, and the mud that sucks at our feet. It is in the yellow rays of the sun and the blue rot of trench-foot. And, above all, it is in the eyes of the men. [Sergeant] Beltsky is gone. A shell fragment sheared off part of a leg; his combat days are over. I am in charge of the platoon. [The platoon's lieutenant had been killed some weeks earlier.] There is no thrill in the promotion. Already we old men feel like fugitives from the law of averages.[21]

---

week before the Germans' attack [of February 16] . . . the Anglo-Americans fired 25,000 rounds daily and received but 1,500 [in return]." A German artilleryman wrote that his side's guns had only "a bare average of two issues of ammunition"— considerably less than what was needed—while the enemy had "a quantitative superiority in ammunition that was horrifying." Eduard Mark, *Aerial Interdiction: Air Power and the Land Battle in Three American Wars*, 136–137.

THE WORLD WAR II COMBAT soldier's life was one of unremitting misery and hardship, far removed from the comforts and experiences of civilian life. He was required to perform his duties no matter how cold or hot or wet or dry or exhausted he was. He was required to carry impossible weights long distances, sleep in holes, attend to bodily functions like a barnyard animal, exist on a substandard diet, swing emotionally from boredom to terror in an instant, endure seemingly ceaseless artillery and machine-gun fire, be confronted with scenes so horrifyingly gruesome that they were impossible to describe, move forward (if he moved at all) into the teeth of the enemy's munitions, and remain alert at all times. It is no wonder that some men cracked under the strain.

A 3rd Infantry Division platoon leader recalled the day that a veteran sergeant, who had spent nearly a year under fire, snapped at Anzio: "He was . . . going to take off running. They had to tackle him and hold him down and send him back. He was the last person in the world you would have thought that would happen to." When a soldier suffered a psychotic break, there was nothing to do but remove him from combat and give him an extended period of rest, sometimes with shots of sodium pentothal (known as a "blue bomber") to knock him out. In rare cases, the affected soldier never recovered.[22]

Nineteen-year-old Bren gunner Private Fred Mason, C Company, 2nd North Staffs, received his introduction to combat at Anzio. He recalled that he

> didn't see the enemy until we moved to the front line about the 6th of February. Most of our time was spent sitting in slit trenches [foxholes], not daring to show our heads because the Germans, in most cases, were only fifty yards away. The conditions in our slit trenches were atrocious. Always damp and most uncomfortable. We used to wear two pairs of socks to keep our feet warm. Also we wrapped ourselves in a couple of blankets. If we were lucky enough to obtain some wood from the farmhouses in the area, we would use it for a roof, which made things a little better.[23]

An American soldier echoed those sentiments: "It was just plain hell all through the day, and the nights were worse. The hole got about six inches of water, and you couldn't do anything but try and bail it out with your helmet. We wrapped shelter halves and blankets around us but they didn't do much good. They got soaked with rain and then you sat on a piece of wood or something and shivered and cussed. . . . You couldn't get out of that hole once the sun came up, or even show the top of your head [because of the enemy]."[24]

The weather remained abominable. Trying to stay dry in his flooded foxhole was Stanley Smith (Company I, 30th Regiment, 3rd Division). He said, "One thing we had to contend with was the weather. I have never seen it rain so long day after day—seemed like there was no end of the rain. And it was a cold rain, and we were soaked to the skin with no way of getting dried out." Smith finally did get dry. He was wounded on February 6 and got to recuperate in a nice, warm, dry army hospital.[25]

Conditions were indeed atrocious, and thousands of troops would need to be evacuated because of "immersion foot"—what in World War I was termed *trench foot*. A form of frostbite, immersion foot occurs when feet remain wet for long periods of time, and that was certainly the case for tens of thousands of troops at Anzio—Allied and Germans alike. They often spent twenty-four hours a day crouching in near-freezing water and mud up to, and above, their ankles. The leather of their boots absorbed the moisture, and it seeped through and into their wool socks. Some soldiers tried building "rafts" or floorboards out of cardboard ration cases or wooden ammunition crates that would keep them above the wet muck, but for most the effort was a waste; there was simply no way to keep warm and dry at Anzio in the winter of 1944. Otherwise, the pain and discomfort were, as more than one soldier put it, as bad as the shelling to which they were subjected.

Immersion foot was not merely an uncomfortable inconvenience; it could also be life threatening. In severe cases, untreated immersion foot can involve the toes, heel, or entire foot and can result in gangrene setting in, which would require the foot to be surgically amputated. Left untreated, gangrene could result in death.[26]

The misery each man exposed to the elements faced is almost impossible to convey in words. Surely, some men, when they learned they were to be posted to Italy, expected blue skies, sunshine, and palm trees, but many parts of Italy in the winter are a far cry from the salubrious posters in the travel agencies. Winter warfare has always been thus. In the previous world war, an American officer in France wrote, "It does not have to be very cold to make soldiering an unpleasant task."[27] Unpleasant, indeed. Frozen ground makes it almost impossible to dig foxholes and other shelters. Bare skin sticks to the metal parts of weapons. Water in canteens freezes.

In 1944 the uniforms and cold-weather gear of the various nations were uniformly inadequate. Troops who were specially trained for mountain and winter warfare, such as the 10th U.S. Mountain Division and German mountain divisions, were issued specialized clothing and footwear, but the average soldier was not. The American GI might receive a knitted wool cap, wool socks, wool scarves and gloves, woolen underwear, and pile-lined field jackets, but the footwear was insufficient to protect a man's feet. Occasionally, rubber galoshes or overshoes made their way to the front, and these were a godsend, and the U.S. Army had a special combination rubber-and-leather boot called a "shoepac," but these were issued in far too few quantities. As a stopgap solution, the army issued tins of "dubbin"—a waterproofing wax compound that soldiers rubbed onto their leather combat boots and shoes in an often futile attempt to keep out the moisture.[28] To make matters worse, as 45th Division artilleryman Jim Bird said, "The rear-echelon people were always siphoning off the gear intended for the front-line troops before it could get up to us."[29]

The suffering of tens of thousands of soldiers in Italy in the winter of 1943–1944 was exceeded only by the suffering of millions of both German and Soviet troops during the insanely brutal conditions along the Eastern Front during the winter of 1941–1942.

EVERYONE KNEW THAT AN UNENDING supply of ammunition was critical to being able to maintain the Anzio forces, but, incredibly, Clark ran into opposition from British Admiral Sir John Cunningham, commander in chief of the Mediterranean Fleet, whom the Fifth Army commander described as being "not particularly happy about the Anzio operation anyway, because it forced him to keep in use craft that he wanted to withdraw in preparation for the coming cross-Channel invasion of Normandy." To speed up ammunition resupply, Clark ordered that trucks fully loaded with ammunition be driven backward onto the LSTs at the port of Naples before being delivered to Anzio; the trucks could then drive off the vessels and head straight for the ammunition dumps without any further handling at the port. "Admiral Cunningham bitterly objected to this," Clark said, "saying that it was dangerous. For our viewpoint, everything touching Anzio was dangerous."[30]

JAMES SAFRIT'S UNIT, COMPANY F, 179th Infantry Regiment, 45th Division, was ordered to move to another sector of the front, and, once there, Safrit and two friends, Turner Brown and Francis "Buddy" Burns, were set to work digging new protective holes into the creek bank. "We had just finished it and were arranging our gear in the bottom," Safrit said. "Turner Brown had come over and was 'shooting the breeze.' He sat on top of the bank far enough down that his head didn't show over the edge. There was the ever-present rumble of artillery, but there was none falling anywhere near us and we were feeling pretty good. We were fairly sure that we would be in this defensive position for a couple of days and we hoped to get a little rest."

Buddy Burns was Safrit's closest friend. He recalled a time when Burns's grandmother, who claimed that she was a psychic, made a prediction about the future. "He named many instances where she had proved uncannily correct in her predictions," Safrit recalled. "Darned if he hasn't got me believing it. She told him that he would go through the war without a scratch, and he firmly believed it. He was just as scared as anyone else while the shells, bullets, and bombs were raining down. But the minute it was over, he would start wisecracking in that screwball Donald Duck falsetto voice of his, and so help me, he could even make me or anybody else laugh."

Suddenly, a salvo of mortar shells came whistling in directly onto Safrit and Burns's position.

One shell landed squarely in our hole. We later found six holes where the shells from a *Nebelwerfer* multi-barreled mortar hit.[*] The shell seemed

---

[*] Bernie L. Stokes, a 45th Division artilleryman, recalled the *Nebelwerfers*: "Germans—they liked to have whistles on everything else they could think of. They had this nest of mortars—I think there was six of them. They'd all go off at

to send the whole spray of shrapnel in a direct line with Burn's [sic] body. The shrapnel missed me completely, but the deafening explosions knocked me silly.

After I shook off the shock, I realized that Burns was trying to tell me something, but blood kept gushing up into his throat. He kept desperately trying to speak. He slumped into my arms and rattled horribly. I was drenched with his blood by now. I was screaming for the medics, but even I could see that no one could help him now. He was dead. I knew from that moment that I would never be the same again. He was a friend like I would never have again. We had been through so much—suffered through the cold and mud of the mountains, and now the hell of Anzio. I sat there huddled in the hole with his limp body in my arms and I just broke down and cried like a baby. Finally, the stretcher-bearers came and carried him away.

How I was spared, I'll never know. I was only a few inches from Burns, yet I wasn't even scratched. And Brown was sitting no more than a couple of feet away from us and in a direct line of the shell; only Burn's [sic] body had blocked the flying steel from hitting him. The rope that Brown had been aimlessly twirling was clipped off neatly close to his fingertips, but he wasn't scratched.

Safrit reflected, "One thing that this convinced me of was that there had to be a God that could cause such a miracle on our part. Brown and I realized that it just wasn't our time to go. Unfortunately for Brown, his time was not long in coming. He was killed in action about a month later at Anzio from a direct hit from a Mark VI tank firing point blank into his foxhole."[31]

---

once and they all had a different sound. They called them the pipe organs comin' through the air. They wasn't very effective but they made a lot of noise. 'Course the 88s, they had that high whistle. If you heard the whistle, you were safe. They had already gone over. And if they went over you—say ten feet—you was pretty safe, too, because they was comin' in at such a high speed all the shrapnel went forward. Hardly ever get anything comin' back." www.6thcorpscombatengineers .com/linksTributeVeterans.

AERIAL PHOTOS TAKEN ON FEBRUARY 6, the first clear day in a week of bad weather, showed that the Germans had been busy increasing their artillery strength. Most of the guns had been emplaced south of the Alban Hills, where they could support an attack either down the Albano Highway or from Cisterna. A large buildup was also noted on the left flank, across from Penney's division.[32]

As the sun rose that day, the men on the beachhead could actually see the yellow ball; a week's worth of rain, mist, and low clouds had at last come to an end, and so the artillery spotters—men in high-wing Piper Cub aircraft known as L-4 "Grasshoppers" that glided like hawks above the battlefield—were able to act as the eyes of the gunners below. Perhaps now, the men hugging the mud down below said, the Allies would be able to pay back the Germans for all of the week's worth of shelling they had endured.

When German soldiers saw an L-4 circling lazily above them, they knew what to expect. "If we make the slightest move," a German POW admitted under interrogation, "all Hell breaks loose." Sometimes the spotter planes were used as decoys to draw German antiaircraft fire— fire that would reveal the positions of the enemy guns and enable Allied aircraft or artillery to take them out. To fool the spotters, the Germans sometimes resorted to constructing dummy artillery positions. It was all cat and mouse.[33]

Robert E. Dodge (Anti-Tank [AT] Company, 15th Infantry Regiment, 3rd Division) recalled the day he saw an L-4 "jumped by two Messerschmitts; he went right down close to the ground and kept twisting around some buildings. The Jerries came in firing, but one couldn't pull up, and crashed. The other pulled up and left. Later, I heard that the pilot of the Cub painted a plane [silhouette] on his cockpit to show his victory."[34]

"NEED REPLACEMENTS BADLY," LUCAS CRIED to his diary on February 6, "but am told there are none to be had. Where are all the troops we had in the United States? We can't fight this kind of war without men and ammunition, and howitzer ammunition is dangerously short." Lucas was convinced that he was losing the war of attrition. His figures said the VI Corps' losses from all causes were almost 800 per day, and 300 a day could not be replaced. This meant that VI Corps was losing its strength at a monthly rate of 9,000 men—mostly infantry. But he added, "I feel entirely confident of our ability to hold what we have and teach the Hun a lesson if he attacks us."[35]

If the British and Americans were short on men and ammo, they had another ally: intelligence in the form of the Italian resistance group headquartered in Rome. Through their efficient network of spies in the various German headquarters, this group had informed Fifth Army and VI Corps that the Germans were planning another major attack that would be launched early on February 7. Armed with this critical information, Lucas and his staff quickly prepared plans for meeting the attack. On the night of February 6, orders were sent out to all frontline units to be alert for a possible attack the next morning; all signs indicated that the initial attack would be directed against Truscott's 3rd Division, followed by an attempt to take control of Aprilia and Carroceto Station along the vital Albano Highway; Clark arranged for air support to be on call. About this, Lucas wrote, "The dope is that the German will attack us with all his strength at 4:00 AM. I am as ready as I can be. I hope it is enough. I must not lose."[36]

A FRONT-PAGE ARTICLE IN THE *New York Times* on February 6 carried the headline "Allies Give Ground." The reporter painted a gloomy portrait of the situation at Anzio: "The overall picture of the 156-day-old battle of Italy," wrote correspondent Milton Bracker, "is not overly encouraging and it is time to say so." Bracker pointed out that, despite Allied air superiority, the Germans continued to bring in thousands of reinforcements to bolster their defensive ring around the Anzio beachhead. "There was nothing to justify the hope of a swift, smashing junction of the Allies' forces and a triumphant march on the capital."[37]

In the unlikely event that Mark Clark saw Bracker's words, he certainly would not have agreed with them. When he visited the beachhead and the major units of VI Corps that day, he found the situation quiet and reasonably well in hand. About the only weak spot he could find in the Allied line was the boundary line between Penney's 1st British Division and Truscott's 3rd Division. Seams between units—especially those of different nationalities—are almost always hard to defend and relatively easy for an enemy to exploit. To shore up the front line, Clark directed Lucas to tell Eagles to send elements of the 45th Division to the villages of Carano and Padiglione, where they were to prepare defenses.[38]

As Intelligence had predicted, shortly before midnight on February 6, the German assault began with 800 rounds of artillery falling on the positions of Lieutenant Colonel Brown's 2nd Battalion, 157th Infantry Regiment, positioned along the Moletta River line on the Allies' western flank. This was followed by a one-company ground assault. An hour of heavy fighting broke out, but the Thunderbirds managed to hold their line while dealing a costly blow to the Germans.[39]

The next day they and all the other units at Anzio would face an even sterner test.

CHAPTER 9

"Do a Dunkirk while you still have time!"
FEBRUARY 7-8

MONDAY, FEBRUARY 7, BEGAN LIKE every day at Anzio—with a wake-up call in the form of an exchange of artillery, mortars, machine-gun bullets, grenades, and every other piece of weaponry and ordnance the two sides possessed. Bone-chilled men in their water-filled foxholes who had had virtually no sleep the night before were again called upon to battle for their lives against enemies seen and unseen.

Elements of Penney's 1st British Division again found themselves the object of the Germans' lethal intentions. Having been warned of the pending attack, the 1st Battalion, London Irish Rifles, stood by in Aprilia with fixed bayonets, but, apart from attempted infiltration by German patrols between the battalion and the 10th Royal Berks on their right, nothing serious developed. Then shelling increased, and enemy aircraft made several strafing raids over the LIR's positions. Radio reports of increasing concentrations of infantry and tanks in areas off the main road two or three miles to the north indicated that perhaps the Germans were massing to break through the LIR at Aprilia.

Shortly after 5:00 A.M., under cover of smoke, artillery fire, and the predawn darkness, the German 65th Infantry Division hit the 5th Grenadier Guards on the left, the London Irish in the center at Aprilia, and the 10th Royal Berks on the right. Casualties among the 24th Guards Brigade units steadily mounted with each and every infantry probe and with each and every shell that exploded in their midst. The men along the front took everything the Germans could throw at them, but it soon became apparent that it was a losing battle, for, no matter how bravely the men fought, the situation for the 1st British Division was deteriorating.[1]

The men of 2nd Battalion, North Staffs, who had taken much of the brunt of the enemy assault for the past week, were barely holding on to Buonriposo Ridge when the Germans suddenly hit them with artillery, mortars, tank fire, and more infantry assaults. Ivor Jones, the batman to Major John Osbourne, C Company commander, recalled, "Of all the units defending the British sector, the most dangerously positioned was my battalion, the 2nd North Staffs, whose mission it was to protect the left flank of the [1st] Division. . . . If the position fell to the Germans, the entire Allied left flank would have been in danger of collapsing."[2]

As the morning wore on, a renewed effort to weaken the Allies intensified, as German aircraft continued to bomb and strafe Aprilia and all the British units arrayed around it. Also in the area were the 168th Brigade with the 3rd Battalion of the 504th U.S. Parachute Infantry, astride the Albano Highway. The 2nd Brigade held the right flank with a squadron of the 1st Battalion, Recce Regiment, and the 1st Loyals. Penney's division reserve consisted of the whole of the 3rd Brigade.

It became obvious that the Germans were about to make another concerted effort to capture Aprilia and Carroceto, for, without them, access to the Albano Highway would be denied, and the Germans needed the highway in order to enable their tanks to avoid the boggy fields and smash the Allies' final beachhead line of defense. In addition, possession of the two towns would anchor the Germans' strong defensive positions as well as create assembly areas from which to launch further attacks.[3]

UNDER COVER OF SMOKE AND a heavy barrage, the Germans came on, first hitting D Company, 1st LIR, and then B Company. The Royal Berkshires to the right of the LIR, and the Guards to the left, also came under fire. Advancing in waves through the mud, the German infantry concentrated on pounding D Company, LIR, with rifle, machine-gun, mortar, and artillery fire. Before long, panzers rolled up and added their voices to the battle. All day the fight raged, with the Germans refusing to halt their attacks and the men of the London Irish Rifles refusing to be broken. But theirs was not the only battle that day.

Nine miles due east of Aprilia, the Americans were also struggling to hold their ground. Truscott's 3rd Division near Cisterna, for example, was critically understrength, having lost 2,400 men killed, wounded, or missing since the landings. At Littoria, on the far-right flank of the beachhead, the Germans had been using a tall concrete water tower as an observation post to spy on the 3rd Division sector and send artillery fire down upon it, but the Americans had had enough. To "blind" the Germans, the XII Air Support Command sent P-40s and A-36s to attack the water tower and put the observers in it out of business.[4]

As if to pay back the U.S. Air Force for eliminating their observation tower at Littoria, at 8:10 A.M. on February 7, the port of Anzio and neighboring Nettuno were attacked by twenty Focke-Wulf Fw 190s and Messerschmitt 109s.* Some of the bombs landed in Nettuno, blowing up three ammunition trucks, destroying several buildings, and leaving countless soldiers dead or wounded.[5]

The Luftwaffe was far from done. At 11:35 A.M., fifteen Focke-Wulf 190s and Messerschmitt 109s bombed and strafed the harbor area, dodging in and out of the steel cables that held aloft the barrage balloons that were supposed to discourage just such attacks. German bombs and bullets found an LCI and an LCT and damaged them while killing thirty men and wounding forty. In spite of the attacks, the enemy paid a heavy toll for their aerial audacity. On that day, antiaircraft gunners

---

* Most of the German aerial attacks against the beachhead were carried out by Luftwaffe Gruppe II of Kampfgeschwader 40—a unit that had been based at Grosseto until October 1943 before it was moved in January 1944 to the south of France. Night attacks against the beachhead were made by the Nachtschlachtgruppe 9, based at Canino in the province of Viterbo, flying both Italian Fiat warplanes and Junker 86 "Stuka" dive-bombers. Two main attacks—on the nights of February 14–15 and February 16–17—were made north of Anzio and in the direction of Aprilia-Anzio by the Fw 190 and Jagdgeschwader (JG 2) coming from bases in the south of France and a field at Canino near Viterbo, where NSG 9 was also based. Other airfields used by the Germans—and by the Italians from the Repubblica Sociale Italiana—were located at Rieti and Perugia. Silvano Casaldi, email to the author, October 24, 2015.

would shoot down seven enemy planes, get credit for six "probables," and damage nine, while American and British fighter pilots accounted for seventeen shot down with a dozen probables.[6]

One especially nasty weapon in the Luftwaffe's arsenal was the "butterfly bomb"—a large, hollow canister filled with small grenade-size "bomblets." Just before it hit the ground, the canister would break apart, scattering the bomblets over a wide area, each exploding with the force of a 60mm mortar round. Described by some soldiers as sounding like "loud popcorn popping," the weapon was particularly dangerous for troops caught in the open. Soldiers quickly learned the importance of adding overhead protection to the tops of their foxholes, and any scrap lumber to be found was quickly converted into roofs and covered with soil for extra protection.[7]

Robert "Doc Joe" Franklin, a medic with Company I, 157th Infantry Regiment, 45th Infantry Division, recalled the devastation that the small but deadly butterfly bombs could cause:

> I heard a loud explosion and ran to the noise and smoke in the air. Lieutenant Lehman, a so-called "explosives expert," had found a butterfly bomb that hadn't exploded. He apparently had been sitting on the ground with three men around him trying to figure out what was wrong with it, and he must have given the little propeller that armed the thing a couple of turns. When I got there, Lehman had no arms or legs, his head was flat as a pancake, and his brains were in a neat pile about a yard away—as if somebody had scooped them out and laid them there. The men around him were dead, too.[8]

To Robert E. Dodge (Anti-Tank Company, 15th Infantry Regiment, 3rd Division), the aerial attacks sometimes took on all the properties of entertainment. "One evening before dark," he said,

> German bombers flew over on their way to the harbor. They came in waves of six. As they approached the barrage balloons on the horizon, tracers and aerial bursts rose up to meet them. Of the first wave of planes, all went down in flames. Other waves did better, but some still went down. You could hear the explosions and see the flashes. The

Jerries must have hit an ammo dump because there were some tremendous flashes. . . . Once hundreds of our bombers flew over, probably bombing around Rome. Later, as they returned, a group of stragglers came last; they had been hit and were flying together for protection. Suddenly one went into a power dive. Five men bailed out, but their chutes, or the men themselves, were on fire. Soon the chutes collapsed and the men were a trail of smoke as they fell. The plane went into the dirt just over the Jerry lines.[9]

One of the American squadrons helping to defend the skies over Anzio was the 99th Fighter Squadron—the famed African American Tuskegee Airmen, known as the "Red Tails" for the distinctive color painted on the vertical stabilizers of their aircraft. On one day, the 99th, flying obsolescent P-40s, downed eight German aircraft over the beachhead, and their "kills" continued to mount. As one historian has written, "In a two-week period, the 99th had achieved a seven-to-one kill ratio in air combat. . . . For the Tuskegee Airmen, the Anzio campaign represented an important milestone—they were no longer apprentice pilots, but seasoned combatants in the air war in Europe."[10]

Additionally, another black fighter group, the 332nd, of the Twelfth Air Force, stationed at Ramitelli Air Field and flying P-39 Airacobras, was assigned to harbor patrol and convoy duty in order to keep the Luftwaffe from attacking ships coming into Anzio's port.[11] So well did the black fliers perform that General Hap Arnold, commanding general of the U.S. Army Air Forces, sent a message of congratulations to Lieutenant General Ira Eaker, commander of the Mediterranean Air Forces, commending the "Negro pilots who downed twelve German planes during the first week of the invasion. . . . My best wishes for their continued success."[12]

ON THE AFTERNOON OF THE seventh, more Luftwaffe raiders arrived, bombing and shooting up Anzio harbor despite the best efforts of anti-aircraft batteries to keep them away. This time, while trying to escape a British Spitfire hot on his tail, a German pilot jettisoned his bombs in order to facilitate his escape back to friendly lines. He apparently did not see the field of tents below marked with red crosses. The bombs splattered in the hospital area of the 95th Evacuation Hospital, next door to the 56th, the fragments shredding the administration and operating tents, killing twenty-eight and wounding sixty-eight others—doctors, nurses, orderlies, and patients.[13]

Chief Nurse First Lieutenant Blanche F. Sigman and two other nurses were administering blood plasma to a patient when the bombs hit, killing all three.* In one of the operating tents a litter bearer, carrying a patient, died when he threw himself over the wounded soldier in an attempt to protect him.[14]

An exhausted Lieutenant Avis Dagit (56th Evac Hospital) had been asleep in her tent after spending countless hours in the operating and recovery wards when she dreamed that airplanes were overhead and guns were firing. Then a fellow nurse burst into her tent and exclaimed, "Thank God, Avis! You're all right!"

"What was all that noise? I could hardly sleep."

"It's so terrible," the other nurse said. "The 95th was bombed. We don't know how many are killed. We're working on the wounded, and surgery is swamped."

"'Was anyone we know killed?' I asked, afraid to hear her answer.

"The chief nurse and a Red Cross worker were killed instantly. Most of the patients in the post-op ward were killed. Your friend Gertrude is critically wounded. The doctors don't think she'll survive. She's in surgery now."

Dagit's friend—twenty-six-year-old Marjorie Gertrude Morrow, from Algona, Iowa—did not survive. Dagit, who had been sleeping a mere 150 yards from where the bombs fell, felt crushed by an enormous weight of sadness and futility and anger—anger at Hitler, the Germans, and the whole damned war. But there was little time for emotions; Avis got dressed and went back to caring for the grievously wounded soldiers.

The next day, the Germans shelled Avis's 56th Evac Hospital, along with the 33rd. Two of the 33rd's nurses—Lieutenants Gertrude Spelboug

---

* Besides Lieutenant Sigman of East Akron, Ohio, the other caregivers killed were First Lieutenant Carrie T. Sheetz, Second Lieutenant Marjorie Gertrude Morrow, and Red Cross worker Esther Richards. Mary T. Sarnecky, *A History of the US Army Nurse Corps*, 226.

and LaVerne Farquar—also lost their lives.[15] A few days later, nurse Lieutenant Ellen Ainsworth was on duty at the 56th Evac when German shells again began dropping among the canvas tents. She was in the process of moving some of the patients to safety when a shell exploded just yards away, throwing a steel splinter through her chest; she died six days later. The twenty-four-year-old was one of the first four women to receive the Silver Star (posthumously) for their bravery.* She is buried in the Sicily-Rome American Cemetery in Nettuno.[16]

Private first class Darrell Harris (509th Parachute Infantry Battalion) was temporarily assigned to be a part of a graves-registration detail. Although picking up corpses from the battlefield was an unspeakably horrible experience, nothing quite prepared him for one particular scene: "It was at Anzio that I saw my first American woman killed by enemy fire. A nurse at the beachhead hospital had been killed by an artillery shell. I think the sight of this one young woman lying there dead devastated me more than all the other dead bodies I had seen."[17]

Private James Aurness of the 3rd Division, who had been recovering from his leg wounds at the 95th before the attack, recalled:

> The tent was packed with patients. Their wounds ranged from injuries like mine to some terrible ones. The guy next to me had been shot in the abdominal area and died that same night. The nurses were truly angelic. They did a tremendous job with our troops. I don't know how they did it. It must have been a traumatic thing to live day after day caring for guys who were filthy, caked with mud and blood, and suffering from horrendous wounds.
>
> I remember one [nurse] in particular, from Minneapolis. She was the first American woman I'd seen in months, and it was like talking to my mother. We talked a lot about home, and she was a great comfort to me.

---

* The others were Elaine Roe, Mary Roberts, and Virginia Rourke. The Wisconsin Veterans Home in King, Wisconsin, and the American Legion post in Ainsworth's hometown of Glenwood City, Wisconsin, are dedicated to their memory. Kathi Jackson, *They Called Them Angels: American Military Nurses of World War II*, 59.

After he was transported back to the States,* Aurness heard about the bombing of the 95th Evac Hospital and wondered if the nurse who had treated him so kindly was among those killed. He would never know.[18]

NOT ONLY WERE THE HOSPITALS on the beach a shambles, but Aprilia was again about to become the scene of pitiless combat. It began strangely. The British picked up a handful of prisoners who gave themselves up willingly because they said they realized Germany could not win the war and decided they did not want to die for their Führer. Under interrogation, the POWs said that their commanders were preparing for another all-out attack to push the enemy out of Aprilia and Carroceto—and all the way back into the sea.[19]

The 1st British Division's front lines were also a mess, and Penney had a juggling act to perform. A gap had developed between the 1st Loyals and the 10th Royal Berks, so a company from the 6th Gordons was sent up to plug it. Aided by three tanks, a local counterattack then drove back the enemy unit that had captured a bridge on the Lateral Road east of Aprilia. But the Germans did enjoy some successes. Combat Group Gräser maintained a position on the right flank near the crossroads, while Pfeiffer's men continued to put pressure on the fragile British positions. A melee of hand-to-hand fighting took place all across Buonriposo Ridge, and the 2nd North Staffs were forced to give ground or be overrun; the battalion, which had begun the day before with forty officers and 664 men, had been reduced in short order to seventeen officers and 364 other ranks.[20]

EVERYONE WAS ON EDGE. ACCORDING to James Safrit (Company F, 179th Infantry Regiment, 45th Division), his unit had been sending out patrols

---

*After recuperating for eighteen months in army hospitals back in the United States, and after the war was over, Aurness gravitated to Hollywood and, despite a lack of training as an actor, was cast in bit parts in dozens of films, including *Battleground* (1949) and as the monster in *The Thing from Another World* (1951). Aurness dropped the *u* from his last name and became James Arness, one of Hollywood's leading actors, most famous for playing the role of Sheriff Matt Dillon in the long-running American television series *Gunsmoke*. James Arness with James E. Wise Jr., *James Arness: An Autobiography*.

every night: "The enemy were very alert to our patrols, and only a few times were we able to return from one without losing men. One of those combat patrols stands out in my mind. There were eighteen or twenty of us who were sent out to determine just how strong an enemy position was, and to pick up prisoners, if possible, for questioning."

Safrit said that the terrain over which they had to cross

was as flat as a pool table and we had to crawl most of the way on our bellies. After what seemed like a very long time, we heard the sound of digging and we saw a large group of figures moving around. We opened fire on them. Some of them returned the fire, but our surprise attack caused a lot of confusion among them and they took off. We moved into their positions and I suddenly stumbled into a foxhole, right on top of a "squarehead" sergeant who was huddled face down like an os- trich. Frankly, it scared me as much as it did him. He started yelling, "*Kamerad! Kamerad!*" I stuck the barrel of my rifle in his ear, and he climbed out very meekly, with his hands on his head.

By this time, the German lines opened up all along the front, so we regrouped and started back the way we had come. The prisoner began to scream, "*Nein! Nein!*" so one of our guys who spoke German asked him what the hell was wrong. He answered that we had crawled through one of their minefields. That was what they were doing when we opened fire on them—they were a mine-laying detail. How fifteen GIs (we had dropped off four or five on the way up to act as a listening post to guard our return route so the Germans wouldn't cut us off) could have crawled through those mines without setting off at least one will always be a mystery to me. Only the "Good Guy Upstairs" could have guided us through without mishap. Believe me, we were thankful.

Just as Safrit expected, the enemy tried to swing around and cut them off,

but our listening post prevented them from doing so. All in all, we were lucky. We lost one man; a burst of machine-pistol slugs killed him. Two others were wounded, none of them seriously. We brought all of them back with us. We had no stretchers, so we carried them on our backs, and with a two-man hand carry, the dead GI, too. The manner that we used to carry the dead soldier—two of us held hands and the corpse sat on our hands. To keep the body upright, so that he would not fall off, we were forced to lay his arms around our necks. His head hung limply forward on his chest. After a while, his arms became stiff and rigid. We took turns carrying him. It was an ordeal I'll never forget.[21]

WHILE THE GERMANS WERE FURIOUSLY trying to eliminate the British hold on Aprilia, they did not ignore the American presence. Jack Hallowell (157th Infantry Regiment, 45th Division) noted that there had been little to indicate that February 7 would be anything other than an ordinary combat day: "3rd Battalion was on the right and in contact with the [2nd Battalion of the] British North Staffordshire Regiment while, on the left, 2nd Battalion troops guarded the coastal road. Between lay a 1,000-yard gap but it was heavily wooded and the few men defending it furnished adequate protection against a breakthrough."

At 9:00 P.M. on February 7, following a firestorm of artillery and mortar barrages, Companies I and L of Major John Boyd's 3rd Battalion, 157th, along with the adjacent 2nd North Staffs, were hit by an infantry and panzer attack. While Company I was fighting off minor probes, the enemy slammed his main thrust between Company L and the left-flank unit of the North Staffs. In a moonlit firefight that lasted over two hours, 3rd Battalion managed to hold its ground but took heavy casualties, one of whom was Boyd himself, killed while making his way forward to the Company K observation post. Boyd's place was taken by the battalion's executive officer, Captain Merle M. Mitchell, who began shifting the companies in preparation for further attacks sure to come.[22]

Hard fighting had also taken place on the seventh in the 3rd Division's sector near Cisterna. Company E, 15th Infantry, attacked north up a road that ran parallel to Femmina Morta ("Dead Woman") Creek, with the objective of capturing a farm east of Ponte Rotto. Meanwhile, Company F, 30th Infantry, attacked from the west to secure the road junction just beyond the Ponte Rotto bridge. Both attacks achieved limited results. That night, panzers and infantry pushed down the road from Cisterna toward Isola Bella. Tank fire destroyed some buildings in which Company G, 15th Infantry, had organized positions; after losing some ground, the company fought its way back before daylight. A second German company-strength attack, supported by tanks, struck Company G, 30th Infantry, but was beaten back.[23]

Late on the frigid evening of February 7, the skies above the German positions to the north of Aprilia and Carroceto lit up as though from a lightning storm, and, seconds later, artillery shells screamed into the two ruined towns. As soon as the shelling stopped, elements of the 65th Infantry Division charged into the 24th Guards Brigade's left flank, spread out on Buonriposo Ridge. The fighting in many places was hand to hand. In the darkness, some Guards units, out of radio contact with higher headquarters, were pushed back to the secondary lines of defense being manned by the 1st Irish Guards and the 3rd Battalion of the 504th U.S. Parachute Regiment. At one point, it seemed as though the Germans were a swarm of army ants making a mad rush over the slopes of Buonriposo Ridge, acting as though death were a minor inconvenience, driving straight for Carroceto and Aprilia, with nothing but Major William Philip Sidney's Support Company of the 5th Grenadier Guards, positioned in a wadi located southwest of Carroceto, standing in their path.[24]

One of Major Sidney's men was an enlisted soldier in the Pioneer Platoon named Sydney Arthur Wright. Wright recalled that he and half the Pioneer Platoon were detailed to go out into no-man's-land to lay antitank mines. The next night, however, the platoon had to go back out and remove the mines so as not to interfere with an order to attack. Before the attack could get under way, the Germans hit them first. The platoon officer was wounded, and the unit became leaderless, at least for the moment. A sergeant named Armstrong took command and ordered the men to begin digging trenches around the perimeter of the wadi. Suddenly, German infantry that had skirted the Guards' forward rifle company northwest of Carroceto began pouring into the wadi.

Collecting the crew of a 3-inch mortar that was firing nearby, Major Sidney personally led a counterattack with Tommy guns and hand grenades, driving the enemy out of the wadi. He then sent the detachment back to continue firing their mortar while he and a handful of men took up a position on the edge of the wadi in order to again stop the enemy, who were renewing their attack in some strength. Sidney and his party succeeded in keeping the majority of the Germans out, but a number reached a ditch 20 yards in front from which they could outflank Sidney's position.

Seeing the Germans trying to maneuver around him, Sidney continued spraying them with his Tommy gun until it jammed. Standing at the edge of an earthen ramp that led down into the gully, he then began throwing Mills bombs* at any Germans who showed themselves. The major then yelled at Wright to bring up a case of the grenades, which Wright quickly retrieved and handed over. Sidney went back and began tossing grenades at the approaching enemy, knowing that he was the last bulwark against the Germans overrunning the Guards' position. When that supply was exhausted, he ordered more; twice Wright went back to fetch more.

As Wright returned with another case of grenades, he said that three Germans suddenly appeared on the lip of the gully—two with rifles and one with a stick grenade. Wright quickly brought his rifle up and fired from the hip, hitting the man with the grenade in the stomach. "He doubled up and fell backwards," said Wright. "As he did so, he dropped the grenade into the gully about eight feet from me. I saw it explode in the mud." The explosion killed one enlisted man and wounded Major Sidney.

At this point, the rest of the company returned with ammunition and chased off the enemy soldiers. Wright and another soldier carried the wounded major about 250 yards to a first-aid post in a cave. Along the way, British 25-pounders started lobbing in smoke shells to cover their escape. "When one landed too near for my liking, I flinched," said Wright. "Major Sidney said, 'Don't worry—they're our shells.'" Wright replied, "Yes, but do the bloody shells know that?"

Realizing that he had dropped his rifle, Wright went back to find it. A figure suddenly dropped down on him. Unarmed, Wright was about to surrender when a voice asked if he had any cigarettes—the voice

---

*The Mills bomb was the British fragmentation grenade that weighed nearly two pounds and was first manufactured in 1915 by the Mills Munition Factory in Birmingham, England. It looked like a plumper version of the American Mark II fragmentation grenade, which weighed one pound, five ounces. Quick, *Dictionary of Weapons and Military Terms*, 305–306.

belonged to an American! In the darkness he had looked like a German. Wright was so relieved that he gave him every cigarette he had.

Before Major Sidney could have his wounds dressed, the Germans struck again, so he staggered back to his unit and, for an hour, helped to hold off the enemy's attacks. Only after the situation was stabilized did Sidney allow himself to be treated. The next day, however, the Germans renewed their attacks on the Guardsmen's positions, and Sidney, although bandaged, bloody, and weak, coolly rallied his men to fight off the fanatical Germans until they gave up their efforts to take the wadi. Because he had demonstrated such "superb courage and utter disregard of danger," Major Sidney was awarded the Victoria Cross, Britain's highest military medal for valor.*

Wright and members of his unit withdrew south to the Flyover and then were pulled back even farther—perhaps a couple of miles to a farmhouse—in order to regroup. Someone saw movement—a person entering the farmhouse. An officer took Wright and a few other men to investigate. They broke down the door only to find the poor old farmer and his wife, terrified at the intrusion. Wright's party apologized and prepared to leave when Wright said that in another room was the farmer's daughter, who had just been visited by her German boyfriend. "He had escaped through the back door. Poor lad, he must have been really in love to come through No-Man's Land and back again. At least it proved that some of the enemy were human."[25]

THE 5TH GRENADIER GUARDS HAD been hard hit during the engagement. David Large, son of Guardsman John R. "Jack" Large, told his father's story:

> My father was captured at Anzio. He was one of 30 survivors of approximately 300 Grenadiers who were killed in the landings. . . . The Germans put them in railway wagons to ship them to Germany. My father, with another Guardsman, broke up the wagon floor in the snow-covered pass

---

* The Lord de L'Isle and Dudley, as Sidney would later be known, served in both houses of Parliament and went on to become the last non-Australian governor of Australia. *London Gazette*, May 12, 1961.

on route and escaped. They were recaptured and beaten, then sent to a [punishment camp] near Altengrabow. The name Gross Scheirstadt rings a bell. He lived in awful conditions then as a slave labourer, seeing others shot and murdered for the least thing. He was put working with two elderly German electricians who, risking death, brought him in a little food each day. . . . He then ended up in hospital with psychoneurosis. My mother often said he came back another person; mentally they killed him.[26]

ON THE NIGHT OF FEBRUARY 7, Lieutenant Richard Evans, the 1st KSLI's adjutant, recalled having a captured German officer shout at him as he was being led away: "Do a Dunkirk while you still have time!" But running away was not an option. At dusk on the following day, two rifle companies of the battalion were pinned down by machine-gun fire, and most of their officers had been either killed or wounded. Evans was sent forward in darkness and pouring rain with orders to contact them. Their exact location was not known, so Evans's mission could have been disastrous. As luck would have it, however, he found them, reorganized their defenses, and made them ready to beat off a German attack the next morning. His citation for the award of a Military Cross paid tribute to Evans's "courage, cheerfulness and determination during fifteen days of bitter fighting."[27]

Ivor Jones, batman for Major John Osbourne, commanding C Company, 2nd North Staffs, said that one of the worst attacks came that night, "when the Germans came over our positions with at least two battalions. They attacked in hordes, fanatically yelling on the ridge, with tanks and self-propelled guns pouring shells into the company area. Two of our three companies were almost surrounded and the battle became a confused pattern of fierce individual hand-to-hand struggles among the slit trenches on the scrub-covered hilltop." Jones said that the battalion suffered 50 percent casualties and that his company became "completely surrounded and eventually ceased to exist" when German infantrymen overran their positions.[28]

As the hours went by, the Germans chipped away at the North Staffs like a sculptor chipping away at a marble block until the stone had been reduced to a fraction of its previous form. With casualties heavy, and his stocks of ammunition nearly exhausted, the North Staffs' 2nd Battalion commanding officer, Lieutenant Colonel A. J. Snodgrass,* had no option but to request permission to retire from the ridge; the 24th Guards Brigade commander reluctantly approved the request, and the ridge was soon in enemy hands.[29]

STAGING A NIGHT ATTACK ACROSS rough and muddy ground is no easy feat, but the Germans were becoming masters at it. By nightfall on the seventh, the situation of Lieutenant Colonel Rupert Good's 1st Battalion, London Irish Rifles, already precarious, was about to become even more so. Arrayed in and around Aprilia, the Germans continued to put British positions under fire and ground attack. Major P. McMahon Mahon's D Company, 1st LIR, still held the town but had been cut off from contact with units on either side of it. Lucas and Penney knew the strategic value of Aprilia—that it controlled the Albano Highway, the only hard-surface north-south road in the area. It was, therefore, imperative that the London Irish Rifles do everything in their power to parry such a thrust until the rest of VI Corps, along with naval and aerial assets, could destroy it.

The ominous rumble and squeak of tanks was heard as the Germans sent a platoon of panzers against the positions of Mahon's D Company. The unit had lost contact with the Guards on their left flank during the day, and, now that darkness had descended, patrols that had been sent out to find them came back with no word on their whereabouts. What was discovered, however, was that the Germans had managed to nearly completely encircle D Company, which had become a salient of its own. Additionally, enemy machine guns had been set up in the town cemetery opposite B Company and were firing on the eastern flank of D Company. Mahon requested permission to try to break out of the encirclement and

* According to Fred Mason of the 2nd North Staffs, Snodgrass "was a strict officer. The only time I saw him was back at B Echelon about the 9th February, when he stood on the bonnet of a jeep and announced that any man running from the enemy would be shot by his officers. He meant it!" Fred Mason, email to the author, November 28, 2015.

fall back to straighten the line between A and B Companies, but this request was denied; the order to all units on the beachhead was that no ground should be given up voluntarily. With their only option to "stand and fight," that is what D Company resolved to do.

Mahon's men were positioned about a half mile north of Aprilia, while Major Jack Cantopher's A Company was located to the west of the town and Captain D. A. Hardy's B Company on the eastern fringe, near the town cemetery and guarding a bridge over the Fosso della Ficoccia. C Company was situated south of town, in battalion reserve, ready to assist the other three companies. Four antitank guns were placed to defend B and D Companies from attack, and mortars and machine guns were also sited to provide covering fire.

Colonel Good and his headquarters staff occupied the lower floor of a house on the southern edge of Aprilia, while Captain Alan Mace and his intelligence section held an observation post in the upper story of the house. The Germans did not immediately suspect that the house was being used by the British, but they could not have been blind to the possibility, either. The exterior stairs leading from the ground to the upper floor, therefore, could not be used during daylight, so communications between the two floors were maintained by telephone. That evening, the German noose tightened around Major Mahon's company; Colonel Good requested that the company be withdrawn from its salient, but higher headquarters once again said no. The LIR still controlled Aprilia, the Albano Highway leading north, and the Lateral Road, which the British had dubbed "Wigan Street," to the east, but no one knew how long that situation would last.

While the efforts to destroy D Company, LIR, were taking place, two companies of Combat Group Gräser attacked C Squadron, 1st Battalion, as well as the Recce Regiment and the right-flank company of the 10th Battalion, Royal Berkshire Regiment, near the intersection where the Lateral Road from Aprilia meets the road to Carano. The Germans' tactics were simple: in the dark, small groups would slip behind the forward British units, cut their communications wire, and then open fire. After the defenders had depleted their ammunition on these stealth targets, the main body of German troops would suddenly emerge and overrun

British positions. But the German attacks were not well coordinated, and, as a result, the British were able to hold the enemy off—for the moment.

Now it became the turn of Captain D. A. Hardy's B Company, LIR, to receive the full force of the attackers—two German battalions, supported by panzers—that penetrated into the heart of Aprilia; Hardy went down with a serious wound. With B Company's complement of officers depleted, Good ordered Lieutenant Richard M. Haigh, second in command of C Company, to take charge of Hardy's men. It was none too soon. Disregarding his own safety, Haigh moved about the B Company area to reorganize the defense and steady the men. Haigh was then wounded in the arm, but he shrugged it off, knowing that the fate of the company, and perhaps the outcome of the battle, rested on his leadership. Haigh learned that the Germans had taken over part of the group of buildings occupied by B Company's headquarters. Without hesitation, he personally led an assault on the enemy in the buildings, firing a PIAT (projector, infantry, antitank) during the fight in which he was again hit but continued to command the company and direct the battle until the Germans were driven out. For his actions, Haigh was awarded the Military Cross.

Colonel Good, seeing that the town was in imminent danger of being lost, shifted Cantopher's A Company from the left flank to reinforce B Company and counterattack the Germans who were pouring into B Company's sector. But A Company's counterattack ran headlong into the German thrust, and it took considerable effort to secure a line along an irrigation ditch a little to the south of the position from which B Company had been expelled. The ability of the London Irish Rifles to hold on to Aprilia was suddenly in grave doubt.

KESSELRING AND MACKENSEN WERE INCREDULOUS at the 1st British Division's refusal to wilt under the constant pressure and launched phase two of their major counteroffensive designed to reclaim Aprilia. At 9:00 P.M. on the seventh, the German ground assault was preceded by a thunderous artillery barrage in order to soften up British positions and deny the defenders any rest. Fifteen minutes later, the fires lifted, and the 2nd Battalion of the North Staffs began reporting that their positions were being rapidly and stealthily infiltrated by small groups of enemy soldiers.

At 10:00 P.M., wireless and telephone communication between company and battalion went dead, a "rescue party" of Sherman tanks* tried but failed to break through to D Company, 1st LIR, and by dawn on the eighth, having heard nothing from D Company for hours, it was assumed that all had been killed or captured.[30]

Despite many displays of courage, the LIR's occupancy of Aprilia was soon at an end. Infiltrating into the ruins of the town that night were members of the 29th Panzer-Grenadier Regiment of the 3rd Panzer-Grenadier Division. Gun battles erupted at close quarters, with every shattered building turned into a stout bunker. Individual life-and-death struggles went on in the dark, but the British were losing their grip on Aprilia.

At the same time, the 3rd Battalion, 157th Infantry Regiment, which was maintaining contact with the 24th Guards Brigade along the Buonriposo Ridge, radioed regimental headquarters that it, too, was under attack by infantry and tanks. The word *ridge* suggests a geographical feature of impressive proportions, perhaps even a portion of a towering landscape. Buonriposo Ridge, a few hundred yards southwest of Aprilia, west of where the "Bowling Alley" crosses the Albano Highway, was nothing of the sort. But in the unrelieved flatness east of the road, anything higher than a pile of cow dung could be considered a position of high ground worthy of taking by force and holding to the end. Such was the case with Buonriposo Ridge.[31]

Night drew a black curtain over the smoldering battlefield. As difficult as February 7 had been for the British, the following day would be an even greater challenge. And the Americans would be in the thick of it, too.

---

* These "Shermans" may actually have been three tank destroyers of the 894th Tank Destroyer Battalion. The platoon leader, First Lieutenant Bernard T. Schaefer, moved his machine so that he could fire on a building that the enemy had occupied. He blew the building apart with his 3-inch gun, and when the Germans came streaming out, he killed forty with his .50-caliber machine gun; another thirty surrendered. For his actions, Schaefer was awarded the Distinguished Service Cross. John Bowditch, ed., *Anzio Beachhead*, 57.

CHAPTER 10

"What a sight a mortar barrage is"

FEBRUARY 8-9

A NEW DAY CLAWED ITS WAY out of the blackness of night, yet the events of the previous night could not be shaken off as just a bad dream. As soon as the sky had begun to turn light on the eighth, Mackensen's brutally simple plan of attack—a one-two punch against the salient—resumed. After another intense preliminary artillery bombardment that wrecked dugouts, observation posts, and foxholes of the forward positions of C Squadron, 1st Battalion, Recce Regiment, and a platoon of the 6th Gordons, Pfeiffer's* 65th Infantry Division struck from the west while Combat Group Gräser simultaneously hit from the east, with Aprilia and Carroceto, invested by elements of the 1st British Division, caught in the middle.

The 1st London Irish Rifles were feeling the pressure but denying the enemy use of the Albano Highway and the approaches into Aprilia offered by the Lateral Road. Laying down lavish quantities of accurate mortar fire, the battalion's mortar section broke up attack after attack. As long as the London Irish's supply of mortar bombs held out, the Germans would not be able to occupy Aprilia.[1]

---

* Pfeiffer, who had been wounded during the battle of Kursk on August 3, 1943, would be killed in action in April 1945 north of Bologna, Italy. www.lexikon -der-wehrmacht.de/Personenregister/P/PfeiferH.htm.

But no sooner had the Germans' artillery barrage lifted than a battalion of the 104th Panzer-Grenadier Regiment, which had been brought up from the Cassino front, supported by tanks, rolled forward and overran the recce squadron and the Gordons, splitting the 10th Royal Berks and the 1st Loyals that were dug in on either side of the Albano Highway. It was a battle that would last all day. The Germans were determined to push all the way to the Lateral Road if they could, but Davidson's 168th Brigade was not about to let that happen. The irresistible force had met the immovable object.[2]

At 6:45 A.M., a group of German paratroopers had leaped not from a plane but into a gully 50 yards from the positions of Lieutenant Richard Haigh's B Company, 1st LIR, at the edge of Aprilia and began blazing away with a machine gun, forcing the company to pull back. Just as it seemed that the B Company command post was about to be overrun, Haigh radioed Good's headquarters with a farewell message: "I am doing all I can, but it looks as if this is our last fight." Immediately after he transmitted that message, Major W. E. Brooks fired a Bren gun from the upper story of a nearby house, putting the enemy gun out of action. Shortly thereafter, Captain Ray Mullins and a small party of men from A Company burst upon the scene and began flinging grenades at the enemy; thirty-three Germans were taken prisoner, but Mullins was wounded during the skirmish. The counterattack regained B Company's lost positions. Saved by the timely arrival of Mullins and his men, Haigh radioed Good: "I must apologise for my earlier despondency."

THE 168TH BRIGADE'S STAND AGAINST the enemy's attempts to take Aprilia on February 7 and 8 had been truly heroic.[3] But no matter how stubborn the 168th was or how determined the men were to hold their line, the Germans were that and more; they refused to give up their incessant attacks, throwing artillery and mortar rounds and their bodies at the Brits, probing Allied lines with patrols and small-scale attacks, feinting with panzers, and mounting aerial assaults by the Luftwaffe. It seemed that the stubbornness of the British and American defenses in and around Aprilia only enraged the Germans more and spurred them on to a greater resolve to "lance the abscess" that the Allies at Anzio had become.[4]

The German attackers were determined to continue to wipe out the frontline British units. The 5th Grenadier Guards, just north of Carroceto, were hit, along with the 1st London Irish at Aprilia and the 10th Berkshires to their right. At first, the attacks were made by infantry only at intervals throughout the day, the enemy probing and testing various points in turn and achieving little, as the defenders fought them off with rifles, bayonets, grenades, and automatic weapons. Once night fell, the attacks intensified, with small penetrations into Aprilia being made. At one point, a Corporal Matthews drove a supply truck loaded with much-needed food and ammunition for Company A, 1st LIR, into Aprilia. Seeing a sentry standing by a house in the dim light, he stopped to ask directions, only to discover the "sentry" was a fully armed German! Without hesitation, the unarmed Matthews punched the German and knocked him down; another British soldier with Matthews dispatched him with a pistol shot.[5]

THE GERMANS WERE ALSO TESTING the seam between the 2nd North Staffs and Company L, 3rd Battalion, 157th Regiment, just west of Carroceto. Out of the morning gloom, panzers appeared and plunged deeply into the North Staffs' positions, reducing the battalion's numbers to just seventy officers and enlisted men; the battalion quickly ran out of ammunition and requested permission to attach itself to Company L, which was fighting on their left flank. But the Yanks, having just absorbed a tremendous artillery barrage, were not in much better condition.[6] "We were right in front of a dairy," recalled Sergeant Glen Hanson (Company L, 157th). "The dairy farm had a reinforced battalion of Germans headquartered there and they tried to split our front with tanks and artillery."[7]

The Germans' thrust did indeed split the seam between the two units, raking Company L with tank and small-arms fire from the right rear. Now was the 157th's turn to hang on by its collective fingernails. Colonel Walter P. O'Brien, the 157th's commander, saw that his right flank, being held by the 3rd Battalion, was in great danger of collapsing due to the increasing weight of enemy fire and ordered Captain Merle Mitchell, now in temporary command of the battalion, to withdraw to a stream running along the southern boundary of the Buonriposo Ridge;

a company of the 179th Infantry was sent up to support it.[8] Mitchell pulled Company L back to the more defensible stream and bent the battalion's right flank to the southeast to better counter the German attack. But, somehow, when the 3rd Battalion pulled back, sixty men of the 2nd North Staffs, who had attached themselves to the Yanks, failed to follow and were soon taken prisoner.[9]

THROUGHOUT FEBRUARY 8, THE GERMANS continued to pound the Allied lines in and around Aprilia, trying to dislodge the Yanks and Tommies, but the Allies were giving as good as they got. In fact, during just a two-and-a-half-hour span that day, supporting artillery batteries fired 24,000 shells of all caliber, and, during that same period, the 3rd Battalion of the 157th went through an entire three days' allocation of machine-gun ammunition. Further, the battalion's mortar crews expended 5,600 60mm and 3,600 81mm rounds.[10]

It seemed impossible that anyone could live through such a saturation of exploding steel and flying lead. Private Harold Lundquist (601st Tank Destroyer Battalion) described the scene: "What a sight a mortar barrage is. It's really something to see if you're not the receiver, and the machine-gun battles were fierce. Tracers were flying everywhere and explosions were rocking the ground all about as orange flame blossomed out under each shell."[11]

Despite the incessant shelling and heavy casualties, the Germans refused to give up their efforts to retake Aprilia and Carroceto Station—two towns that were essential to Kesselring's goal of defeating the invaders. Written records are yet to be found that describe how the German leaders were able to motivate their men to leave their places of cover and relative safety and head toward the Allied lines or how the men felt about being ordered to commit certain suicide on foot. But somehow— whether because of superb discipline, inspiring speeches, or the effects of alcohol and drugs—it happened.[12]

General Penney was decidedly worried, but he fervently hoped that his line could hold. To shore up his left flank, he directed Lieutenant Colonel Leslie G. Freeman's 3rd Battalion, 504th U.S. Parachute Infantry Regiment, which was under his temporary command, to move from its position just north of the Overpass/Flyover to south of Carroceto, where it could be used, if necessary, as a counterattack force in support of the 24th Guards Brigade. The 1st Scots Guards, meanwhile, were ordered to move back to the 504th's former positions.

Pfeiffer's 65th Division continued its southeasterly assault against the Buonriposo Ridge, finally taking it after losing hundreds of men. Other German units managed to penetrate across the Albano Highway and had almost reached Carroceto and Aprilia before they were wiped out by stiffening American and British resistance. The Allied air forces also hit back at the two huge railroad guns that continued to harass the troops, but the guns, safely ensconced in their tunnels in the Alban Hills, were impervious to air attacks. German warplanes, too, were active over the crowded beachhead, bombing and strafing the ships in the harbor, the docks themselves, ammunition dumps, hospitals, and wherever a concentration of soldiers could be spotted.

AT 2:00 P.M. ON THE eighth, Penney threw his divisional reserve, Brigadier J. R. James's exhausted and decimated 3rd Brigade—which was hardly in a condition to be combat effective—into the fray to regain the positions that the 2nd North Staffs had been forced to relinquish on Buonriposo Ridge. For their counterattack, the 3rd Brigade employed two battalions: the 2nd Sherwood Foresters and the 1st Battalion of the King's Shropshire Light Infantry Regiment attacking abreast, with armored support provided by a squadron of the 46th Royal Tanks and a platoon from Company C, 894th U.S. Tank Destroyer Battalion. The 2nd Foresters made good initial progress in clearing the lower end of the ridge, but the 1st KSLI ran into fearsome machine-gun fire on the upper end and was stopped cold. The Germans were well dug in and eventually repulsed the attacks by both battalions, inflicting heavy casualties on the Brits.

The 104th Panzer-Grenadier Regiment was now consolidating its control of Buonriposo Ridge, leaving Penney a few moments to reorganize his forces. With the 1st KSLI and the 2nd Foresters clinging to the left flank, Penney ordered Brigadier Eric E. J. Moore's 2nd Brigade to temporarily transfer the 6th Gordons to the 3rd Brigade to help fill a dangerous gap that had opened between the 10th Royal Berks and the 1st Loyals. To strengthen the 6th Gordons, which was now down to two companies following the costly battle for the Campoleone salient, the

238th Field Company, Royal Engineers, and an ad hoc company made up from 3rd Beach Group personnel were added. The 1st Battalion, 180th Regiment, 45th Infantry Division, was moved to near Padiglione, where it could be employed either as a reserve or as a counterattack force.

While Lucas and Penney were working feverishly to stabilize the front line west of Aprilia, Lieutenant Colonel Leslie Freeman began rushing his 3rd Battalion, 504th PIR, into position to counterattack west of the Overpass/Flyover and relieve pressure on the 5th Grenadier Guards. The paratroopers' counterattacks retook a portion of the lost ground; more important, they bolstered the hard-pressed 24th Guards Brigade and gave the British hope that perhaps the German onslaught could be stopped.[13]

TWENTY-THREE-YEAR-OLD CORPORAL PAUL BERT HUFF of the 509th PIB was leading a six-man reconnaissance patrol into no-man's-land near Carano, about four miles east of Aprilia, to locate a German unit that was threatening the exposed right flank of his company. As Huff and his men were advancing across open terrain, a German machine gun opened up on them and sent the men to ground. The mortar rounds then began exploding in their midst; several of Huff's men were hit. He could have done the prudent thing and pulled his patrol back, but he had been given orders and was determined to carry them out. Leaving men behind to take care of the casualties, Huff crawled alone into the mud, drawing fire from not one but three machine-gun nests, plus an Oerlikon 20mm cannon. To add to his difficulties, he discovered that he was also crawling through a field loaded with mines.

Realizing that trying to withdraw would expose himself to even more danger, he continued on until he got close enough to the first nest to be able to kill the crew with a burst from his Thompson sub-machine gun— all the while being fired upon by the other German positions. Having determined the size and location of the enemy's positions, he managed to crawl back to where the rest of his patrol was sheltering and led them back to their own lines. With the information Huff provided, American artillery shelled the Germans, killing twenty-seven and routing the rest of the company.

The Tennesseean's heroics were one reason his unit performed so well at Carano that it was awarded the Presidential Unit Citation and why he would receive the Medal of Honor—the first American paratrooper of World War II to earn the award. His citation reads, in part, "For conspicuous gallantry and intrepidity at risk of life above and beyond the call of duty . . . Corporal Huff's intrepid leadership and daring combat skill reflect the finest traditions of the American infantryman."[14]

Not to diminish in any way acts of bravery such as exhibited by men such as Corporal Huff, but thousands of British and Americans deserved Victoria Crosses and Medals of Honor (and, for that matter, the Ritterskreuz for the German soldiers). But acts of valor at Anzio were so plentiful that it would have been impossible to recognize each and every deserving soldier. Of the 1945 battle on the Pacific island of Iwo Jima, U.S. Admiral Chester Nimitz said, "Among the men who fought on Iwo Jima, uncommon valor was a common virtue."[15] Substitute *Anzio* for *Iwo Jima*, and one has a fitting tribute to everyone who served there.

Throughout the day the Germans continued to swamp the front with stupendous cascades of artillery, mortar, and tank fire and then sent their infantry charging out across the smoke-shrouded battlefield in scenes reminiscent of the human-wave attacks into no-man's-land that characterized the bloody, futile slaughters of the Great War. American and British gunners mowed down the gray lines of great-coated figures until their gun barrels glowed red hot, but more came on to take their places, as though they were part of some ghastly human conveyor belt extending from Germany itself.[16]

To the east of where Penney's 1st Division along with the 45th's 157th Infantry Regiment and the 504th paratroopers were heavily engaged, the Germans made a solitary thrust at the 3rd Infantry Division and the 509th Parachute Infantry Battalion near Carano. Members of the airborne unit killed twenty-five Germans and captured ten prisoners—most of whom were from Lieutenant General Alexander Bouquin's 114th Light (*Jäger*) Division.[17]

ALTHOUGH THE QUANTITY OF GERMAN artillery fire was heavy, the Allies' firepower was even greater, as was demonstrated on February 8. VI

Corps artillery, including the guns of the 1st British Division, the 1st U.S. Armored and 45th Divisions, and the 976th Field Artillery Battalion, engaged in a coordinated program of counterbattery fire against all known enemy gun positions on the west flank of the beachhead. Added to this strength were the 5-inch and 6-inch guns of two British cruisers, the HMS *Orion* and *Phoebe*, and one American cruiser, the *Brooklyn*—plus the fighter-bombers of the XII Air Support Command and the guns of the 68th Coast Artillery Regiment. In support of the 3rd Division in the Cisterna area, forty-eight B-25 Mitchell medium bombers saturated German positions.[18]

At 10:00 that night, Lieutenant Colonel Good (1st Battalion, LIR) paid a visit to the forward companies and found the men in their positions but their numbers reduced and the men exhausted; some had even been captured by the enemy when they had fallen asleep at their posts. Good requested that his battalion be permitted to withdraw slightly to positions where mutual support could be given, but his request was denied.

Perhaps most in danger was Major P. McMahon Mahon's D Company in Aprilia. Patrols tried to reach D Company from the road junction held by B Company to their right but were prevented by strong German forces that had inserted themselves between the two companies. Additionally, Haigh's B Company was being annoyed by small probing attacks that prevented it from maintaining contact with the 10th Berkshires on their right. Just as worrisome was a gap in the Fosso della Ficoccia sector that the London Irish could not close with mines and that the Germans were using to infiltrate deeper into the British ranks. It seemed just a matter of time before something big—very big—would happen.

Night after night and day after day, the dance of death was played out in a vast, muddy ballroom, with the dancers—American, British, and German—twirling around to the unending beat of the timpani provided by the artillery section, the mortars, the grenadiers, and the aviators, while the high notes were carried on the whine of shells and bullets, the staccato rhythm of the machine guns, and the low rumbling of tank engines that maintained a steady thrum. A choir of unholy voices—the voices of badly wounded men left abandoned in the no-man's-land between the opposing forces—screamed into the night, pleading for someone to save them. Or put them out of their misery.

LATE THAT NIGHT, A GERMAN patrol crept close to the London Irish mortars before a corporal named Allen discovered them and, coolly propping his mortar almost vertically on top of ammunition boxes, launched the mortar bombs with uncanny accuracy and, according to the London Irish history, "succeeded and wrought great damage to the enemy." The German infantry and tanks continued to press the attack but did not dislodge the LIR from their positions and could not retake Aprilia, the northern and eastern approaches to which they controlled.[19]

As February 8 came to a close, elements of Penney's division were still desperately trying to hold on to Aprilia and Carroceto, but a new opponent had been identified—the I German Parachute Corps, with elements of four different divisions with a total of six regiments. Additionally, more panzers and artillery had been brought into the area despite Allied efforts to interdict them while in transit. The positions held by the Royal Berks and the London Irish astride the Lateral Road and in Aprilia itself were under constant artillery and tank fire. Trying to keep the German buildup from becoming too great, the British frequently counterattacked and broke up enemy formations that appeared to have a chance of succeeding. Still, these parry-and-thrust maneuvers did not give Penney or Lucas confidence that the Germans would give up their efforts anytime soon.

THE WEATHER GODS, TOO, SEEMED to be on the Germans' side, playing a major role in depleting the Allied ranks. Cold rains, whipped by fierce winds, slashed down on tired troops trying in vain to stay dry and alert in mud-and-water-filled foxholes or the roofless remains of shattered buildings. Trench foot also became a growing malady, as did body lice. Palatable food and potable water were at a premium. And, of course, the constant artillery barrages took their toll, both physically and mentally.

No one who has never been on the receiving end of an artillery barrage can truly appreciate its physical and mental effects. The concussion wave from an artillery shell, moving at thirty times the speed of sound, can rupture the eardrums, often causing deafness, and can also burst heart and lungs within the chest and cause instant death even though no outward sign of injury is present; many soldiers were killed by the shock wave alone rather than from shell fragments.

The mental strain is also immense. A soldier—even one huddling deep in his hole—has the peculiar sensation that every shell is aimed directly at him and it is only a matter of moments before it blows him to smithereens. In too many cases, he is right. Prolonged shelling can also cause madness and complete emotional breakdown—what was called in World War I "shell shock." As one 1st Scots Guards officer said, "How I hate shells. I have seen strong, courageous men reduced to whimpering wrecks, crying like children. . . . I would sooner have a thousand bullets or even dive bombers than a day's shelling."[20]

Fred Mason (2nd North Staffs) echoed that sentiment. "To be under artillery fire is very scary," he said,

> and that is putting it mildly. The scream of the shells, the *CRUMP* when they explode, the whistle of the shrapnel—a complete and utter nightmare. Needless to say, we were all very frightened and prayed a lot. But the fear of being wounded or worse was not to the fore in my mind—just relief when the barrage stopped. The Germans had mortars which we named "Moaning Minnies"* because of the awful scream as the bombs came down. You ask how we managed without going mad. I think we were all a little mad by the time things went quiet again.[21]

Vere "Tarzan" Williams of the 45th Division recalled, "You just never got used to artillery—no way. Each time a shell went off anywhere near you, it was like getting hit in your chest and ears with a huge boxing glove with a horseshoe inside. You went deaf for a while."[22] Anthony Stefanelli (36th Engineer Combat Regiment) said that after a while, the troops on the line became somewhat inured to incoming artillery. "We learned to stop ducking whenever a shell went by. If you heard the swish,

---

* Mason was referring to the *Nebelwerfer*, a multibarreled rocket-firing German weapon of which there were several varieties and configurations.

then the shell was either to the right, left, or over your head. You never heard the shell meant for you."[23]

The expenditure of ammunition at Anzio was truly prodigious. Bill Mauldin, a soldier with the 45th Infantry Division who drew cartoons for the division newspaper before he was "bumped upstairs" to draw for the *Stars and Stripes*, recalled, "Anzio was unique. It was the only place in Europe which held an entire corps of infantry, a British division, all kinds of artillery and special units, and maintained an immense supply and administration setup without a rear echelon. As a matter of fact, there wasn't any rear; there was no place in the entire beachhead where enemy shells couldn't seek you out." At one point during the battle, Mauldin said that an American artillery battalion of 155mm guns "fired 80,000 rounds of ammunition . . . and there were dozens of these battalions."[24]

MUCH TO THE DISGUST AND disdain of their enlisted men, generals throughout history have always commandeered the grandest quarters for themselves—usually a mansion, chateau, palace, or castle—and lived in safe luxury with fine food and drink, hot and cold running water, and a bevy of servants, while the poor common soldier is forced to sleep in the open or the shelter of a half-demolished building, lie in a muddy hole dug in the ground, get rained or snowed upon, eat cold food (if he eats at all), use an empty C-ration can or his helmet for a toilet, and be subjected to death and dismemberment at the random whim of enemy (and sometimes friendly) munitions.

Such was the case for Harold Alexander and Mark Clark. The finest accommodation in Italy—indeed, one of the finest in all the world—was the royal palace at Caserta, built in the 1700s for King Charles III of Bourbon, who wanted a palatial estate that would surpass in sheer size and extravagance his cousin's palace at Versailles, and so he commissioned the leading baroque architect of the day, the Neopolitan Luigi Vanvitelli, to come up with something that would, had the term been in existence during that period, "blow the minds" of peasants and aristocracy alike.

Not long after the invasion at Salerno in September 1943, and the subsequent capture of Naples that allowed the Allies to reach Caserta,

Alexander and Clark felt that the estate was ideal for the headquarters for both the Fifteenth Army Group and the Fifth U.S. Army, and thus the ultraextravagant 1,200-room baroque palace was commandeered for that purpose. The most exquisite food for the Allied commanders and their staffs was prepared in massive kitchens by soldiers who had been professional chefs in civilian life and carried to the dining rooms on fabulously ornate silver servers by a brigade of uniformed waiters. Only the best wines flowed in endless rivers. Broad hallways, soaring ceilings, and marble staircases adorned the rest of the building; just the private Palatine Chapel alone would have been the pride of most Italian cities. Outside, the opulence went on and on. A huge formal garden surrounded by office buildings in the same Italian baroque style greeted important visitors, while, in back, a vast formally landscaped garden featuring an incredible artificial river, lake, and sculpture-filled waterfall literally stretched as far as the eye could see.[25]

Hundreds of miles to the north of Caserta, in February 1944, John Lucas lived less grandly. With the cities of Anzio and Nettuno coming under increasingly heavy German artillery fire, the VI Corps commander did not feel safe in his aboveground headquarters located in an old Italian artillery barracks building at 39 Via Santa Maria. He probably could have taken a cue from his superiors and installed himself and his headquarters within the sumptuous seventeenth-century Villa Borghese palace at Nettuno but had earlier chosen instead the safer, if less glamorous, surroundings of ancient, musty wine caves located beneath the forest of the Villa Borghese.[26] But when Mark Clark moved his forward headquarters from Caserta to Nettuno, it was into the Villa Borghese that he moved it.[27]

At the opposite end of the scale, Audie Murphy, 3rd Division, dug into the mud near Cisterna, did not know comfort and opulence. Consumed by pessimism, he was more concerned with simply living than with luxury:

> Through our hearts and minds, resignation and futility crawl like worms. We cannot advance. And we cannot retreat another yard without adding further peril to the slim security of our beachhead. Rumors slide from

hole to hole. The British are pulling out while the pulling is good, leaving us holding a gigantic and ferocious wildcat with a very small grip on a very short tail. The Germans are only waiting until our build-up is worthy of a major attack. They will then thrust through the middle of our defenses, split our forces, and drive us into the sea. We believe nothing; doubt nothing. Our function we know. It is to hold the lines until enough men and material arrive to try again cracking the iron wall that lies before us. We listen to the moan of the wind, curse our existence, and snarl at one another. There is no escape with honor except on the litter of the medics or in the sack of the burial squads.[28]

While Murphy et al. worried about imminent death and injury, General Robert T. Frederick's 1st Special Service Force seemed not to care about such mundane things and was itching for a fight ever since landing at Anzio a week earlier. On the night of February 8–9, they got their wish. Sneaking into Sessano, between Littoria and Cisterna, under cover of darkness, they overwhelmed the German garrison, captured the town, and took dozens of prisoners.[29]

AS A DECORATED GERMAN GENERAL of Prussian nobility, Eberhard von Mackensen was not accustomed to having anyone deny him what he wanted, and the stiff, hard-faced Prussian certainly wanted Aprilia back—and the 125,000 men he now commanded were about to do his bidding. At 1:30 A.M. on the ninth, he launched another assault to retrieve the town from Rupert Good's 1st London Irish Rifles. So weary were Good's men after two solid days of nearly nonstop combat and no sleep that the Micks could barely keep their eyes open. Yet they had to, as the Germans, after pounding the ruins of the town with a cascade of artillery shells, came at them in waves. This time it was Pfeiffer's 65th Infantry Division—slipping, sliding, stumbling, and screaming its way across the mud in another attempt to regain the rubble.

The two remaining platoons of the LIR's D Company—Major P. McMahon Mahon's men—summoned every ounce of strength and drop of adrenaline they still possessed to hold off the attackers, but it was like trying to hold back an avalanche. A troop of Sherman tanks was hurriedly dispatched in an attempt to reach them but was stopped by antitank guns.*[30]

DAWN ON FEBRUARY 9 BROUGHT the same dull, depressing pattern to the troops on the beachhead. Their holes were full of water, their boots and clothing were soaked, their feet and fingers were numb, a relentless chill filled their bodies, their stomachs growled for a decent meal, and their eyes were bleary from lack of sleep. The men opened their eyes, blinked, saw the men next to them, and realized, with a wonder, that they were still alive. Yet the horrible reality was that there was no letup in the Germans' attempts to kill them.

Even before the sky had lightened, a profusion of German mortar and artillery shells screamed into the American and British positions in the salient, like Valkyries signaling another ground attack. Men of Penney's division gripped their rifles, peered over the rims of their foxholes, and tried to make out the shadowy forms heading their way. On the western flank, guarded by the 5th Grenadier Guards and 1st Scots Guards, the 65th Infantry Division was back, once again trying to penetrate the British line. They marched ahead with the sullen urgency of men who have been condemned to death, heedless of the British fusillade, their lines buckling and then falling, only to be replaced by more. During the heavy firefight, the 5th Grenadiers were forced to give ground and withdrew back to the area around the Carroceto railroad station and the Overpass. The Germans along the Buonriposo Ridge also shoved what remained of the 1st KSLI and 2nd Foresters back to a stream south of the ridge.

When this softening up was complete, the four regiments constituting Combat Group Gräser† launched the main thrust against the British who were covering Aprilia and the Lateral Road to the east. The

---

* Major Mahon was the last remaining officer in the company; he was taken prisoner by the Germans. London Irish Rifles Association, "The London Irish at War, 1939–45," https://www.londonirishrifles.com/index.php/second-world-war/the -london-irish-at-war-1939-45/.

† The units were the 725th and 735th Infantry Regiments of the 715th Infantry Division, the 29th Panzer-Grenadier Regiment of the 3rd Panzer-Grenadier Division, and the 104th Panzer-Grenadier Regiment of the 15th Panzer Division. Bowditch, *Anzio Beachhead*, 60.

fighting became furious, and the 168th's grip on the front lines began slipping. To the east of Aprilia, the 29th Panzer-Grenadier Regiment knifed between the 1st London Irish and the 10th Royal Berks, while the 104th Panzer-Grenadiers overran the right-flank company of the Berks, thus clearing the way for their panzers and self-propelled guns to come roaring down the Lateral Road and push the British out of the trophy, Aprilia. The trophy may have been demolished, but it was still a trophy worth keeping.[31]

Gräser's attempts to destroy the 5th Grenadier Guards and the 1st Scots Guards on the left flank of the Guards Brigade front were less successful. The morning's attack was thwarted by a timely counterattack launched by the 3rd Battalion, 504th U.S. Parachute Infantry, which helped the Brits hold their positions around Carroceto. Also adding its voice to the battle was Harmon's 1st Armored Division, which counterattacked German forces at Buonriposo Ridge with two companies of tanks. (Harmon became known as the "Fireman of Anzio," because his division was always being called upon to put out "fires.") But once off the paved Albano Highway, the Shermans and Stuarts became mired in mud and were knocked out by mines and accurate antitank fire; Harmon lost seven tanks in that action but was not yet done. Unfortunately for him, neither were the Germans.[32]

At noon on the ninth, another company of Shermans rattled up the highway beyond Aprilia, only to be stopped by a minefield covering the highway. Skirting the mines, the Shermans managed to knock out one panzer and two antitank guns and helped drive back two battalions of infantry. Continuing on, Harmon's tankers destroyed two Mark IV panzers north of Aprilia before dark forced their withdrawal—but not before helping the 1st LIR eliminate the enemy penetration east of the town. As part of their assault, the Germans sent small, tracked remote-controlled vehicles, packed with explosives and known as "Goliaths,"* crawling into the ruins; these weapons proved ineffective because of the rough, rubble-strewn ground and the marksmanship of the handful of defenders.[33]

---

* The B-1 Goliaths, cable-controlled demolition vehicles made by Borgward, were packed with 130 pounds of explosive. Hogg and Weeks, *Illustrated Encyclopedia of Military Vehicles*, 234.

Friedrich Hummel (29th Panzer-Grenadier Regiment, 3rd Panzer-Grenadier Division) recalled, "We got a new weapon, two so-called 'Goliaths.' They were very small tanks, fifty centimeters in height, full of explosives. They were radio controlled. The first one arrived nearby but overturned. The second went under an American tank and with a powerful explosion put it out of battle. The other tank made a reverse movement at full speed and we didn't see it any more. This gave us new courage—we were hoping to receive many more miraculous weapons, as the Führer had announced to us and promised."[34]

James Safrit (Company F, 179th Infantry Regiment) called the Goliaths "doodle bugs" and remembered how his unit knocked them out: "Today, the Germans sprang their secret weapon at us. It was a 'doodle bug' tank—a small, unmanned tank filled with high explosives which was guided electronically. We spotted the damn things and opened fire with everything we had. The explosions were terrific when they blew up. Scratch one secret weapon. We didn't see any more of those things."[35]

THE ALLIED TROOPS ON THE ground received some much-needed support from naval and air assets. Lying offshore, cruisers began pounding suspected German positions. While laying a smoke screen for the cruisers, the British destroyer *Loyal* was damaged by a shell from a German shore battery, forcing it to withdraw to Naples for repairs.[36]

In combat interservice rivalries were forgotten. Donald Greener (1st Armored Division) said, "The ships in the harbor gave us supporting fire many times to keep Jerry from driving us off the beachhead." John Piazza (45th Infantry Division) too expressed his thanks to the navy gunners: "The naval gunfire saved the day during a huge German offensive."[37] Air support also poured in: 104 fighter-bombers, 84 medium bombers, and 36 light bombers were sent up to bomb and strafe German assembly areas around Campoleone. Aiding in the effort, another 84 American bombers that were on a mission to hit German supply dumps between Valmontone and Palestrina were diverted to bomb the enemy troop concentrations besieging Aprilia. Somehow, though, with all this firepower, the Germans remained undaunted and continued to press home their attacks.[38]

One of the Germans was Felix Reimann, a corporal in a Combat Group Gräser unit, whose Sturmgeschütz III (StuG III) assault gun was supporting an infantry advance against the British in Aprilia. "We fired [while] on the move," he recalled, "and I kept a careful eye on the ruins as we approached. We were vulnerable and the traverse of the gun on the StuG was not too good.* . . . Then from the right I saw a flash followed by a massive white explosion right in front of my eyes. An anti-tank round had caught us. I was blinded but could hear the screams of [fellow crewmen] Scherling, Paulsen, and Weber as they burned to death." Reimann somehow managed to escape, collapsed, and woke up in a German field hospital two days later.[39]

The intensity of the day's fighting was impossible to sustain; both sides had suffered heavily, and so, by late afternoon, the two weary opponents paused to consolidate, reorganize, recover casualties, and replenish ammunition stocks. But there was no denying that, no matter how tired, bloody, and depleted they were, the men of Combat Group Gräser had won the main prize: Aprilia itself. As the London Irish survivors straggled out of Aprilia, the job of holding on to the town passed to the Germans.[40]

THAT NIGHT THE 45TH DIVISION'S 180th Infantry Regiment, under Colonel Robert L. Dulaney, was brought up to relieve Brigadier Eric E. J. Moore's battered 2nd Brigade on the right flank of Penney's division; Moore's dispirited men were pulled back and placed into division reserve. One of the 2nd Brigade officers, Second Lieutenant Ted Lees of the 6th Gordons, recalled, "All told during that period, from my platoon of thirty, plus replacements, some thirty-six were killed or wounded, including some of those who were on the way to us as replacements. You could say that I was rather lucky, without a scratch."

Lees remembered the 180th Regiment coming to the relief of his unit; it was time for the tattered remnants of his battalion, now reduced to

---

* In fact, the gun had *no* traverse. Because it could point only straight ahead, the entire twenty-four-ton machine had to be turned in order to aim the 75mm gun. Hogg and Weeks, *Illustrated Encyclopedia of Military Vehicles*, 142–143.

less than a full company, to head south to B Echelon for some much-needed rest and recuperation. During the march back, Lees said that he discovered that he could fall asleep while marching. While he was taking a break on the side of the road, he said, "I was quite sure that I had left my body and was looking down on myself from above (hallucinations?) but I never reported it to anyone else."[41]

With the 2nd now out of the line, Penney had three brigades remaining—the 3rd, 24th, and 168th—at the front, but, with all the casualties, his division's strength had been reduced by half. That night all frontline units began unspooling huge coils of barbed wire in hopes that it would slow down the next German attacks that everyone knew were coming—quite assuredly the next day.

IT WAS NOW THE 45TH Division's turn to feel the full force of the Germans. On the night of February 9, Lucas met briefly with the 45th's commander, Major General William Eagles and told him to do whatever he could to relieve the 168th Brigade near Aprilia (two battalions of the 45th's 157th Regiment were already on the far western end of the line).[42] Without going into detail, Lucas ended the conference with Eagles by saying, "Okay, Bill, you give 'em the works" and then promptly left the meeting.[43] Exactly what "give 'em the works" meant was open to interpretation.

Intelligence could not say exactly how strong the Germans were in the Aprilia-Carroceto area, but Eagles figured it was a job for an entire 3,000-man regiment; he told Colonel Malcolm R. Kammerer to send his 179th Infantry Regiment northward to relieve the 168th. But Kammerer, for reasons unknown, selected only one battalion for the task: Lieutenant Colonel Wayne L. Johnson's 1st Battalion, plus two companies of the 191st Tank Battalion. Companies A and B of Johnson's battalion, with C in reserve, would advance with the tanks. They were to move out before dawn on February 11 and cross the soggy fields to replace what was left of the 168th around the ruins of Aprilia. It was, like so many other orders issued at Anzio, easier said than done. The regiment's historian noted, "The odds were 1,000 to 1 against [the 1st Battalion] before it jumped off."[44]

CHAPTER 11

"Battle is kind of a nightmare"
FEBRUARY 10–12

A MEMBER OF THE 1ST BATTALION, Scots Guards, by the name of McIntosh recalled, "General Lucas seemed unwilling to take the war to the Germans so they came looking for us." Shortly after midnight on the bitterly cold and moonlit night of February 9–10, some fifteen panzers and a German infantry battalion struck the 1st Scots Guards, holding the ground about a mile north of Aprilia at a location the troops called "Dung Farm" or "Smelly Farm" due to an overabundance of manure. After radioing for help, M-10s of Company B, 894th U.S. Tank Destroyer Battalion, came to the rescue. Artillery rounds were also dropped onto the scene, forcing the panzers and infantry to pull back temporarily.

McIntosh noted that the fighting was "fierce and vicious, especially around [Aprilia], which we took and lost and took again." McIntosh's unit suffered several casualties when one of their Bren gun carriers drove over and exploded a crate of grenades. Then German mortars and artillery began to rain down. "We became surrounded in this position and had to fight our way out." Taking refuge in a house, McIntosh said, "I was talking to my corporal in the doorway of the house when he suddenly collapsed; a German sniper had hit him in the head. That night the Germans attacked with tanks and blew the front of the house down."

The 1st Battalion of the Scots Guards regiment had gone into Anzio at full strength—about 800 men; over the next few weeks, they were reduced to sixty. The battalion commander would be killed, and all the company commanders would either be killed, wounded, or captured. McIntosh, who also became a prisoner, recalled that, during just one morning's fighting, the unit had lost two officers, twelve sergeants, and forty guardsmen. "I lost a lot of friends that day," he said.[1]

NIGHT FELL, BUT GERMAN ATTEMPTS to destroy the British around Anzio did not slacken. In the dark, the 145th Grenadier Regiment of Pfeiffer's 65th Infantry Division hit the 2nd North Staffs hard. Thirty-year-old Major Peter Henry "Skipper" Mornement, commanding C Company, was wounded in the leg and taken prisoner. Three nights later, he was allowed by his captors to write a letter home to his mother:

> From the start I want you to produce that little extra bit of courage that you say I have imparted to you, and which you have stored away for an emergency. I fear you have been notified by various army means that I am where I am, and dread to think of the alarm and worry and distress which it must have caused you, and I also dread to think how long my letters will take to reach and reassure you. I, too, of course will not hear from you for months now—a soul-tearing thought. . . .
>
> Three days ago, or rather three nights, my position was overrun and I was hit in the right leg by a splinter and could not participate in the fight to regain our ground. All night long it was touch and go, and Scales, who took over command, did very well. But in the morning we had enemy dug in all round us, and our ammunition was exhausted, and not quite half my lot were taken prisoner, quite a number wounded. Now I have been well looked after and my leg is better, and I shall in time catch up with the others. Then we shall wait with courage until we are repatriated, and that will not be too long.

Unfortunately, the repatriation would never take place, nor would Major Mornement see his mother, wife, or son again. He died of his wounds in the Ospedale Civile in Mantova on April 20, 1944.[2]

BACK IN HIS PALATIAL HEADQUARTERS at Caserta, Mark Clark was receiving desperate reports from Lucas that the Germans had "stepped up attacks which they had been pressing sporadically for several days against the British 1st Division along the Albano Road sector." Clark noted, "In the new and stronger thrusts, they made a number of penetrations and seized the little village known as the Factory [Aprilia], which stood like a fortress above the road and now gave the enemy a good jumping-off place against our left flank."[3]

Possession of Aprilia and Carroceto had become an intense battle of wills. For the time being, the Germans were in firm possession of the two towns, but regaining them was of prime importance to the Allies because the breakout, whenever it came, could not take place without their being in Allied hands, and that did not appear to be in the cards.

Worrying Penney and Lucas was the condition of both Moore's 2nd Brigade and Davidson's 168th Brigade. Both had suffered heavily trying to hold Aprilia and keep the Germans from plunging south and splitting the bridgehead. In fact, so battered was the 2nd Brigade that Lucas had pulled it off the line on February 9 and relieved it with the 45th's 180th Infantry Regiment. Now Davidson's 168th Brigade needed relief. The men of the 168th—the 1st London Scottish, 1st London Irish Rifles, and 10th Royal Berks—had given all that soldiers could humanly give, but their numbers were now just too few—less than one-third of normal strength.

Like the little Dutch boy who had too many leaking holes in the dike and not enough fingers, Lucas was scrambling to find units fit enough to plug the gaps in the line while he pulled other units out for a brief but much-needed rest. Battered, bruised, and bleeding, the 168th Brigade would be relieved from its position along the front and sent back to B Echelon for a breather. What was left of Good's battalion was replaced by a single Thunderbird company whose numbers, although depleted, were greater than those of the British battalion.[*4]

---

*The LIR's "rest" period proved illusory; B Echelon was within range of German guns, and the Luftwaffe made nightly forays over the wooded area, strafing and dropping butterfly bombs, causing additional casualties in this place of supposed rest and safety. London Irish Rifles Association, "The London Irish at War, 1939–45," https://www.londonirishrifles.com/index.php/second-world-war/the-london-irish-at-war-1939-45/.

AT 4:30 A.M. ON THE 10TH, the American 504th paratroopers' 3rd Battalion (isolated north of Aprilia) and the 5th Battalion of the Grenadier Guards (holding out west of Aprilia and north of Carroceto) were attacked from three sides and were able to maintain their positions only because of the timely arrival of an armored squadron from the 46th Royal Tank Regiment. But contact with the two forward companies of the 1st Scots Guards (north of Aprilia and between the 504th and Grenadier Guards) had been lost. The remainder of the Scots Guards, in danger of being cut off, withdrew to the Overpass/Flyover. To cover the British withdrawal, a company of American M-10 tank destroyers was brought up and kept the Germans at bay.[5]

At Carroceto elements of Pfeiffer's 65th Infantry Division attacked the hamlet and expelled the British. The 5th Grenadier Guards counterattacked and drove out the Germans. (Combat Group Gräser would countercounterattack later that evening and retake the town.)[6] An hour later, a harried General Penney radioed Lucas to say that his exhausted troops had been fighting all night and were running out of ammunition and that his division would cease to exist unless fresh troops immediately relieved it. Lucas told Penney to hold on, that help would soon be on the way.[7]

"Things get worse and worse," complained John Lucas in his diary. "I am trying to get the 45th in to relieve the British. . . . I would also give a great deal for some M-1 howitzer ammunition. This is a national scandal. We have been at war, or preparing for it, for four years, and soldiers must die because the guns have nothing to shoot. Where has it gone?"[8]

Besides ammunition, the beleaguered Lucas, virtually devoid of reserves by now, ordered Colonel Thomas H. Stanley's 36th Engineer Combat Regiment to become an infantry outfit and take over a portion of the line along the Moletta River on February 10, relieving two battalions of the 157th Infantry, which were then moved up to support the British. The 36th was well acquainted with war by this time, having first been blooded at Algiers in November 1942, then during Operation Husky—the invasion of Sicily—and most recently during Operation Avalanche at Salerno. Although the 36th Engineers specialized in the construction of defenses, bridges, and roads and the elimination of enemy mines, obstacles, and booby traps, by taking over a relatively quiet portion of the front, they released infantry troops needed to bolster the critical central sector.*⁹

THE MEDICAL FACILITIES AT ANZIO continued to come under both deliberate and accidental enemy attack. On February 10, shells fell into the 33rd Field Hospital area, killing one nurse and wounding several other personnel. To somewhat protect hospital patients and caregivers from being killed or wounded, shallow rectangular pits were dug as far down as the high water table would allow, tents erected in these pits, and walls of sandbags used to build revetments and blast shields around them. This helped reduce casualties within the hospital areas, except for direct hits and antipersonnel butterfly bombs bursting above them.[10]

For the combat medics themselves, crawling onto the still-raging battlefields to administer whatever medical care they could, life was difficult both mentally and physically. Ray McAllister had been a bazookaman in Company C, 180th Regiment, 45th Division, but in the mountains near Cassino had been transferred to become a platoon medic—"the poor SOB who follows the platoon in combat, picking up or bandaging up the fallen members with no one to pick up the medic—a very lonesome position," he said. Very little training went along with the transfer. "All the medics with the company had been killed or wounded. I guess their life in combat was five or ten seconds."

He heard about a medic who took a bullet right in the middle of the red cross painted on his helmet. "Another medic was in a deep foxhole with two wounded men, one German and one American, when a Tiger tank came up on the hole and locked one tread and went round on the other, grinding the wounded and the medic into pulp. Great enemies! We painted out the red crosses on our helmets and some guys even carried weapons. When they kill medics, the rules of the Geneva Convention do not count."

---

*The men of the 36th would find themselves occupying this stretch of the line until they were relieved on March 24 by the 15th Regiment of the 3rd Infantry Division. During all that time, the 36th was subjected to ceaseless artillery fire and infantry probes but never broke—a testament to their courage and fighting abilities. "History of the 36th Engineers," http://www.6thcorpscombatengineers .com/docs/36th/36th%20History%20WDRB.pdf.

McAllister, who would become a physician after the war, recalled once going out to bring in casualties from the shelling.

> The first man I saw was bleeding and bubbling from multiple punctures in the chest. He was begging me to do something. I guessed that he had been hit in the lungs. I pulled out a morphine syrette to relieve his pain. I stuck the syrette in his muscle and squeezed and nothing happened. He died in my arms in agony and all I could do was try to comfort him. When I got back to the rear aid station with the less-seriously wounded, I found out that one had to puncture a metal seal on the syrette before the morphine would flow. I had done him no good. As I said, we got precious little training.[11]

"THIS IS A HELL HOLE," complained Paul Brown of the 179th to his diary on Thursday, February 10; it was a sentiment shared by virtually everyone at Anzio. "Very little sleep last night. Enemy flew very low last night, serving personnel bombs. . . . Our Regiment has moved up directly in rear of British 1st [Division]. We will probably go through them tonight or tomorrow for much belated push. 170 [Allied] planes dropped eggs [bombs] on enemy roads and railroads yesterday afternoon. . . . Nettuno is becoming a wreck with shells, bombs hitting it continuously. Our cemetery is becoming very large. Planes down: 5—ours 2, theirs 3."[12]

IT BEGAN RAINING LATE THAT night and was still pouring when Wayne Johnson's 1st Battalion, 179th, relieved what was left of the 168th Brigade south of Aprilia. Johnson was then ordered to continue on and assault Aprilia with the assistance of tanks from Lieutenant Colonel Percy Perkins's 191st Tank Battalion.[13]

A member of Company B, 1st Battalion, 179th, Sergeant Brummett Echohawk, a Pawnee Indian from Oklahoma, recalled that he and another sergeant—a Potawatomi named Turtle Head—reported to the command post. "It is midnight, and raining," he said. "The captain fills us in on the situation. We are to take the 'Factory.' We'll have tank support. The captain pauses and looks at us. Battalion, he adds, wants two Indian sergeants to lead the attack. We are it. We alert the men. They are in two-man slit trenches with a shelter-half stretched over as protection from the rain. Some sit hunched over in raincoats and steel helmets out-side, for their slit trenches have long filled with water."[14]

The sopping-wet Yanks left their line of departure shortly before 2:00 A.M. on the eleventh and moved toward Aprilia. The assault was supposed to begin with a fifteen-minute barrage, courtesy of the 189th Field Artillery Battalion, starting at 6:15 A.M., along with armor support. Right on schedule, the artillery concentration began roaring.[15] Echohawk remembered, "At the start line, we wait. Still dark. Rain has stopped. It is 'brass-monkey' cold. . . . Then American artillery opens fire. Word is passed to fix bayonets. Sergeant Turtle Head and I start forward. The men follow. We maintain interval and slosh through mud." But the promised tanks were nowhere to be seen. At least the fifteen-minute ar-tillery preparation took place on time. Grumbling that they could have also used the services of the U.S. Air Force and a few warships as well, Johnson's men trudged forward. Lo and behold, the morning sky grew loud with wave after wave of scores of Corsica-based planes coming to plaster German positions.[16]

As the planes expended their ordnance and departed and the barrage lifted and the infantrymen advanced to within sight of Aprilia, the Ger-mans' 725th Infantry Regiment, holed up in the basements and rubble of the town, emerged and opened fire, sending the Thunderbirds sprawling into the fields and water-filled ditches. Mortar rounds dropped in, splat-tering the advancing GIs with mud, blood, and shrapnel. Then, from behind Carroceto, came a roaring noise—the sound of tank engines rev-ving to life. Within seconds the panzers were on the Albano Highway, firing their main guns and stitching the air with their machine guns, rumbling straight toward the Americans.[17] As men tried to burrow into the cold sludge, Echohawk and Turtle Head yelled, "Don't lay down—run!" The group took off, heading for Aprilia with bayonets affixed—but without tank support.[18]

The frightened infantrymen gave it their all, moving forward in short rushes, only to be cut down by the murderous German fire. Somehow, a few Thunderbirds such as Echohawk and Turtle Head made it to the ruins—the broad space called the Piazza Roma surrounded by the Saint Michael Church, the city hall, the local Fascist Party headquarters build-ing known as the House of Fascism, and the barracks of the Carabinieri (national police force). A block away was the school where the Germans had a strongpoint. There were also enemy soldiers inside the crumbled remains of the post office, the cinema, a hotel and bar run by Carlo Calabresi and brothers Laurino and Silvestro Carboni, Zafferino Olivieri's bakery and grocery store, Quirino Cirilli's butcher shop, a tobacco store managed by Clelia Tofani, Antonio Arrigi's stationery shop and emporium, Mario Santarelli's hardware store, Romualdo Palma's tailor shop, and more—each building its own fortress.[19]

"At the 'Factory,'" Echohawk continued, "we now stood toe to toe with the German Panzer-Grenadiers to slug it out. For hours the battle raged on, with us taking the stronghold only to lose ground to German counterattacks minutes later. A real shoot out. German infantry chased us out of there, only for the company to regroup and retake the ground immediately. The Germans continued to fight, running us out of the 'Factory' once more."[20]

No matter how hard the Americans fought, the Germans, securely in possession of Aprilia, fought back harder, as though they were defending Aachen, Munich, or Berlin. At last, to break the stalemate, the Germans, like a cavalry charge of old, threw an assault by tanks out from behind Carroceto, where they had been taking shelter. Following in the panzers' wake was a phalanx of screaming, counterattacking infantry. Without the 191st's tanks that were supposed to be supporting them, Johnson's men, fearing annihilation, abandoned their small gains. The pathetic remnants of the infantry stumbled back from the factory of death to their original lines, their faces and olive-drab wool uniforms caked with mud, their eyes glazed with the horror they had witnessed, their hands trembling from the shock of battle; all of the company's officers and half of its enlisted men were either dead, wounded, or missing.

That night Johnson tried to reorganize his 1st Battalion for another attack, but it seemed hopeless; the shaken survivors of the day's battle were in no shape to launch another strike anytime soon. Besides being physically and emotionally spent, the ammunition they would need was nearly gone. Perhaps other companies would have better luck. Johnson told the commander of Company C to get ready—they were next up to bat. And, despite their physical and mental condition, what was left of Companies A and B would be thrown in, too, along with Company L of 3rd Battalion.[21] If Johnson was a literary man, he might have quoted from Tennyson's *The Charge of the Light Brigade*: "Theirs not to question why; theirs but to do and die."

General Lucas, perhaps not realizing that the attack had been turned back, wrote in his diary that evening, "The attack against the 'Factory' is progressing but I am afraid it doesn't mean much as it is too hot a spot for us to stay in if we get hit. The enemy can't either."[22]

Alas, there was no rest for the weary—the battle for Aprilia resumed shortly before 4:00 A.M. on the twelfth. But at least now Company A of the 191st Tank Battalion finally had arrived. The Shermans and the 179th infantrymen crossed their line of departure but did not get very far. The tanks were heading up the Albano Highway in single file when the first one was knocked out by a direct hit; the second blew up 200 yards farther, and there the attack stalled.[23] At 8:30 A.M., the dwindling number of Shermans laid down a thick smoke screen so that they could pull back, leaving the infantrymen basically on their own. Company A, 179th Infantry, after mortaring the southwest corner of Aprilia, withdrew under that smoke screen without even getting close to the town.[24]

For the remainder of the morning and into the early hours of the afternoon, the American infantrymen repeatedly tried to breach Aprilia's defenses but were stopped each time. It was not until 1:00 P.M., after Johnson's men had been fighting alone for two hours, that the 191st's tanks tried again. Brummett Echohawk recalled that five Shermans rolled up, but he and other infantrymen yelled at the tankers to get away; they were drawing too much enemy fire. Shells started slamming into the tank hulls, turning the tanks into infernos. "I have one thought: get the hell away from that tank," Echohawk said. "Too late. An 88 belts the lead tank. There is no explosion as expected but a vibrating thud—armor-piercing shells. The man in the turret gathers himself and jumps. A hail of bullets catch him. The tank rocks with another hit before smoke boils up. Another tank has its turret blown off; its motor keeps running."[25]

Still the Americans pressed on. Johnson radioed for a smoke screen, and soon white phosphorous shells blossomed like cotton balls on the near horizon, billowing like a bride's veil on her wedding day, drawing a gauzy curtain across the battlefield that would obscure the Americans' movements from the Germans. The Thunderbirds and the handful of tanks advanced behind the white curtain, but as the smoke drifted away, they became easy targets for German antitank crews, which proceeded to pick off the Shermans. Ahead of them, American artillery continued to crash into the ruins of the village, enabling the Yanks to get closer.[26]

For a brief moment, it appeared as if the attack might succeed. By early afternoon, a few Thunderbirds had penetrated Aprilia's southeast corner and were trying to root the Germans out of their positions. More hand-to-hand combat took place in which men used knives, bayonets, and grenades at close range, but it was no use; courage alone was insufficient. Then the sound of German tank engines filled the air as more panzers burst onto the scene, sticking their armored snouts into the huddled masses of the American infantrymen and blasting away at point-blank range. Streams of bullets flew up and down the streets from German machine guns hidden among the piles of rubble. The men of the 179th were unable to overcome the Germans' superiority in numbers and weapons and were sent fleeing.[27]

Brummett Echohawk scrambled over dead comrades before taking cover in a watery cow path outside of town, his heart pounding. He said, "I struggle backward like a crawdad. I make it back to the roadside ditch. My sides heave like an eared-down bronc. I hear mortar shells. They rustle like dried leaves, then explode. They had us. Tears come." The other attackers were also pinned down, unable to move. A bolt of pain ripped through Echohawk. He was one of the lucky few; soon he would be evacuated for wounds sustained during the assault on Aprilia.

Back at one of the Anzio hospitals, Echohawk made friends with a pretty, dark-haired nurse. "I liked her, she liked me," he said. "That night the Germans hit the beachhead with a heavy air raid and fire from a railroad gun we called 'The Anzio Express.' My tent was hit. The nurse I liked was decapitated."[28]

AFTER PAUSING FOR A FEW hours to catch their breath and to strategize their next move, the commanders of Companies A and B of the 179th, along with the 27th Armored Field Artillery Battalion, decided to try another frontal attack. The attack began before dawn. This time, Company B of the 191st Tank Battalion rolled up to support the 179th's Company

B and reached the road junction southeast of Aprilia, where they lined up and began pumping shell after shell into the pile of rubble until they ran out of ammunition and had to pull back. It seemed like a waste of good ammunition, for the Germans, although deaf, dazed, and dirt covered, were ready and waiting. As the American infantrymen advanced under fire into the rubble, both Companies A and B began slugging it out with the Germans in furious hand-to-hand combat that lasted all day and into the night. But Aprilia remained German property.[29]

CHURCHILL WAS FURIOUS. HE WAS informed that the landing forces had nearly 18,000 vehicles on shore. He sarcastically growled in a cable to Admiral Cunningham, "How many of our men are driving or looking after 18,000 vehicles in this narrow space? We must have a great superiority in chauffeurs."

Why the Allies weren't making progress was an aggravating mystery to him. As both the father *and* the mother of Operation Shingle, Churchill feared that his progeny had become an unruly, disappointing offspring looked after by nannies who did not have the same emotional investment in its development that he did, and he wanted to give it a few parental whacks in order to set it straight on life's path. After all, Shingle, like a child, was fast becoming a reflection of its parents, and Churchill did not want to be criticized for its upbringing.

The frustrated prime minister, trying to prod Alexander into being more forceful in his dealings with the Americans, sent him a message telling him to "order" and not merely "urge":

> I have a feeling that you may have hesitated to assert your authority because you were dealing so largely with Americans and therefore urged an advance instead of ordering it. You are however quite entitled to give them orders, and I have it from the highest American authorities that it is their wish that their troops should receive direct orders. . . . American commanders expect to receive positive orders, which they will immediately obey. Do not hesitate therefore to give orders just as you would to your own men. The Americans are very good to work with and quite prepared to take the rough with the smooth.[30]

Churchill was also growing increasingly dissatisfied with Lucas and, indirectly, with Clark, too; a movement was afoot to get rid of the VI Corps commanding general. Alexander, in his memoirs, asked rhetorically: "There still remains the question, what went wrong with the Anzio operation, seeing that we gained almost complete surprise?" He answered his own question: "The answer is clear." What was clear to Alexander was what he viewed as Lucas's failings: too slow, too cautious, not aggressive enough; he spent too much time building up the beachhead instead of pushing out, and fretting about a lack of reinforcements.[31]

Alexander, wishing to assign blame elsewhere, failed to mention that both he and Clark might have had some responsibility in not making clear to Lucas that a swift thrust toward Rome—at least to the Alban Hills—was expected—and in their not being unable to supply Lucas with all the troops and landing craft that were required to make such a coup de main possible. Instead, Alexander sent a cable to his irascible boss, Field Marshal Alan Brooke, the chief of the Imperial General Staff, to complain about what he regarded as Lucas's poor leadership and pessimistic outlook and to request permission to do something about it. Brooke, who held a dim view of Americans in general, agreed that Lucas must go. But who would replace him? Alexander suggested "a thruster" like Lieutenant General George S. Patton Jr., who had been relieved of command of Seventh Army in Sicily after slapping two hospitalized enlisted men whom he had accused of cowardice and malingering.

Brooke proposed Patton's name to Eisenhower, but Ike felt such a move would have deflated Patton's ego; going from being the commander of Seventh Army to commander of a corps simply wasn't done. But, a few days later, at Supreme Headquarters Allied Expeditionary Force, Ike summoned Patton, now with him in England secretly preparing the Third U.S. Army for the invasion but publicly pretending to be the commander of the fictitious First U.S. Army Group in hopes of deceiving the Germans. Ike said, "You may have to take command of the beachhead in Italy and straighten things out."

Patton claimed that he did not care about the loss of prestige; just the possibility of getting back into the war in any capacity was good enough for him. Patton considered the possibility "a great compliment because I would be willing to command anything from a platoon up in order to fight." Ike had even put two airplanes on standby in case the proposal was accepted and Patton decided to fly immediately to Italy.[32] But the appointment never took place; it was nixed the next day, and Patton never learned why. Fifth Army would have to find someone else to command VI Corps. Luckily, the perfect man for the job was right under everyone's noses.[33]

AS BATTERED AND DEPLETED AS it was, Wayne Johnson's 1st Battalion, 179th, was ordered to resume the assault on Aprilia and Carroceto the next day. The plan this time was for the Thunderbirds, along with the 191st Tank Battalion, to first hit Carroceto Station and retake it before turning east and advancing upon Aprilia. What the Americans did not know was that the Germans had intercepted a radio message mentioning the coming attack; Gräser moved more reinforcements into Carroceto and Aprilia to lie in wait for the arrival of Johnson's men.[34]

The attack by the 1st Battalion, 179th Infantry, had come close to retaking Aprilia. But "close" does not count in battle. By the time the two companies straggled back to their line of departure some 500 yards south of Aprilia, they had been severely beaten. Company A was particularly hard hit, having been reduced to three officers and forty enlisted men. Grizzled infantrymen were crying, and angry, too—angry that they had been led into an ambush by commanders who had no idea that an overpowering enemy had been lying in wait for them and angry that the armored support they were expecting had shown up two hours late.

It seemed like the end for Johnson's battalion. Never before had they fought so fiercely against such unequal odds. Never before had they been forced to concede a battlefield that they had almost won. And never before had they suffered such heavy casualties—not in Sicily, not at Salerno, not at Venafro. The Germans shoved what was left of the American unit back toward Anzio; only by desperate measures did Johnson's men keep the Germans from driving through and all the way to the seashore.[35]

IN THE 2ND BATTALION, 179TH Sector, south of Aprilia, the men could hear the sounds of battle that had involved the 1st Battalion, but they had not been ordered to take part. Sergeant Lee Anderson (Company F, 179th) was in a foxhole with a buddy when a panzer suddenly appeared outside his foxhole. "My rifle got run over by the tank," he said, "so we got out of there. Our unit fell back to a canal and composed ourselves." Later in the day, after conducting a patrol, Anderson and others returned to a wooded area for the debriefing. "We were gathered in a group to critique the mission. We were exposed and not under cover. A barrage came in and I got a big slash in the back of my helmet. As I recall, two others were hit by that same barrage." He was evacuated to a hospital in Naples with his wound. It took until June 2 for Anderson to recover and rejoin his unit.[36]

Like most infantrymen, James Safrit (Company F, 179th) anticipated attacks with fear and trepidation:

The only way we can advance is for the artillery to pound the hell out of the Germans, and then we move up as close as possible. . . . I've learned to crawl like a snake! I have had plenty of spent bullets and shrapnel slap into me. I would welcome a small wound just to get back to a hospital and take a bath. I don't feel sorry for anybody who gets hit, no matter how bad; at least they are out of it. That's more than I can say. Gee, you should see the relief on the faces of those who are heading to the hospitals.

An ordinary civilian could never understand how a man feels who has been through hell, beaten down, knowing fear in his heart countless times; a man who has forced himself to do a task while his mind and soul are screaming for him to turn around and run, and never stop running until he is safe at home in his mother's arms, like he did when he was a child. But a man with any self respect can't do that and still live with himself, so he just keeps plugging along.

The idea of the "million-dollar wound" became attractive to Safrit:

Many times I imagined how it might happen, how I might get out of this hell: Suddenly, unexpectedly, there's this ripping burst of machine-gun fire, or an explosion that comes out of nowhere, then a searing, burning pain. A feeling of panic and shock hits your brain, and you realize that what you have secretly hoped for has happened. You have been wounded—how bad doesn't matter. All you care is that you have been honorably relieved from this hell on earth. Nobody can keep you here any longer. A fierce pride floods through you, and calmly, you wait for the medic to take you away. Other guys pass you moving up. They envy you and you can feel it. . . . At least that is the way *I* would feel.

Safrit recalled the day a new man in the unit named Smithers died in his arms while his unit was making a resupply run in the snowy mountains at Venafro a few weeks earlier. A mortar barrage struck, and Smithers "was hit bad, a big hole in his stomach and blood oozed from his chest. The rest of us were assigned the unpleasant task of carrying the wounded down the mountain to the battalion aid station. I helped to carry Smithers. He was conscious and asked for a cigarette, so I threw a raincoat over us and lit one. He took a deep drag into his tortured lungs. I knew he was dying and, for the life of me, I couldn't refuse his last request."

By time the group reached the base of the mountain,

Smithers had begun to rattle horribly in his chest. Just before we reached the aid station, he gave a long, tortured sigh and never uttered another sound. Another good guy "gone west." He had traveled 4,000 miles to die on a muddy stinking hill on his very first day of combat with no one to comfort him or really care, but such is war. You just can't dwell on a friend getting killed. If you do, it will drive you stark raving mad. Death was nothing new to me by then, but seeing a buddy go like that with only a few hours of combat behind him made me realize even more how close and how quickly the "Grim Reaper" could snuff out your life. One minute full of vibrant, healthy life, and the next, a misshapen, lifeless hulk that seems to shrink after life has fled from the body.[37]

"THERE IS A HAUNTING UNREALITY to a battle area which is difficult to explain," said 1st Armored Division commander Ernie Harmon. "Battle is kind of a nightmare, with alarums and excursions, bravery and hysteria, but many men adjust themselves to it. It is the juxtaposition of war and peaceful routines which bothers men most. Even in those first weeks, when our occupancy of the beachhead was most in hazard, sheep grazed calmly right beside my truck. Cattle and mules wandered, seeking grass among the minefields."[38]

AS FEBRUARY 12 CAME TO a close, despite the Allies' best efforts, Pfeiffer's 65th Infantry Division and Combat Group Gräser were in firm control of the piles of rubble that had once been Aprilia and Carroceto. Three days of bitter, merciless fighting had torn the Allies' earlier gains from their hands, and the Albano Highway, cratered and littered with broken and burning vehicles and dead bodies, was closed to the Allies. The British and Americans would not be marching into Rome anytime soon.

Mackensen's interim victory, however, had been costly; hundreds of his troops were dead, wounded, or missing. It is estimated that Mackensen had committed the equivalent of more than six full regiments, practically exhausting his supply of reserves. But at least his men had pushed back their enemies. Now, if only Kesselring could send him additional troops, perhaps he could fulfill his mission and shove them all the way back into the sea.[39]

Again, the unspoken question that loomed over the battlefield like a barrage balloon: How much more would the Allies be expected to take?

CHAPTER 12

"Do not kill any cows!"
FEBRUARY 13–15

THE 1ST BRITISH DIVISION HAD been kicked around like an old football for three weeks and it could no longer take the pounding. Ever since the landing, the division had been the spearhead that had pushed north of Aprilia to the outskirts of Campoleone and had given everything that VI Corps and Fifth Army had asked of it. Penney's men had absorbed a level of punishment that few divisions before or since have had to absorb. The men had performed magnificently in the face of overwhelming odds, but battalions were now reduced to the size of companies, and most companies were now no larger than platoons. The division desperately needed time off the line to rest and receive fresh replacements. To accomplish that, a new division would need to be brought in to replace the battered 1st.

Lucas had requested fresh troops, but no "fresh" troops were available.[1] Clark fretted, "I didn't have another infantry division to send except those that were exhausted [on the Cassino front], and I didn't have any shipping in which to send one. . . . I did the best I could and, after shopping around, decided to send the British 167th [and 169th] Brigade of the 56th Division in view of the fact that X Corps [on the Gustav Line] was in a position where it could make very little progress on the Fifth Army front until something happened at Cassino. I informed Alexander of my decision and, although surprised, he agreed."[2]

Clark told Lucas that arrangements had been made to bring the rest of Major General Gerald Templer's 56th British Division[*] to Anzio, a fact that allowed Lucas to emit a small sigh of relief. But the two new brigades of the 56th would do little to rescue the situation. If anything, the arrival of the 56th was merely an exchange of one depleted, battle-weary division with another, just another pile of coal to be shoveled into the frightful maw of the flaming furnace known as the Anzio beachhead.[3]

BEFORE THE 56TH ARRIVED, HOWEVER, another attempt was made to take Aprilia. Shortly after midnight on February 12–13, Lieutenant Colonel Wayne Johnson, commanding the 1st Battalion, 179th Infantry, woke his exhausted men and gave them the bad news: at 2:00 A.M. they were to storm Aprilia once more. After the requisite bitching and moaning, the men accepted the inevitable, strapped on their equipment, grabbed their weapons, and headed across torn-up fields strewn with torn-up bodies from the previous day's battle. This time it would be Companies B and C thrown into the cauldron; what was left of Company A would be in reserve.

Accompanied this time by Company C of the 191st Tank Battalion, the 1st Battalion, 179th's Company B began approaching Aprilia from the south and Company C from the southwest, while Company I from 3rd Battalion provided flank cover farther to the east. The tanks did not get far; they reached the road junction southwest of Aprilia when they were again stopped by a minefield that the enemy had laid during the night; one tank had its track blown off. The other tanks pulled off the road and, taking cover behind a group of farm buildings, shelled the town as

---

[*] The 56th "Black Cat" Division (so named for its sleeve insignia showing a silhouette of Dick Whittington's black cat on a red square background) was composed of three brigades: the 167th (London) Infantry Brigade, 168th (London) Infantry Brigade, and 169th Infantry Brigade. The 167th was made up of the 7th Battalion, Oxfordshire and Buckinghamshire; 1st Battalion, Royal Ulster Rifles; and 8th and 9th Battalions, Royal Fusiliers. The 168th Brigade, already at Anzio, was composed of the 1st Battalion, London Irish Rifles; 10th Battalion, Royal Berkshires; and 1st Battalion, London Scottish Rifles, a.k.a. Gordon Highlanders. Making up the 169th (Queen's) Brigade were the 2nd Battalion, 5th Queens Regiment; 2nd Battalion, 6th Queens Regiment; and 2nd Battalion, 7th Queens Regiment. D'Este, *Fatal Decision*, 199.

Companies B and C fought their way into Aprilia and kicked out the German occupiers. As the sky began to grow light, the Germans returned
and forced Johnson's battalion to fall back to a position approximately
500 yards south of the town. The infantrymen also soon found themselves without armor support; the tank company was ordered to withdraw because, in two days of fighting, the battalion had had eight tanks
totally destroyed and several others damaged (an armored division had
an authorized strength of fifty-three Sherman medium tanks and seventeen Stuart light tanks). The effort to retake Aprilia had to be suspended.[4]

THE DECISION WAS MADE TO blast Aprilia, Carroceto, and Campoleone
from the air. With clear weather finally forecast, two waves of dive-
bombers dropped their ordnance, followed by thirty-four B-17s and
nineteen B-24s that saturated the area with 145 tons of bombs. Three
shell-shocked members of the 145th Grenadier Regiment of Pfeiffer's
65th Grenadier Division staggered into Allied lines and surrendered;
they said they could not take the pounding any longer.[5]

The Germans, having taken every counterpunch the British could deliver and staggered by the unexpectedly stubborn resistance, also needed
a moment to catch their breath and devise new ways to overcome their
enemy. But it was still Aprilia that Mackensen considered his most important intermediate objective—and, hence, the most important one for
the Allies.

With both sides pausing to stock up on fresh supplies of both men
and munitions, the clashes around Anzio devolved into a brief ceasefire. During the pause, forty-five-year-old Gerald Templer* and his 56th
British Division began arriving piecemeal from Naples. First to arrive
was Brigadier J. Scott-Elliott's 167th Brigade, composed of the 7th Battalion, Oxfordshire and Buckinghamshire Light Infantry Regiment (better
known simply as the "Ox and Bucks"), and the 8th and 9th Battalions,

---

* Templer had led the 56th during the fighting in North Africa and was highly regarded by his peers and superiors. So highly regarded was Templer that, after the
war, he would be knighted and named chief of the Imperial General Staff. D'Este,
Fatal Decision, 238; Wynford Vaughn-Thomas as quoted in John Ellis, *The Sharp
End: The Fighting Man in World War II*, 35.

Royal Fusilier (City of London) Regiment. While the Ox and Bucks was a relatively young regiment, created in 1881, the predecessor of the Royal Fusiliers (City of London) Regiment was formed in 1685 after the English Civil War and had fought in every war since then.

At the outbreak of World War II, the Royal Fusiliers were shipped to northern Iraq to protect the oil fields from possible capture by the Germans; the impending defeat of the Afrika Korps in North Africa precluded that possibility, so the regiment was sent to help the Eighth Army finish off Rommel and his desert foxes. The regiment next saw action during the invasion of Sicily and then participated in the Allied invasion at Salerno and the long, hard slog up the peninsula to Cassino and the Gustav Line. Like the 7th Ox and Bucks, the 7th and 8th Battalions of the Royal Fusiliers were battle weary from weeks of fighting along the Gustav Line; Anzio was the last place they wanted to be.[6]

The 8th Battalion, Royal Fusiliers, took up their positions southeast of Aprilia, in the center of the line; the 9th Battalion was to the 8th's right, and the 7th Battalion, Ox and Bucks, was on the left, in contact with the 157th Regiment of the 45th Infantry Division.[7] A new member of Z Company, 8th Battalion, Royal Fusiliers, was a young subaltern named Eric Fletcher Waters.[*] He had joined the unit at Monte Damiano just a month earlier but, like so many of his fellow fusiliers destined for Anzio, would not have much longer to live.[8]

The 7th Battalion, Ox and Bucks, reached Anzio on February 13, and its commanding officer, Lieutenant Colonel Shaw Ball, received orders that his men would take over the area at the front currently occupied by the 1st Foresters and 1st KSLI; these battalions would then fall back to B Echelon. Ball's men had seen much hard fighting in early January in the rugged mountains near Cassino and at the Garigliano—a river that ran red with the battalion's blood. What they needed was a good, long rest, not more combat, but a rest was not in the cards.[9]

---

[*] Waters's wife, Mary, had given birth to a son on September 6, 1943, just three days before the Salerno invasion. The child was named George Roger Waters. Many years later, dropping the "George" from his name, Roger Waters would be one of the founding members of the British rock band Pink Floyd. www.roger waters.org.

LIFE FOR THE BRITS AND Yanks at the front, being bombed, shelled, and fired at every day, was bad enough, but there were more depredations. Men were cold and wet and covered with sticky, stinking mud—and stayed that way for days, sometimes longer. The lice were a silent, omnipresent enemy, too, burrowing into the seams of the men's uniforms and causing almost unbearable itching.

For the troops on the front lines, life was miserable in the extreme and stretched to the limit men's ability to endure the unendurable. For example, the high water table at Anzio made digging a foxhole a difficult proposition, as one could dig only a foot or less before the hole began filling with water like a bathtub.

Within a very short period of time, once the men realized that the invasion had stalled, they began to get creative with their semipermanent living arrangements. Depending on one's location, it was possible to dig deeper and thus build a relatively warm, dry, and secure shelter. Bernard Kahn, a German-born machine gunner with Company H, 157th Infantry Regiment, 45th Division, recalled, "Our sleeping holes were the most comfortable we had had during the war up to that point. Being dug into the side of the bank [of the Mussolini Canal] and having shelter-halves rigged on railroad ties, we were able to keep the ground completely dry. . . . It was actually possible to sleep without boots on."[10]

Not everyone thought removing one's boots was such a good idea. Victor Wade (3rd Division) made the mistake of taking off his one night: "The next morning my feet were swollen and I had great difficulty getting my boots back on. I don't think I have ever been so cold in all my life as I was on that particular night."[11]

Bill Mauldin observed that the European mud, especially in wartime, is unlike mud found anywhere else in the world. "Mud . . . is a curse which seems to save itself for war. I'm sure Europe never got this muddy during peacetime. I'm equally sure that no mud in the world is so deep and sticky or wet as European mud."[12]

A GI fighting in northern Germany in late 1944 wrote another description of mud that applied equally well to the conditions at Anzio: "It is amazing what a little mud in the wrong place can do. It will make your rifle a worthless piece of junk. It will jam it just when you need it most. It will ooze through your shoes and through your socks and eat away at your feet. It will make your foxhole a slimy, slippery, smelly jail. It will creep into your hair, your food, your teeth, your clothes, and sometimes your mind."[13]

Audie Murphy (Company B, 15th Infantry Regiment, 3rd Division) reflected on the fact that the rain "is not without its blessing. As long as it keeps the ground swampy, enemy armor bogs down and cannot move against us." Relieving oneself in a battlefield environment was a particularly unpleasant and tricky necessity, as Murphy also noted: "Often we must use ration cans as chamber pots, hurling them from the holes like grenades after they have served their purpose."[14]

"The toilet function was indeed a hit-and-run proposition," recalled Bernard Kahn.

> There was the chronic problem of getting a decent distance from one's own dugout and yet not dig a latrine hole at some other soldier's doorstep. Everybody was always sensitive, alert, and ready to yell discouragement to all infractions, as everybody apparently had been through the experience of stepping on an innocent piece of ground only to discover that it was a freshly covered latrine hole. . . . It was par for the course to be out in the open, pants down in a squatting position, only to receive such yells of welcome as "Get the hell away from here" or, worse, to be caught in a mortar barrage.[15]

Then there was the food—barely enough to keep a man alive. Ted Lees of the 6th Gordons recalled:

> Our rations until [March] were COMPO packs, each a wooden box for twelve men for one day. They included corned beef, beef stew, a mixture of tea, sugar, and milk known as compo-tea, tinned cheese, biscuits, loo [toilet] paper. Our cooking equipment was our own mess tins (two) and a mug. To heat up any food we had some instant fuel in small rounds which we balanced on two bits of metal, with this we could make some kind of cake/bread by digging a hole in the side of our bunker and using it like a primitive oven. Water came in old jerry cans which had at one time held petrol, and they were never really satisfactorily cleaned, so the water always had a petrol flavour.[16]

Sometimes, if a frontline position was under fire, the runners carrying cans of food from the kitchens in the rear areas to the front lines were too frightened to deliver them. On occasion, an Italian cow or sheep might get killed by bullet, shell, or land mine and become a delicacy that relieved the sameness of the bully beef and K and C rations, but trying to build a cooking fire without the smoke or flame giving one's position away was always a challenge. Then, too, some of the abandoned farmhouses were treasure troves of all sorts of food (and drink) that added variety to the otherwise monotonous combat diet.[17]

First Lieutenant Bill Whitman (commanding Company B, 180th Regiment, 45th Division) recalled that his unit was one of the fortunate few to be getting fresh meat:

> We were putting many wandering Italian cows out of their 'misery' (some had been hit with artillery). . . . Our jeeps would pick it up on their return to the kitchen in the rear and deliver the cow to the cooks who would make us steak sandwiches and send them up to us. The order came out: "Do not kill any cows!" One day [battalion commander Lieutenant] Colonel [Daniel K.] Ahern was at my company when the steak sandwiches were delivered from the kitchen. The colonel was furious! He asked me why I was permitting my men to kill cows in direct violation of orders. I explained to him that the cows were stepping on mines and this was something that we could do nothing about.[18]

Major General Ernest Harmon noted with tongue in cheek, "Cattle were protected by Army orders, but the life expectancy of beef dropped sharply. Canned rations are monotonous and fresh beef tastes good. At Anzio, cattle seemed to have a habit of attacking soldiers. Anyway, the soldiers always maintained they shot in self-defense."[19]

Lieutenant Russell W. Cloer (Headquarters Company, 7th Infantry Regiment, 3rd Infantry Division) said that although the civilians had been evacuated from the Anzio area, the farmers "were not allowed to take their cattle with them. The cattle now roamed the fields aimlessly until they were killed by enemy shellfire. The dead cattle had to be buried because the odor became unbearable after a few days in the sun. This had to be done at night, of course, because of enemy artillery observers."[20]

THE MEN STANK, TOO. WOOL clothing that had been slept in and sweated in and rolled around in the mud in gave off a foul odor that made men barely able to stand their own body odors, let alone those of other men.

Personal hygiene became the first victim of the protracted struggle at Anzio. The American staff officers had it best. Lieutenant Charles F. Marshall, of the 3rd Division's G-2 (Intelligence) Section, recalled, "One of the privileges of being a staff officer was that of being able to get a hot bath once a week. Each officer was allotted ten minutes for his ablutions. Two GIs had the sole duty of heating water and scrubbing out the tub for the next officer. No matter how much bombing, shelling, and strafing might be going on, few officers ever skipped the luxury of that bath. As a morale maintainer, it was second to none."[21]

Enlisted men and British line officers rarely enjoyed that luxury. Green Howards Lieutenant Raleigh Trevelyan complained that he had had only one shower in two months.[22] George Avery (84th Chemical Mortar Battalion) recalled that Truscott's 3rd Division "set up a shower in Padglione Woods where we would be sent, five at a time, to get a hot meal and a hot shower and a change of uniform. I used these facilities *once* in four months, so you can understand how welcome the chance to 'go to the showers' was."[23]

And, of course, there were other smells: the omnipresent, nauseating stench of death—dead cattle, dead horses, and dead men—as well as the distinct aromas of manure and discarded ration cans moldering in the fields and the acrid taste of cordite and gunpowder wafting across the battlefields and the overpowering odor of unwashed feet when the boots came off in the foxholes. In the hospitals there was the overwhelming smell of the putrefying flesh of the wounded.

A British officer recalled going to visit one of his wounded men at one of the Anzio hospitals. After stepping into the tent and searching lines of beds, he went past "bottles of blood plasma dripping into cinder-colored bodies, past enamel buckets full of dirty swabs and bandages, past piles of twisted sheets. . . . The farther I moved from the door, the more oppressive became the smell, so that before I had gone halfway around the ward, I had to return to the [nurse]."[24] Everywhere one turned, it seemed, there was a symphony of smells to assault the senses and sicken the stomach.

Despite the lack of proper bathing and washing facilities at the front, some units still expected their soldiers to be clean shaven; others were a bit more informal and relaxed the rules about personal grooming. First Lieutenant Bill Whitman, one of the latter, said that his battalion commander "ordered me to 'bust' a sergeant for not shaving. The sergeant was on an outpost where there was no water to shave with. The colonel and I went round and round about this matter. So, much later, without the colonel's knowledge, I got the sergeant transferred to our Service Company to save his stripes."[25]

Lieutenant Trevelyan, one of the former, said, "I insisted that everybody should have a shave and brush his teeth. (It's surprising how physical appearances affect morale.) We had great difficulty coping with a tough nut called Crocker, a real old soldier. He hadn't shaved once since we'd left B Echelon, and would only do so when Sergeant Chesterton threatened to put him on permanent latrine duty the moment we returned out of the line." The water for shaving came from a muddy pond teeming with mosquito larvae.[26]

Malaria had not been completely eradiated from the Pontine Marshes, either—despite Mussolini's efforts to accomplish that feat, a number of the soldiers came down with the disease. One of them, George Avery, 84th Chemical Mortar Battalion, recalled that malaria gave him "a fever and hallucinations, and so I spent some days at a hospital on the beachhead. We called this hospital 'Hell's Half Acre.' It was semi-underground with the tents set up in pits surrounded with sand bags. This area received some shelling and nurses died there." Malaria was considered a "non-battle casualty," so, when his fever broke, Avery was sent back to his unit that was dug in along the Mussolini Canal. No Purple Heart medal was awarded, either.[27]

SOME MEN LOST THEIR MINDS or were reduced to a nonfunctional state after being subjected to the unrelieved shelling and awful living (and dying) conditions at Anzio. Months after the battle had been concluded, the U.S. surgeon general distributed a report, *Prevention of Loss of Manpower from Psychiatric Disorder*. In it the surgeon general noted that, in Italy, infantry battalions lost 50 percent of their original strength killed, missing, or wounded in 120 days in combat. This figure would have been higher still had not many soldiers been removed as exhaustion cases before they could become casualties. "While the British count a man's combat usefulness as 400 days, twice the US estimate, they relieve their troops every twelve days or less for a four-day rest. In Italy, the American soldier was kept in the line as long as eighty days without relief."[28]

One of the things absolutely essential for boosting morale was a letter from home. The mail, when it could be delivered to the men on the front lines, was always a welcome break from the constant gut-churning fear of combat. Many of the soldiers' families and loved ones wrote on a daily basis to keep up their servicemen's spirits. Being thousands of miles from home and forced to live in subhuman conditions added to the misery of soldiers on both sides of the line at Anzio. But being subjected to the random death that was continually dispensed by combat had by far the worst psychological effect on those who were there.

OF ALL THE DIRTY JOBS that had to be performed on the battlefield—rifleman, machine gunner, artilleryman, tankman, medic, and so on—arguably no one had a worse job than the men of the Graves Registration Service. It was their gruesome duty to crawl out onto the battlefield, usually at night, to retrieve the often-mangled corpses of soldiers—both friend and foe—and bring them back for burial. And no retrieval duty was more sickening than crawling into the still-smoldering wreckage of a tank—American or German—that had been destroyed by an armor-piercing round; inside were the burned and ripped-apart bodies of the crewmen that had to be extracted, sometimes in pieces, from their armored tomb. The GRS men were sometimes called ghouls,* but it was a term of respect, for theirs was one of the most harrowing, dangerous, and agonizing jobs around. Many GRS men "went to pieces" after having to collect the shattered remains of fellow human beings. Many of them also resorted to alcohol to blunt the emotional impact of what they had to see, feel, and smell.[29]

Paul Brown, 179th, was one of the "ghouls" or "buzzards." He recalled in his journal the particularly memorable night of February 13–14 when

---

* Even more inelegantly, the GRS crews were sometimes referred to as the "buzzard detail." Audie Murphy, *To Hell and Back*, 119.

he and his GRS unit, commanded by the Service Company commander Captain Robert L. Richmond, were sent out to gather the remains of men killed during recent fighting: "Went to same place as night before last. Enemy tanks sighted in on us where I was turning truck around. I thank God I am alive after that. All of us were scared but I was driving the damn truck. Truck has several holes in it. Shells dropped in 25 yards [away]. Bombers dropped flares then lay eggs to their hearts content. Picked up 5 boys last night."

For Brown, too, becoming inebriated was the only way he could deal with the macabre nature of his duties. Various diary entries noted, "Hell hit again last night but I had so much rum in me I would have never known what hit me. Sure was sick this morning. We [picked up] one boy last night; there are many more but we cannot get to them yet. . . . One hell of a night, my nerves are just about shot. . . . Got 3 more 157th boys last night. Shemp & Gernard were drunk and went with us. . . . Drank vino again last night, sure got drunk. . . . Was drunk again last night. . . . Got drunk again. . . . Was drunk again last night. . . . Left vino jug alone last night. . . . Got drunk again, and I mean drunk!"[30]

Although alcohol was not readily available to most soldiers on the beachhead,[*] some soldiers such as Paul Brown managed to scrounge bottles of vino and rum from their British counterparts. Second Lieutenant Francis E. Liggett, an artillery forward observer in the 45th Division, also had his share:

> The British were on our left flank and we were fairly close to some of them. After getting acquainted, we visited back and forth. We didn't get a liquor ration and they did, so one evening they invited Olsen and me over to drink and visit. Their hole lived up to their motto, "As long as you have to go, you just as well go first class." They had dug a hole about ten feet deep and had about four feet of dirt over the top of it. Also electric lights like we had, powered from a nearby vehicle.

---

[*] One British soldier noted that, while the enlisted men received rum, the officers received a ration of one bottle of Vat 69 scotch per month. Ted Lees, "Anzio— Beach Head," www.bbc.co.uk/history/ww2peopleswar/stories/16/a2059616.shtml.

While sitting down there, we heard a loud thud up above and dirt started shaking down on us. We went outside to see what happened. On top of the hole lay a huge projectile from the big (280mm) railroad gun that the Germans had up near Rome—the "Anzio Annie," as we called it. It had apparently hit a tree that deflected its trajectory so it landed on its side without hitting the fuse on the end of it, which would have caused it to explode. Had it exploded, it would have made a hole big enough to bury a truck in.[31]

Fred Mason of the 2nd North Staffs recalled, "As far as I can remember we received our rum ration at different times. It was issued with our food, but not every day—probably once a week. Of course it was very welcome because of the awful cold. Also when we were going into an attack. We were only allowed small rations, because of the obvious. It was a spirit to keep the spirits up."[32]

SOMETIMES THE DEAD GAVE UP their secrets. Lieutenant Charles F. Marshall, a fluent German-speaking intelligence officer assigned to the 3rd Infantry Division, noted, "The greater the butchery, the larger was the capture of documents. I was always a bit repulsed when handed a batch of bloody papers with a buckslip reading, 'From good Germans—dead ones.' This was our 3rd Infantry Division's trademark.

"The study of documents was engrossing work, because one never knew what one would find. There was also a tantalizing element: In which batch would we hit the jackpot? Meticulous examination leavened by serendipity and *voila*!—there it could be!" Marshall and his team (three native-born Germans and one American of German ancestry) were never happy handling the blood-soaked documents that were often brought in by the mail-sack load, but the perusal of a thousand documents might reveal in one information about the enemy's plans and enable the Allies to thwart those plans, thus saving Allied lives.

Marshall noted that certain aspects of reviewing the contents of an enemy soldier's pockets were anything but pleasant:

Before eating . . . I scrubbed my hands thoroughly, not only for sanitary reasons, but to get rid of that odor of death that, no matter how much I scrubbed, seemed to linger with an irritating pervasiveness. We thought then, and I still think now, that we were making a significant contribution to the battle to undo Hitler. Our work revealed that Germany was running so short of manpower that sixteen- and seventeen-year-old kids were being drafted and given only two months of basic training before being thrown into the front lines. This policy was criminal. Sometimes I felt like weeping as I went through their papers and pictures. To my parents I wrote: "They're not soldiers. They're just children in uniform. They are now pulling their kids directly from the *Hitler Jugend*. I can't help wondering how long before they take them from the kindergarten. I don't see how Germany can go on much longer. We have overwhelming air power, manpower, and production."

There was also a treasure trove of photographs and other personal items with entertainment value: birth certificates, baptismal certificates, family pictures, pictures of their girlfriends or wives, diaries, driving licenses, and any of a hundred more or less standard items—including, as a rule, a batch of personal letters.

Marshall noted that some of the dead "carried nude pictures of their wives or sweethearts—stimulating reminders of the joys awaiting their return. One PW had half a dozen seductively posed shots that, according to the letter found with them, had been taken by the woman's father. Such photos, triggering salivating appraisals, lightened the day's chores and were gleefully passed around, getting as much critical inspection as a captured map."[33]

IT WASN'T JUST SOLDIERS WHO were exposed to the horrors and the dangers of the battlefield; noncombatants, too, felt the effects. E. O. Bowles, a driver in the 137th Ambulance Company, American Field Service, admitted that he "never before knew what fear meant. I mean, really being physically afraid. It is quite an experience, and it makes most of the prewar worries and anxieties look pretty unimportant. It isn't a fear of death or of anything tangible—it is just fear. Almost everyone here is afraid, and it is no emotion to be ashamed of. Bravery, after all, doesn't consist of a lack of fear but of an ability to carry on and do your job even when you're so afraid you can hardly hold the wheel of your ambulance."[34]

WHILE FEAR MUST HAVE BEEN equally rampant in the German camp, preparations were nevertheless being made for the Fourteenth Army's next attempt to drive the Allies out of the Anzio-Nettuno beachhead once and for all. The other attempts had come close, but it was now or never for Kesselring and Mackensen. They decided that February 16 would be the start of the major effort to bulldoze VI Corps off the beachhead and into the sea. If this effort failed, then perhaps the entire campaign would be lost. And if the Italian campaign was lost, then could the Fatherland's defeat be far behind?

"At the [Anzio] bridgehead," Kesselring later wrote, "the struggle was still in progress, the American 6th Corps aiming to break through to the Alban Hills, and Mackensen to get a preliminary grip on Apulia* [*sic*] before launching our main counterattack. The Allied assaults were repulsed with heavy casualties on both sides, our counterattack leading to the occupation of Apulia on 8–9 February and to the capture of Corroceto [*sic*] on 9–10. Allied counterattacks misfired."[35]

On the Allied side, General Lucas observed, "This is becoming a war of attrition. Until I am considerably reinforced, I can't do much about it."[36] As events would prove, Lucas's chances of obtaining considerable reinforcements were slim to none.

THE SITUATION ON THE FRONT lines was unnervingly like the calm before the storm. Except for some light shelling following the February 11–13 slugfest, the Germans were being strangely inactive. Taking advantage of the unexpected lull, the beachhead forces were shuffled to give some of the most hard-hit units time to recuperate. The 157th Infantry Regiment of the 45th Infantry Division relieved its 1st Battalion with its 2nd. After the staff officers from Templer's 56th British Division arrived at the front, they were briefed by General Eagles and his staff and then went forward to reconnoiter the positions they would take over from the 157th before midnight on the fourteenth. All seemed to have gone

---

* Kesselring wrote his memoirs secretly while in an Allied prison after the war; thus he was working from memory and not from any diary, notes, or official reports. He therefore misidentified Aprilia, calling it Apulia, which is a province in southeast Italy constituting the "heel" and "Achilles' tendon" of the boot-shaped peninsula.

smoothly and without a hitch. But all good things must come to an end, and the quiet along the front was about to be violently shattered.[37]

The Germans upped the tempo of their air raids and artillery fire on the eve of the big attack. On February 15 there were eight air raids in the Anzio area that hit an LCT loaded with fuel and a Liberty ship, and heavy-caliber shells blew apart Anzio's summer hotels and palatial villas along the harbor and seashore.[38]

Sergeant Vere "Tarzan" Williams (Company K, 157th, 45th Division) recalled an enemy shelling that day that cost his unit dearly. While his company was moving to occupy a new area of the front, a shell came in and wounded one man. "Two men ran to him when another shell came in and wounded *them*," he said. "When we started back to our area, another shell came in and hit a big tree. There were nineteen men hit by that last shell, including me. I remember seeing my helmet rolling slow in front of me." Shell fragments had hit Williams in the neck and shoulder; he spent the next several weeks in the hospital.[39]

Corporal Al Bedard (Headquarters Company, 157th) recalled losing a buddy, George S. Viereck Jr., a Harvard graduate:

> George and I were on an observation post when, all of a sudden, the Germans started to shell us. One of the soldiers yelled out that he had been hit. I went up and saw he had caught a piece of shrapnel. It just missed a vein but shattered his leg. While I was attending to him, George ran back to the CP [command post] and got a couple of guys with a litter and came back to where I was. We got this fellow on the litter and the four of us carried him. On the way back from the CP, the Germans lobbed in a couple of mortar shells. George got hit with a fragment across the temple. He died in our arms; he just bled to death. He kept asking us, "Please help me, please help me." There wasn't a thing we could do for him.[40]

AT ANZIO, BRITISH AND AMERICAN troops lived and fought together side by side, their units often intermingled, as they had not been on most battlefields before—or would be again. As a result, the chance for rapport between allies was great. Nineteen-year-old Private Fred Mason, a Bren gunner with C Company, 2nd North Staffs, had positive things to say about the Americans sharing the beachhead with him: "They were good soldiers, and very friendly. We had a great deal of respect for them. Sometimes, when it was possible, they came over to us, and they always had something to give us—K rations, chocolate, etc." Mason also noted, "Sometimes we could hear one of their men sending mortar shells over and every time he put a bomb into the barrel, he shouted, 'Count your men, Kesselring!'"[41]

It took some Americans longer to warm to their British counterparts, however, probably because of Clark's antipathy toward the British that rubbed off on them. George Fisher, 180th Infantry Regiment, noted, "While the British sometimes made one want to wring their necks, we had to admit that they were brave, even to the point of being foolishly stubborn and brave. When everything would go wrong and the British troops would be in a highly dangerous predicament, a question addressed to a British officer or enlisted man as to how things were going would invariably bring the reply, "Tis a bit sticky, but we're having a good shoot.'"[42]

THE INCREASED LEVEL OF LUFTWAFFE aerial attacks and Wehrmacht artillery concentrations signaled that something very big was about to take place. In addition, "Ultra" intercepts (the Allies' code-breaking efforts) had revealed that Hitler had ordered nine divisions shifted from the Balkans to the Anzio-Nettuno area. Although Alexander and Clark were privy to these top-secret decodings, Lucas was left out of the loop. All Lucas knew was that his superiors had told him to be ready for a German counterattack—something that he had been doing ever since the January 22 landings.[43]

A prisoner of war from a parachute regiment told his captors that an attack was scheduled for February 16 "to reduce the bridgehead or split it down the center." The center of the bridgehead was the Albano Highway that ran through Aprilia all the way to the harbor. Consequently, every unit within the entire area was put on alert.[44]

ON FEBRUARY 15 GENERAL ALEXANDER, commander of the Fifteenth Army Group, paid a visit to the London Irish Rifles' 1st Battalion that was taking a few days' rest beneath the tall umbrella pines at B Echelon. Alexander was an old friend of the LIR from prewar days, and he

Lieutenant General Mark W. Clark (left), head of Fifth U.S. Army, confers with Fifteenth Army Group commander Field Marshal Sir Harold Alexander while Alexander's chief of staff, U.S. Brigadier General Lyman Lemnitzer (center), looks on. (U.S. NATIONAL ARCHIVES)

Major General John P. Lucas, U.S. VI Corps commander, was criticized for being "too cautious." He ultimately was replaced by Clark in favor of Lucian Truscott. Here, smoking his trademark corncob pipe, he is pictured with his deputy corps commander, British Major-General Vyvyan Evelegh, February 17, 1944. (U.S. NATIONAL ARCHIVES)

Aerial view of Anzio (foreground) and Nettuno (right). (U.S. National Archives)

Apparently unworried about enemy opposition, a line of British "Tommies" smile for the camera as they leave Anzio and head north on the Via Anziate in the direction of Rome which, as the sign says, is only 57.6 kilometers away. Unfortunately, it would take the Allies four months to get there. (U.S. National Archives)

Mark Clark and Colonel William O. Darby, former commander of the 6615th U.S. Ranger Force, photographed in April 1944 after Darby had been assigned to lead the 179th Infantry Regiment of the 45th U.S. Infantry Division. An Army censor has obscured the 45th Division insignia on Darby's sleeve. (U.S. NATIONAL ARCHIVES)

A German, dressed in a mixture of military and civilian clothing, lies dead beside his shot-up *Kubelwagen* after being ambushed by members of the 1st SSF, January 24, 1944. (U.S. NATIONAL ARCHIVES)

War correspondent Ernie Pyle (center, with goggles on cap) chats with American GIs at Anzio. (U.S. NATIONAL ARCHIVES)

Field Marshal Albert Kesselring, commander of Army Group C in Italy. (U.S. National Archives)

General Heinrich von Vietinghoff, commander of German Tenth Army that successfully stalled Allie's progress at the Gustav Line. (U.S. National Archives)

Colonel-General Eberhard von Mackensen, head of German Fourteenth Army that was responsible for the defense of the Anzio sector. (U.S. National Archives)

A Tiger I of the 508th Heavy Tank Battalion on its way to Anzio. (U.S. National Archives)

Major General William W. Eagles, commander of 45th U.S. Infantry Division (shown while assistant division commander of the 3rd U.S. Infantry Division). (U.S. National Archives)

1st U.S. Armored Division commander Major General Ernest N. Harmon. (U.S. National Archives)

Major General Lucian K. Truscott, former commander of the 3rd U.S. Infantry Division, photographed after taking command of VI Corps. (U.S. National Archives)

VI Corps underground headquarters in Nettuno. (U.S. National Archives)

While soldiers climb the canvas to erect a hospital tent behind her, a U.S. Army nurse smiles for the camera as she digs a foxhole for protection from German bombs and shells. (U.S. National Archives)

An anti-tank "sticky bomb" being removed from its carrying case. (Screen shot from Signal Corps film, "A Report from the Anzio Beachhead," U.S. National Archives)

Brigadier General Robert T. Frederick, commander of the 1st Special Service Force (a.k.a., the "Devil's Brigade"). A destroyed Sherman tank smolders in the background. (U.S. National Archives)

British humor on display at a dugout. Troops lived for months in water-filled holes as protection from German shelling and aerial attacks. (U.S. National Archives)

The nearly completed "model Fascist town" of Aprilia, ten miles north of Anzio, which was dedicated by Italian dictator Benito Mussolini on October 29, 1937. The severe modernist design of the buildings and the two towers led many American and British soldiers to think that this was an industrial complex—hence the nickname, "the Factory." (Silvano Casaldi collection)

Raymond Saidel's sketch of a GI handing a water canteen to a wounded German soldier being helped to the rear by a comrade. Note barbed wire atop the edge of the sunken road and a log dugout in which a soldier is resting. (USAMHI)

American soldiers work to extract a jeep stuck in Italian mud near Cassino. Bill Mauldin observed, "I'm sure Europe never got this muddy during peacetime." (U.S. National Archives)

Bodies of German soldiers lie in a water-filled ditch after one of their failed attacks against Allied troops. (U.S. National Archives)

A GI covers the bodies of two buddies killed during the fighting. (U.S. National Archives)

The battle-damaged structure known as the "Overpass" to the Americans and "Flyover" to the British. (U.S. National Archives)

Major General John "Iron Mike" O'Daniel, commanding officer of the 3rd U.S. Infantry Division. (U.S. National Archives)

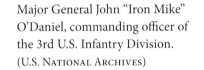

German POWs transport a wounded comrade under armed guard. A knocked-out Sherman tank burns behind them. (U.S. National Archives)

An artist's depiction of the battle of the caves. (U.S. National Archives)

The volcano Vesuvius erupting in March 1944. The eruption affected U.S. aerial operations when hot ash covered an American air base near Pompeii. (U.S. National Archives)

American reinforcements arrive at Anzio harbor aboard LSTs in preparation for the May breakout. (U.S. NATIONAL ARCHIVES)

A 1st Special Service Force 3.5-inch rocket launcher team attacks a German-held house during the breakout. (U.S. NATIONAL ARCHIVES)

German prisoners taken by the 7th Infantry Regiment, 3rd U.S. Infantry Division, during the capture of Cisterna, May 25, 1944. The original caption says that the Germans "sniped at U.S. soldiers until ammunition gave out." (U.S. National Archives)

Men of the Japanese-American 100th Infantry Battalion, attached to the 34th U.S. Infantry Division, move up to assault the town of Velletri, May 28, 1944. (U.S. National Archives)

Although Kesselring had declared Rome an "undefended open city," the first contingent of 88th Division troops to enter the city come under German fire. (U.S. National Archives)

While driving down the Via della Conciliazione, Lieutenant General Mark W. Clark stops to ask an American Catholic priest from Detroit for directions to Rome's City Hall. St. Peter's Basilica is in the background. (U.S. National Archives)

The American Military Cemetery at Nettuno. (Author photo)

came to congratulate them on their fine performance during a very critical period of the battle. His visit did much to cheer the battalion and prepare it for the difficult days ahead.

While the London Irish were resting, British and American forces were still attempting to drive the enemy off Buonriposo Ridge and also out of Aprilia and Carroceto. The two towns, which had already been pounded severely, were again hit with heavy artillery bombardments and bombing raids by the air forces, but the Germans refused to be dislodged and, in fact, were reinforcing their hold on the area.[45]

Although Alexander had nothing but praise for the London Irish, he was less than pleased with the corps of war correspondents. On the fifteenth, he met with a group of reporters to give them a piece of his mind. Concerned that the British and American publics were losing heart about the situation in Italy because of a series of negative, but realistic, news reports from the front, the usually very proper, upper-crust British officer said, "There is absolutely no Dunkirk here—there's no basis for pessimistic rubbish. I assure you the Germans opposite us here are a very unhappy party. The Germans realize they've lost the battle, though events have not gone as swiftly as we ourselves hoped. . . . As it is, we are near the end of the second round and we are winning it. . . . I am delighted to find the troops so full of fighting spirit and of such high morale."[46]

Alexander's attempts to castigate the media, put a good face on the situation, and buck up home-front morale notwithstanding, the Germans were still very much in the fight. More and more units were being moved in under the cover of darkness to occupy their waiting places within the rubble of Aprilia, Carroceto, Cisterna, and the wadis, canals, and gullies that cut through the area. Ammunition was issued, and the artillerymen stacked their wooden cases full of shells near their guns in readiness for the big attack that would "lance the abscess" once and for all.

Edward Heard (London Irish Rifles) said, "Reports came of constant traffic on the roads and railways into Rome and on the roads leading south and south-east into Albano and Genzano. Much activity was observed in the German rear areas, and it was safely deduced that their build-up for the next phase of the all-out offensive ordered by the Führer was soon to come. According to prisoners, a final crushing blow was planned to split the beachhead in half and to break through to the sea at Nettuno."[47]

The prisoners spoke the truth. What was intended to be Kesselring's and Mackensen's final crushing blow was about to take place.

SIXTY-FIVE MILES DUE EAST, AT a pinnacle known as Monte Cassino, rising above the sleepy town of Cassino, a tragedy was about to be enacted. Because a month of ground attacks had all failed, and because they firmly believed that German troops were using it as an observation post, the Allies decided that the Benedictine abbey on top of the mountain had to be eradicated.

This decision was reached after Major General Francis Tuker, commander of the 4th Indian Division, an element of Lieutenant General Bernard Freyberg's New Zealand Corps, had been selected to make the next assault. He had asked higher headquarters to authorize his plan for a wider maneuver to attack the hill from the flank, but his request was rejected; he was told that he must, like all the other divisions that had already expended themselves trying to assault up the steep southern face of the mountain, try the frontal approach again. The word *suicidal* was not mentioned in these orders, but that was the hidden message.

Tuker relented, but on one condition: the monastery first must be obliterated by aerial bombardment. Alexander and Freyberg agreed, and, on the fifteenth, several waves of American bombers from the Twelfth and Fifteenth U.S. Air Forces overflew the abbey and released their lethal loads, dropping nearly 1,000 tons of bombs and blowing the monastery's hallowed halls and walls apart. The Allies also contributed 190,000 artillery shells to the effort. (Fortunately, the Germans, working in conjunction with the abbot, had previously removed all the pieces of portable art for safekeeping.)

With the historic building now pulverized, the Germans on Monte Cassino had no qualms about taking up fighting positions within its collapsed walls. Clark was furious; he had not wanted the abbey bombed, but Freyberg had gone over his head to get authorization straight from Alexander. In the event, the destruction was all for naught. The next day, the 4th Indian Division once again stormed the summit but, after

much hard fighting, had to pull back with the stench of another failure clinging to their torn and bloody uniforms. The stalemate at Cassino remained. It was beginning to look to the Allies that the war in Italy was unwinnable.[48]

HITLER, ENSCONCED IN HIS BUNKER deep in the woods in Rastenburg, East Prussia, cared nothing about the loss of the abbey, but he was becoming apoplectic about the situation at Anzio. He railed, screamed, threatened, and foamed at the mouth, demanding that the British and Americans be bulldozed into oblivion. His personal message was read aloud to all the troops, demanding that the Allied beachhead be eliminated in three days.[49]

Responding to his boss's demands, Kesselring gave the code name *Morgenrote*—"Red Morning" or "Dawn"—to the February 16 operation designed to destroy the Anglo-American forces. The February 8 and 11 counteroffensives against the entrenched Allies had very nearly succeeded. Perhaps one more division or twenty more tanks or a hundred more guns might have made the difference and achieved the breakthrough to the water's edge. Triumph at Anzio had been within Germany's grasp on February 8 and the three days that followed, yet it had slipped away like a golden nugget falling through one's fingers into a bottomless mineshaft. Kesselring and Mackensen were convinced that one more massive counterattack would tip the scales in their favor. It *had* to. If it failed, then defeat for Germany in Italy was only a matter of time.

Mackensen's plan of attack was a classic pincer maneuver. A thrust by four infantry or motorized divisions, augmented by eleven combat battalions, backed up by two mobile divisions (the 26th Panzer and 29th Panzer-Grenadier), and spearheaded by Hitler's pride and joy—the elite instructional and demonstration unit known as the 309th Panzer-Grenadier Regiment (also called the "Infantry Lehr Regiment") from the Infantry School at Döberitz—would come barreling south at dawn toward Aprilia and the Flyover/Overpass. According to plans subsequently taken off a German officer prisoner, a hundred panzers and a variety of assault guns and self-propelled howitzers would come straight down the Albano Highway from the direction of Campoleone. Anything in their way would be crushed, pulverized, and pushed aside.[50]

To reduce the impact of American air superiority, in the first few minutes of the assault, German guns would pound the airstrip at Nettuno to render it unusable, and every airworthy Luftwaffe plane would be up and bombing and strafing every Allied position below.[51] The eastern half of the force would then hit the 45th Infantry Division in and around Aprilia, while the western half would concentrate on destroying the 56th British Division at Carroceto and the Wadi Country west of Aprilia. With those units crushed, the Germans would have total control of the main north-south highway and could then plunge all the way down to the shoreline.[52]

Or so the German thinking went.

For Kesselring and Mackensen, February 16 would be *der Tag*—"the day"—the day of decision. The February 8 offensive had not accomplished its objectives, so Morgenrote—the second counteroffensive—was launched. If the Germans could burst through that small opening beneath the Overpass/Flyover, their chances of reaching the rear areas and pushing the Allies into the sea were slim. But unless they could accomplish such a herculean feat, their hold on Anzio would not last much longer and the Allies would have won.

For the Germans, everything depended on this all-or-nothing effort. For the past four weeks, more units had been rushed in along with replacements for the units that had been severely reduced in their previous assault. More trains filled with shells for the artillery pieces had arrived at the rear areas along with more fuel and spare parts for the panzers, more bombs for the Luftwaffe, more food, more bandages, more of everything the Germans would need to make victory theirs. There had been shipments of brand-new weapons, too—eighty PzKpfw V Panther tanks, the sixty-five-ton Ferdinand heavy tank destroyers designed by Porsche and called the Elefant; and even the little Goliath B-1 cable-controlled demolition vehicles. Four hundred and fifty-two pieces of artillery also were in place.[53]

The Allies at Anzio-Nettuno knew this, of course, tipped off by their Office of Strategic Services (OSS) spies and the Italian partisans who risked torture and death to report the departure of troop trains and supply trains from Rome. But knowledge of what an enemy is planning to do is one thing; being able to stop them from doing it is quite another.[54]

None of the British or American soldiers living like rats in the mud at Anzio gave much, if any, thought to the fact that they were all actors in a drama that could be compared as a larger version of the 24th of Foot's stand at Rorke's Drift, in which 140 defenders held off a 3,000–4,000-man Zulu army, or the 1836 battle of the Alamo, in which 250 Texans and other *Norte Americanos* faced 1,800 soldiers of Santa Anna's Mexican Army.[55]

No one wanted to bring up the fact that the Alamo defenders had all been wiped out.

CHAPTER 13

"The shrill, demented choirs of wailing shells"
FEBRUARY 16 (MORNING)

THE MEN LAY IN THE wet, muddy darkness in the cold that comes before the dawn, filled with the fear that always chooses that time in which to make itself felt. One man coughed, then another. It was the damned waiting that played hell with one's nerves. Once the fighting started and the bullets began to fly and the shells began to explode, then animal instincts took over, propelling the body forward with blood-chilling screams, as though the insanity of war had driven everyone mad.

The men lay in the wet, muddy darkness in the cold that comes before the dawn, fingering their rifles, checking their ammunition pouches, feeling for their grenades, making sure one more time that their bayonets were firmly affixed to the barrels of their rifles. The cold and wet had seeped into the marrow of their bones during the night, stiffening their joints and numbing fingers and toes, making it even too cold to think. Their mouths were as dry as the sands of the Libyan desert, and more than a few canteens were unfastened from belts and swallows taken. Bottles of alcohol, too, were passed around. Somewhere down the line someone was reciting the rosary. A few were vomiting and crying softly, trying not to be heard, fully aware that this was probably their last morning on earth. It was always like this, the tenseness before the attack, the silent wondering if you would make it through unscathed or if you would end up a torn and blasted piece of meat, feeling your blood oozing into the rich, black soil that smelled just like the farms back home.

The men lay in the wet, muddy darkness in the cold that comes before the dawn, looking at their best friends lying next to them, their faces illuminated by the occasional flare and star shell, mud smeared but unlined, the strong faces of youth and the recruiting posters, the face you fear you will never see again. Down the line a couple of the new replacements, just teenagers, really, are crying, sobbing that they don't want to die, that this is nothing but mass suicide. The sergeant tells them to shut up.

The men lay in the wet, muddy darkness in the cold that comes before the dawn, listening to their corporals and sergeants and lieutenants squishing past them in the water-logged field, telling everyone to stay calm, to conserve ammunition, to keep moving forward no matter what happens around them, to remember that their wives and mothers and girlfriends back home are immensely proud of them, even if they should not make it home, that their country, *der Vaterland*, and leader, *der Führer*, are immensely proud of them, that the future of Germany depends on their courage, their steadfastness. Someone is singing quietly to himself, as if to inspire himself and remind himself why he is here in this soggy hellhole so far from home: *Deutschland, Deutschland, über alles* . . .

HITLER HAD DEMANDED THAT FOURTEENTH Army launch the final and definitive assault that would shove the Allies into the sea or die trying, so try it would do. Kesselring had approved Mackensen's plan to strike on either side of Aprilia this day and drive southward, supported by two secondary attacks. Against an Allied force of 100,000 men Mackensen would throw 125,000 Germans into the attack—nearly as many men as the Allies would use to storm the beaches of Normandy come June.[1]

Hitler maintained his micromanaging style, even down to telling his field commanders what units must be used. For the assault on the sixteenth, Hitler insisted that his pet unit, the Infantry Demonstration Regiment 309 (Infantry Lehr), which demonstrated tactics at the Infantry School at Döberitz, be the spear point of the attack, "and this on a very narrow front so as to guarantee a pulverizing effect on the part of our artillery bombardment," Kesselring later wrote.[2]

However, Hitler's handpicked Infantry Lehr was not ready to lead the assault. Originally scheduled to leave its line of departure before dawn on the sixteenth, the unit would not begin moving out until the day was fully light; because the regiment knew nothing of the terrain, it needed daylight to attack across the unfamiliar landscape. In their place, Gräser's 3rd Panzer-Grenadier and Hildebrandt's 715th Motorized Infantry Divisions were hurriedly moved to the front. To their right were the 4th Parachute and 65th Infantry Divisions, the latter aimed at the seam between the 157th Infantry Regiment, 45th Division, and the 167th Brigade of the 56th British Division.

THE PRECURSOR TO THE APOCALYPTIC onslaught of February 16 was an eerie silence. The night had not been filled with the usual sporadic rain of German artillery shells that the Allies had come to expect. It was almost as if the Germans were using the hours between midnight and dawn to gather every shell in their arsenal and quietly load them into every gun along the front, getting ready for the big moment when all would be unleashed like a pack of vicious dogs ready to tear the throats out of the invader.

The deck of clouds dissipated, and the predawn, already cold, turned bitter. Americans and British soldiers who had been shivering in their freezing foxholes while trying to catch a few moments of sleep sensed something different in the air. Either the Germans had packed up and moved out during the night, or else something massive was about to happen. Men quietly made sure their frost-covered rifles were loaded, their machine guns had full belts of ammunition seated, their mortar rounds were close at hand to their tubes.[3]

The eastern sky had barely begun to lighten when, at 6:30 A.M., hundreds of German artillery pieces, mortars, and *Nebelwerfers* began flashing, hurling their shells in the vicinity of the Overpass. At first it sounded like the booming rumble of thunder that accompanies a fierce storm, but this was no meteorological event. The booms were swiftly followed by the almost ethereal sounds of hundreds of shells simultaneously tearing, whistling, and screaming through the air—a sound described perfectly by World War I British officer and poet Wilfred Owen as "the shrill, demented choirs of wailing shells"—concluding with ungodly concussions and the violent trembling of the earth that signaled the arrival of the end of the world.

If they weren't already in their holes or bunkers, men on the receiving end of the barrage dove into any depression in the ground that would shield them from the white-hot steel splinters that started ripping through the air with every shellburst. The cries of the wounded soon pierced the cacophony of noise, yet the explosions, heedless of the pleas for mercy, would not stop. It was as if every shell the Third Reich possessed had somehow been transported to the gunners at Anzio and was being hurled at the Americans and the British.

The barrage caught the Allies by surprise. Lieutenant Bill Whitman (Company B, 180th Infantry Regiment, 45th Division) said that he had just crawled out of a shell hole to brew a cup of morning coffee "when a tank shell came screeching in and went through the top of the frontal bank and right through the hole that I had just gotten out of. Everyone got quite a kick out of it except me. The sky was suddenly filled with artillery, tank, and mortar shells. The tank fire was the worst. The German tanks stood off and fired direct cannon fire into us. Men were hit all around within a few minutes. The pounding kept up. We hugged the sod."[4]

Lieutenant Colonel Ralph Krieger, commanding the 1st Battalion, 157th Infantry Regiment, 45th Division, also recalled the day's opening barrage: "It was hell, I'll tell you for sure. I lost quite a few people, including my orderly. We were in an advanced CP in a ditch and the Germans started shelling us. He got hit by a direct hit on his foxhole; I was right alongside him. How I got missed getting hit, I don't know."[5]

Had the shelling that went on relentlessly for an hour and a half been the only thing directed at the Yanks and Tommies, it would have been more than enough. But, no, there was more to come. As the bombardment abruptly halted, whistles blew and German officers and NCOs shouted and the men of the 3rd Panzer-Grenadier and 715th Motorized Infantry Divisions took one last deep breath and started on their way toward the 157th and 179th Infantry Regiments' positions.

Suddenly, as the smoke from the barrage drifted away, there came a new sight: rank after rank of German infantry in ankle-length greatcoats accompanied by their panzers. Across the flat, smoke-shrouded fields, endless ranks of gray figures, rising up like thousands of ghosts from the graveyard, surged forward. Say what one will about the evil regime for which they fought, no troops ever fought with more astonishing courage than did the German soldiers that morning. Across the slick, slippery morass the Germans came—past knocked-out tanks that lay in the mud like the carcasses of dead elephants, insanely yelling and screaming, a scene out of Gettysburg, a Pickett's Charge with panzers.

"Here they come!" a Yank yelled, and those soldiers who could still hold a rifle or man a machine gun or a mortar pulled themselves out of the muck and mire and began firing furiously at the approaching forms, knowing that their lives—and perhaps even the outcome of the war— depended on their stopping the German attack. Hundreds of artillery pieces also opened up, saturating the front.[6]

Gotthold Schwegler, a machine gunner in the 145th Regiment of the German 65th Infantry Division, recalled that terrible morning: "On the 16th we started. The . . . allies covered us with continuous fire, as had never happened before. After about a hundred meters, the attack remained on open ground, in sight of the enemy. Around us the shells were falling and tracers hissed above us so that we couldn't lift the head. The wounded shouted; the medical men were not able to help them. If the wounded got up from the terrain, they became again a target for the snipers. We stayed this way until late afternoon, almost stiffened by the cold, in the rottenness."[7]

By the time Infantry Lehr was assembled for the attack at midmorning, they were nothing but cannon fodder. Hans Schuhle, a member of 7th Company, Infantry Lehr, remembered that his regiment was supposed to lead the charge from Aprilia down toward the Overpass—a distance of two or three miles—but their late start was immediately met by the seemingly endless barrage of Allied shells, including those of the navy and bombs dropped by the Twelfth U.S. Air Force. "The terrible fire had already completely demolished us before the attack," Schuhle said,

and our morale was destroyed. With guns we were threatened by our officers and non-commissioned officers and forced to leave our shelters and go into the attack. It was already 9:00 AM when we began with this attack. Through deep swamps, always looking for a new shelter, we hardly reached the escarpment of the railroad. At that time the enemy artillery became even stronger and we could find shelter only in the shellholes.

It was then that I found myself with an American in the same hole. We looked at each other. . . . We stared into each other's eyes, neither of us reacting. I then understood that the American infantry were under the fire of their own artillery.

Schuhle had the presence of mind to take the American soldier prisoner and took him back to his own lines, refusing an order by an officer to kill the Yank.*[8]

Kesselring later wrote that he had to pay for the mistake of agreeing to use the Infantry Lehr to spearhead the attack. "I cannot acquit myself of a share in the blame. Even though [Infantry Lehr] was put to me as a crack one, I should not have accepted this just on mere hearsay, but should have known a home defence unit with no fighting experience could not stand up in a major action." The regiment, as Kesselring put it, was "thrown back disgracefully."[9]

Siegfried Westphal, Kesselring's chief of staff, said much the same thing, noting that Hitler even "laid down the breadth of the front, namely, a narrow strip only six kilometers [3.7 miles] wide. . . . Hitler set great store by the success of this attack. If the enemy could be thrown back into the sea now, it would be bound to have an effect on the invasion plans in the West. Hitler hoped that his adversaries would . . . be unable to launch their invasion in France in 1944. This would mean a gain of time that was most desirable."[10]

The Germans, holding positions in Aprilia, had excellent observation of the 2nd and 3rd Battalions of the 179th Infantry, located to the south and southeast of the town, as well as the 2nd Battalion, 157th Infantry,

---

* The next day, Schuhle learned that his regiment "did not exist anymore." He also heard that a German tank detachment had lost forty-eight tanks in the first few hours. "We were taken away from the front line and for almost two days we had to carry our dead comrades and their sad remains back to a road." Hans Schuhle letter, September 2, 1990.

positioned just to the west and astride the Albano Highway. The hollow husks of demolished buildings made excellent ad hoc bunkers in which German tanks and infantrymen could hide, relatively safe from Allied bombardments, while being able to take targets under fire. The network of roads that fed into Aprilia from the north also allowed the Germans to bring in small detachments of panzers, blast the American positions, and then withdraw to reload. It seemed, too, that no matter how many German infantrymen fell, more continued to take their places.[11]

FROM IN FRONT OF THE Embankment that carried the Overpass above and across the Albano Highway that was, by now, as badly cratered as the farmers' fields, the Allies' return fire responded. Rifles and machine guns opened up with a cascade of noise, mortar tubes coughed, and the main 75mm guns of the few Sherman tanks stationed along the line barked. Behind the Overpass, American mortars and artillery lobbed shell after shell into the fields being swarmed by the Germans. The reply from the Germans was equally thunderous. It was as though the land-scape had been transformed into a vision of hell: leaping, jagged crests of red and orange flame tearing the world to pieces, great spouts of filthy earth blasted skyward. Nothing could live through such a maelstrom. And yet. . . .

It is easy to dismiss the ranks of German soldiers shouting and stum-bling and slipping across the glutinous morass toward the Allied lines as a faceless, nameless horde *Sieg Heil*–ing like automatons and willing to die gloriously for their Führer and for Greater Germany. Yet each one of them, whether old or young, was somebody's son, father, uncle, brother, lover, husband, fiancé. Each one of them had hopes and dreams and plans for the future, once the war was over.

Like the Yanks and Tommies, the Germans came from a variety of backgrounds. Some, before getting caught up in the war, had been stu-dents, teachers, shopkeepers, and factory foremen. Some were former policemen, firemen, apprentices, businessmen. They had been truck drivers and train conductors. They had worked in hospitals and butcher shops, painted houses and pictures, repaired shoes and watches. They once were construction workers, laboratory assistants, and farmers. They carried in their pockets letters and sentimental photographs of their parents, girlfriends, wives, children. They all hoped to go home once the war was over. They were, in many ways—as was a generation of Americans, British, Russians, and Japanese—just ordinary young men who happened to be born at precisely the wrong time and place in history.

Most of them, wearing the eagle-and-swastika emblem sewn above the right breast pocket of their tunics and a swastika decal on their steel helmets, were not hard-core Nazis. They were, like the boys on the other side in British and American uniforms, just doing their patriotic duty. Some were not even German but had somehow been conscripted into the army that had conquered their homeland; they, too, did not want to die, but neither did they want to shirk their duty or disobey orders, for they knew the consequences—such as facing a firing squad—could be as harsh as battle.

There was a time, too, especially at the beginning of the war, when they, as small cogs of the giant German war machine, were considered part of the finest army in the world. Hitler had instilled in them the idea that they were unique, special, destined to rule the world, and they had certainly started out like that—quickly and relatively easily invading and reoccupying the Rhineland, taking over the German-speaking Sudetenland border regions of Czechoslovakia, entering Austria to frenzied cheers after the *Anschluss*, defeating Poland, Norway, Denmark, Belgium, Holland, Luxembourg, and France. They had marched into those countries as conquerors, and some of the civilians—even in the Ukraine after Germany invaded the Soviet Union—welcomed them as liberators, going so far as kissing their cheeks and thrusting flowers into their arms.

The years 1940 and 1941 were the heady days for Hitler's soldiers—the high-water mark for the Third Reich. German submarines had nearly severed the tenuous lifeline of cargo ships crossing the Atlantic to keep alive the faltering hopes of the British and Soviets. Germany had nearly brought England to its knees and had been within a hair's breadth of defeating the Soviet Union. The German army had seemed unstoppable.

But two major defeats loomed for Hitler: North Africa and Russia. The British battled alone and heroically against Rommel and his Afrika Korps, chasing each other back and forth across Morocco, Algeria, Tunisia, and Egypt, until the Brits were bolstered by the arrival of

the Americans in November 1942. Hitler's biggest power grab of all—
the successful 1941 summer invasion of the vast and unforgiving Soviet Union—was his downfall as the offensive sputtered to a halt the
following winter. Since that time, it was one setback after another for
the Wehrmacht, the Waffen-SS, the Luftwaffe, even the Kriegsmarine.
Yet, like a cornered tiger, the trapped, desperate animal can be the most
dangerous.[12]

CHURCHILL NOTED IN HIS MEMOIRS:

> The expected major effort to drive us back into the sea at Anzio opened on
> February 16, when the enemy employed over four divisions, supported
> by 450 guns, in a direct thrust southwards from Campoleone. . . . The
> attack fell at an awkward moment, as the 45th US and 56th British Divi-
> sions, transferred from the Cassino front, were just relieving our gallant
> 1st Division, who soon found themselves in full action again. A deep,
> dangerous wedge was driven into our line, which was forced back here to
> the original beach-head. The artillery fire, which had embarrassed all the
> occupants of the beach-head since they landed, reached a new intensity.
> All hung in the balance. No retreat was possible.[13]

The courage required by the Germans to cross that open ground between Aprilia and the Overpass should not be dismissed lightly. There
were no trees or rocks to shelter behind. If a soldier felt the urge to find
a place safe from the wall of lead and steel being flung his way, his only
option was behind a tank or into one of the innumerable craters blown
into the ground by munitions. Even then he could not tarry long, for an
officer or NCO—themselves with probably only moments left to live—
was sure to roust him out, give him a swift kick in the backside or a prod
with a bayonet, and get him going again in the direction of the Flyover/
Overpass. Anyone who chose to retreat to his own lines was in danger of
being shot by his own superiors, for the German soldier should not be
seen to run away from danger and thus cause a mass exodus to the rear.

General Harmon noted, "The Germans had 120,000 troops in the
area. The combat units were the finest in the Reich's army—I was not to
see their equal later in Belgium and Holland and Germany. When the

attack came, it was propelled by Hitler's personal order that the 'abscess in Italy' must be removed."[14]

But it is not clear if either Kesselring or Mackensen appreciated what would happen if and when their troops actually reached the Overpass/Flyover. Certainly, their troops would pile up like sand in the bottleneck of an hourglass, with thousands of men to the north of the tiny gap. This jammed heap of humanity would present an immense target of opportunity for every Allied ship, gun, and warplane in the area, much as the fleeing German Army Group B clogging the narrow country lanes at Falaise, France, would do in the coming August. Anyone who survived the onslaught of Allied munitions while approaching the Overpass/Flyover would surely be torn to pieces if he managed to reach the other side. There was not the slightest possibility that the Germans, no matter how brave or hopped up they were, would have succeeded at driving the defenders into the sea.

WAVE AFTER WAVE OF PANZERS and foot soldiers came rolling like a gray tide across the churned-up fields, heading directly for the right flank of Company E, 157th, holding positions along the railroad track, and Company G, whose left shoulder was touching the 167th Brigade west of the Albano Highway.[15]

At Company G's (157th Infantry) position, it was a knock-down, drag-out, no-holds-barred brawl. In addition to infantry, the Germans, who continued to come on as though they were possessed, also sent in four panzers, each of which was destroyed by the timely delivery of artillery. Although G's 3rd Platoon was nearly wiped out, the rest of the company, fighting off every attempt to infiltrate its positions, held its ground.[16] The German artillery fire that thundered down on the 2nd Battalion, 157th, lying astride the Albano Highway just west of Aprilia, was reaching a terrifying intensity. The earth shook and trembled violently, and the massed explosions blotted out every other sound. Thunderbirds who thought they couldn't press themselves any deeper into the mud discovered that they could.

Slamming into the Americans' forward positions with the force of a runaway freight train, the Germans, against all odds, had survived their advance through the hellish barrages intent on taking out every foxhole and machine-gun nest, every mortar position and observation post. In the center of the action was Company E's commander, Captain Felix L. Sparks. Through the smoke and haze of the shelling, Sparks could see vague forms moving toward him. Thinking that they might be members of the neighboring 179th, he radioed battalion headquarters for clarification. Informed that what he saw weren't friendlies, Sparks ordered his men to open fire.

The forms were accompanied by tanks, and Sparks knew that he had a real battle on his hands. A ten-minute artillery bombardment that seemed like an hour hit his company's positions; luckily, Sparks's men were well dug in along the Albano Highway, and they suffered few casualties. He said, "Just as soon as the barrage lifted, they sent three tanks through us. They were over on my left; they didn't come down the main road, which was where my 3rd Platoon was. They came so fast I couldn't believe it."

A couple of M-10 tank destroyers were parked near Sparks's foxhole, and he directed them to engage the panzers, but the TD commander hesitated, thinking they were British armor. "Hell, no!" Sparks shouted. "They're German tanks!" The TD's main gun opened up immediately at almost point-blank range, knocking out the first two enemy tanks. "It was like they disintegrated," Sparks remembered. "Parts were flying everywhere." The third panzer pivoted and took off for the rear.

But the fight had just started. "Right after this," said Sparks, "one of the TDs moved a little to the left, maybe fifty to seventy-five feet off the highway. I don't know why—maybe he was trying to find a position where he'd have a longer field of fire. That was a mistake. There was a German tank waiting there and it knocked him out. He went up in flames and burned me out of my foxhole." Five minutes later, a wave of German infantry came rushing across the muddy field directly toward Company E. Sparks said:

I don't know if they were drunk or what, but they were yelling and screaming—what they were saying I don't know. But we cut them down. Some got in with us but we killed every damned one of them.

Over on our right the Germans were hitting the 179th at the same time. I couldn't see what was going on but I could hear the firing. The

Germans botched up the attack on us but good. The first time they had tanks but no infantry. The second time they had infantry but no tanks. About thirty minutes later they came again. This time they had tanks *and* infantry. That's what killed us. The tanks went right up to our foxholes and blew my men right out of them.

At the height of the battle, another American tank destroyer rolled up next to Sparks's position and singlehandedly tried to halt the German attack. Sparks recalled that one of the crewmen

strapped himself to the .50-caliber machine gun that normally was used as an anti-aircraft weapon. It was mounted awkwardly on the side of the tank destroyer, and the gunner had to put a big leather strap around himself so he could lean back while firing up in the air. This sergeant strapped himself on and was firing the gun down into the attacking waves of German infantrymen. But they got him with what we call a "burp gun."* I watched the dust spurt out the back of his jacket as the bullets hit him. He was killed, but he stopped the Germans right at the edge of my foxhole."

The attack went on, however, and the single remaining tank destroyer, nearly out of ammunition, was forced to pull back. With the TD gone, Sparks resorted to desperate measures. Yelling to his men to get as low into their holes as possible, he got on his radio and ordered an artillery strike—right on top of his company's positions. The Germans swarming into his area were suddenly torn to pieces.[17]

Alvin "Bud" McMillan, a sniper in nearby Company K, 157th, was concentrating on picking off officers and NCOs at ranges up to 500 yards. "You pretty well had your choice of what you were going to shoot at," he said. But a shell burst overhead, and a fragment hit him in the right thigh. "I took off my belt and tied a tourniquet around my leg and I

---

* An MP-40 machine gun—technically known as a 9mm Parabellum machine gun, but often called a "Schmeisser," after its designer, Hugo Schmeisser. It had a full-automatic firing rate of 350–450 rounds per minute. Quick, *Dictionary of Weapons and Military Terms*, 192.

kept on fighting. There really wasn't but about nine or ten of us doin' any shootin'—the rest were either gone or in hidin'. . . . Just to our immediate front there must have been a hundred or more Germans runnin' right at us."[18]

Sergeant Daniel Ficco (Company C, 157th) told his men to hold their fire until a line of 200 charging Germans got within range. "Then I gave the order and we fired. We had some mortars and the ground was almost black with Germans coming at us. I was firing an M-1 Garand and it got so hot I could hardly touch it; I don't know how many rounds I put through it."[19]

Watching the German onslaught continuing to unfold and overrun some of the forward foxholes, Captain Kenneth Stemmons, commanding Company B, 157th, also called an artillery strike down on his company's own positions. "I asked for quite a bit of it and they replied, 'We'll give you a little bit to see if that's what you really want,' but we were all in our holes and the Germans were running around us in the open. We got the artillery and the Germans suffered terrible casualties."[20]

THE SITUATION WAS ALSO DETERIORATING by the minute for elements of the 179th Infantry Regiment, being pummeled by the 3rd Panzer-Grenadier Division. Two companies of the 2nd Battalion—Companies F and G—were spread out along a gully of Carroceto Creek near Aprilia and were being relentlessly hammered; Company F, gathering together the remnants of its scattered force, reported that it was down to thirty men and that all its machine guns had been put out of action. This necessitated the battalion commander, Lieutenant Colonel Edward E. B. Weber, telling the companies to pull back a short distance—no easy feat while being shelled and shot at.

Within the 3rd Battalion, too, there was fear that the men of Company I were in danger of being encircled, so a platoon from Company L was sent forward to assist in their extraction. The 179th managed to hold, however, and, with the considerable help of Allied artillery, halted the Infantry Lehr's charge, throwing the elite unit back with heavy casualties.[21]

At the same time, three German regiments of panzers and infantry hit Major Merlin O. Tryon's 3rd Battalion, 179th, pushing back two of the companies—F and G—and inflicting heavy casualties. Company L attempted to come to their aid, but the panzers stopped it cold. The battle went on for hours. "A shell dropped into a hole about two or three holes over from me," said Daniel Witts, Anti-Tank Company, 179th. "It just blew the hell out of them."[22]

Witts's buddy in the AT Company William H. Gordon recalled, "The Germans practically ran us over. In fact, several of our positions had to pull back to where I was. Everybody was scared. We thought about running—but we didn't run."[23]

The panzers were everyone's greatest fear. A German Mark IV Tiger tank looks menacing when it is just sitting still. When it is moving toward you, like a mobile bunker, it is downright terrifying, and it takes every ounce of courage a man possesses to keep from running away. The twenty-five-ton Mark IV Tiger, or, in German, *Panzerkampfwagen* IV (abbreviated PzKpfw IV), was the most numerous tank produced by the Germans from 1936 to 1945—8,800 of them rolled off the assembly lines of several manufacturers. The wide tracks, squarish body, MG-34 forward machine gun, and high-velocity 75mm main gun protruding from the turret made it a formidable opponent on the battlefield, and the three-inch-thick frontal armor made it virtually impervious to anything the American Sherman could throw at it.[24]

"We counted twenty-six German tanks out there. We called for anti-tank help, but nothing came," said Lieutenant Robert LaDu (Company F, 179th). "They broke through our lines like nothing, and there were so many of those Germans; they came in almost like a battalion parade formation. Our artillery was landing among them—you'd see a rifle flying through the air, or an arm or a leg. It was just a slaughter."[25]

Lieutenant Charles Reiman (Company G, 179th) recalled seeing an American M-5 Stuart tank rumbling down the road when it suddenly "burst into flames. No one got out." Not long afterward, Reiman's platoon came under fire from a self-propelled artillery piece. "This vehicle fired between five and ten rounds at the G Company CP and hit it every time. I started to unlimber our bazooka but my men got very nervous, so I didn't use it; I wasn't sure that I could hit it at 200–300 yards, anyway. We did not fire at the vehicle." It withdrew back around a hill and disappeared from sight; Reiman speculated that this vehicle was the one that had knocked out the Stuart earlier. Later that day, when the rest of Reiman's company surrendered under duress, he played dead and avoided capture.[26]

TO KNOCK OUT AN OPPONENT'S artillery, armies rely on counterbattery fire, and on February 16 the Germans delivered the heaviest counterbattery fire yet experienced at Anzio. In the early-morning hours, the fire was concentrated on the 45th Division artillery; it then shifted to the positions of the corps artillery. To prevent the American artillery spotters in the Piper Cub aircraft from directing Allied fire onto German gun batteries, the Germans made a concerted effort to shoot down the L-4 Grasshoppers by ground fire and fighter planes; at 10:00 A.M., the 3rd Division's observation plane had been knocked out of the sky. Although the division urgently requested fighter protection, VI Corps could guarantee no immediate aid, as German guns had hit the Nettuno airfield and destroyed four Spitfires as they were about to take off, thus causing the field to again be abandoned for use during daylight hours. Fighter protection would have to be provided from fields in the Naples area.[27]

During the morning of the sixteenth, the 179th Infantry beat back all attacks against it with heavy losses to the enemy. The 45th Division's 160th Field Artillery Battalion brought the fire of its guns to bear on a large concentration of German troops near Aprilia* and stopped them cold. While the German infantry had suffered heavy losses during their morning attacks, the panzers, too, were taking a beating.

One of those who accounted for a number of German dead was the 45th's First Lieutenant Donald E. Knowlton, a forward observer for the 160th Field Artillery Battalion. He had set up his radio next to a farmhouse southeast of Aprilia and was calling in artillery strikes as the

---

* The *36th Engineer Combat Regiment's Operations Journal* noted that 800 infantrymen and an unspecified number of panzers had assembled on the north side of Aprilia in preparation for an attack before artillery broke up the gathering. *36th Engineer Combat Regiment Operations Journal*, February 16, 1944, www .6thcorpscombatengineers.com/36th.htm.

enemy came into view. That morning, when the American infantry outposts were being forced back by enemy tanks and infantry, he knew he
couldn't withdraw but would have to stay at his post to continue adjust-
ing the artillery fire. As Germans began closing in on his position, he
picked up his carbine and killed two of the enemy and possibly a third
before a bullet struck his helmet and briefly knocked him unconscious.
Left for dead by his men, Knowlton came to just as the Germans, stum-
bling like drunken, determined men across the stinking, slimy fields,
were nearly on top of his OP. He grabbed the handset to his radio and
called down artillery fire on his own position; within seconds the shells
came screaming in, killing many of the enemy and forcing the survivors
to withdraw. Luckily, the badly wounded Knowlton was eventually discovered by other American troops and carried back to friendly lines. His
actions resulted in his receiving the Distinguished Service Cross.[28]

Another forward observer with the 160th Field Artillery, First
Lieutenant James M. Sherrick, was directing artillery fire from a half-
demolished building when an infantry liaison officer crawled up and
informed him that the Germans were pushing the 179th's front line
back and that higher command had ordered all outposts withdrawn. But
Sherrick saw that the only hope of stopping the Germans that had nearly
completely encircled him was to remain at his post and keep directing
artillery fire down upon them. With the enemy closing in—close enough
that he could see the insignia on their collars—Sherrick made the ultimate decision: he yelled, "Drop the range 400 yards!"—thus, like Captain Sparks and Lieutenant Knowlton before him, calling artillery fire
down on his own position. Just as the Germans were about to overrun
his OP, a half-dozen shells erupted, blowing the enemy to pieces and
wounding Sherrick. Once the smoke had cleared, more Germans came
up and angrily took the stunned Sherrick prisoner. Although he spent
the rest of the war in POW camps, Sherrick's courage, like Knowlton's,
earned for him the Distinguished Service Cross.

Onward rolled the German tank-and-infantry juggernaut, bent on
crushing everything in its path. The 179th Regiment had been hard hit
in the assault and was forced to fall back to a position more than a mile
south of Aprilia. It was even worse than the beating the regiment had

taken a few days earlier when it had tried to capture Aprilia. The last line of defense was made up of American tank destroyers and batteries of 105mm and 155mm artillery, and they acquitted themselves well. The panzers and their accompanying infantry were unable to advance through the curtain of exploding steel and flying lead, and the pause enabled the shattered Thunderbird lines to recompose themselves. Not only recompose, but to prepare to launch a counterattack![29]

CHAPTER 14

"This was the big attack"
FEBRUARY 16 (AFTERNOON)

SIMULTANEOUSLY WITH MACKENSEN'S EASTERN PINCER attack directed against the Thunderbirds, his western pincer hit Templer's 56th British Division, which was holding the left flank of the central beachhead defense line. Here the enemy's efforts seemed to gain traction. The 3rd Battalion, 12th (*Sturm*) Regiment, from Trettner's 4th Parachute Division, attacked across the Moletta River against the 8th and 9th Battalions, Royal Fusiliers, followed by the 10th Parachute Regiment attacking from the Buonriposo Ridge against other British positions. Two German companies managed to penetrate all the way to the Lateral Road before the 8th Royal Fusiliers counterattacked and the tanks of the 46th Royal Tank Regiment appeared to halt the drive.

But the damage had been done; the forward companies of the 8th Royal Fusiliers and the 7th Ox and Bucks had been overrun, and the Germans had driven a wedge into the center of the 167th Brigade line. The 8th Royal Fusiliers had been in position at Anzio for less than a week when they took the full brunt of the attack being led by the 3rd Panzer-Grenadier and 715th Infantry Divisions; behind them came the 26th Panzer and 29th Panzer-Grenadier Divisions. Company X of the 8th Royal Fusiliers was overrun; only one officer and twenty men survived. Company Y was hit even harder, with but one officer and ten men making it back to friendly lines. The remnants of Company Z were still in position, battling for their lives.

Luckily for the British, perhaps because of heavy German casualties, sheer exhaustion, or because it was just a diversionary attack to support the major offensive down the Albano Highway, the Germans failed to make an effort to exploit the penetration.[1] But there seemed to be no letup in the German attacks, and no one—not Alexander nor Clark nor Lucas nor the individual soldier in his muddy foxhole—knew how much longer the Yanks and Tommies could hold out. Yet the day was only half over.

VIEWING THE BATTLE THROUGH BINOCULARS from atop a barn was Reynolds Packard, a war correspondent with United Press International. He wrote that he could "see tank battles and infantry fighting all along the skyline. German wounded and dead are so numerous as to actually hamper their attacks as advancing waves of Nazi infantry walk over a gruesome carpet of their own dead and dying."[2]

Also observing the German attack was Lieutenant Colonel William P. Yarborough, commander of the 509th Parachute Infantry Battalion: "The Germans launched an all-out attack which came down the divisional boundary between the 3rd and the 45th [Infantry Divisions]. It was aimed at the 45th Division. And since I was right on that boundary, I could see the whole thing deployed, like on a sand table with the advance elements, the armor units following up, the Kraut infantry, the whole damn thing, and I was able to call Corps artillery onto that operation."[3]

The German advance could have been a scene out of the Napoleonic era, with Kesselring's and Mackensen's finest troops marching upright into the teeth of American artillery and machine guns and being torn to shreds as though they were marching on parade. Sergeant Lawrence Butler (Company I, 1st Armored Division) said, "German infantry would walk at us, standing tall, firing their rifles. They were hopped up on wine or something."[4]

Yarborough continued, "That was one hell of a fight and we thought the German attack was going to really roll over our final protective line. . . . All the Corps artillery that we had was churning up the ground out in front of us. The Germans came forward in their usual disciplined way and tried to dig in their weapons and move forward but, boy, the stuff was flying into the air around there. Nothing could live."[5]

Sergeant Phil Miller, a tank driver in the 191st Tank Battalion, was astonished by the scenes of courage and carnage that he witnessed in the fields in front of the Overpass:

> It looked like the whole German army had risen up out of the ground and, standing straight up, came charging at us. We hit them with every- thing we had and still they kept coming. I lost another tank from a direct hit from a German 88. My assistant gunner and I were the only two that got out; the three men in the turret were killed in the blast and fire. We were later told that [the enemy infantrymen] were given a pill as a last ef- fort by the Germans to push us into the sea. . . . The firing finally stopped and the dead were buried in trenches dug by a bulldozer.[6]

Staff Sergeant Charles W. Keyser, in charge of three tanks of Com- pany A, 191st Tank Battalion, was located behind a farmhouse 600 yards from Aprilia when a shell seemingly from nowhere screamed in and knocked out his platoon's Number 2 Sherman. Keyser's men suddenly were in a fight for their lives. At noon on the sixteenth, enemy infantry worked down the ditch beside the road to the farmhouse. Spotting the infiltration from his tank, Keyser fired a 75mm shell that exploded in the enemy's midst, while a second attempt to take the house was broken up with hand grenades. Two enemy tanks then approached down the road. Concealed by the cloud of dust around the house, Sergeant Keyser, in tank Number 3, charged toward the two panzers, knocking out one with three rounds and setting the other on fire with four rounds; well-placed shells killed the crews as they attempted to escape.

At 2:30 P.M., Keyser's tank received a direct hit that disabled his SCR-506 radio that he depended upon to direct artillery fire and that caused him to fail to receive the "withdraw" order from his platoon leader. At 4:15 six more panzers appeared. Laying down his own smoke screen, Keyser tried to make a run for it across the fields, but, 300 yards from the house, his tank was hit and his driver killed. Badly burned, Keyser crawled out through the tank's escape hatch and hid in a ditch until after dark, when he managed to return to his battalion. Altogether, for the loss of seven tanks, the 191st Tank Battalion had destroyed fifteen of the enemy's. For his actions, Sergeant Keyser received the Distinguished Service Cross.[7]

WHILE THE GERMANS WERE PUSHING the Americans back from around Aprilia, they also sent the 4th (Fallschirm) Parachute and 65th Infantry Divisions against the 167th British Brigade, which was holding positions in the ravines and gullies of Wadi Country to the south and west of Aprilia. Although it was only a feint, the sudden German thrust unnerved the 167th, which unexpectedly pulled back, thus leaving the 157th's left flank dangerously exposed.

Captain Felix Sparks's Company E, 157th, 45th Division, was also having its difficulties; he wasn't sure if his men could hold against another of a series of human-wave attacks. A head count revealed that his company was down to fewer than twenty men.[8] Through the smoke drifting across the fields, Sparks saw a German armored vehicle coming his way, flying a white flag. When it reached his position, an officer emerged, and Sparks approached him. "Captain, you have a great number of wounded here," the German said in excellent English, "and we have a number of wounded. Would you agree to a truce of thirty minutes so we can evacuate our wounded?" Sparks agreed, and so both sides began picking up their casualties. At the thirty-minute mark, hostilities resumed.

Once again the enemy came at Sparks's men with panzers and ground troops—with mortars and artillery thrown in for good measure. Just as it seemed the Germans were about to overrun Company E, Sparks said, "I called in the artillery fire on our own positions. Sometimes an artillery barrage will completely disorient some soldiers. They completely lose control. You hear this crash, crash, crash that goes on for five or ten minutes. I've seen soldiers go insane from a barrage."[9] Luckily, the American barrage stopped the German assault—but only temporarily.

For the remainder of the afternoon in front of the 45th Division's positions here, the Germans continued to probe, looking for a weak spot, a place that they could exploit and gain an advantage. Panzers rolled to and fro, firing their main guns, reversing, swiveling their turrets, and firing again. Both sides pounded the other with stupendous amounts of artillery, the battlefield looking and sounding like the thundering climax of a Fourth of July fireworks show, an orgiastic frenzy that seemed to be an expression of Hitler's iron will to annihilate his enemies. It did not seem possible that anyone could live through this battle—one of the most intense of the entire war.[10]

THE GERMAN ATTACK OF FEBRUARY 16 was general and widespread. In addition to assaults against the 56th British and 45th U.S. Divisions, the 3rd Infantry Division farther east was also struck with deadly force. Two companies of the Parachute Demonstration Battalion, attached to the Hermann Göring Parachute-Panzer Division, and supported by nine Mark IV tanks, launched an attack from northwest of Ponte Rotto directly at the seam between the 2nd Battalion, 7th Infantry Regiment, and the 3rd Battalion, 30th Infantry Regiment, but the assault proved disastrous; virtually all the Germans were either killed by artillery fire or captured.[11]

PRIVATE FRED MASON, A BREN gunner with the 2nd North Staffs dug in near the Overpass/Flyover, recalled seeing a farmhouse in which a group of Germans had taken shelter being subjected to a terrific shelling. During a brief lull, six of the soldiers came out of the house and across the road

> with hands on their helmets. Some looked very young. When another 150 prisoners gave themselves up that day, they looked bewildered, tired, and frightened. They also looked pleased to be out of it. I think I might have envied them a bit and felt sorry for ourselves because they would be going to a nice, safe prisoner-of-war camp while I and my mates were stuck at Anzio with the prospect of more battle to come.
>
> Fighting around the Flyover was incessant. It was shelled, mortared, bombed, and there was little of it left after the battle. German positions were on the Rome side, and Americans and British on the Anzio side. Sometimes we were only fifty or sixty yards from one another. We could not move during daylight. Many lives were lost in that vicinity. We had

an observation post on the banks of the Flyover. The Germans knew this, of course, and wanted it for themselves, but we managed to hold on.

When we later moved back to B Echelon for a so-called rest, we still had to live in holes in the ground, but the cover was better than up at the front. But it could still be dangerous. One day a Cockney fellow—I don't remember his name—stood up in the woods at B Echelon and waved at the German shells going over. Unfortunately, he did it once too often; he was killed by an incoming shell.[12]

AT DUSK ON THE SIXTEENTH, having somehow survived the day's events, Everett W. Easley (Company F, 179th) was trying to recuperate in his foxhole when he saw a

white flash from artillery or a tank. They laid three shells on my hole within arm's reach and didn't hurt a thing. Blew our rifles all to hell, but didn't hurt us. It was a hell of a mess, though, I'll tell you. That night, we got orders to withdraw, and some withdrew and some didn't. We were all disorganized then. I stayed with my friends. The Germans came running down this ditch and we just kept shooting them as fast as they came. There were three German tanks that came down the road. About every two minutes they'd fire their machine guns about a foot-and-a-half high above the road. I scrambled across the road and there were Germans all over the place. In the dark they must have thought I was one of them.

Easley managed to escape capture—or worse.[13]

As nightfall approached, frontline observers saw movement ahead; the Germans were bringing up more tanks and infantry and getting prepared for one last determined effort to drive the Allied forces off the beachhead.[14] At 10:30 that night, the 157th's Anti-Tank Company reported that thirteen enemy tanks operating in the dark along the Albano Highway had knocked out a complete section of 57mm guns. At midnight, contact was made with the 7th Battalion, Ox and Bucks, operating to the left of the 157th, but the British unit was in an even more precarious position than the Yanks. There was every reason for the Allies to believe that they were at the end of their rope and that one more concentrated German effort would succeed in destroying VI Corps.[15]

THE MAIN GERMAN ATTACK

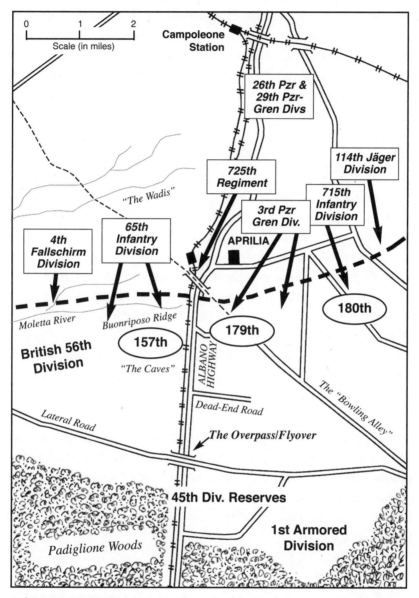

February 16, 1944: The Germans launched their heaviest counteroffensive to date, nearly succeeding in destroying U.S. and British troops around Aprilia. (Positions approximate)

"FEBRUARY WAS A BAD MONTH," said Cordino Longiotti, 179th, with considerable understatement. "The Germans were throwing everything they could find at us, and as we were retreating our casualties were mounting, especially for the frontline troops. After a short rest of one day, on the night of 16 February we moved to the front lines again with the rifle company, which we were supporting, and dug in along the Albano Road. We were to hold that line at all costs." Longiotti noted that his company's previous commanding officer had been wounded at Venafro, so they received a replacement captain who turned out to be too frightened to lead his troops. "He remained behind and under whatever protection from fire that he could find."[16]

For Corporal Ray Sherman (Company K, 179th), February 16 was the day he went from being a soldier to a prisoner of war. He said that his unit was "completely overwhelmed, and our commander sent word down the line to dismantle our weapons and surrender. The enemy kept some of us right on the front lines to go out and pick up their dead. We did this mostly at night. We just piled them up like cordwood. Lots of them had had a bowel movement when they died, so we didn't enjoy the job." It was during this period that Sherman began to suffer from the effects of frostbite. The Germans allowed their captives to shelter in a barn or stable in the daytime to rest and warm up.

Sherman said, "The enemy didn't make any attempt to feed us so I ate the remainder of a K-ration. I went through my pack and gas mask and left my home address in it. I buried a good hunting knife in cow manure so the Germans wouldn't find it and use it on me." Waiting to be evacuated to a POW camp in the rear, Sherman recalled that he and another American, named Simpson, were sitting in a building with some German guards

and watched tracers and artillery go by for some time. An American had just taken a couple loaves of bread inside when a shell hit the back side [of the building] and another demolished a shed about twenty-five feet from us. After aiding the wounded American, two of us took off to the rear on our own. Simpson and I were together, staying in the ditch alongside the road as much as possible. About thirty-five other POWs and their guards joined us. A British Spitfire saw us and strafed us as we followed the ditch. Tracers missed me by about five feet.

We were taken to a building and questioned. We only gave them our name, rank, and serial number. Our officers were separated from us and we walked until about 11:00 PM. We descended into a deep valley and spent the night in a vineyard. Because I could speak a bit of German, one of the guards took two of us under his blanket with him. It was very cold. We left the valley at about 8:00 AM [February 17] and walked all day without any food. We were finally put on trucks that delivered us to a house where we were locked in an upstairs room and given a quarter of a loaf of bread, a dark heavy rye, and some green tea in our canteen cups about noon. We slept on straw and were very cramped for space.

We were interrogated again and gave them our name, rank and serial number. They knew our family history and outfit. We left about 8:00 PM and walked about five kilometers [three miles] to the "Film Studio [Cinecittà]," where warm food, etc., was promised. There was a twelve- to fifteen-foot-high barbed-wire fence with about an eight-foot space and another outer fence, with wooden guard towers on all four corners with armed guards. The space between the fences was patrolled with dogs and armed guards. We signed a book, which was said to be for the Red Cross so they could contact our loved ones.*

---

*Cinecittà was one of the more unusual prisoner-of-war encampments. The sprawling ninety-nine-acre movie studio complex with over two dozen sound stages on the southern outskirts of Rome was dedicated by Mussolini in 1937 and intended to be a production facility whose output—both propaganda and feature films—would rival those in far-off Southern California. Called "Hollywood on the Tiber," the studio, which is still operating, has turned out thousands of films, including *Scipio Africanus* (1937), one of the most elaborate, expensive, and spectacular productions of all time. In the postwar era, such films as the 1959 Academy Award–winning *Ben-Hur* and *Cleopatra* (starring Elizabeth Taylor) in 1963, as well as other epics and films by such celebrated directors as Federico Fellini, Vittorio De Sica, Luchino Visconti, Roberto Rosselini, and Martin Scorsese were filmed here. Allied bombs destroyed part of the complex in 1943, but enough remained so that the backlot and sound stages could be used to incarcerate Allied prisoners of war. Author visit to Cinecittà, 2015.

From Cinecittà, Sherman and the rest of the prisoners were sent to various POW camps. He eventually ended up in Stalag VII-B in Memmingen, Germany, then on to a slave-labor camp in Augsburg. Despite several escape attempts, Sherman remained a prisoner of war until April 26, 1945, when the camp was liberated by a U.S. armored unit.[17]

ANOTHER AMERICAN, ROBERT JAGODA, WAS also captured on February 16 and taken first to Cinecittà, along with hundreds of others from the 45th Division. He said that the camp "was so crowded that many of the men had to sleep standing against walls. Eventually, the POWs were transported to a military camp in Laterina in the province of Arezzo, a place that held 8,000 prisoners during the war. That is where the starvation began. I got down to seventy-nine pounds."

For two months, all the prisoners received for breakfast was a loaf of black bread that was shared between five men before heading out on work details beyond the barbed wire. The evening meal was much the same as that given to concentration camp inmates: an unpalatable "stew" of water, lard, and cabbage leaves. Diversions were hard to come by. Jagoda recalled the day that the former world champion heavyweight German boxer and paratrooper Max Schmeling came to the camp to put on a boxing exhibition. The fighter promised that if any of the prisoners—by now little more than living skeletons—would spar with him, he would provide them with steaks. "Of course, he did not keep his promise," Jagoda said. Jagoda was later transferred to a POW camp in Germany.[18]

BY THE TIME NIGHT HAD covered the grotesquely splayed corpses on the battlefield, the 45th's line had been badly dented but not broken, nor had the 56th British Division been shoved back. But Lucas and Clark worried that another big push could fracture the fragile front line and send the Germans plunging toward the seashore. They were still waiting for Kesselring's main force to strike.[19] Clark acknowledged the vital part played by the Thunderbirds on the sixteenth: "The brunt of the attack was borne by the 45th Division, which held a six-mile sector astride the Albano-Anzio road," he wrote in his memoirs.

He also noted that "Mackensen worked furiously to regroup his troops and at dawn [on the seventeenth] the Germans came on again with everything they could muster. The advance continued, following for the most part the road network, and by midmorning the beachhead troops were fighting desperately to hold the last line—the original D-day beachhead line about seven miles from the water."[20]

In addition to fighting the Germans, Lucas was also fighting desperately to hold his job, but Churchill, Alexander, and Clark finally had had enough of him. The VI Corps commander was just not displaying the type of aggressiveness that they had hoped and expected that he would. Alexander said to Clark on the sixteenth at their Caserta headquarters, "I am very much dissatisfied with General Lucas. I have no confidence in him and in his ability to control the situation. I very much fear that there might be a disaster at Anzio."[21]

"You know," added Alexander gravely, "the position is serious. We may be pushed back into the sea. That would be very bad for both of us— and you would certainly be relieved of your command." In his elliptical way of commanding, Alexander's inference was that Clark had better replace Lucas with some younger, more dynamic officer—and quickly— or face professional disgrace.[22] Clark could not disagree. In his memoirs he wrote that Alexander was unhappy about Lucas's leadership of VI Corps, and Clark was beginning to have his own doubts. "My own feeling was that Johnny Lucas was ill—tired physically and mentally—from the long responsibilities of command in battle. I said that I would not under any circumstances do anything to hurt the man who had contributed so greatly to our successes since Salerno and our drive northward to Anzio."[23]

That evening, in his command post, a weary, dispirited General Lucas confided to his diary, "This was the big attack . . . and it came from the north directly south toward Anzio. It was launched with tremendous power. . . . I knew that five or six divisions were actually involved in the attack and it was on a narrow front."[24] In his memoirs, he added, "This was a desperate, bloody battle where men fought hand-to-hand with whatever weapon was available. The dust and smoke and confusion were such that little could be seen and many events occurred which will never be part of recorded history."[25]

Back at the darkened beachhead, along the 45th Division's line, the enemy's attacks had finally come to a halt for the day. By the time the battle was spent, the muddy ground in front of the American and British positions was thick with dead Germans, lying as still and motionless as felled logs. Although the Germans had fought with undeniable courage, they had been slaughtered in great numbers. American and British troops, their ears ringing, faces blackened with dirt, and minds numbed from the day's events, could not believe that the enemy could possibly find the strength, or the numbers of men, to renew the battle the next day.

ON THE EVENING OF THE sixteenth, Mackensen wrestled with a huge decision, the most important decision of his military career: In light of his heavy losses and only limited successes that day, should he call off the attack scheduled for the seventeenth or commit his last reserve of two divisions? One part of him felt that, no, he should not throw the dice again and perhaps suffer an even more serious reversal—but perhaps the Allies were nearly beaten and it would take only one more push to send them into the abyss. Kesselring, himself similarly conflicted, thought the attack should go forward. But even if both Germans felt strongly about canceling the assault, they knew that Hitler would countermand their orders and demand that the enemy be hurled back into the blue Tyrrhenian, no matter what the cost—for every German soldier must continue fighting, even unto death.[26]

Kesselring and Mackensen decided that an even greater effort must be made. It would come the next morning.

CHAPTER 15

"I do not feel that I should
have sacrificed my command"

FEBRUARY 17-18

NO DOUBT, EACH THUNDERBIRD—or, for that matter, each Allied soldier—wondered how much more punishment he could stand or how long it would be before help would arrive to bolster the 45th Division's positions. But there were no fresh troops, no reinforcements, to be had. The units already fighting for their very lives at Anzio would need to hang on until the Germans were all dead—or they were.

From the lowest private in his foxhole to Lucas and Clark in their headquarters, it was plainly obvious that *today* was the Germans' ultimate moment of truth, the day that Kesselring and Mackensen would achieve their glorious, hard-won breakthrough—or go down in ignominious defeat.[1] The narrator of a U.S. Army Signal Corps film documenting the battle said, "The Germans have only one last hope—to make our victory so costly that we will weaken, compromise, make a deal with them and their Axis pals."[2]

Operating along the Carano Road on the right flank of the 45th's sector, the 180th Regiment had been spared most of the heavy blows that had hammered the 157th and 179th Regiments on the sixteenth. But on the morning of the seventeenth, a force of approximately 200 German infantrymen, closely supported by numerous panzers and preceded by a fearsome artillery barrage, materialized through the battlefield smoke and hit the 180th's positions—an attack that bore all the hallmarks of the human-wave assaults that had rolled across Flanders's fields in the previous world war. No sooner was one wave of tanks and infantry stopped than another appeared to take its place. On the 45th Division side, communications were knocked out and leaders went down dead and wounded. But the Thunderbirds, knowing that to break and run meant certain death (as well as dishonor), remained at their posts and kept up an unending fusillade against their attackers.[3]

The situation in the 157th's sector that same morning was verging on critical. The Germans had tried infiltrating, probing, bombing, and saturating the Thunderbirds with artillery and airplanes but had been unable to force them from their positions. In the early afternoon, a Luftwaffe raid on the 157th regimental headquarters knocked out communication with the forward units. But it was Lieutenant Colonel Lawrence Brown's 2nd Battalion that was in the most danger. At midmorning his men had repulsed an attack and suffered a few casualties when the Luftwaffe swooped in and bombed and strafed his positions. By afternoon the Germans could be seen trying to completely encircle the 2nd Battalion—and seemed on the verge of succeeding.[4]

To the 157th's right, the 45th's 179th Regiment was undergoing a crisis of its own. In military parlance, the word *relieved* means fired from one's position (British: *sacked*). At 2:15 P.M. at this crucial point in the battle, the regimental commander, West Pointer Colonel Milton R. Kammerer, described by the regiment's historian as "popular" and "too humane," was suddenly relieved of his duties. Reasons for his relief remain vague, although some accounts have referred to him as being exhausted by the strain, too kind, too compassionate, and not tough enough on those under his command. Or perhaps it was because his superiors felt that he had failed to send in a sufficiently large enough force to take and hold Aprilia, in the event allowing a thousand of his men to be captured. Whatever the reason, he was quickly replaced by Ranger commander Colonel William Darby, who no longer had a Ranger unit to command. Could Darby rally Kammerer's shaken troops?[5]

Truth be told, there wasn't much left of the 179th for Darby to command; one battalion was seriously understrength, another was at less than half strength, and the third was nearly devoid of men still capable of fighting. If ever a military organization needed a shot in the arm, it was the depleted and demoralized 179th Infantry Regiment, and the energetic Darby was that shot.[*6]

An apocryphal story is told about Darby. It is said that shortly after he took over the 179th, a despondent lieutenant colonel, on the verge of tears, came to him and confessed that his battalion had been shot to pieces. "I guess you will relieve me for losing my battalion," he said to his new commander. "Cheer up, son," Darby supposedly told him, patting him on the shoulder. "I just lost three of them, but the war must go on."[7] Perhaps the story is true, but the flippant remark seems out of character for an officer who so deeply loved his men and was so greatly affected by the loss of them.

AT 7:00 A.M. ON FEBRUARY 17, elements of Glaxo Murray's 24th Guards Brigade was moved up from 1st Division reserve to take over the forward positions occupied by the 1st London Irish Rifles, which would then pull back to a reserve position west of the Albano Highway and south of the Buonriposo Ridge. Here the ground was intercut with deep and steep wadis and ditches, with a mass of tangled undergrowth at the bottom. The London Irish had hardly reached their new position when orders came to move again—to the Buonriposo Ridge area to try to locate the 7th Oxfordshire and Buckinghamshire Light Infantry—the Ox and Bucks—who, during the night, had been surrounded and cut off and were in very real danger of being destroyed piecemeal.

Sergeant William Heard (7th Ox and Bucks) recalled that, during the night, his battalion had moved into a new position located in a wadi. At dawn on the seventeenth, the Germans hit the outnumbered unit's position with a heavy mortar barrage and ground attack, but the Ox and Bucks stood their ground. Suddenly, machine-gun fire coming from the battalion's rear erupted, and Heard and his company were encircled. For the next five hours, they fought off attack after attack, doing everything possible to keep themselves from being overrun. But the Germans were

---

* Darby would keep this job for two months before the War Department decided that it had other plans for him. William O. Darby and William H. Baumer, *Darby's Rangers: We Led the Way*, 175.

unrelenting in their shelling, perhaps demonstrating their anger at being denied victory. But the Ox and Bucks had no time to pat themselves on the back; they were rapidly running out of men and ammunition. The battalion commander, Lieutenant Colonel Shaw Ball, had been wounded two days earlier, as had his second in command; the battalion was now led by a Major Norcock. Even the injured, if they could, had to bandage their own wounds. Each man knew that if he failed to perform his duty, it might mean the end, not only for the battalion but for the entire beachhead.

For three more hours the attacks went on, each one deepening the fissure in the Ox and Bucks' positions; two companies were obliterated. Then, suddenly, the attacks unexpectedly ended, and the battalion was given a reprieve. Insistent orders from brigade said that it was imperative that the 1st London Irish Rifles find the battered 7th Ox and Bucks and take over their positions. But, in the wadis, the LIR suffered heavy casualties that they could ill afford. In fact, A and C Companies, LIR, were both down to about thirty-five men. In addition, some of the LIR platoons, while trying to locate the Ox and Bucks, had themselves gone missing within the many wadis, some of which were not marked on maps. In the event, despite heroic and costly efforts, the 1st LIR were unable to make contact with the Ox and Bucks.[8]

AS THE GERMAN OFFENSIVE BECAME more and more threatening, and doubts about the Allies' ability to stop it grew to worrying proportions, American officials considered evacuating the nurses from the beachfront hospitals to keep them from possibly falling into enemy hands. Knowledge of what German troops had done to Russian women when they invaded the Soviet Union was uppermost in their minds, but the idea was soon abandoned—their presence at the beachhead, sharing danger and hardships with the men, was a great morale booster. The women, too, believed that they were needed and insisted that they be allowed to stay. Plans to evacuate them were scrapped.[9]

NEAR CISTERNA, TRUSCOTT'S MEN HAD turned back a serious German assault, but, after this attack faltered and failed, the reconnaissance battalion from the Hermann Göring Parachute-Panzer Division was thrown in as the second wave. This move gained some success, penetrating 300 yards between two regiments. Near noon on the seventeenth, to break up the attack, the commander of Company K, 30th Infantry, called for an artillery strike on his company's positions—a strike that slaughtered the Germans and stopped the assault in its tracks.

More of the enemy, however, continued to keep up the pressure until, at midafternoon, with their numbers severely reduced by artillery, mortars, and machine-gun and small-arms fire, they withdrew, leaving the field covered with the dead and dying—as well as littered with their broken rifles, punctured ammo cans, shattered field radios, helmets, boots, bits of uniforms hanging on the strands of barbed wire, and other detritus of war. As the day wore on, five panzers and a half-track were also destroyed by the 751st Tank Battalion. That evening a counterattack by the 30th Infantry restored the regiment's original line.

Smaller German units also tried attacking bridges over the Mussolini Canal that were being held by Frederick's 1st SSF and the 504th PIR arrayed along the canal, but they had no better luck. The paratroopers and Forcemen were supported by Company C, 894th Tank Destroyer Battalion, that pumped out shell after shell and knocked out three panzers and a self-propelled gun.

Having failed on the ground, German aircraft and long-range artillery were called in to loosen the Allies' grip. The Luftwaffe flew nineteen missions and 172 sorties that day, but the results were negligible, with only an Allied ammunition dump the major casualty. The Allies, on the other hand, struck back hard from the air. A U.S. bombing mission originally scheduled to hit Cassino was rerouted to the Anzio battlefield, where thirty-four missions and 468 sorties bombed German positions. Enemy troop concentrations at Aprilia and Carroceto were especially hard-hit by dive-bombers and B-25 medium bombers, while the B-17s and B-24s unloaded their ordnance on the long lines of German trucks and tanks trying to reach the area.[10]

WEST OF APRILIA, ALONG THE Albano Highway and about two miles northwest of the Overpass/Flyover, Lieutenant Colonel Brown's 2nd Battalion, 157th Regiment, 45th Division, found a series of large chambers that had apparently, until recently, been part of a mining or gunpowder-manufacturing operation—carved deeply into a ridgeline; the tunnels that interconnected the caves were thousands of feet long. Thinking that the caves would be an ideal place in which to establish a command post, aid station, supply point, and fighting positions, Brown ordered his four companies to take up positions in and around the entrance.[11]

Henry Kaufman (Company H, 157th) described the caves: "There were some six caves in all. . . . These particular caves were very large, about a normal city block long, half a block wide, and about fifteen feet high. Each cave contained maybe fifteen ten-by-twelve rooms. The cave I was in sheltered me and five other members of my company, as well as at least fifty Italian women of assorted ages, some with babies. They were all refugees from nearby Aprilia, trying to survive the bombing and shelling."[12]

Captain Felix Sparks received orders to pull back and insert what was left of his Company E, 157th, into these caves, located a few hundred yards south of his current position. Sparks's men emerged from their holes, their faces blackened by all the flying dirt and powder, their uniforms filthy, torn, and stained, their ears ringing or deaf, their eyes filled with terror. With help from a couple of Shermans from the 191st Tank Battalion, they began hurrying to the rear to set up fighting positions outside the caves. No sooner had Company E settled in than the enemy could be seen advancing across hundreds of yards of open ground, where they were picked off by tank, rifle, machine-gun, and mortar and artillery rounds. Nevertheless, as quickly as one wave of German infantry and armor was decimated, another took its place.[13]

Sparks's men wondered: Would the caves be a defensible place of safety—or a catacomb where their bodies would be left to rot?

ON FEBRUARY 17, GENERAL PENNEY was nearly killed. While in his mobile command post (a trailer, called a "caravan" by the British) parked in a wooded area, a German shell exploded in a nearby tree and blasted metal fragments through the thin walls and into his back. After Penney was evacuated, Gerald Templer assumed temporary command of the 1st Division in addition to his own 56th. (Penney returned from the hospital six days later and regained command.) Templer was highly regarded as a forceful, energetic commander—unlike Penney, who, although a dependable officer, was seen by many as being cast from the same uninspiring mold as John Lucas.*[14]

AS ALEXANDER AND CLARK BEGAN to plot the dismissal of Lucas, on the seventeenth they removed Lucian Truscott from command of his beloved 3rd Infantry Division and installed him as deputy commander of VI Corps. Clark had had several officers under consideration to take over the corps. Three were British: Penney, Templer, and Major General Vyvyan Evelegh, the latter Lucas's deputy corps commander. But the bulk of the troops at Anzio were Americans, and it was decided that the corps commander should also be an American. The brash, outspoken Ernie Harmon was briefly considered but then rejected because, as one historian put it, "he had a genius for saying the wrong thing, for rubbing people the wrong way. . . . He could hardly be a good choice for a sensitive position in a coalition venture." To take Truscott's place as head of the 3rd Division, Clark would promote Brigadier General John "Iron Mike" O'Daniel, whose rugged countenance alone looked like it could terrify the enemy.[15]

Clark recognized that "the situation was rather critical that afternoon [the seventeenth]. We had suffered heavy losses of men and matériel. We were back to a line that had nothing much behind it except the beaches and the sea. We were obviously going to take it on the chin with everything Mackensen could throw at us. . . . I told Truscott that he would take command of VI Corps as soon as the crisis was passed. All Truscott had to do was make sure he had a beachhead to command when the crisis was over."[16]

Lucas, of course, was dismayed to learn that Truscott was coming in to be his deputy—but not especially surprised. To him, such a move meant only one thing: his tenure as commander of VI Corps was about to come to an end, despite Clark's advice or order to not stick his neck out and "forget this goddam Rome business." "I hope I am not being

---

* After the war, Field Marshal Sir Gerald Templer would be the military governor of the British zone of occupied Germany. He also led the British fight against Communist insurgents in Malaya in the 1950s. Obituary, *New York Times*, October 27, 1979.

relieved of command," Lucas wrote gloomily in his diary. "I have done my best. I have carried out my orders and my conscious is clear. I do not feel that I should have sacrificed my command."[17]

Changes in leadership—whether in the military, government, or business—usually mean one of two things: either a bad situation is about to change for the better, or things are about to get worse. It is said that it is unwise to change horses in the middle of a stream, and it can be even equally unwise to change commanders in the middle of a battle. Therefore, Lucas would remain in command of VI Corps a little while longer, for the Germans were even at that moment about to resume their counteroffensive against the beachhead forces.

Clark held Lucian Truscott in high regard, saying that "of all the division commanders available to me in the Anzio bridgehead who were familiar with the situation, he was the most outstanding. A quiet, competent, and courageous officer with great battle experience through North Africa, Sicily, and Italy, he inspired confidence in all with whom he came in contact." And at that critical moment, confidence was exactly what everyone at Anzio—and beyond—needed.[18]

THE GERMANS CONTINUED TO MOUNT attack after attack, and they followed the predictable pattern: artillery, panzers, infantry. 1st Armored Division commander Ernest Harmon noted that the enemy, out of desperation, threw every soldier they had—able-bodied or not—into the attack: "German prisoners later told us that even soldiers sick with dysentery were routed out of their beds and thrown into the line."[19] Many prisoners arrogantly told their captors that the Allies stood no chance, that the Germans were the superior force, the master race, and soon more soldiers in overwhelming numbers would be arriving at the beachhead to annihilate the Yanks and Tommies.[20] Still others smiled and smirked for the Signal Corps photographers after their capture, as if to say, "You can't defeat us."

As on previous days, the Allies refused to be moved. Each attack on the seventeenth was beaten back. That evening, Lucas wrote in his diary, "This is the second day of Jerry's all-out effort to drive us off the beachhead. His main blow today [was] against the 45th Division. We have lost a little ground but not too much. The struggle is bitter and our losses have been heavy, but [the enemy's] have been much heavier. . . . This battle must be won. I figure today and tomorrow will see it through. It may be the decisive battle of the Italian Campaign."[21]

Forty miles to the north, the lights in Mackensen's Rome headquarters burned into the stormy late hours of February 17. Once again the Germans had expended a maximum effort to destroy the British and Americans, and once again the effort had fallen short. Were the soldiers capable of another maximum effort? Would another attempt succeed, or was it also doomed to failure? Mackensen didn't know, but there was only one way to find out: try again on the eighteenth.

MACKENSEN'S ORDERS WENT OUT. AT dawn on the eighteenth, what was left of his infantry and panzers and stocks of artillery ammunition would once again be hurled at the Allies. As depleted as they were, the 65th Infantry and 3rd Panzer-Grenadier Divisions, accompanied by tanks, would throw in everything they had to force a human wedge between the 167th Brigade and the 2nd Battalion, 157th Infantry, to the west of Aprilia. The 114th and 715th Infantry and 26th Panzer and 29th Panzer-Grenadier Divisions would then do their utmost to overpower the 179th Regiment located between the "Dead End Road" and the Overpass. Farther to the west, the 4th Parachute Division would endeavor to assault and annihilate the 36th Engineer Combat Regiment manning the left flank, while, on the eastern side of the beachhead, the Hermann Göring Parachute-Panzer Division would smash into the 3rd Infantry Division and the American paratroopers. It was to be an all-out assault. Failure was not an option.[22]

Fortunately, the Allies at Anzio had a secret friend in Rome: the OSS.* This unit had set up a clandestine watching service of partisans

---

*The Office of Strategic Services, the forerunner of today's Central Intelligence Agency, was created to gather intelligence about the enemies of the United States. Major General William "Wild Bill" Donovan was its founder and leader from July 1941 until September 1945. At his death in 1959, Donovan was the only American to have received America's four highest awards: the Medal of Honor, Distinguished Service Cross, Distinguished Service Medal, and National Security Medal. George C. Chalou, ed., *The Secrets War: The Office of Strategic Services in World War II.*

that surveilled the twelve main highways that led out of the capital; five times daily they radioed VI Corps headquarters with information about the Germans that their agents had picked up. The OSS even had a spy within Kesselring's headquarters and another who served as a liaison officer between the Gestapo in Rome and the Italian secret police. The intelligence proved invaluable.

As an OSS spy, Peter Tompkins wrote, "At a critical moment in the battle, the Rome team flashed word of an imminent German counterattack along the Anzio-Albano axis. This attack was hurled back only because G-2 [Intelligence] at Anzio knew where and when it was due. Colonel Langevin, G-2 of the VI Corps, stated that OSS might well be said to have saved the beachhead. . . . To what extent these [Italian] partisans contributed to saving the Anzio Beachhead remains for historians to settle."[23]

THE "MISSING" 7TH OX AND Bucks was surrounded on Buonriposo Ridge but, amazingly enough, still holding out. On the afternoon of the seventeenth, the German attack on their positions on the ridge suddenly halted but resumed again at midnight. Ammunition was running low and some machine guns were completely out, but the fighting spirit never wavered. They would be tested again the next day.[24]

FEBRUARY 18 OPENED WITH THE usual heavy ear-splitting, ground-shaking bombardment by the Germans, followed by the familiar on-rushing charges by troops and tanks through a downpour. "We couldn't understand how the Germans could keep doing this, where all their manpower was coming from," recalled Lieutenant Colonel Ralph Krieger, 1st Battalion, 157th. "But as long as they kept coming, and we had the ammunition, we would keep killing them. We had no other choice."[25]

The 179th Infantry Regiment, under its new commander, Bill Darby, soon found itself in the crosshairs of the 715th Motorized Infantry Division. So concerned was Darby about his new command's ability to hold the line that he requested of Eagles that he be allowed to pull back to more defensible ground, but Eagles said no. The 179th must stand its ground; there were no reserves behind the regiment. Although the 179th's positions were being pummeled by artillery fire, Darby set about reorganizing to meet the threat. The 1st Battalion moved up to the 2nd Battalion's left, and Darby borrowed the 157th's 1st Battalion to bolster his right flank. The 2nd and 3rd Battalions were reinforced with personnel from the service company, the maintenance battalion, the military police, the cooks and clerks. Every man who could hold a rifle was thrust into action. No sooner had the hasty realignment been completed than the Germans struck, splashing across the glutinous bog as American bullets and shells tore into their ranks.

The rain was coming down in sheets, but the intensity of the battle, like the rain, showed no signs of slackening. If anything, both grew more intense as both sides tried desperately to gain the upper hand. Morning changed into afternoon, and still there was no letup in the attacks. Somehow, Darby's men hung on, fighting off one savage assault after another, hunching their shoulders against the unending cascade of artillery shells that continued throughout the night and until dawn the next day.[26]

Heading across open ground for the Overpass/Flyover, the 3rd Panzer-Grenadiers were trying to spear their way through, but Company I, 157th, refused to let them. Despite the low ceiling, American airpower, too, was called in to break up the enemy formations. Men fell in droves, but the Germans kept up their attacks as though the bombing and strafing warplanes were just so many pesky mosquitoes.

Sergeant Brummett Echohawk (Company B, 1st Battalion, 179th Regiment) had been discharged from the hospital and returned to duty just in time for the enemy's final concerted attempt to break through at the Overpass. "The front flashes and rumbles like an electrical storm," he wrote. "Enemy barrages continue as fierce as ever. . . . After a near hit, we find ourselves helping each other dig out. We cough and spit mud, but continue to rise and fight back, holding the line. Chaos ensues as Germans, in long overcoats, swarm forward. . . . Accurate rifle fire drops them and stops the few that continue their advance."[27]

THE 157TH SOMEHOW ENDURED THE unendurable, watching buddies blown apart by direct hits or shot through the head or medics killed as they tried to aid the wounded. Men wept as their nerves could no longer stand the strain. At the caves, the Thunderbirds found themselves in an increasingly untenable situation. One of the men, First Sergeant

Harvey E. Vocke, recalled, "One morning I carried a wounded man down to the caves and was going to bring back a can of water but when I was coming out of the caves, Jerry opened up with machine guns and knocked the cans out of my hands. They made assault after assault on the caves that day and night. It seemed everywhere I looked I would see a GI getting killed by machine-gun fire."

Machine-gun outposts, tanks, and forward observers formed a semicircle outside the caves' entrances, where they could bring fire on anyone approaching. Inside were the 2nd Battalion's medical detachment, under Dr. Peter Graffagnino and his medics, along with German doctors and aid men who had been captured, working on wounded men from both armies.[28]

An officer from the 2nd Battalion found a letter on a German corpse outside the caves. "Shortly after you get this," the soldier had written to his mother, "I will be dead. Our officers have lied to us. We are low on ammunition and low on food. The war is lost. Germany is lost."[29]

"We were trapped by the Germans," said Henry Kaufman (Company H, 157th), "and unable to move more than fifteen or twenty feet outside of the cave. On the 18th we were attacked by the enemy in very close hand-to-hand combat, with fixed bayonets, right outside the entrance to our cave."[30]

Al Bedard (Headquarters Company, 157th) recalled:

The Germans attacked us night after night with one outfit or another, and we broke up their attacks for a week. Every morning I'd look out and there'd be German machine-gun crews lying dead behind their guns where our interlocking fire had cut them down during the night. They had us surrounded and we couldn't get out, but we kept breaking up the center of their attack every time they tried to hit us. Finally, they threw everything they had at us. The last couple of nights we called down our own artillery on our positions to break up the attacks. They were swarming all over the tops of these caves out in the open.[31]

The Germans continually tried to attack across the flat, muddy ground that was now a ghastly carpet of dead and wounded, and each time they moved out from their cover they received the full force of American and British firepower. What was left of the Infantry Lehr Regiment 309 was thrown back into the battle but was hit so hard that it shuddered, stopped, and then fell back in disorder.[32] Kesselring was supremely displeased with the conduct of the Infantry Lehr and held himself responsible for having relied on hearsay that Hitler's elite demonstration unit "was invincible."[33]

James Safrit (Company F, 179th Infantry Regiment) said:

We just found out that we have been fighting Hitler's crack commando regiment [the Infantry Lehr Regiment] that had been sent to break through our lines. They were special troops trained for special missions. Their orders were to wipe out the 45th Division and seize the beachhead. We had already sampled some of their grisly tactics. A few nights earlier, two men in the 2nd Platoon were in a slit trench—one was on guard and the other was asleep. The next morning, the sleeping soldier awoke and found his partner with his throat cut. Those Krauts had slipped in and murdered one man and left the other to find him—a very demoralizing tactic. After that, we were forced to pull the pin on a grenade and sit up and hold the handle down. I guarantee no one went to sleep holding those grenades.[34]

ACTS OF EXTREME BRAVERY PROLIFERATED all over the beachhead. Private first class William J. Johnston (Company G, 180th Regiment, 45th Division), from Colchester, Connecticut, was manning his .30-caliber Browning machine gun in a position near Padiglione. Coming under assault by an attacking force of approximately eighty Germans, he mowed them down, leaving at least twenty-five dead and wounded scattered in front of his position and forcing the rest of the attackers to temporarily flee. Determined to eliminate the stubborn Johnston, the Germans resorted to mortar, artillery, and sniper fire. When two Germans crawled so close to his position that his machine gun was ineffective, he pulled out his pistol and killed one German and the second with a rifle taken from another soldier.

After a daylong battle with the Germans on the eighteenth, Johnston was informed that his platoon was pulling back, but he volunteered to stay behind to cover the withdrawal. As darkness descended over the battlefield, Johnston remained at his post, picking off at least seven of the enemy whenever they showed themselves. As the last man off the front line, he carried his gun to a new position and maintained an all-night vigil. In the dark, though, the Germans drew near again, and this time their shots found their mark, one of them wounding him near his heart and forcing him to crawl away from his gun. A passing soldier found him and stopped to aid him. Refusing to be led to safety, Johnston asked the soldier to help him resume his position behind the machine gun, which went back into action for about ten minutes before going silent.

Although assumed to be dead, Johnston slowly and painfully worked his way back from his overrun position through enemy lines on the morning of February 19 and provided valuable information about the enemy's positions. For his heroic determination that aided in halting the German attack, he received the Medal of Honor.[35]

AT ABOUT 4:30 A.M. ON the eighteenth, the 7th Battalion, Ox and Bucks, sent a wireless message to brigade headquarters: "Mother and child are doing well"—meaning that the battalion headquarters and B Company, the last remaining company, were hanging on. B Company then decided to do something extraordinary: it would counterattack the Germans!

Sergeant William Heard said, "We stormed some houses occupied by the enemy and from where snipers had been giving us continual trouble. Near these buildings Major Norcock was wounded and Captain Close-Brooks took over command of our very small, exhausted, but by now exceedingly aggressive band of soldiers."

Angered by the impertinence, the Germans fought back fiercely in a battle that lasted all of the eighteenth and well into the night. But B Company's reduced numbers meant the odds of success were too great and so a final message was sent that indicated B Company was just about to be overrun. Five stragglers—Heard being one of them—made it back to battalion headquarters. Out of food and nearly out of water, the few remaining members of the battalion realized that they could surrender or stay and fight to the last man; they chose the latter. Gathering every bullet they could find, the men crouched behind coils of barbed wire and waited for the Germans to come and get them; if they were to die, they would take as many of the enemy as possible with them.

At least the battalion wireless set and Allied artillery were still func-
tioning, allowing fearsome barrages to be called in whenever the Germans got too close. "When the enemy finally withdrew," Heard recalled,
"their casualties had been heavy, with dead and wounded lying everywhere." Again, the reprieve was only temporary, for the enemy quickly
returned to continue to batter the few remaining Ox and Bucks. "At odd
intervals," Heard said, "a heavy German tank would move up onto a
nearby road to literally within a few yards of our position. From there it
would attack positions to our rear. It was so near that the shouted orders
by the tanks crew and the sound of each spent shell case clattering on the
floor of the tank could be clearly heard. We couldn't help but think that
the next round would surely be the one to land in our midst."

The Germans, like the British, refused to give up, and the infantry
attacks and shellings continued into the next day—the fifth day of nearly
nonstop fighting. The 7th Ox and Bucks was now down from 800 to
about 100 men. On the fifth night, a British tank managed to get through
with a supply of ammunition, rations, cigarettes, and batteries for the
wireless set. Heard said, "With these we continued to hold the enemy
until, later the next day, we were relieved." When the battalion pulled
out, there were only about sixty men left.

The 7th Ox and Bucks' stand was one of the most extraordinary in a
battle filled with them. But the survivors did not learn until much later
that the 1st Battalion, London Irish Rifles, had been expending every
effort to come to their aid.[36]

EARLY ON THE MORNING ON February 18, a group of about fifty Germans
again assaulted Z Company, 8th Royal Fusiliers, but was beaten back. A
few hours later, a larger contingent attacked, inflicting heavy casualties.
One of the officers killed that day was Lieutenant Eric Fletcher Waters;
his body was never recovered.[*37]

---

* Roger Waters was deeply affected by his father's death. At the core of his disturbing, surrealistic 1982 film, *Pink Floyd: The Wall*, is a dramatization of the battle
of Anzio. His song "When the Tigers Broke Free" also pays homage to the battle.
Review of *Pink Floyd: The Wall*, *Chicago Sun-Times*, February 24, 2010. The mu-
sician also installed a small monument that stands near the place where the 8th
Battalion fought and where Waters is believed to have lost his life.

ONE DID NOT NEED TO be on land to be in harm's way. On February 18, the British light cruiser *Penelope* was on her way from Naples to Anzio when a German submarine—the *U-410*—intercepted her and put two torpedoes into her. The ship sank, carrying the captain, George D. Belvin, and 416 other officers and men to their doom; 206 survived.[38]

Meanwhile, Mark Clark returned to VI Corps headquarters in Nettuno to discuss with Lucas, Truscott, and Harmon ideas for striking back at the Germans. Ever the aggressor, Truscott said that he wanted VI Corps to counterattack as soon as possible. Clark thought that was a fine idea, but what forces would he employ? Harmon proposed that elements of 1st Armored could mount a counterattack up the "Bowling Alley" and hit the Germans in the flank as they were attacking down the Albano Highway and the fields around it. "I proposed that we knife through the Germans and try to cut them off," he said. "The plan was approved and set for the next morning." The plan called for the 6th Armored Infantry Regiment to accompany the tanks on the south side of the Bowling Alley and the 30th Regiment of the 3rd Division on the north. Harmon added, "All the VI Corps artillery, arrayed behind us, was to attempt to make life unlivable for the enemy in front of us."[39]

Still wracked by caution, Lucas opposed the counterattack, Truscott said, "for he had always been reluctant to commit his Corps reserve. Now that General Clark favored the counterattack, Lucas reluctantly agreed, and we set to work."

It was decided that two forces—Force H, under Harmon, and Force T, under Templer—would be formed to hit back at the enemy the next morning. Force H would consist of several tank battalions flanked by the 30th Infantry Regiment from the 3rd Infantry Division and the 6th Armored Infantry Regiment, while Force T would employ the 169th Brigade as soon as all elements had arrived from Naples. Force H, with regiments abreast, would sweep up the Bowling Alley to seize the ground north of the Dead-End Road, while Force T would push northward from the Overpass/Flyover with the mission of seizing the western end of the Dead-End Road where it intersects with the Albano Highway and make contact with the 157th's 2nd Battalion, which was still in the caves and nearly surrounded. "These forces would be supported by all the artillery we could muster," said Truscott, and Clark said that he would try, weather permitting, to get as many Allied planes into the air as possible.[40]

Harmon said, "It was an eventful afternoon and evening as we prepared for the all-important slugging match. After darkness fell, tanks began to move forward into position." The heavily laden infantrymen, each weighed down with 130 rounds of ammunition, however, "had to march five miles in ankle-deep mud to get to their jump-off positions."[41]

Lucas wrote in his diary that evening that Clark "was not critical. He seemed a little worried. He is certainly doing all he can to help me. What we want is lots of nice weather so the air [force] can help us. Raining today." Lucas also commented on the fact that Anzio harbor was temporarily closed to shipping because the Luftwaffe had sown the waterfront with mines and that he had to send elements of Harmon's 1st Armored Division up to help the British because of the lack of ammunition that the mining of the harbor had caused for Penney's men. He also noted that Harmon's attack on the eighteenth had been successful, caused many German casualties, and brought in some 500 German prisoners.[42]

VI Corps' plans had been made. The next morning, February 19, the Germans would get a taste of their own bitter medicine.

CHAPTER 16

"The stakes are very high"
FEBRUARY 19–MARCH 22

A T 2:00 A.M. ON THE nineteenth, General Harmon was rousted out of his bunk in his 1st Armored Division mobile command headquarters; VI Corps was on the phone. The caller said that the Germans had stolen the march on him and were already beginning to move south toward the Overpass/Flyover. Harmon said, "It was suggested that perhaps our sortie [up the Bowling Alley] be called off and the armor pulled back to meet the advance head on. I disagreed emphatically, and got permission to proceed with the original plan."[1]

Elements of Smilo Freiherr von Lüttwitz's 26th Panzer Division and 15th Panzer-Grenadier Division were headed straight for Lieutenant Colonel E. Fulbrook's 1st Battalion, 1st Loyal (Lancashire) Regiment of Brigadier Eric E. J. Moore's 2nd Brigade, and Lieutenant Colonel Wayne L. Johnson's 1st Battalion, 179th Infantry, that were outposting the Albano Highway, north of the Overpass/Flyover. The British, dug in near the Lateral Road, or "Wigan Street," in front of the Overpass/Flyover, did not realize the German juggernaut was rolling their way. Suddenly, explosions erupted all around. Second Lieutenant Ted Lees (6th Gordons) recalled that his platoon was in foxholes when a direct hit on one of them killed two of his men. "At one point . . . a shell landed quite near and I saw pieces of shrapnel fly past; they were white hot in the dark, and I was rather lucky that I was not in the way of any of this shrapnel."

He took a patrol out to see if a gully was occupied by the Germans, bypassing several dead enemy soldiers and avoiding trip wires to mines and was crawling over some barbed wire when a German opened up at close range. "The bullets missed me and killed the bloke behind. Then came a couple of stick grenades, the ones with long throwing handles, which also missed me. Instead of being very brave and firing back, I threw a smoke grenade and got out over the wire rather quickly. I didn't have time to check on the bloke who was killed, and was told off later as I should have taken his name tag or something." For many years afterward, Lees would wake up with a nightmare of that incident.[2]

FORTUNA, THE ROMAN GODDESS OF luck, was beckoning seductively to the Germans. The opportunity to break the stubborn defenders had at last come. Every battle has a pivotal moment, a tipping point, in which the outcome is decided. Such a moment—when the attackers overwhelm the defenders or the defense repels everything the attackers can muster—may last a minute or an hour or a day. Realizing that this was the pivotal moment, that it was now or never, Mackensen directed Gräser to throw all the remaining elements of his 3rd Panzer-Grenadier Division into the battle; the Americans and the British seemed to be tottering on the brink of collapse. Victory or defeat stood in the balance.

In the predawn darkness and downpour, the Germans crashed into the 1st Loyals positioned near the Lateral Road, forcing them back.[3] There, with the fighting swirling in rain and confusion, the 701st U.S. Tank Destroyer Battalion arrived at the exact perfect moment, broke up the assault, and knocked out seven attacking panzers.[4]

Wayne Johnson's 1st Battalion, 179th, arrayed at the Overpass, was also coming under great pressure. The Germans charged across the mud, screaming, firing, and throwing grenades. During the skirmish, a shell exploded, breaking both of Johnson's legs and killing his aide; he applied tourniquets to his injured extremities and refused to be evacuated. Continuing to direct his battalion's actions, Johnson was, as the 179th's commander Bill Darby[*] later said, "the major factor in preventing the complete collapse of the 179th Infantry."[5]

The Loyals, too, as the Lancashire Infantry's historian wrote, "fought back valiantly and held their ground until, on the afternoon of the 19th they were able to mount a successful counterattack. This was the turning point of the battle."[6]

AS DAWN BROKE, GENERAL HARMON was near the head of his armored column, could see the smoke and explosions of the battle up ahead, and was urging his men forward to hit the enemy's flank. Templer's Force T had been delayed getting started, so the outcome of the battle depended on Harmon and his men. The guns of the 27th and 91st Armored Field Artillery Battalions were about to open up on the Germans in front of the armored spearhead. Then, as Harmon noted, "I received a message which was responsible for the toughest decision I ever had to make. My chief of artillery reported that a battalion of the 45th Division, for reasons unknown, was in front of what we called the 'No Fire Line.' In other words, if we laid down our barrage, we would kill our own troops. There are times when the responsibilities of a military commander are, in the true meaning of the word, awful. This was one of them."

He realized that if he ordered the artillery to commence firing, it "might mean the death of many fine, brave American soldiers. To abandon the artillery attack would be to abandon sorties upon which, I was convinced, the saving of the beachhead depended. The brutal, naked choice seemed to be between the loss of some hundreds of men and the loss of many thousands. Backed up by headquarters, I gave the order to fire." The landscape suddenly erupted in flashes, smoke, and great columns of muddy earth, blossoming like giant dirty mushrooms, being flung skyward; the Allied barrage had caught the Germans in midstride.

---

[*] On April 30, 1945, while serving as assistant division commander of the 10th Mountain Division, Darby was killed by German artillery in the town of Torbole, at the northern end of Lake Garda. Flint Whitlock and Bob Bishop, *Soldiers on Skis: A Pictorial Memoir of the 10th Mountain Division*, 172–175.

His tanks and infantry columns dove into the enemy, blasting them to oblivion.

To Harmon's great relief, he learned later "that the 'doomed battalion' was not a battalion, but a platoon, and that platoon, fortunately, was not where, in the confusion of battlefield communication, we were told it was. This, however, does not change the reality of the decision I had to make."[7]

Harmon also recalled that the Allies' artillery, naval gunfire, and fighter-bombers saturated the Germans. "The German division had been destroyed. Ruined vehicles and dead and wounded men littered the landscape. We took 1,700 prisoners. Allied artillery, in addition to supporting our advance, had plastered German rear assembly points. Naval guns on ships at sea, anti-aircraft guns, and more than 200 medium bombers and fighter-bombers concentrated on the same ground with deadly effect. An escaped American prisoner told us that while being marched up the Albano Road, he had seen enemy dead stacked up like cordwood in piles of 150 each. Bulldozers were digging mass graves."

What had happened was, just as Gräser's men and vehicles charged into the attack and seemed to be on the verge of splitting the defensive lines, out of the morning smoke and fog Ernie Harmon's tanks came roaring to the rescue and, according to the 1st Armored Division commander, "broke the back of the German advance. . . . By 3:30 P.M. enemy troops were disorganized; an hour later our infantry had reached its objective. Unbeknownst to us, a German division [the 3rd Panzer-Grenadiers] had been on its own way down the Bowling Alley to strike at our lines when the tremendous Allied barrage began. By the evening we knew we had won our battle. What a difference a will to win can make! . . . Now it was the Germans who were disorganized, disillusioned, and at the end of their offensive strength. . . . We no longer needed to worry about being driven into the sea."[8]

Johnson's 1st Battalion, 179th, had done its part, too. Captain Hurd L. Reeves and First Lieutenant James H. Cruickshank Jr., commanders of C and B Companies, respectively, had their men keep up a murderous fire throughout the afternoon, causing great casualties among the Germans and sending them fleeing. According to the 179th's history, "For the first time in four days, the line became stabilized."[9]

There was no stability farther to the southwest of Aprilia where Z Company, 8th Battalion of Royal Fusiliers, 56th British Infantry Division, was in the fight for its life. The day before, the company had barely managed to hold off its attackers, the 26th Panzer and 29th Panzer-Grenadier Divisions, but on the nineteenth the enemy was back with renewed determination to eradicate this irritant. The company commander, Captain Harry Witheridge, soon found his position isolated and surrounded; no relief was possible. Therefore, after hours of heavy fighting, Witheridge and his men, almost out of ammunition, were forced to surrender.[10]

THE BATTLE OF THE CAVES was also reaching its climax. After a week in the caves, under continual German attack, the men were running very low on food, water, and ammunition. Only at night could parties leave the caves in search of water in drainage ditches that, according to one officer, was "the dirtiest water I ever drank."[11]

Henry Kaufman, a member of Company H, 157th, was one of the cave dwellers. "On February 19, the 2nd Battalion of the Queens Royal Regiment started to fight its way to the caves. They were totally unsuccessful since, with the exception of the caves, the Germans commanded all the ground at Anzio. This was definitely one of the worst battles ever fought, as entire companies of men completely disappeared without a trace."[12]

Captain Felix Sparks later learned that General Eagles had asked for British support; although having little to spare, they sent the 2nd and 7th Battalions of the Queen's Royal Regiment, part of the 56th British Division, in to help. With his characteristic bluntness, Sparks said, "That was about the stupidest thing I'd ever in heard my life; we were completely surrounded and cut off, but the British were going to relieve us and we were supposed to go to the caves and consolidate all the men we had left in the battalion. The British were then going to take over our positions and the following night we would withdraw. The only problem with that grand scheme was that the British were almost annihilated trying to get up to us."

When the handful of British reached his position, Sparks took his men—all sixteen of them—back to the caves. "Out of around a thousand men originally in the battalion, there were maybe three or four hundred men left. The wounded were all in the caves, too," Sparks said.[13]

THERE WAS NO JUBILATION IN Kesselring's headquarters when February 19 came to a close. The Allies had still not been driven off. Siegfried Westphal, his chief of staff, noted, "Two days of heavy fighting resulted only in a slow and costly advance. German troops penetrated to within twelve kilometres [7.4 miles] of the beach, and some units still nearer, though these, left to themselves, must have been eventually overwhelmed, for there was no more news of them. The Army Group and Army commands decided that they could not be responsible for further heavy losses and called off the attack."[14]

AT ANOTHER PART OF THE beachhead at this time, another Thunderbird was about to make history. The 45th Infantry Division was notable for the number of Native Americans that were in its ranks—some 3,000 to 4,000—which is not all that surprising, since the division was made up of Oklahoma and Colorado National Guard regiments and the American Southwest—especially Oklahoma—has a high Native American population.

One of those was Second Lieutenant Jack Montgomery (Company I, 180th Regiment), a Cherokee from Broken Arrow, Oklahoma. At dawn on the twenty-second, near Padiglione, Montgomery's half-strength platoon was pinned down by a force three times its size. The nearest enemy position—four machine guns and a mortar—was hammering Company I's position. This made Montgomery mad, and so he decided to take the situation into his own hands. Telling his platoon to cover him, he crawled out into the flat field ahead of him and began lobbing grenades and firing his rifle at the closest enemy position, killing eight and forcing four more to surrender.

As he was escorting his prisoners back to his platoon's position, he spotted another group of Germans clustered around a farmhouse. After calling artillery down upon the house, and while the barrage was still going on, he returned to the battlefield and killed three more Germans, knocked out two more machine-gun nests, and took seven more prisoners. Still not finished, he headed for another house some 300 yards distant where he saw movement; despite the artillery falling all around him, he captured twenty-one prisoners. "I had no intention of doing what the Army said I did," Montgomery confessed.

That night he went out to make contact with an adjacent company. "I was always going somewhere I didn't have any business going," he said. "I was coming back alone through a big ditch when a shell hit. I don't remember much about it. I was hit in the left leg and right arm and right chest. It wasn't very long before my medic found me. Your medic was the one person you had to have confidence in. I knew he would find me."

Evacuated to a beachhead hospital (where he said he was more frightened of enemy shelling than he was out on the battlefield), he was operated on and then sent to Naples and finally back to the United States. In January 1945, Montgomery was notified that, because he had killed eleven Germans and taken thirty-two prisoners, he would receive the Medal of Honor; President Roosevelt personally decorated him with it at the White House.[15]

AT 2:00 A.M. THE NEXT morning, now that the British had arrived and taken up positions at the northern openings to the caves, Lieutenant Colonel Lawrence Brown decided it was time to try to effect his 2nd Battalion's escape out through the southern entrances, which faced the sea. Sending his companies out one by one under cover of darkness, he hoped to extract what few men remained. The first to slip out was Company G, followed by F, Headquarters, Heavy Weapons, Sparks's E, and the walking wounded; the battalion surgeon, Dr. Graffagnino, elected to stay behind with the nonambulatory wounded and take his chances as a POW. He spent the rest of the war in prison camps.[16]

Through ravines and brambles the men went, trying not to make a noise, but in the darkness no one knew where they were going. Suddenly, a German machine gun ripped the night; the 2nd Battalion had walked into the encircling Germans. Men screamed and fell. In the confusion that followed, Sparks led a group of about forty men into a canal or a ravine and, by dead reckoning, stumbled into a British artillery unit, who then pointed the way to the American lines. The British unit that suffered heavy casualties while trying to come to the aid of the 2nd Battalion in the caves also managed to slip back to friendly lines.[17]

A few soldiers remained in the caves when the others moved out. One was Henry Kaufman (Company H, 157th). He recalled that the Germans shot tear gas into the caves in hopes of forcing the Americans out. When that didn't work, they resorted to flame-throwing tanks; he was burned on the arm. Still the GIs refused to give up. Finally, when their ammunition was expended, they waved a white flag. Kaufman said that when the Germans entered the caves, they were furious. They came in with rifles and machine pistols drawn and herded the GIs out. Suddenly, there were shooting, panic, and screaming. A few Italian women who had been in the caves were shot by the Germans, who called them collaborators. An officer abruptly ordered his men to cease firing. On his way out, Kaufman noticed about twenty-five or thirty dead Germans around the cave's entrance; he and the other POWs were ordered to pick up the bodies and carry them back to an area that contained about fifty other dead Germans.

After a short while, Kaufman and the other men from 2nd Battalion, 157th, were herded back to an area that held hundreds of other American and British prisoners. The group was then told to begin marching to the north, toward Rome. During the march, friendly fire began to drop onto the road, forcing the POWs to run for cover. A shell went off near Kaufman, and he recalled, "One of the British soldiers, running alongside me, was hit directly in the face by shrapnel. I couldn't see his facial features. I only saw a mass of blood. His entire face seemed to have been blown off."

After going a few more miles, the line of POWs was attacked from the air by American P-47s and British Spitfires, which added to the Allied death toll. For the rest of the day, the prisoners were pushed northward by their guards, the road lined with dead Americans. If a prisoner couldn't keep up the pace, the guards shot and killed him.

At last, toward nightfall, Kaufman and the group came to a large encampment where barbed wire and guard towers surrounded a compound of sturdy, permanent buildings; they were ordered into a building the size of an aircraft hangar. It wasn't long before the prisoners learned that they were in the prisoner-of-war camp at the Cinecittà motion-picture studio. It was the first of numerous camps that Kaufman would be in until the end of the war.[18]

AFTER SPARKS MADE IT BACK to friendly lines, a flood of fresh-faced, scared-looking youngsters directly from the States and the replacement depots was given to him to mold into a new Company E. However necessary replacements were to reconstitute battered, depleted units, they were never quite the same as the veterans who had been lost. Sparks also had the sad duty of writing and expressing his condolences to the families of men wounded, killed, or listed as missing in action. No matter how a man died, no matter what the truth was, the letter home invariably told the bereaved family that the dead soldier had performed heroically until the last moment and that his death was instantaneous and painless.

One day Sparks received a letter from a frantic mother whose son, Sergeant Robert L. Fremder, was a member of Company E and had gone missing. She wrote, "The last time I dreamed of Bob was the night before we got the telegram [from the War Department]. . . . In that dream I was over there with him . . . in a queer-looking stone house and shooting through the windows and any place to get at the Germans. Then a bomb burst just where he was. I saw him go up in pieces."

She begged Sparks to give her more information about what had happened to her son, but, for the life of him, Sparks could not recall a Sergeant Fremder.[19]

ON FEBRUARY 23, A SMALL, quiet ceremony was held at VI Corps headquarters. Johnny Lucas, looking old and tired, was ushered out as corps commander with a few short speeches and courteous handshakes by Clark and Truscott.*[20]

---

* After being relieved of command, Lucas served as Clark's deputy for three weeks and then returned to the United States, where he commanded the Fourth Army, a training command headquartered at Fort Sam Houston, Texas, until 1946. After the war he served as chief of the U.S. Military Advisory Group to the Nationalist Chinese government during China's civil war. He then became deputy commander of the reactivated Fifth Army at Fort Sheridan in Chicago. On Christmas Eve 1949, while at a party in Chicago, he suffered a heart attack and died at age fifty-nine. He is buried at Arlington National Cemetery. He wrote his memoirs, but they were never published. D'Este, *Fatal Decision*, 538; Martin Blumenson, *The Gamble That Failed*, 130; Martin Blumenson, *United States Army in World War II: The Mediterranean Theater of Operations—Salerno to Cassino*, 419–432; www.ww2gravestone.com/people/lucas-john-porter-old-luke/.

THE GERMANS, WHO HAD USED glider bombs so effectively in January, used them again on February 25. The Luftwaffe Unit II/KG100, flying Dornier Do-217 bombers, known as the *fliegender Bleistift* ("flying pencil") because of its slim fuselage, had been specially equipped with another of Hitler's "wonder weapons"—radio-controlled Hs-293 glider bombs. The glider bombs, each with a payload of 1,000 pounds of explosive, were released out of range of the antiaircraft guns and steered by radio signals directly onto their targets. Eric Alley, aboard the British destroyer HMS *Inglefield*, which was being used as a floating artillery platform to bombard German positions, said that aerial attacks took place nearly every night just at dusk, and on February 25 it was the turn of his ship to be attacked. Sitting three miles off the Anzio lighthouse, the destroyer was bobbing up and down in the heavy sea when a glider bomb slammed into the ship. "We abandoned ship into these extreme conditions," he said. Thirty-five men of the ship's company of 192 were lost that night. Rescue ships—minesweepers and other destroyers and the American salvage vessel USS *LCI12*—moved in to pull Alley and his surviving shipmates from the water.[21]

LIKE A WOUNDED, DYING ANIMAL, the German Fourteenth Army at Anzio still possessed enough strength to lash out at its tormentors one last time. In preparation for the assault, scheduled to begin on the 29th, Mackensen shifted Lüttwitz's 26th Panzer Division to the Cisterna front and moved Walter Fries's 29th Panzer-Grenadier Division into army reserve. Pfeiffer's 65th and Gräser's 3rd Panzer-Grenadier Divisions, under the control of the I Parachute Corps, remained holding the front that included Aprilia, Carroceto, and Campoleone. The 114th Light (Jäger) Division, reinforced by the 1028th Panzer-Grenadier Regiment (from the 715th Infantry Division), faced Carano. Controlling Cisterna were the repositioned 26th and Hermann Göring Parachute-Panzer Divisions, plus a newly organized unit—the 362nd Infantry Division—made up of a hodgepodge of regiments and battalions gathered from the Adriatic front. The 4th Parachute Division was positioned at the Moletta River line in Wadi Country. All told, the Germans had nine divisions—five of which were slated to attack the 3rd U.S. Infantry Division on the twenty-eighth. This time, instead of using the Albano Highway as his main axis of attack, Mackensen decided to punch through the front being held by O'Daniel's 3rd Division and 504th Parachute Infantry Regiment, arrayed along the Mussolini Canal.

During the evening of the twenty-eighth, German artillery fire began to grow in intensity, starting first along the British-held western flank and shifting to the east, where the shells began falling in the 3rd Division sector. O'Daniel countered this fire with barrages of his own from the guns of the 27th and 91st Armored Field Artillery Battalions in the vicinity of Conca. German artillery stocks were badly depleted, but weeks of resupply had filled the ammunition dumps of the Allies; it is estimated that for each shell fired by the Germans, the Americans returned twenty. In fact, the Germans estimated that Allied artillery fired 66,000 shells—more than double the number fired on any single day in the big offensive of February 16–20.

Even in the face of this overwhelming firepower and the suicidal nature of their attack, the Germans began to roll toward American positions behind a heavy smoke screen. Unlike riflemen, the American gunners did not need to see their targets in order to take them under fire. The shells tore unseen into the advancing ranks, blowing men and machines apart and causing the attacks to falter and fall back. Only in the sector manned by the American paratroopers did the Germans make any appreciable gains.[22]

The 106-man* Company B, 509th PIB, attached to the 30th Infantry Regiment, was dug in on a low hill about a mile northeast of Carano. First Lieutenant John Martin, who had taken command of the company just a few days earlier after the previous commander became a casualty, said that the sixty replacements he had just received were not much better than raw recruits. "Over half of them had never fired an M-1," he lamented, and none had had any training on mortars or machine guns. And most of them had just been released from the hospital and were still recovering from wounds. But beggars, Martin realized, could not be choosers; into the foxholes they went—and none too soon, for, at 5:30 A.M. on the twenty-ninth, a heavy barrage dropped into Company B's positions,

---

* An infantry company normally had about 200 men.

followed by the 1028th Panzer-Grenadier Regiment charging from out of the smoke screen. In the dark that morning, German sappers had cut through some of the barbed-wire entanglements in front of the paratroopers' position, and now the panzer-grenadiers were pouring into the gap, firing point-blank at anyone who showed himself. Martin tried to call for artillery but communications were out.

"Grenades were falling all over the place," he said. In the dark nobody knew who was friend or foe, "and everybody was all mixed up together swinging rifles and firing pistols. Then that crowd went right through us and into the reserve platoon area, where everybody went at it again." Then a second wave of Germans arrived and "began rolling over us, and those of us left around the CP were engaged again at close range by twenty-five or thirty of them. We were forced down into the creek with grenades falling all around us." Martin was wounded and knocked unconscious until a couple of men pulled him out of the water in the creek; they were then taken prisoner. One of the platoon leaders, seeing that the command post had been obliterated, ordered his men to withdraw, but only he and twenty-two enlisted men made it to the rear. Lieutenant Charles McKinney, one of Company B's survivors, recalled, "When the fight was over that morning, you've never seen so many bodies in your life lying on that field, dead."

After swarming over Company B's positions, the panzer-grenadiers, who outnumbered the paratroopers 3 to 1, continued on, heading straight for the 509th PIB's main line of resistance near Carano, where Lieutenant Dan DeLeo's Company A, down to ninety-six men, was waiting for them. Artillery rained down on the Germans as the paratroopers opened up with rifles and machine guns and mortars. The panzer-grenadiers, courageous though they were, did not stand a chance. American tanks finally arrived on the scene, and, in midafternoon, the skies had cleared enough to allow Allied warplanes to make an appearance, bombing and strafing the enemy. As the Germans fell back in confusion, the paratroopers attacked with bayonets, rifle butts, and even fists and regained their lost positions. For their steadfast role on February 29, the battalion earned a Presidential Unit Citation. A doctor with the battalion aid station surveyed the bloody battleground afterward and shuddered. "The sights I saw that day can unravel a guy," he said, without elaboration.[23]

Although the Germans had inflicted many casualties on the Americans, Kesselring was unhappy with the results. "Today's successes did not meet our expectations," he told his commanders, "despite the fact that we achieved surprise, that enemy artillery fire was light, and his air raids delayed. . . . We will succeed only if officers and men regain their former self-confidence as in olden days, inspired by an impetuous urge to attack."[24]

ON MARCH 1, WITH THE weather improving, Allied warplanes were up and bombing German positions with increased ferocity. General Mackensen urged Kesselring to give up the devastatingly costly ground assaults and go on the defensive, but Kesselring would not hear of it. No, he told Mackensen, he should again concentrate his next attack on the eastern flank, where the 3rd U.S. Infantry Division was still trying to take Cisterna.[25]

So, for a few blessed days at the beginning of March, while Kesselring and Mackensen wrestled over what to do, there were no massed charges of panzers and infantry against the Allies. Shells continued to saturate the front, however, and probes by infantry patrols remained as a way of the Germans telling the Allies that they were still there and not planning on leaving anytime soon. The relative quiet, however, played hell with American and British nerves, for the lack of enemy offensive action only made the troops worry that Kesselring was building up his forces again for another, even greater, run at them.

THE MEN IN THE AIR were also required quite frequently to prove their mettle. On March 2, Staff Sergeant Thomas M. Moriarty, the ball-turret gunner in a B-17 Flying Fortress nicknamed *Leakin' Lena* (96th Bomb Squadron, 2nd Bomb Group, Fifteenth Air Force, based at Foggia, Italy), was on his fiftieth and final mission. (At this time, the number of combat missions flown before an airman was eligible for stateside rotation was fifty.) The squadron's target for the day was a concentration of German troops north of Anzio.

Leakin' Lena and the squadron took off and headed for Anzio at an altitude of 19,500 feet. When they reached the IP (initial point—the coordinates where a bombing attack begins) and began to drop their bombs, a wall of flak hit them, knocking out the two starboard engines; the nose was also hit and partially destroyed. The mission leader, Colonel Elmer J. Rogers, riding aboard the B-17, was wounded in the foot. The plane lost altitude and issued a "May Day" alert, and the crewmen began strapping on their parachutes in preparation for bailing out but were then informed that the plane would have to ditch in the sea. "We started throwing everything out that was not nailed down," Moriarty said. "We then began to assemble in the radio room to follow the ditching procedure. The plane was shaking like a jackhammer."

The pilot, First Lieutenant Thomas R. Degan, and copilot, Second Lieutenant Benjamin E. Nabers, ditched as well as could be expected. Moriarty said, "We braced ourselves for the crash. We hit very hard and came to a stop at once. Water was rushing in fast . . . and we started sinking." He was second to the last one out and stepped down on the wing but soon found himself in the water. "Before the undertow pulled me down, I saw [waist gunner William E.] 'Red' McNichol standing on the upturned wing." When Moriarty popped to the surface again and spit saltwater out of his mouth, he began swimming toward a dinghy bobbing about 20 yards away. "We all made it except Red McNichol. We saw him in the water about 100 yards away. Ben Nabers said he was a good swimmer and was going after him. It looked like Red was hanging on to a ration box. Nabers was told it was useless to go after him but he went anyway. He got out a ways from the dinghy and seemed to stop to grab something and call out to McNichol but there was no response. We just kept drifting away very fast; the water was rough and cold."

Then it was time to grab the injured Colonel Rogers and haul him into the dinghy. The survivors floated for nearly four hours, at one point waving their white scarves at a passing plane that turned out to be German. Luckily, the enemy pilot did not see them. Then a British "Wimpy" Wellington bomber was spotted on the horizon. "He just kept making circles, larger and larger," Moriarty said. "The Wimpy finally made a big swing and we shot up a flare. In seconds he was dropping flares around us and in less than a couple of minutes, a British Air-Sea Rescue boat was alongside of us."

The rescuers pulled them aboard and gave them dry clothes and rum. The search for the two missing members went on for a while, but the colonel needed medical help for his wounded foot; he was transferred to a British destroyer. The rescue boat then took the remaining men to the island of Ponza, south of Anzio and west of Naples, where they were fed and treated for shock and exposure. Moriarty noted, "I was treated for back injuries, Lieutenant [Robert A.] Brienza also for back and neck injuries. He seemed to be in bad shape and extreme pain. Lieutenant [William] Popoff and Lieutenant Degan for injuries, also." The next day the survivors were all taken to a hospital in Naples. Moriarty was released three days later and returned to his base, from which he was taken back to the States. His war was over.[26]

ON THAT SAME DAY, MARCH 2, Staff Sergeant Audie Murphy (Company B, 15th Regiment, 3rd Division) earned the first of his two Bronze Star medals. While his small patrol was engaged in a firefight, Murphy crawled a hundred yards across open ground to knock out a partly disabled panzer. Firing several rifle grenades at it, he knocked it out. When the Germans became aware of his presence, they turned their machine guns on him. Murphy wrote, "The operation stirs up a hornet's nest. Two enemy machine guns bark. Tracer bullets streak about me. I follow the ditch as far as possible. Then I kick caution out of the way and take off like a jackrabbit. My comrades, hearing me coming, get a fifty-yard start on me. But I catch up before we pause to rest our aching lungs a quarter of a mile away." Luckily, he was able to lead his men back to safety.[27]

March 2 also saw the return of Number 9 Commando to Anzio. After arriving at Peter Beach on January 22, Lieutenant Colonel Ronnie Tod's Number 9 Commando had a few skirmishes with the enemy in Wadi Country during its short two-day stint at Anzio and then were packed up and sent back to Naples, where they were then used in operations along the western Garigliano. Arriving along with Number 9 Commando on March 2 was a newcomer: Number 40 Royal Marine Commando. Commanded by Lieutenant Colonel J. C. "Pops" Manners, Number 40 Commando had started out as a component of the Eighth Army fighting on Italy's east coast at Termoli before being selected for

Anzio. The two Commando battalions were assigned to augment Templer's 56th British Division and conduct hit-and-run raids into German territory in the vicinity of the wadis.[28]

A member of 40 Royal Marine Commando, "Knocker" White, recalled that March 2 "was filthy, wet, and cold, and everywhere a quagmire. First night there, somewhere up at the front, I don't know where as we hadn't seen any maps, or the territory in daylight, we ('Y' troop) were called up to do a fighting patrol. I remember we waded up a river, water knee-deep, for some two hours until we came to an army post on top of the river bank." White's commanding officer told the men that some Germans were holed up in a group of farm buildings and the Commandos' mission was to eliminate them.

Just as the mission was set to go, a tremendous thunderstorm, full of lightning and a heavy rain, hit the area. "I didn't mind," said White, "because I'd often found that the filthier the weather, the more likely you were to get away with it, and so it was. The going was hard, as every yard was pitted with mortar and shell craters, and then suddenly there were the buildings, and we were in among them before they knew what had hit them. They were all killed, except one whom we took back as a prisoner."[29]

ALTHOUGH STILL UNHAPPY WITH THE Allies' progress, Churchill was astonished at the courage and resilience of the Allied soldiers at Anzio. He sent a cable to Roosevelt:

> I must send you my warmest congratulations on the grand fighting of your troops, particularly the United States 3rd Division, in the Anzio beach-head. I am always deeply moved to think of our men fighting side by side in so many fierce battles and of the inspiring additions to our history which these famous episodes will make. Of course I have been very anxious about the beach-head, where we have so little ground to give. The stakes are very high on both sides now, and the suspense is long-drawn. I feel sure we shall win both here and at Cassino.[30]

In the March 3, 1944, issue of *Yank* magazine, war reporter Sergeant Burgess W. Scott wrote of the Anzio beachhead: "This little Allied colony on the shinbone of the Italian boot is only a few weeks old, but it is rapidly becoming one of the hottest corners of this struggling earth."[31]

That sentiment was echoed by Jon Clayton (G-3 Section, 3rd Infantry Division) in a letter to friends back in the States:

> This beachhead has become a hot spot. Every day sees our bombers conducting sorties upon the enemy; and damage must be great because the vibrations [from the explosions] can be felt many miles away. The enemy takes his turn at night. Attacks, counterattacks, and constant shelling combine to make the fighting intense. . . . I'll just relate one incident. . . . It was just after dinner one day that a Jerry plane zoomed low and began strafing the road outside our bivouac. The boys got him in their sights and shot off his tail. Unable to control the plane, he crashed into a small hill. His bombs exploded and we found him and his plane well distributed over quite a large area. A clean, white hand was found nearby, some unidentifiable bones were buried in the ground, part of the skull was about fifty yards away, while a shoulder was perched upon the hay stack of a farm nearby.[32]

WHILE THE MEN WERE PROUD of having been able to withstand every German attack up to this point, homesickness ate away at many of those stuck at Anzio; their only relief were the letters they received from their wives and sweethearts back home—letters that took two or three weeks to arrive.

And, of course, it is unrealistic to expect that every Allied soldier on the beachhead was brave and steadfast, willing to die to derail Hitler's plan for world conquest. Most—perhaps all—were frightened out of their wits, sticking to their posts for only two reasons: they didn't want to abandon their buddies, and there was no place for them to go. Wracked by fear, by cold, by loneliness, by the sheer misery of Anzio, some soldiers resorted to the self-inflicted wound. Medic Robert "Doc Joe" Franklin, Company I, 157th Infantry Regiment, 45th Infantry Division, remembered one particular casualty. "He was a new boy with one of the other platoons, and he had shot himself in the foot. He said he was cleaning his rifle and accidentally shot himself. It wasn't my job to tell him what a liar he was. I just got him evacuated."[33]

THE GERMANS WERE STILL TRYING all sorts of tricks and subterfuge against their enemies. For example, on the morning of March 4, the 167th British Infantry Brigade reported that a group of Germans waved a white flag, indicating that they wanted to surrender. When the British troops went out to take in the prisoners, they were fired upon. The word went out: "All ranks should be warned and must not be taken in by this trick."[34]

No one realized it then, but March 4 marked the final major effort by the Germans to evict the invaders from the Anzio-Nettuno area. Anzio had ceased being a *battle* and had turned into a *siege*. Kesselring and Mackensen no longer had the strength to break through the Allies and drive them back into the sea. Nor did the Allies have the capability of breaking out of their encirclement. All the Germans could do at this point was inflict as many casualties as possible with localized attacks on the Yanks and Tommies in the hope that the bloodletting would so disgust the American and British civilians back home that they would demand that their governments abandon Roosevelt's call for Germany's unconditional surrender and negotiate an armistice with Hitler.

For their part, Kesselring and his chief of staff, Westphal, assessed their troops' capabilities and were none too pleased with their conclusions. Westphal confessed in his memoirs, "About this time, our strength was no longer adequate. We were not capable of aggressive action. . . . The [German] soldiers had accepted every hardship and suffering that the fighting in the Pontine marshes and the hellish war of attrition had imposed, but it had all been in vain. What value was sacrifice if success remained unobtainable?"[35] By the time the latest series of suicidal assaults finally ended, Mackensen's Fourteenth Army had been reduced by thirty tanks and a further 3,500 men—men the Germans were hard-pressed to replace. At that point, the Germans went over to the defensive and restricted themselves to small-scale attacks, incapable of mounting anything greater than localized pinpricks.[36]

KENNETH WILLIAMSON, A PAYROLL CLERK with the 45th Infantry Division, recalled that the time had come to pay the troops. He said, "Even at the extraordinary conditions existing at Anzio, they wanted [to be] paid. So, Captain Ernest E. Brown, two other enlisted men, and I struck out for Anzio [from Naples in an LCI] with a field safe full of payrolls and money." The troops were paid in scrip.*

"Although the troops demanded some money in their hand, even where there was no place to spend it, they sent most of their money home—to families, to banks, etc. Each soldier probably kept an average of twenty to thirty dollars just to goof off [that is, drink, gamble, and spend on women]."[37] Many also piled their extra scrip into collection plates at church services.[38]

SIX WEEKS AFTER THE LANDINGS, Alexander sent out a dispatch to counter the criticism that still hung over the operation:

> From various reports I have read from home, it appears that public opinion imagines that after the initial landing no effort was made to advance further. This is most distressing to me and the troops. Reference should be made to the many casualties sustained by the British in taking Campoleone where they were finally held at the foot of the Colli Laziali, and also the losses suffered by the Americans in trying to take Cisterna, where all attacks failed.
>
> After this, superior German forces attacked us in strength and threw us onto the defensive and we had a bitter struggle to maintain the bridgehead intact after being driven back from Campoleone. A man may enter the back door of a house unperceived by the kitchen-maid who raises the alarm. But unless the inhabitants hide upstairs, there will be a fight in the passage for possession of the house. We are now fighting in that passage.[39]

Lucian Truscott's VI Corps troops, after having endured six weeks of nonstop bombing, shelling, and human-wave attacks, were at the end of their tether. Everything the Germans could throw at them had been fought off, but at a tremendous price. The temporary American cemetery in a field at Nettuno was growing, and the British, too, were dealing with a mounting death toll. The beachhead hospitals were full to

---

* The GIs were not paid in American currency but, rather, in military scrip—small bills that looked like "Monopoly" money, as scrip was supposed to reduce black marketeering. It never did.

overflowing, with hundreds of wounded men being taken by ship every week to Naples, home of the 17th, 37th, 45th, and 300th General Hospitals, which were at capacity.[40]

THE ALLIES SUSPECTED THAT THE enemy had also suffered greatly, but did not know to what extent. What was learned later was that Mackensen's Fourteenth Army continued to receive reinforcements that brought the total number of German forces up to 135,698 by mid-March. Kesselring had considered mounting another major offensive, but Mackensen convinced him to conserve troop strength in order to counter an expected Allied spring offensive.[41]

Angered by Hitler's continued micromanaging of the situation in Italy, in which the Führer made incessant demands for Kesselring to perform miracles beyond his power, the field marshal dispatched Westphal to meet with Hitler personally to try to explain the realities on the ground. "I made my report to Hitler on the Obersalzburg during the evening of March 6," Westphal wrote. "For more than three hours I unfolded the reasons which had made it impossible to throw the enemy back into the sea, despite all our reinforcements. After five years of war the troops had become exhausted to a frightening degree. The heavy losses had seriously handicapped the commanders of all ranks. For instance, it was now only seldom possible really to co-ordinate the fire of the various weapons."

Instead of exploding with rage as he usually did whenever a general gave him bad news or declared that something Hitler had demanded was impossible, the Führer at last seemed to comprehend that men, no matter how well trained and superbly disciplined, simply could not stand up to unrelenting torrents of bullets, bombs, and shells just because their leader had ordered them to do so. Westphal continued:

Hitler made frequent interruptions, but I was able to keep him to the subject. At the end, he said, with obvious emotion, that he knew well how great was the war-weariness which afflicted the [German] people and also the Wehrmacht. He would have to see how he could bring about a speedy solution. To do so, however, he needed a victory. A victory on a large scale—for instance on the Eastern Front—was impossible, for we had not the strength. That was why he had hoped that success would attend the Nettuno assault. I left the room with the feeling of having met with understanding. [Field Marshal Wilhelm] Keitel [chief of the Oberkommando der Wehrmacht (OKW)] later bade me farewell with the words: "You were lucky. If we old fools had said even half as much, the Führer would have had us hanged."

"Hitler did appear to be in a depressed mood that evening," recalled Westphal. "But looking back, it seems possible that he deliberately showed sympathy for our difficulties in Italy in order to put our minds at rest. On the two following days he questioned the officers from the front, who could only confirm what I had already said. The hoped-for consequences, however, were not forthcoming."[42]

THE ALLIES AT ANZIO, OF course, knew nothing of this meeting and could not believe that circumstances were so dire for the Germans. No matter how many Germans the British and Americans killed, there always seemed to be more to take their place. The deaths and the fighting seemed endless, a battle that would go on forever, a nightmare from which one could not awaken.

Men at the lower echelons struggled to keep themselves from going to pieces. Letters from home were essential to this process. Paul Brown, the Graves Registration Section member in the 179th Regiment, wrote that letters and photos from his fiancée were about the only things that kept him sane. Then he got back to describing his state of mind that day: "The shells were too thick for us to go up to front last night but got 2 KIAs in Regiment Area. The rest dugouts are almost ready for use. Hope no bombs hit them, no shells can hurt them. We put a full-length mirror and plenty of chairs, reading material in each—a damn good thing. To be used when boys return off 5 days in lines & wet foxholes. No news of relief for us anywhere."[43]

THE ALLIES DID NOT KNOW that the Germans had shot their bolt and that no further major attacks would be launched against them, and so they continued to rotate exhausted, understrength units out of the line in exchange for units only slightly fresher.

So beat up and depleted was Templer's 56th Division that Truscott pulled it off the line and sent it back south to Naples on LCIs for some much-needed rest and recuperation.[44] The 5th British Infantry Division, commanded by forty-five-year-old Major General Philip G. S. Gregson-Ellis, a graduate of Sandhurst and a veteran of the Great War,[45] was shipped in from Naples to relieve them. The 5th Division was made up of the 13th Infantry Brigade (consisting of the 2nd Battalion, Cameronians; 2nd Battalion, Royal Inniskilling Fusiliers; and 2nd Battalion, Wiltshire Regiment), the 15th Infantry Brigade (1st Battalion, Green Howards; 1st Battalion, King's Own Yorkshire Light Infantry [KOYLI]; 1st Battalion, York and Lancaster Regiment), and the 17th Infantry Brigade (2nd Battalion, Royal Scots Fusiliers; 2nd Battalion, Northamptonshire Regiment; and 6th Battalion, Seaforth Highlanders). In addition, there were three Royal Artillery battalions, an antitank regiment, antiaircraft regiments, a reconnaissance regiment, a machine-gun battalion, and four companies of Royal Engineers. Gregson-Ellis's division had been fighting its way northward from Italy's heel since September. Brigadier J. Y. Whitfield's 15th Brigade, a part of the 5th Division, replaced Brigadier J. Scott-Elliott's worn-out 167th Brigade.[46]

Twenty-year-old Lieutenant Raleigh Trevelyan (1st Battalion, Green Howards) was one of the British soldiers who found themselves moved up to a terrain feature at Anzio dubbed "the Fortress," on the extreme left position in the British sector, near the ancient town of Ardea. "All night long," he recalled, "the artillery and mortars of both sides kept up a non-stop barrage. The screeching and whirring of the shells over our heads might have been some furious gathering of witches on Walpurgis Night. Sometimes the explosions were close enough for us to see shreds of flames spurting upwards in the dark, and the shrapnel would come hissing at us from all sides."[47]

SOMETIMES NEW MEN WOULD BE assigned to a unit and killed before anyone knew who they were. On March 7, Private first class Charles Schindler (a member of Lieutenant Bill Whitman's Company I, 180th Infantry Regiment, 45th Division) wrote in his diary, "We moved up to the front last night, which was about a two-and-a-half-mile hike cross country. . . . I was appointed as the BAR man for the 3rd Squad. Today a shell landed in one of the fellow's holes and three were killed—two I had only met once and don't know their names. They had come up as replacements on the same day as I, and it was their first time on the line."

Whitman said that on the evening of March 7,

The Germans hit us hard. They pounded our positions with tanks, assault guns, self-propelled howitzers, artillery, and mortar fire. This kept up for at least thirty minutes. When it lifted, most of our platoon telephone lines were knocked out. The Germans then attacked with two companies of infantry. They were cutting our scarce barbed wire, crawling under and through it, and some were trying to climb over it. A German officer with a flame-thrower was trying to run and jump over when our riflemen shot him down.

Now, more Germans were turning on their flame-throwers, the liquid fire spurting over our positions. Other Germans were throwing hand grenades to pin our men down so that they could advance their flame-thrower men close to us where they would be effective. Our men shot them down by the scores, and then the artillery and the other supporting fires came in with a roar that sounded like the earth exploding. . . . It seemed like Hell had been moved to this particular spot. The screams and explosions rent the night air. Cries in German and our own men calling "Medic, medic!" or "I'm hit, I'm hit," could be heard from time to time. Things quieted down. . . . We had been fighting almost all night.[48]

BY MARCH 11, GLAXO MURRAY'S 24th Guards Brigade (1st Irish Guards, 1st Scots Guards, and 5th Grenadier Guards) was a battered shell of its previous self. More than a month on the front line had seriously reduced its numbers, and replacements were becoming harder and harder to find. The decision was therefore made to withdraw it from Penney's 1st Division and bring up the 18th Infantry Brigade, commanded by Brigadier A. D. McKechnie.

This unit consisted of the 1st Battalion, Royal East Kent Regiment (known as the "Buffs"); the 9th Battalion, KOYLI; and the 14th Battalion, Nottinghamshire and Derbyshire Regiment (the Sherwood Foresters). As a result of the fact that the brigade had spent the past several months in Tunisia, which had been secured in May 1943, it was a well-rested force—just what VI Corps needed for the trials ahead.[49]

AS AN ELEMENT OF THE 168th Brigade, the 1st London Irish Rifles' war at Anzio finally came to an end as it packed up, left the port, and sailed back to Naples. During the 1st Battalion's nearly six-week ordeal at Anzio, its casualties in killed, wounded, and missing amounted to thirty-two officers and 550 other ranks. "Only twelve officers and 300 other ranks embarked, and many of these had just returned to the battalion from hospital," said the battalion's historian.

A week later, after the regimental band rejoined the LIR from the east side of Italy and Italian washerwomen had cleaned and pressed their uniforms, the men formed up and received their medals and awards on parade from Field Marshal Alexander. He followed up with a letter to the battalion's commanding officer:

> I do so heartily congratulate you on having such a splendid battalion. It was a real joy to me to be with them today, and I thought they looked just fine. Smart, proud of themselves—in fact, just what one wishes and expects Guardsmen to look like. It must have impressed all the on-lookers very much, like it did me.
>
> The Micks were always good (the best in the whole Brigade), but I really believe they were better today than ever they were or ever have been. I am only so sorry that I could not remain longer with you . . . but as you know I have this important and tricky battle of Cassino in full swing, and it must be won. . . . Good luck to you all.

The battalion marched straight off parade to enjoy a monumental dinner and then prepared for returning home. The 1st Battalion, London Irish Rifles, never fought again. They went home, immensely proud of their many defensive stands at Anzio and glad to be well out of it.[50]

THE BENEDICTINE ABBEY THAT HAD crowned Monte Cassino since AD 529 had already been destroyed a month earlier, but the ides of March—the day Julius Caesar was stabbed to death in 44 BC—was also the day that spelled doom for the German-held town of Cassino below it. The Allies had tried to take the town, which controlled Highway 7 that led into the Liri Valley and then into Rome, but the Germans refused to relinquish it. The miserable, cold, wet weather was no help, either. Totally frustrated, the Allies decided to bomb the town into submission. On the fifteenth, with the weather having slightly improved, the Mediterranean Air Force was called upon to obliterate Cassino. In several waves, B-25s, B-26s, B-17s, and B-24s—a total of 435 aircraft—unloaded almost a thousand tons of ordnance; the town disappeared behind a wall of exploding dust and dirt.* From 8:30 in the morning until noon, the aerial bombardment went on.

The Allies were sure that nothing could have survived the horrendous saturation of high explosive, but, just for good measure, after the final plane had departed, the artillery—746 guns—opened up. For forty minutes, the cannonade lasted. When the firepower demonstration was at last complete, the Allies noticed one small detail that apparently everyone had overlooked: the streets were so choked with rubble—in fact, there *were* no streets—it was impossible to move vehicles through Cassino to get to Highway 7 and the Liri Valley.[51]

AS IF ITALY HADN'T ALREADY seen enough turmoil and destruction, on March 17 the volcano Vesuvius, located less than ten miles to the east of Naples, rumbled to life, sending a red river of molten lava flowing down the western slopes toward Naples. Over the next few days, the old mountain roared and shook the earth with mighty tremors. People living nearby started packing their belongings in case Vesuvius was preparing for the kind of full eruption that had buried Pompeii and Herculaneum 1,865 years earlier.[52]

---

* In actuality, only about 300 tons dropped by the B-17s and B-24s hit the town; the rest splattered all over Monte Cassino itself, the ruins of the monastery on top, the surrounding countryside, and Allied-held areas, killing and wounding soldiers and civilians. Bombs even accidentally hit Venafro, ten miles away, and killed seventeen soldiers and forty civilians. Blumenson, *Salerno to Cassino*, 441.

THE 504TH PARACHUTE INFANTRY REGIMENT was holding a position along the Mussolini Canal near the town of Sessano, a German stronghold; orders came down to eliminate that stronghold. It would not be easy. The town was protected by a double apron of barbed wire and a thick minefield. Machine-gun barrels sprouted from the windows of almost every building in town, and mortars were known to be zeroed in on all avenues of approach.

But the paratroopers did as they were ordered. On the afternoon of March 18, American 155mm howitzers were called upon to blast holes in the minefields and barbed wire and to knock down the buildings. Despite the heavy shelling, the Germans refused to retreat and laced the area with machine-gun and mortar fire whenever movement was spotted. Using drainage ditches, the paratroopers advanced on their objective but were kept at bay. One 504th officer reported, "The attack did not penetrate the defenses of the strongpoint, but the diversion it created drew [German] reserves from critical portions of the line." The officer declared, "Mission accomplished."

The paratroopers were relieved on March 23 and sailed back to Naples, having suffered 120 killed, 410 wounded, and 60 missing in action during their sixty-one days at Anzio. Now the 504th would head to Great Britain, where it would rest and ready itself to jump into Holland in September in an operation code-named Market Garden—forever known as "a bridge too far."[53]

THE GERMANS WHO HAD WORMED their way into the wadis west of the Albano Highway needed to be rooted out, or so the top brass decided, and it was Number 9 Commando that was selected for the job, which was scheduled for March 19. The British Commandos were keen for the task; they had had enough of being pummeled by German munitions and were itching to finally be let off the leash to conduct some violent raids into enemy territory—the very thing they had joined up and been trained to do.

Number 9 Commando had an authorized strength of about 450 men and was commanded by Lieutenant Colonel Ronnie Tod. The unit, formed in the fall of 1940, had taken part in a number of spectacular raids—perhaps the most famous of which was the raid on the German-held St. Nazaire naval dockyards on March 5, 1942. Although many of the men had been killed or captured, their exploits had become the stuff of legend. Assigned to the British 2nd Special Service Brigade in Italy, the remnants of Number 9 Commando were augmented by new blood and continued their career of specializing in hit-and-run raids—until taking part in Operation Shingle, where they basically held a defensive sector for most of their time at Anzio.

The mission for Tod's men was to clear out an infestation of Germans who had been using the wadis as a staging area to attack British units holding the western side of the beachhead. On maps the particular wadi in question, located about eleven miles north of Anzio and two miles west of the Albano Highway, resembled the letter *U*, and the Commandos had labeled the geographic formation with three names. The left vertical side of the *U* was named "Haydon," the right side was "Laycock," and the lower curved portion dubbed "Charles." The action commenced before dawn on March 19 with B and C Squadrons hitting Haydon; A and Headquarters Squadron followed as reserves. But the Commandos quickly ran into heavy opposition and were forced back by machine guns, sniper fire, and a strong counterattack. It soon became clear that the Germans were considerably stronger than the Commandos had anticipated, and battling in the darkness, with its attendant command-and-control problems, proved chaotic, just as darkness had earlier proved deadly for Darby's Rangers.

Radioing the unit behind him, one of the Commando captains shouted, "Hurry up or you'll be too late to throw your grenades at the Germans!" During the battle, when a bullet ruptured a water bottle worn by one of the officers next to him, Tod saw the fountain of spurting water and exclaimed, "Good God, he's been hit in the bladder!"

Supplies were running low, and the wounded needed to be evacuated. Fortunately, the Germans respected the display of Red Cross flags during the removal of the casualties. But the effort to capture the wadi could not be sustained; higher headquarters ordered Tod to pull his men back. By the time the Commandos had returned to their base and roll call was taken, the grim tally became known: nineteen dead, fifty wounded, and four missing. Shortly thereafter, Number 9 Commando was withdrawn from the Anzio area and sent to Molfetta on the Adriatic side to rest and refit. They never returned to Anzio.[54]

ON A BEAUTIFUL SUNDAY IN March, Robert Dodge (Anti-Tank Company, 15th Infantry Regiment, 3rd Infantry Division) was persuaded by a buddy to attend a religious service in the dunes near the beach. "We walked through the sand to the service," Dodge said, "and sat in the sun. A GI played a portable organ as we sang. The chaplain was getting ready for communion—*WHAM*—a 280mm shell slammed in close by, throwing sand everywhere. The chaplain grabbed the cross, took off running, and hollered that he thought it the Lord's will that we disperse. We all took off running; more shells came in, but I don't think that anyone was hurt."[55]

Besides the medics, another—even smaller—group of noncombatants must be singled out for praise: the chaplains. In every army during wartime, soldiers far from home and facing death are likely to seek solace in their religion. No truer phrase than "There are no atheists in foxholes" has ever been uttered. The World War II generation was a much more religious and churchgoing society than the secular one today. The vast majority of Americans (as well as British and Germans) of that era often reverted to their faith and the comforting words of a chaplain to get them through their travails. Chaplains of every denomination were called upon to administer last rites to the dead and dying, to be a "shoulder to cry on" when visiting the sick and wounded in hospitals, or to just act as a sympathetic sounding board for soldiers who were homesick, had their hearts broken by a "Dear John" letter, or just needed a compassionate friend during a particularly trying time.

Father (Captain) Joseph Barry was a Roman Catholic chaplain assigned to the 157th Regiment of the 45th Infantry Division. Although soft spoken and diminutive in stature, he was a giant when it came to providing the spiritual sustenance that the troops required in their daily confrontation with death. Barry once wrote to a fellow priest, "I can say that every day and night on this battle-front is a constant reminder of Death," and he noted that, as each exploding shell "came a little closer, each prayer became a little more fervent."

Father Barry brought religious comfort to the young men who had been taught that it was a sin to kill, young men who faced violent death on a daily basis and saw their buddies killed and grievously wounded, young men whose hearts became hardened by all the death and destruction around them, young men who risked turning into killing machines who had lost all concept of humanity. A sergeant wrote, "On the Anzio beachhead where a person couldn't stick his head above ground in the day-time, Father Barry crawled through canals and drainage ditches to bring us spiritual encouragement. More than ever before in our lives, we needed courage, pitting the perishable body against formidable engines of indestructible steel. More formidable than steel, however, is the immortal soul of man."[56]

MARCH 21 HAD BEEN A relatively quiet day—a few shells traded between both sides, a few skirmishes here and there, but nothing of great significance—except for those who were killed or wounded or taken prisoner. Then, at 4:00 A.M. on the twenty-second, the morning opened with a violent crash, or, rather, a series of them. Nurse Avis Dagit (56th Evac Hospital) was sleeping fitfully in her tent when suddenly the night was split open "at two-second intervals as 88mm shells 'walked' toward us. I lay paralyzed with fright as the bursts passed overhead toward Anzio. About forty shells fell in the hospital area and the 15th Evac suffered the heaviest damage. One hospital ward received a direct hit that killed seven patients and wounded many others."[57]

The prospect of death could not be escaped even when one was no longer in combat.

CHAPTER 17

"They liked to send us out to stir things up"

MARCH 23–MAY 21

FRIDAY, THE TWENTY-THIRD OF MARCH, was a warm, quiet day in Rome. The talk in all of the *taverne* and *ristoranti* was the mighty eruption of Mount Vesuvius, 360 miles to south, that had begun six days earlier. The volcano, which had buried, and thus preserved, Pompeii and Herculaneum in AD 79, continued spewing flaming lava and pumice and shaking the surrounding countryside—almost as though it were a living, breathing entity reacting with pain and anger at the fury of war raging across Italy's surface. Luckily, the plume of smoke and ash that billowed several miles into the atmosphere avoided teeming Naples; several feet of black pumice did blanket the towns and fields around Pompeii, though, and wiped out the village of San Sebastiano.[1]

The eruption also seriously affected the operations of the Twelfth U.S. Air Force's 340th Bomb Group at the Poggiomarino (Pompeii) Air Field near Terzigno. Between seventy-eight and eighty-eight B-25 Mitchell bombers were destroyed by the hot pumice, putting the base and squadrons of the group temporarily out of action.[2]

An eruption of a different—and far more deadly—nature took place in the heart of Rome on March 23. On that day, Italian partisans, using an improvised explosive device, killed thirty-three SS policemen marching along the Via Rasella near the Barbarini Palace. When Hitler was informed of the ambush, he angrily demanded that thirty to fifty Italians be executed for every German who was killed.

Civilians in the neighborhood were rounded up, an angry German officer threatened to blow up all the buildings in the area, and Kesselring's headquarters was called to inform him of what had happened. But the chief was out, visiting troops at the Anzio front.* In Kesselring's absence, Mackensen, as the next-highest-ranking officer, took it upon himself to reduce the punishment; only ten Italians (most with no connection whatsoever to the attack) would be killed for each dead German. Once Kesselring arrived back at his Monte Soratte headquarters that evening, Siegfried Westphal filled him in on the partisans' attack and Hitler's demand for swift retribution. Kesselring approved Mackensen's decision; Kesselring's involvement in the Kappler massacre would ultimately lead to postwar charges of war crimes.

After pulling criminals at random out of the city's prisons, Lieutenant Colonel Herbert Kappler of the SS, head of German police and security personnel in Rome, had 335 men trucked to a large, abandoned mine along the Via Ardeatine on Rome's southern perimeter. There, on March 24, each victim was dispatched with a pistol shot to the back of the head. The entrance to the cave was then dynamited to seal it from the outside world.[3]

ON OR ABOUT THE SAME day that the civilians were executed, war correspondent Ernie Pyle left Anzio. In his final column from Italy he wrote:

> As for all the rest in that Mediterranean Army of ours—it was wonderful in a grim, homesick, miserable sort of way to have been with them. There was not one single instance, from private to general, when they were not good to me.

---

* Kesselring had wanted to launch another counterattack as a way of finally dislodging the Allies there, but during his tour of the front he found that German strength and morale were even worse than he had first thought, while the Allies were growing ever stronger. He would prepare a report to that effect for Hitler, and the Führer would reluctantly accept the fact that a German victory at Anzio was no longer possible. Robert Katz, *The Battle for Rome*, 219–230.

I hated the whole damned business [of war] just as much as they did, who suffered so much more. I often wondered why I was there at all, since I didn't have to be, but I found no answer anywhere short of insanity, so I quit thinking about it. But I'm glad I was there. . . .

I've written many times that war isn't romantic to the people in it. But there in that plane, all of a sudden, things did seem romantic. . . . It was one of those moments impossible to transmit to another mind. A moment of overpowering beauty, of the surge of a marching world, of the relentlessness of our own fate. It made me want to cry.[4]

Ernie Pyle was on his way to England and then to France, where he would cover the biggest war story of all—the Allied invasion of Normandy. Then, in early 1945, he would go to the Pacific to write about the common American soldier fighting for one island after another. On the tiny island of Ie Shima, on April 18, 1945, he would be killed by a Japanese bullet.[5]

THE ANZIO AREA WAS STILL a dangerous place to be in the two months after the initial landings. Both sides were still sending out patrols to grab prisoners and cause trouble, and both sides periodically lobbed artillery and mortar shells at each other but without the earlier intensity. Each side used the cover of night to repair telephone lines that had been damaged or destroyed, pick up the dead and wounded, and strengthen their positions with barbed wire and minefields. When the weather was flyable, the British and American pilots would fly combat sorties over German positions; the Germans would reply in kind, but in far fewer numbers. Allied warships would also occasionally unleash a salvo at German gun positions and troop concentrations. Many of the men on the ground no doubt felt that this was how the Anzio operation was going to end—static warfare with little or no gains being made by either side, reminiscent of the trench warfare of World War I. A whimper instead of a bang.

Clyde Easter (7th Infantry Regiment, 3rd Division) recalled that in the darkness of March 23-24, he headed out into the barren fields with a small night patrol: "There were maybe eight of us, just a small squad. When it got quiet, they liked to send us out to stir things up. They liked to know where the enemy was. It was around this little village of Isabella [*sic*—Isola Bella]." Easter's patrol was trying to knock out a German machine-gun nest, but somehow the Germans heard them coming and began firing.

> One guy got a flesh wound in the shoulder and I got shot through the hand. We got down in this ditch or creek line. We're lucky it was there or we'd have all been dead. They caught us wide open, maybe only 150 feet away.
>
> The bullet hole was between my thumb and my index finger. The sergeant tried to clean it up and put some sulfa powder in it. The other wounded guy and I started walking back. Honestly, that was as danger-ous as being out front. You always worried about friendly fire, especially at night. But we made it back. I passed out shortly after that. I'm sure it was from the pain. It started out as more of a burning, but then began working its way up the nerves in my arm—very painful.

Easter spent about a month recuperating in a hospital back in Naples.[6]

GENERAL CLARK CAME TO VISIT Truscott and the beachhead again on March 29. The VI Corps commander and his staff (as well as the staffs of every major headquarters on the beachhead) had been busy for the past several days working on plans for offensive action—the long-awaited breakout. Intelligence brought reports that the Germans had weakened their front by withdrawing the Hermann Göring, 26th, and 29th Panzer-Grenadier Divisions, leaving only six or seven divisions to surround the beachhead. As a result, Truscott was confident that not only could his forces withstand any attacks the enemy might throw at him, but VI Corps stood a good chance of punching through the enemy line when the time came. But the Eighth British Army was not yet ready for its final assault on the Gustav Line; everything was put on hold until their preparations were complete.[7]

Kesselring, meanwhile, was trying to imagine what new plans the Al-lies might be formulating. Taking into consideration the fact that both the German navy and the Luftwaffe had been reduced to near-total inef-fectiveness, he came to the conclusion that Fifth Army would probably make another amphibious landing, likely in the La Spezia–Livorno area. Such a move, he thought, would spell the end for the German Army Group C, which no longer had the strength to hold off attacks at both Anzio and the Gustav Line *and* oppose another landing—especially now that good flying weather would enable the Allied air forces to pound any movement of German troops on the highways or railways.[8]

WAR ON THE SEAS WAS still a danger that could not be ruled out. On March 30, Gunner's Mate Ian Billingsley was returning from Anzio to Naples aboard the destroyer HMS *Laforey* for some routine maintenance when orders were changed to join four other Royal Navy ships to hunt for a submarine—the *U-223*—off Stromboli. Although it was night, the U-boat was soon spotted on the surface, and the pursuing British ships began firing their deck guns. The *Laforey*'s captain switched on the searchlight, which illuminated the destroyer for the U-boat. Billingsley said:

> Suddenly there was a deafening explosion and I found myself hurtling upwards and then landing with a thud on the Oerlikon's safety rails. The U-boat had torpedoed us and I was conscious between bouts of blackness and pain, that *Laforey* was breaking up in her death throes [*sic*]. I tried to stand but had no movement in my legs. Using my elbows, I managed to propel my body to the ship's side. *Laforey* was sinking and I clung to the rigging as she started her final plunge. Frantically, I tore myself free and with arms working like pistons, propelled myself as far from the inevitable whirlpool of suction as possible. Suddenly, like a cork, I was whirled round and round and drawn towards the vortex where our beloved ship had finally disappeared beneath the waves. Fortunately, my half-inflated life belt kept me on the surface.

With three fractures in his spine, and paralyzed from the waist down, Billingsley was rescued, but 179 of his shipmates lost their lives. The *U-223* itself was sunk by the other destroyers; there were 17 survivors.[9]

DESPITE THE SLACKENING OF HOSTILE action in March, casualties continued to pile up. In just the 3rd Infantry Division alone, exploding shells caused 83 percent of the division's casualties that month; other units suffered similar rates.[10] How much longer would they be forced to endure their situation, the men on the Anzio beachhead wondered. Yet they used their slack time to improve their trenches, foxholes, and dugouts, while waiting either for the Germans to renew the attack or for the orders to come down directing them to attempt their breakout.

The British and American soldiers stuck at Anzio in their muddy foxholes probably did not yet realize it, but they had pulled off a remarkable feat. Those who were still alive had fought off some of the most severe attacks in recorded history. They had persevered against horrendous artillery barrages and aerial assaults. They had held fast against waves of infantry and panzers. They had seen their buddies killed next to them and die in horrible ways. They had suffered grievous wounds yet returned to their duty stations. They had lived in mud and squalor, surrounded by foul smells and even worse sights, with absolutely no guarantee that they would prevail in the end. They, as a group, had taken every punch the Germans could land and were still standing—bloody but unbowed. They had, in short, accomplished the impossible.

There was, of course, no way to predict the future. No one knew if the Germans would come back against them in even greater numbers and turn their up-to-now heroic defensive stand into an ultimately tragic defeat. No one knew if the war might end with them still holding on to their ragged parcel of beachhead land, and absolutely no one knew if they would be called upon to duplicate the Germans' all-out assaults across the shell-cratered mud of no-man's-land.

It would not be long, however, before they would find out.

AS MARCH MELTED INTO APRIL, the two sides, like a pair of prizefighters in the twelfth round, leaned against each other, utterly spent, too exhausted to administer the knock-out blow yet unwilling to concede the bout, their seconds yelling at them to keep punching, their weary arms making the obligatory ineffective jabs at kidneys and ribs—except, at Anzio, the jabs consisted of periodic shellings, bombings, air raids, and patrols. The dirty, deadly business went on.

In the third week of March, the 1st Battalion, King's Own Yorkshire Light Infantry of Gregson-Ellis's 5th British Division, had been moved up to relieve the 36th U.S. Engineer Combat Regiment in a patch of woods, who were then moved to the rear to prepare for the breakout. At 3:30 P.M. on April Fool's Day, the KOYLI, which had missed the heavy fighting in February and the first week of March, was hit by a punishing barrage, followed by an intense ground assault—including flamethrowers—by a German parachute battalion.

The close-quarter three-hour battle, also employing grenades and bayonets, was one of the most desperate of the entire war, but the Yorkshiremen refused to give ground. The Germans got the worst of the fight; the next day twenty German bodies were found in the area (no doubt many others were carried off, as the Germans were skilled at retrieving their dead) as compared to one English officer killed and eleven men wounded. But that violent action was the exception in April, not the rule.[11]

"LIFE AT ANZIO WAS NEVER dull, easy, or quiet," remarked Major General Lucian Truscott.

> German artillery and aircraft continued to strike almost daily. While mass raids of fifty or more aircraft practically ceased during April, hit-and-run raids by one or more planes persisted. Nor was there any part free from the daily scream of artillery projectiles in flight, the crash of bursting shells, or the thud of bursting bombs. Life was tense as it always is when men live close to death. But we learned how to survive. The men found some means of making life more comfortable, and even discovered precarious forms of entertainment to relieve the tedium of congested living and battle tensions.[12]

It is said that war consists of long periods of boredom interspersed with brief periods of intense terror. At Anzio, from January 22 until the beginning of April, it was the exact opposite: long periods of terror interspersed with brief periods of boredom. But now, with the coming of spring, feeling returned to the mud-caked, waterlogged, half-frozen soldiers who had begun to believe that they would never be warm again. Men emerged from their holes and dugouts, their pale, squinting faces turned upward at a bright, unfamiliar object in the sky: the sun. Fingers and toes gradually thawed, there was hot water with which to shave and shower, and creaky bones and stiff muscles slowly became renewed. The slackening of random artillery bursts ended the troglodytic existence.

Ad hoc unit newspapers began to proliferate. Some thirty news sheets, ranging from dailies to biweeklies to weeklies—with such mastheads as *Beachhead News*, *Red Devil*, *The Sea Horse*, and *Flakky-Wackky*—began to be churned out on unit mimeograph machines and distributed to the beachhead residents. A feature story in the May 1 issue of the *Stars and Stripes* said, "Their make-up would make the *New York Times* shudder, their exaggeration and distortion of fact would shame the tabloids, but for reader interest, they all rate Pulitzer Prizes."[13]

Sports, too, began to occupy idle moments. The Americans braved the occasional falling shell or strafing Messerschmitt to enjoy pickup baseball games, while the British were able to play a few soccer matches and get in some cricket. Dice, card games, and other forms of gambling—such as betting on the outcomes of rat, beetle, and donkey races—also proved popular. Other diversions included the playing of guitars, harmonicas, and phonograph records, plus group singing, listening to Axis Sally's propaganda-rich radio broadcasts, swimming in the sea, writing letters home to loved ones, and attending shows and concerts provided by entertainers coming up from Naples. Church services in the field, also, were well attended. Then, too, there was the constant cleaning and servicing of weapons, for no one believed that this extended "rest period" could possibly last much longer.[14]

Truscott said that he would "always admire the trait in the men and women who served which prompted them always to seek relaxation in the normal pastimes of peacetime living, reminding them of home. Without this I do not see how men could have survived the terrific tension under which they lived at Anzio."[15]

The coming of spring also meant the coming of spring flowers, and Truscott saw to it that bouquets of roses, clipped from bushes that grew outside his command villa, were delivered to the field hospitals crowding the beachhead. "Among my much-treasured mementoes of Anzio," he reflected, "are the notes of appreciation sent to me by the chief nurses."[16]

The U.S. Army's official history says little about April other than to indicate that it was a time of rest, renewal, and reflection. Men still lived in their swampy underground dugouts but made major improvements to them with wooden floors, electric lights, and substantial roofs. Pinup pictures from *Yank* magazine adorned the walls. The ever-present specter of death, though, was never far from anyone's mind. Artillery continued to fall, even during times of little other activity. One of those wounded during the April lull was George Courlas (Company G, 157th):

> I was nicked in the arm by enemy artillery. I failed to remain in the foxhole and was left exposed. My foxhole partner noticed the blood and, with the sleeve ripped on my left arm, advised me accordingly. By then, I could feel the sting. Upon the advice of the platoon sergeant and company medic, I reported to the aid station at battalion headquarters. They patched the arm and pulled out a piece of metal, then [the doctor] made his report—a Purple Heart, which was eventually to be the first of three by the end of the war in May 1945. I reported back to duty after a good lunch at the aid station.[17]

THE GERMANS WERE STILL DOING whatever they could to contain the Allies in what Axis Sally called "the world's largest self-sustaining prisoner-of-war camp," but it was not easy.[18] Germany was still fighting for its life on the Eastern Front and preparing for an Allied invasion somewhere in the West. Therefore, units throughout southern Europe were combed for soldiers who could be brought in to bolster the Anzio-Nettuno front. One of those replacements was Karl Muller, who had been stationed with a training company in Avranches, France; he was assigned to the 3rd Panzer-Grenadier Division. He recalled his road trip to Anzio in April with a group of other replacements:

> It was night and our driver turned off the headlights. The officer ordered us to wear helmets, do not smoke, and do not show lights since we were under the curse of enemy artillery.
>
> The truck stopped and in a low voice came a new order to maintain calmness. We found ourselves in the zone of operations and we followed our officer single file, keeping a distance of some meters in our file. Streaks of lightning were tearing the sky in every direction. Going down slowly into a gorge full of water, we reached a position where soldiers

were draining their holes in the ground. All of them asked if we were ready. We answered, no, that we are replacements assigned to 6th Company, 29th Regiment, 3rd Panzer-Grenadier Division.

"Damn crap, damn shit," the usual reaction to the word "replacement."

We reached our new unit without trouble. The day after we also dug our foxholes, trying to dig them in hard ground. I saw that many soldiers around me had burn holes in their uniforms, riddled by the rain of phosphorous that had fallen on them.

Although he was now on the battlefield, Muller's thoughts were about his father, mother, and sisters, Christine and Maria, back home, who must have been sick with worry about his welfare—thoughts that "caused me physical pains. I prayed, 'Oh, my God, please let me see my parents and my sisters again. I don't ask this in my interest, but theirs.'" Karl's brother had died on the Eastern Front in 1942, and he knew his family's sorrow was immense.

Two days later, he wrote a letter home: "Dear parents and dear sisters, I am now unexpectedly at the front line. We are near Aprilia. The Americans are about 70 meters from our position. It's quiet now. The enemy artillery is not shooting at us, as it could be dangerous for their own men. The food is good. Willi Stolz and I are in the same group. We are both healthy and well, but covered with dirt. I salute you and wish you well. Yours, Karl."[19]

ON EASTER SUNDAY, APRIL 9—a dreary, rainy day—the 56th Evac Hospital said farewell to Anzio. It was being replaced by the 750-bed 38th Evac Hospital; the 56th had been ordered to head for the harbor, board ships, and sail down to Naples, from which it was trucked to Nocelleto, a small town about twenty-eight miles northwest of Naples—and a long way from the fighting—where it would set up a new facility.[20]

Nurse Avis Dagit had mixed feelings about leaving Anzio, for some of her fondest and bitterest memories were forged there. "I was leaving some of my heart at Anzio," she said, recalling the many friends she had lost. "We had prayed continually for relief from the hazardous duty, but not by leaving the beachhead before we finished the job. No one wanted to be a quitter. We had lived like prairie dogs scurrying from one hole to another for so long, it was difficult to imagine living in the sun. The prospect dazzled us momentarily. We had survived more than 500 air raids along with shellings day and night for the past two months and a half. More importantly, we had cared for thousands of sick and wounded."

As the LCT carrying the hospital personnel pulled out of the harbor, the Germans fired a few shells at it in a parting gesture; luckily, they all missed. A destroyer answered back.[21]

THE 36TH ENGINEER COMBAT REGIMENT'S operations journal for April has day after day of the notation, "Nothing to report." Only occasionally does an entry appear that describes "light shelling" or "intermittent shelling" or an "air raid." Action picked up on April 10, and the soldier keeping the journal reported, "Intermittent shelling during day. Heavy shelling during night in 2nd Battalion [area]. E Company had one EM [enlisted man] killed and one EM wounded. F Company had one EM killed and two wounded."[22]

A member of the 84th Chemical Mortar Battalion noted that a wounded lion still had teeth:

Daily shellings were becoming nerve wracking and April 13 brought the worst going over that the men of the 1st Platoon had ever experienced. Shelling of the position greeted the early morning, lasting only a short time to more or less prepare the men for what was in store for them. After three hours of peacefulness, the enemy unleashed a barrage of 88mm and mortar fire on the ranged-in target. A smoke shell landed in a little grass shack adjoining the house, and immediately bloomed into a raging inferno. There was ammunition and the platoon jeep housed in the shack, so with little hope of stopping the fire, the men stayed in the shelter inside the house to avoid the unceasing hail of shells.

Huddled under the shelter, the men could hear a shell puncture the wall of the house on the second floor once occupied by the company CP, then one through the roof. The gas in the jeep exploded to throw more of the spreading flame to nearby ammunition which shortly went up with a rocking blast that was certain to let the enemy know there was really something of target value in the area being shelled. Either spreading flames or a direct hit set off another pile of ammunition to completely black out the inside of the shelter. The tremendous concussion blew all the plaster from the outer wall of the barn, knocking over a small tree and brought down the remaining shingles of the roof damaged by the action of March 22.

After the barrage had ceased and an investigation could be made, all haystacks were observed to be burning in the barnyard, while craters marked the once nicely piled heaps of ammunition. The ammunition for No. 3 gun, amounting to 40 rounds HE [high explosive] and 20 rounds WP [white phosphorous], left a hole some 30 feet in diameter and 15 feet deep. Some of the unexploded shells were thrown for a distance up to 700 yards from the gun position, and nearby 81mm mortar men had to take cover to avoid the falling debris.[23]

Enemy shelling then slacked off but did not entirely cease until the sixteenth and seventeenth of April, when several more casualties were caused by German artillery fire. Things then went relatively quiet again until the twenty-third and twenty-fifth, as heavy shelling again dropped into the 36th Engineers' area, causing several more men to be wounded.[24]

IN HIS DIARY, PAUL BROWN (Graves Registration Section, 179th), as usual, mixed the mundane with the horrific:

April 18: Everything is running fine, shows, showers, ball games, card games, etc. until 5:00 PM when one Company was in formation a shell killed 4, injured 24. Isn't that hell? Could have come 50 yds. more and killed 100 who were in show tent! We played a AT [antitank company]. Won 15 to 10. Baseball.

April 19: GRS never rest. A body floated in from the sea. Was an awful job. Movies are still going strong.

April 23: Had Regt. memorial service, very good thing. I have no sorrows for those boys gone, just high praise. We are getting ready to go back into action in a few days. . . . Won another ball game last night.[25]

April 23 was also the day that Private first class John C. Squires (Company A, 30th Infantry Regiment, 3rd Division) of Louisville, Kentucky, became the eighth of thirty-nine men within his division to earn the Medal of Honor in World War II—making the 3rd the U.S. Army division with the most recipients of the nation's highest decoration. His company was given the mission of dislodging a meddlesome enemy position in and around Spaccasassi Creek, near Padiglione, on the night of April 23–24.

Squires, the platoon messenger, was participating in his first offensive action but did not allow the enemy's artillery, mortar, and anti-tank-gun fire to prevent him from investigating the effects of an explosion that hit the leading platoon. Starting out across 50 yards of open ground ahead of the advance element, he seemed to lead a charmed life as he was missed by a flurry of shells directed his way. Squires reconnoitered a new route of advance and returned to inform his platoon leader of the high number of casualties sustained and pointed out an alternate route. Acting without orders, Squires then rounded up stragglers, organized a group of lost men into a squad, and led them forward.

When the platoon reached Spaccasassi Creek and established an outpost, Squires, knowing that almost all of the NCOs were casualties—and disregarding enemy machine-gun, machine-pistol, and grenade fire that covered the creek draw—placed eight men in a defensive position. The enemy fire continued to take its toll; when his forty-man platoon had been reduced to fourteen men, he twice brought up reinforcements. On each trip he had to crawl through barbed wire and across a German minefield, all the while under intense artillery and mortar fire.

Three times in the early-morning hours of April 24 the outpost was counterattacked, but, each time, Squires ignored intense machine-gun fire and grenades that exploded all around him while he fired hundreds of rounds of rifle, BAR, and captured German machine-gun ammunition at the enemy, killing many Germans and helping to stop the attacks. He then moved 50 yards to the south end of the outpost and engaged twenty-one German soldiers in individual machine-gun duels at point-blank range, forcing all twenty-one to surrender and capturing the enemy's machine guns.

After questioning a captured German officer, Squires positioned the captured guns and instructed other members of his platoon how to operate them. The next night, when the Germans attacked the outpost again, he killed three and wounded more with captured "potato-masher" grenades and fire from his German machine gun. His courage was honored with the Medal of Honor, posthumously, because in one month the nineteen-year-old soldier would lose his life during the breakout.[26]

KARL MULLER (3RD PANZER-GRENADIER DIVISION) had indelible memories of April 24:

A [German] assault company is attacking at the ditch. It is serious. We are at the front with the attackers and carry wounded back to a makeshift aid station in the ditch. Dead are only carried as far as the Nebelwerfer battery. On the way I meet a seriously wounded comrade. He is shot through the mouth. I have to take out the whole clot of clotted blood from his mouth with my fingers so that he does not suffocate. His shoulder is also injured and this comrade also has a shot in the knee. I have to pause every few meters along the ditch. I bring him to the dressing-place and fall with exhaustion.

In the morning, I am among the *Nebelwerfer*s. There is total peace. I know that since 9 o'clock a ceasefire has been negotiated. We can retrieve our dead in the position conquered by the Americans. I find among them comrade Willi Meier and soldier Weber. It can be seen that they have fallen in close combat. They have terrible deaths. During this close combat at least 15 comrades were killed. From comrades we learn that our mates Kunze, Breichle, and Lehn have been captured. The fighting resumes again about 4 PM. My war morale is getting a heavy blow. Towards evening, more and more of our troops are attacking. A flame-throwing unit also attacks with its device. They are told to camouflage their device well against aerial observation; it could otherwise be disastrous if the Americans discovered this. In the night of 26 April, we have five dead and several wounded.

About the only thing that gave Muller hope was seeing long lines of American POWs being herded to the rear. A few days later, after burying a dead American soldier in a roadside grave, Muller came to an ominous conclusion: "How are we going to chase the Americans back to the United States? It is unambiguously clear that the war is lost for Germany."[27]

WITH THE ARRIVAL OF MAY, the men of the 36th Engineer Combat Regiment ceased being infantrymen and returned to their usual duties: repairing roads and bridges, widening culverts, digging ditches, painting signs, revetting tents and adding fly screens on tents in the hospital areas, and constructing Nissen huts. When not kept busy by these activities, the engineers honed their marksmanship skills with weapons such as rifle grenades, bazookas (3.5-inch rocket launchers), and 57mm anti-tank guns.[28]

The two sides also continued to lob shells at one another. Sergeant James R. Bird (Battery A, 160th Field Artillery Battalion, 45th Infantry Division) said, "The epithet, 'rear-echelon commandos,' did not exist on the beachhead of Anzio—everybody on site and offshore was vulnerable. . . . Anzio could be compared with a 'lost weekend.' War service, especially in a place like Anzio, is like living in the city—you seldom know what your neighbor does, much less of what happens a block away."

Bird also recalled that, about this time, his battery "started to be supplied with 'proximity' fuses. These fuses were designed to explode the artillery shell about thirty feet above ground as it was landing. These fuses were seventy percent effective. That is, seven out of ten exploded as designed, some only when they hit the ground and the rest at the top of the apogee as they began their downhill drop. It was quite a sight at night to see a few exploding way up in the sky as they began to fall."[29]

The improving weather, the profusion of poppies and other wildflowers emerging across the cratered battlefields, the increasing music of songbirds, the arrival of better rations, and the relative lack of combat elevated everyone's mood at Anzio. Yet deep down, there was the gnawing awareness that good times in war do not last. Periods of inactivity and relaxation are almost always replaced by the anticipation of violence so cataclysmic that it keeps men up at night shivering with deep-seated worry and thoughts of mortality.

Everyone knew that, sooner or later, unless the Germans suddenly surrendered (and no one gave that a reasonable chance), the day of reckoning was fast approaching. One only need look at the harbor and see the vast mountains of supplies that were building up; March had already seen more than 157,000 tons delivered to the beachhead.[30] There were also more tanks and artillery pieces and reinforcements by the thousands streaming in. The breakout that everyone was simultaneously hoping for and fearing was at hand. The months of being on the defensive—of being the punching bag for the Germans—was about to end. The time for offensive action—the breakout—was fast approaching.

AS SPRING PROGRESSED, THE MOSQUITO and fly situation at Anzio grew to intolerable proportions. The flies, of course, were gorging on the decomposing corpses of men and animals left out on the battlefields, but the mosquitoes, too, were having their own feast on living flesh.

Gunner Bert Reed (24th Field Regiment, Royal Artillery) recalled, "The weather was getting warmer and the area was being sprayed for mosquitoes. Some of the lads had caught malaria, some caught dysentery. They had to stop troops going to the hospital because it got so overcrowded with malaria and dysentery patients—there was no room for casualties. So you just had to really suffer at your place of duty."

Reed's unit had set up a collapsible toilet in a clearing where the flies were huge and had a vicious sting; the men used gasoline in an attempt to keep their population down. Reed said:

> Every day an orderly poured petrol down on the waste then set fire to it to keep the flies off. Our position was shelled just after the orderly had poured down the petrol. He had to run for cover and had no time to light the petrol. When the shelling stopped, I decided I wanted to go to the loo, so I lifted up the flap and sat down, lit a cigarette, and threw down the lighted match. The petrol fumes had built up so—*WHOOOOMPH!*—I was thrown off my throne. Everyone else thought it a huge joke. I had to laugh myself.[31]

IN HIS DIARY, PAUL BROWN noted on May 3 that the Germans were still out there making life miserable for him and his buddies: "We sure got hell last night (all night). I didn't sleep but one hour. Bombs tore up my clothes on the line 25 yds from my and Puter's hole. Killed two boys in hole 50 yds away. They had 40 bombers, all flew in low under antiaircraft. Also picked up two KIAs in lines. Put more sandbags on top also. Makes about two feet. Hope they give us a rest tonight."

Two days later he wrote: "No air raids last night. Three KIA from 1st & 3rd Bn. It sure is getting tiresome bringing in our boys. Got sort of drunk on distilled vino. Artillery was plenty busy all night. Our bombers sure did raise hell all day over enemy lines; it kept the ground in a tremble most of the day. The jazz band played this afternoon. They sure are good."[32]

THE GERMANS WERE CONVINCED THAT the Allies would begin their offensive at any time and were fixated on the idea that it would likely be preceded by another amphibious landing—this time farther up the coast, in the La Spezia–Livorno (Leghorn) area. General Westphal noted that, because the Germans lacked any sizable naval assets, the Allies were free to do as they pleased "without significant hindrance either before or during disembarkation." With such a landing, the Allies could swiftly move inland and block the escape routes of German armies fleeing northward through the Apennines.

"Such an operation would have brought about the collapse of the front in Middle Italy and delivered a fatal blow to the Army Group," he wrote. "The fact that, with improving weather, Allied air power would also be called upon to deliver decisive blows that would mean the end for Kesselring's army. . . . There was nothing in the Po Valley that could be called 'troops.' The whole Apennine peninsula would then have been in Allied hands in the summer of 1944."

Adding to the Germans' woes, Westphal admitted, "Ammunition was always short, and we were scarcely ever able to shoot off at more than a fifth or tenth of the enemy's rate of fire. Nor, of course, was there any superfluity of petrol, spare parts, or clothing. . . . The enemy air forces attacked the railways day and night. . . . After our inferiority in the air, it was these supply difficulties which caused the German leadership in Italy the most concern."

Nevertheless, the Hermann Göring Parachute-Panzer Division, whose command had changed in the middle of April from Lieutenant General Paul Conrath to Major General Wilhelm Schmalz, was pulled out of the line at Anzio and sent up to Livorno to forestall another Allied invasion.[33] The movement turned out to be a wild-goose chase, for, unknown to the

Germans, the Allies possessed neither sufficient naval transport nor sufficient extra ground forces available to make such a move possible. Operating in the looming shadow of Overlord, the Italian campaign would soon be relegated to "minor theater" status.

U.S. Army Chief of Staff George C. Marshall had received reports that Clark had become worn and frazzled and so arranged for him to have a two-week respite back in Washington, DC, in mid-April to recharge his batteries and get him ready for the all-important battles ahead. Clark welcomed the break, enjoyed a few days at a West Virginia resort with his wife, Renie, and briefed President Roosevelt on the general plan for the next phase of the Italian campaign. He then flew back to Italy refreshed and with his cocker spaniel, Pal, by his side.[34]

TO END THE TWIN STALEMATES that had developed both at Anzio-Nettuno and along the Gustav Line sixty-three miles to the south, the Allies began planning their massive two-pronged assault that would break through the German defenses and continue the march to Rome that had begun many months before. Knowing that the great invasion of France would come in early June, and wanting to grab some of the glory that would accrue to the conqueror of Rome before Normandy wiped the Italian campaign off the front pages of the world's newspapers, Mark Clark, with Alexander's approval, gave the order to begin preparing for Operations Diadem (the cracking of the Gustav Line) and Buffalo (the breakout from Anzio).[35]

As Alexander envisioned it, the Eighth Army would make an all-out assault to blast through the Gustav Line at Cassino and drive up Highway 6 into the Liri Valley toward Frosinone and Valmontone. As this attack gathered momentum, VI Corps would make a maximum effort to break through the encircling forces at Anzio and also head toward Valmontone. There the two Allied forces would meet, block the German Tenth Army's escape routes up Highways 6 and 7, and then turn left and continue the march, arm in arm, to jointly liberate Rome.

Clark, of course, had different ideas. Valmontone was northeast of Anzio, Rome to the northwest. Therefore, in order to beat the British to Rome, Clark would have to disobey Alexander's wishes while not appearing to do so. He told Truscott to devise four axes of attack:

straight to Rome; north to the Colli Laziali; northeast through Cisterna to Valmontone; and southeast along the coast to link up with the rest of the Fifth Army coming from the western end of the Gustav Line. To fool Alexander into thinking that he was making his major move toward Valmontone, Clark ordered Truscott to send part of VI Corps in that direction but make the major thrust toward the Alban Hills and then execute a sharp turn toward Rome with all the American units; the British contingent of VI Corps would protect the corps' left flank but would not be invited to share in the entry to Rome.[36]

General Alexander, whom Truscott called a "charming gentleman and magnificent soldier," visited VI Corps headquarters on May 5; Truscott briefed him on the four different possible axes of attack that he and Clark had devised for the upcoming breakout. Alexander shook his head and told Truscott in no uncertain terms to forget the alternate plans; there was to be only one axis of attack: from Cisterna northward to cut Highway 6 at Valmontone. The Fifth Army's drive to capture Rome was *not* to be considered at this time.

When Clark dropped in on Truscott the following day, he was incensed to learn that Alexander, whom he despised, had been "interfering" with his American chain of command and his plans. "The capture of Rome is the *only* important objective," Clark stressed to Truscott in no uncertain terms.[37]

In his diary, Clark wrote, "I know factually that there are interests brewing for the Eighth Army to take Rome, and I might as well let Alexander know now that if he attempts any thing of that kind, he will have another all-out battle on his hands, namely, with me."[38]

Truscott noted, "While [Clark] agreed that the Cisterna-Valmontone assault would probably be the most decisive, he also thought that the quickest way into Rome might be via Carroceto-Campoleone [that is, northward up the Via Anziate], passing west of the Colli Laziali. Clark was determined that the British were *not* going to be the first in Rome."[39]

This declaration would have dismayed Churchill, for the prime minister wrote later in the month, "The capture of Rome is a vast, worldwide event, and should not be minimized. I hope that British as well as Americans will enter the city simultaneously."[40]

ON MAY 6, PAUL BROWN wrote in his diary:

> The Artillery raised Hell again starting at 11:00 PM. Our beachhead has
> 2,900 Allies and 400 Germans in its cemetery. Good size. The [Graves
> Registration] boys picked up 6 KIA plus 1 Jerry. A very bad odor from
> them due to 6 weeks in open. Received word that I am soon to go home.
> Am being put in Training Co. as instructor. Our Regt. is coming off line
> tonight, 157th going in. No big push as yet. Don't think they will for
> awhile.
>
> May 8: April quota left this morning for home. I am now training
> these replacements till my time comes. Oh happy day! Had a little trou-
> ble last night at ball game between Service Co. & Band. F.G. slugged
> Capt. S. & Sgt. V.—Capt. filed charges, will see what I can do to help F.G.
> He was very drunk. Took several pictures today of the gang. Nothing im-
> portant on line, just constant patrolling and slight enemy action. Plenty
> of Artillery all time of day & night. No air raids for several nights.[41]

KARL MULLER (3RD PANZER-GRENADIER DIVISION) was at a position near
Aprilia that the Germans called "House 8," close to Spaccasassi Creek.
After digging a foxhole during the night next to the house, a sergeant
named Jakob told him, "The Americans are in front" and cautioned him
to be on his guard. Muller recalled:

> Right on the street, about ten meters away, sat a shot-up Sherman tank.
> The turret with the cannon tube lay in the ditch. One of our soldiers
> hoped to get cigarettes and food out of the tank and went, of course, at
> night into the tank. There were firefights going on, so he could not leave
> the tank. Then it was day and he had to stay until the next night. He had
> not found anything, but the dead soldiers of the tank crew made his stay
> agonizing.
>
> Once we received a canister with twenty liters of wine. Everyone
> fell to the ground, one after another, drunk. Sergeant Jakob was excited
> about it. "If I did not know where we were, I would sing," he said, and
> then sank into a deep sleep. The Amis could have carried us away. Ten
> meters behind the house I found a dead German soldier; he did not be-
> long to our unit. A lieutenant came and told me that he had learned that

I had found the missing soldier. After I told him that the soldier had a machine gun next to him, this officer had realized that he had found his soldier and the uncertainty was gone, and he could now notify his relatives. "I thank you a thousand times," the lieutenant said to me.[42]

ALTHOUGH MOST OF THE HARD fighting seemed to have dissipated, there were still small pockets where intense skirmishes and individual heroics took place. On May 8, 3rd Infantry Division Sergeant Audie Murphy earned his second Bronze Star after he crawled out onto the battlefield near Cisterna with a grenade launcher attached to his rifle and used it to destroy a partially disabled panzer that the Germans were still using. By the time the war was over, Murphy would be the most decorated American soldier of World War II—including a Medal of Honor for his actions in France in January 1945.[*43]

On Tuesday, May 9, Paul Brown wrote, "No bombers, but Artillery came in as usual. Am sure playing safe. I will probably be leaving before 25th of month. There is sure to be a big push."[44] Brown was right about the big push. The simultaneous attack all along the Gustav Line by both the Fifth U.S. and the Eighth British Armies, originally scheduled for May 10, was about to begin. Lucian Truscott wrote:

> The Eighth Army was to break through the Cassino defenses and drive up the Liri Valley, while the Fifth Army broke through the mountainous areas west of the Garigliano River to turn the flank of German forces opposing the Eighth Army in the Liri Valley. The beachhead forces [at Anzio] were to be prepared to attack on twenty-four-hours' notice in the direction of Cisterna-Valmontone to cut Highway 6 in the rear of the German main forces. These operations were to destroy the German

---

* After the war, fascinated by Audie Murphy's heroics and his boyish good looks, Hollywood cast him in more than forty films, including *The Red Badge of Courage* (along with fellow Anzio veteran Bill Mauldin) and *To Hell and Back*, the latter film in which he played himself (his 1949 memoir bears the same title). But, suffering from post-traumatic stress disorder and alcoholism, he died in a small-plane crash on May 28, 1971, at the age of forty-six. He is buried in Arlington National Cemetery. www.arlingtoncemetery.net/audielmu.

forces and drive the remnant far north of Rome. The capture of Rome was the important immediate objective.

Of course, this was what the combined Fifth and Eighth Armies had been trying for months to do—all without success. Would this new effort be any different?

For Operation Buffalo, the VI Corps' portion of the operation, Truscott decided, because the British forces under his command had been bled white, that the main thrust would be made by John O'Daniel's 3rd Infantry Division, Ernie Harmon's 1st Armored Division, and Charles Ryder's 34th "Red Bull" Infantry Division, which had been brought up from the Cassino front on March 25 and assigned to VI Corps.* The 45th Infantry Division would form the left flank of the thrust; the British would try to hold in place any German units in front of them.[45]

Assigned to the 133rd Regiment of the 34th Division was the 100th Infantry Battalion, a primarily Nisei unit composed mostly of Japanese American members of the Hawaii National Guard, which had suffered heavy casualties trying to take Castle Hill, below Monte Cassino, a few weeks earlier.[46]

By this time, the Allies at Anzio numbered approximately 90,000 troops (with about 2,000 tanks on both fronts), with more arriving daily, while the German strength had been whittled down to about 70,400—not exactly the 3-to-1 ratio of attackers to defenders that instructors of tactics stress as the ideal, but it would have to do.[47] To deceive the Germans as to the Allies' true intentions, Truscott prepared a deception plan called Operation Hippo, which called for the 1st and 5th British Divisions to make a strong "demonstration" on the beachhead's left flank a few hours before the main offensive began around Cisterna on the beachhead's right flank. With the enemy's attention focused on

---

* The 34th Division, a National Guard division from the northern plains states, is credited with being the first American infantry division to land in North Africa in November 1942 as part of Operation Torch. It also holds the distinction of having spent more time in combat (611 days) than any other U.S. Army division in World War II. "History of the 34th Division: World War II, 1941–1945," www .34thinfantry.com/history/history-34th.html.

the British jabs on the left, Truscott thought that perhaps the Germans would not be expecting the Americans' right cross.[48]

PAUL BROWN CONTINUED HIS JOURNAL on May 10:

> Another hell of a raid. Was reported 15 planes came over. Flak was falling all around. No bombs fell close. Our Regt. is moving back on line tomorrow night. My good friends have been stopping in to congratulate me on my going home. Will send box of my stuff home tomorrow.
>
> May 11: Had good night's sleep for once. All was quiet. Am sure anxious to leave, yet do not want to leave the old gang. One Bn. moved back in lines last night. No KIAs so far.[49]

AT AMERICAN AND BRITISH ARTILLERY batteries all along the Gustav Line, battery commanders stood by their guns, right arms raised, looking intently at their watches. As the carefully synchronized watch hands reached 11:00 P.M. on May 11, the men simultaneously dropped their arms and yelled, "Fire!" Suddenly, the black night lit up with flashes too numerous to count. An unearthly thunder, seeming as though the world was splitting apart, battered eardrums and engulfed every sense. An unholy wind expelled from hundreds of artillery barrels and mortar tubes kicked up dirt; sent leaves fluttering, sleeping birds flying, dogs scurrying, and rattled windows for miles around. The great counter-offensive called "Diadem" had begun, literally, with a bang—thousands of them.

Within seconds, the projectiles that had been launched reached out with their long fingers and began finding their targets. Men in Wehrmacht-gray uniforms screamed as the cannonade crashed to earth, ripping through vehicles, buildings, and flesh, sending everything flying in violent convulsions. It seemed impossible that anything could have lived through such a hellish upheaval, but here and there across the darkened landscape forms began moving, forms covered with dust and debris, forms that spit the dirt from their mouths and wiped it from their eyes as they stumbled around, trying to find their weapons and their comrades. There was no time to lose. Then another avalanche of shells came crashing down. And another and another. Men, driven insane by the shelling, left what few places of safety there were and dashed to the rear, only to be torn apart by more explosions. Was there no end to the madness?

A few miles from the barrages, the American and British infantrymen were crossing their lines of departure, moving toward the bright flashes lighting up their objectives, heading into the walls of smoke and dirt being blasted skyward and drifting over them. The Yanks and Tommies had had more than enough of the stalemate that had gone on along the Gustav Line since October 3, 1943. It was now time to pay back their tormenters in spades. "Let's go, men!" shouted captains and lieutenants and sergeants. And so their men, terribly frightened but also exhilarated and flushed with adrenaline, got up and went, shouting and yelling to give themselves courage. It was literally now or never.

The radio reports from the southern front soon came crackling into Truscott's VI Corps headquarters in Nettuno. He recalled:

> The Eighth Army had slow going in the Cassino area. Cassino and the Monastery were not taken until the night of May 17th by Anders' Polish Corps.* Meanwhile, the advance of the French [Expeditionary] Corps and Keyes' II Corps was off to a good start, the French Corps in particular was beginning to outflank the Germans in the Liri Valley. The Eighth Army now had three bridges across the Rapido River, and we expected the drive up the Liri Valley in full force. The question now was: would the Germans be able to stop the advance in front of the "Adolf Hitler Line"—their defensive position across the Sacco River south of Frosinone?

If the Allied advance was halted, no doubt the breakout from Anzio would be postponed and the stalemate would go on.[50]

---

* Lieutenant General Władysław Anders's II Polish Corps consisted of the 5th Kresowa and 3rd Carpathian Infantry Divisions and considerable tank, vehicle, and artillery assets—a total of about 50,000 men. Władysław Anders, *An Army in Exile: The Story of the Second Polish Corps.*

Joseph Menditto (2nd Battalion Headquarters, 351st Infantry Reg-iment, 88th U.S. Infantry Division) would never forget the morning that his division's assault on Minturno began: "The colonel's command group was advancing forward, ducking the machine guns and mortar fire. The Germans kept firing parachute flares into the sky . . . and bar-rages of artillery and mortar fire deafening our ears and deadly machine guns blasting away."[51]

Realizing that this was the start of the Allies' big offensive along the Gustav Line, Kesselring, knowing that Vietinghoff's Tenth Army—facing eleven Allied divisions—could not take much more pounding, decided to pull the army out of the line and have it make a quick, fighting withdrawal toward Rome, using Highways 6 and 7 and every other route that was open to them.[52]

AS DIADEM CONTINUED TO ROLL, Truscott turned to his task of preparing VI Corps for its own offensive, dubbed Operation Buffalo, which was now scheduled for Monday, May 21. To help add weight to the opera-tion, the 36th "Texas" Division, which had been hard hit on January 20 in its abortive crossing of the Rapido, would be brought up to Anzio by ship on May 22; the 85th U.S. Infantry Division was also put on alert. As events turned out, Buffalo would be delayed for forty-eight hours, not beginning until May 23.[53]

The Americans had a few tricks up their olive-drab sleeves—or at least Harmon did. For one thing, his engineers had devised "snakes"—a new twist on the old Bangalore torpedo—which were 300-foot steel pipes filled with 6,000 pounds of explosives, several of which could be connected together, slid into minefields or beneath coils of barbed wire, and, when detonated, blow a fifteen-foot-wide gap in the line.[54]

The other invention was the "battle sled." Sherman tanks would pull metal containers—one-hundred-gallon water drums cut in half length-wise and chained together; two soldiers could lie in each sled. During practice trials, the infantry expressed their dislike for the sleds because of the dust kicked up, the bumpy ride, the exhaust fumes, and the heat generated by friction with the ground. Nevertheless, the experiment was declared successful and would be employed during the breakout.[55]

Lieutenant John Shirley was a green replacement just assigned to
Company I, 15th Infantry Regiment, 3rd Infantry Division. He said:

I was nineteen years old. I welcomed the adventure and excitement, but
didn't want to die. I had strong feeling about duty, honor, and country,
but I couldn't help wondering how I would react under fire for the first
time. The Army calls it your "Baptism of Fire" and warns it can be terrifying. The commanders as well as the foot soldiers were worried about
the attack, and studied various strategies that might give us an advantage. One of the many ideas of our Division Commander, General John
O'Daniel, would involve me. His idea was to transport special assault
teams forward on low sleds pulled along the ground by medium tanks.
The teams were to become known as "Battle Sled Teams."[56]

PAUL BROWN WROTE:

May 12: Plenty of Artillery all night. Our lines are same as for months.
We will push most any day now. No KIA last night. Have radio for our
house. Sure swell music.

May 13: 5 killed last night. One was old friend. Sure wish I could get
off this beachhead or have my name off the list. Artillery came in close as
hell again all night. News from Russian front is fine, also Cassino front.
Now it's our turn.

May 14: 4 more KIA last night. Bombers came over at 5:30 AM, no
damage. Our Corps Artillery raised hell for ½ hour at 8:30. British troops
on Cassino marched 14 miles. Played cards and listened to radio as usual
last night. Got beer and Coca-Cola yesterday. Sure good.

May 15: 4 KIA last night. Who is next? Went to Hospital to hear 1st
Armored band, a real bunch of musicians. Drew PX supplies today for
weather is wonderful. Artillery sure did pour it out last night. No shells
came in for a change. Had rumor we will leave before 25th.

May 18: No news for today. Am sure anxious to leave. Our bombers
are now becoming active. The drive should start soon.

The next day he noted, "Bad news today. Two old Service Co. boys
went up to line for eight days. Duke DeCharles was killed outright, Tom

Dare was wounded. They had no business going up. All boys in Serv. Co. feel bad. Duke was first to go that way."[57]

GOING INTO BATTLE ACCOMPANIED BY a stirring march was not a common occurrence in World War II, but it was also not unheard of. Piper Bill Millin would play the bagpipes as Lord Lovat's 1st Special Service Brigade waded ashore at Sword Beach on D-Day, June 6, 1944, and headed for what would become known as Pegasus Bridge, but the 3rd Infantry Division received a rousing send-off on the evening of May 21. Leaving their encampment near Nettuno and approaching the main road to Cisterna, the 3rd Division infantrymen found themselves being serenaded by a rendition of "Dogface Soldier"—the Marnemen's jaunty march performed by the division band.[58]

As the men swung into step, each one stood a little taller and felt a surge of pride go through his body as he contemplated the historic nature of this occasion. In the very near future—perhaps as early as morning, the decisive battle that would mark the conclusion of the Anzio phase of the Italian campaign would be fought. And each man no doubt wondered if he would be alive to take part in a victory parade.

CHAPTER 18

"I told the aid man to fix me up"

MAY 22–25

DESPITE THEIR BRAVERY, KING LEONIDAS'S 300 Spartans, sprawled dead on the coastal plain at Thermopylae, had been unable to hold against Xerxes's 100,000 men. The 250 defenders of the Alamo had all been slaughtered before they could break out and attack Santa Anna's Mexican Army. The survivors at Rorke's Drift could only watch as their frustrated Zulu foes marched away, conceding the field to the 24th of Foot. Something extraordinary was about to take place at Anzio, something that was nearly unique in military annals: a besieged force was about to break out of its encirclement and turn from being the hunted into the hunter.

It was May 22—the day everyone at Anzio had been anticipating with equal amounts of hope and dread. The ammunition had been issued to the infantrymen, the artillery batteries, the tankers. Warplanes had been armed and fueled. The ammunition lockers of the ships offshore had been replenished. The hospitals were standing by.

Everything was in readiness. General Truscott had sent his order of the day regarding Operation Buffalo to "the Officers and Men of the Allied Beachhead Force." It read:

> For more than four months you have occupied the most dangerous and important post of any Allied force. You have stopped and defeated more

than ten divisions which Hitler had ordered to drive us into the sea. You have contained on your front divisions which the enemy sorely needed elsewhere. . . .

Now, after four months, we attack. Our comrades of the Fifth and Eighth Armies—Britons, Poles, French, Americans, Italians—have achieved a great victory on the south front. They are driving the enemy to the north. They have set the trap—it is for us to spring that trap and complete the destruction of the right wing of the German 10th Army. . . . Our comrades in the south are fighting their way toward us. The eyes of the world will be upon us. Be alert—be vicious—destroy the hated enemy. Victory will be ours.[1]

Fine and inspiring words, but would words be enough when the time came to leave the safety of the trenches and the dugouts and march fully exposed across the same blood-soaked ground that had been covered by the torn corpses of thousands of Germans who had given their all trying to destroy *their* hated enemies? The world was about to find out.

THE KEY TO BREAKING OUT of the Anzio beachhead remained the capture of two key towns that had given the Allies so much trouble and cost so many lives—Aprilia and Cisterna. Once they had fallen, three more would take their place: Lanuvio, Velletri, and Valmontone. For the Germans, it was equally important that none of these towns be given up.

The Operation Buffalo plan was fairly complex and relied on everyone "hitting their marks" in the proper sequence. On May 23—Buffalo's D day—the 3rd Infantry Division, assisted by the 1st Special Service Force, would assault Cisterna. The 36th Division behind them, along with elements of 1st Armored, would then leapfrog past them toward Valmontone—ten miles to the northeast of Velletri on Highway 6 or fourteen straight-line miles from Cisterna—swamping any enemy forces in Cori or Artena along the way. Harmon's 1st Armored Division, to the left of the 3rd Infantry Division, would head cross-country straight for Velletri on Highway 7 at the point where that highway turns abruptly left and heads for Rome. Velletri lies seven and a half miles north-northwest of Cisterna and directly south of looming 3,000-foot Monte Artemisio, a feature of the Alban Hills.

Three days later, to the left of this thrust, the 45th Division, reinforced by the 135th Regiment of the 34th Division, would kick off its portion of the plan, skirting Aprilia and heading north toward Lanuvio—nine miles north-northeast of Aprilia and six miles due west of Velletri—with the intention of capturing Albano and then angling around the west side of the Alban Hills and marching directly for Rome; the 1st British Division, with the 5th Division on its left flank, had Aprilia in its area of responsibility. The two British divisions also had the task of making certain that the 4th German Parachute and 65th Infantry Divisions did not strike the 45th Division's advancing flank.

Alexander had expected that Clark would follow his directive and make the major push toward Valmontone and cut Highway 6, but Clark had no intention of doing that; the Valmontone thrust was more of a feint than a full commitment of his combined II Corps–VI Corps force. The real objective was to get his Fifth Army onto Highway 7, where it could wheel sharply to the left and make the shorter run for Rome.[2]

MAJOR GENERAL ERNEST HARMON WANTED every man in his 1st Armored Division to be well briefed before going into battle. To this end he arranged for all company and platoon leaders to be flown over the beachhead in small planes to get a bird's-eye view of the terrain over which they would soon be attacking. Further, he had his engineers construct a detailed scale model of the terrain, showing the Cisterna-Cori-Valmontone sector "with every hill, every stream, every bridge, every road, even the color of the rooftops reproduced on this model. We placed a boardwalk above the exhibit, which was about fifty feet square, and the troops, in installments, came to study it minutely. . . . The knowledge of where they were going to be during battle might mean, in emergency, the difference between life and death."[3]

To pin down the Germans west of the Albano Highway and prevent them from slamming into the left flank of the striking force, it was planned that the 1st British Division would launch a feint northward toward Campoleone late on May 22. As expected, this attack was met by stiff opposition, and the battle went on all night.[4] As the British and Germans were tangling in Wadi Country, the main act of Operation Buffalo began like Diadem had twelve days earlier—with a fearsome forty-five-minute artillery barrage that left the gunners' ears ringing and temporarily deaf and shook the ground beneath Anzio, Nettuno, Aprilia, and everywhere else around the beachhead as though the son of Vesuvius was about to blow a giant chasm through the earth's crust at Anzio.[5] The fanfare never ceased, as every gun in the American and British sectors fired as quickly as it could be reloaded. Tens of thousands of shells tore through the dawn sky and cascaded down upon German positions.

"There was a crash of thunder and bright lightning flashes," wrote Truscott, who was standing with Clark at one of the corps' artillery observation posts, "as more than a thousand guns, infantry cannon, mortars, tanks, and tank destroyers opened fire. That first crash settled into a continuous rumbling roar. Some distance ahead, a wall of fire appeared as our first salvos crashed into the enemy front lines, then tracers wove eerie patterns in streaks of light as hundreds of machine guns of every caliber poured a hail of steel into the enemy positions."[6]

Then the fires lifted, and as many as 750 B-17 and B-24 bombers roared overhead and blanketed the enemy with tons of bombs.[7] After the bombers had expended their ordnance and turned for home, the artillery opened up again. Much of the attention was focused on Cisterna, which Truscott said was "a key locality in the German plan for containing the beachhead." If the enemy opposition in and around Cisterna could be smashed, then the Americans would be able to pour out of the right flank of the beachhead like wine pouring from a ruptured cask and grab Highway 6, the escape route for the Tenth German Army, retreating from the Gustav Line.[8]

The plan for taking Cisterna called for a pincer maneuver: the 7th Infantry Regiment would assault Cisterna directly, while the 30th Regiment would hit it from the division's left flank and the 15th Regiment from the right. Harmon's tanks, clad in sandbags to absorb the impact of the enemy's antitank weapons, would then move up through the 34th Division and push the explosive "snakes" into the German minefields ringing Cisterna. Once gaps in the minefields were blown, more tanks and the 3rd Division would begin advancing toward Cisterna.[9]

The Hermann Göring Parachute-Panzer Division, which had been rushed up to Livorno to prepare for a possible Allied landing there, had to be rushed back down to Anzio and was preparing to launch a counteroffensive on May 26, but Operation Buffalo stole a march on Kesselring; instead of a counteroffensive, the Germans were now being unmercifully pummeled and fighting for their very existence.[10] The division was particularly hard hit. During a 220-mile forced march from Civitavecchia to the front, the unit was bombed and strafed so unmercifully by Allied warplanes that their value as a military unit had been almost totally destroyed.[11]

BUT DISLODGING THE GERMANS FROM Cisterna would be a herculean task. In the nearly four months that the battle for the area had gone on, Cisterna had been reduced to rubble, and the rubble gave the defenders the advantage of cover and concealment—"a veritable fortress," as Truscott put it. "Deep ravines and canals on either side of the town afforded defilade from our fires, and numerous irrigation ditches were barriers to tank attack. Extensive caverns underneath the town protected the defenders from our heaviest artillery and air bombardments." Everywhere the advantage was to the defender.[12]

The start of the 7th Regiment's assault on Cisterna did not begin auspiciously. Just as Colonel Wiley H. Omohundro's regiment began moving out from its line of departure, German artillery began crashing into the area, sending men diving for cover and delaying the attack for three hours. When the fire slackened, the men got up, ears ringing and angry as hell, and advanced toward the shattered town, their movements covered by a smoke screen and supporting artillery. Seeing the Americans advancing, the Germans mounted a small counterattack with tanks and infantry, but this was blunted and soon beaten back.[13]

Still, the Germans—the 955th Regiment of the 362nd Division and elements of the 715th Division—refused to give up Cisterna. Firing from under and around piles of rubble at anything in olive drab that moved, the defenders took a heavy toll on the 7th Regiment; Company K had two commanders killed within the span of a few hours, and scores of enlisted men also became casualties. Everywhere along the front, O'Daniel's Marnemen were running into dogged resistance that required grenades and even a bayonet charge to overcome. To the 7th Regiment's right, the 15th Regiment task force of tanks and infantry, led by Major

Michael Paulick, trying to get past Cisterna and on to Valmontone and Highway 6, was supposed to maintain contact with the 1st Special Service Force but was having tough going; German resistance was stronger than anticipated. During the first three hours, Company L lost 110 of the 150 soldiers who had started the attack.[14]

LIEUTENANT JOHN SHIRLEY (COMPANY I, 15th Infantry Regiment, 3rd Infantry Division) and his platoon were literally dragged into combat within their battle sleds. He said:

> The day we broke out of the Anzio/Nettuno beachhead, May 23, 1944, was one of the worst single days of fighting any U.S. Army division endured. Nine hundred and ninety-five 3rd Division men were killed or wounded in a very short time. The next day another 625 men met the same fate. About an hour after the attack started, a radio message called us to battle. We laid on our stomachs, head down, in our sleds, and moved onto the road and toward the front. Then we went into an open field and the tanks turned right and stopped. The squad leader yelled to get out and move forward. As I climbed out of the sled, I kept a very low silhouette, as bursts of German machine-gun bullets were chopping into the stalks of wheat only inches above my head. After I passed a minefield, I scrambled down into a ditch. Just after I arrived at the ditch I saw for the first time a man killed in battle.

While taking cover in a ditch, another lieutenant said to Shirley:

> We must do something, and asked me to look over the edge of the ditch towards the Germans to see what I could see. I returned to him and reported about the flamethrower and the broken trees, piles of rubble, broken buildings, and barren landscape in front of us. The lieutenant gathered his team and planned an attack. I had the BAR man from my squad following me. Some of the men were killed by the Germans who were firing at us. About twenty feet in front of me was a zig-zag trench. A dead German soldier was stretched out, face down, just behind the trench. We took an empty house and then we moved to a nearby trench. This trench made a turn every ten to fifteen feet.

Cautiously making his way down the trench, Shirley turned a corner and saw "a German rifleman firing to his front towards the anti-tank ditch. I fired a burst from my tommy gun into his back. I had just killed my first enemy soldier."[15]

Harmon's tankers, operating just to the west of Cisterna, had mixed progress. On the western flank of the division's thrust, Combat Command A, with infantrymen from the 135th Infantry Regiment, 34th Infantry Division, riding atop the Shermans, passed through the 45th Division's lines and pushed their snakes into enemy minefields, blowing paths for the rest of the attackers to follow. Stunned Germans in their forward positions were killed or captured; a few of the enemy attempted to charge the tanks with grenades, but the Shermans' machine guns cut them down. In the wake of the tanks came tank destroyers, performing their deadly work whenever a panzer unwisely showed itself. Soon Combat Command A's armored wave had crested over the railroad embankment and rolled about 500 yards north into the fields beyond before it was halted by darkness.

Combat Command B's advance was not as relatively easy. Its commander had chosen not to employ the snakes and so was held up by the minefields the Germans had spent months emplacing. The 34th Division, too, had been unable to clear the "friendly" minefields in front of it because no one had thought to provide the division with an accurate map showing where the devices had been planted. As a consequence, many of the Shermans had their tracks blown off, halting the advance.

The men of the 3rd Battalion, 6th Armored Infantry Regiment, and 16th Armored Engineer Battalion moved ahead of the disabled tanks, slowly using mine detectors and probing with bayonets to uncover the hidden explosives while enemy fire ripped through their ranks. American artillerymen took the enemy's artillery pieces—along with three or four panzers and a self-propelled gun near the hamlet of Ponte Rotto, less than a mile west of Cisterna—under fire and soon put them out of action. Combat Command B's advance resumed, but much time had been lost; the command did not reach the railroad embankment until after dark.[16]

THE 45TH INFANTRY DIVISION'S PUSH through Carano was also running into heavy opposition. Medic Robert "Doc Joe" Franklin (Company I,

157th) recalled seeing Captain Ralph Barker, CO of the adjacent Company L, after his foot had been blown off by a mine. Somebody expressed sympathy, but Barker took it in stride; "That's all right—that's the one that was always getting cold." Franklin also noted that after his unit had overrun some German positions and taken a few prisoners, one of the stunned captives looked at him. "He spoke English and said that he had been on the Russian front but had never experienced anything as vicious as our breakout from Anzio. He said it was the most vicious thing he had ever seen."[17]

At Carano, the tomb of Menotti Garibaldi, the son of Giuseppe Garibaldi, considered one of the "fathers of modern Italy," became a hotly contested feature. Company B, 157th, established its CP inside the small marble-clad mausoleum. Captain Ken Stemmons, the company commander said:

> I assumed it was like a national park. Inside the mausoleum itself, it was about ten feet wide by twenty feet deep. It was about ten feet tall and had marble inside and had family members entombed in caskets in the walls. In the center there was a flat marble piece with Garibaldi's name on it, and a big, ornate brass rail around it. The Krauts knew we were in there and were firing their tanks' guns at us. They were firing armor-piercing shells and the shells would come in one side and go out the other before they would explode. It tore up everything inside [including the corpses in their crypts].

Stemmons and his men discovered a subtomb twenty feet beneath the marble slab and set up their CP down below out of the direct line of fire. "There were six or eight of us in there. We were so far down, somebody back at battalion called me the 'submarine commander.' We had candles going for light, and when the Krauts would fire and hit the building, the concussion of the explosions would suck out all the air and the candles would go out." Stemmons's men stayed in the vicinity of the tomb for two days, fighting off one German attack after another. He recalled that his company had gone from 193 men at the start of the breakout to only 34 by the time the battle was over.[18]

RARELY IN THE HISTORY OF the U.S. military has one day produced so many Medal of Honor recipients, but May 23, 1944, was just such a day.

On that dismal, drizzly day whose dark clouds mingled with the smoke of battle and hung like a funereal shroud over the battlefield, twenty-four-year-old Staff Sergeant George J. Hall (Company B, 135th Infantry Regiment, 34th Division) displayed a level of courage and determination that few other men have demonstrated. Once the Allies at Anzio began moving out of their assembly areas shortly after 6:00 A.M., three German machine guns near Cisterna started barking at Hall and his company, sending them to ground.

"I don't know exactly why I did it," Hall said later. "Somebody had to knock out those machine guns. The platoon was back of me, and I guess I figured it was up to me to do it. Then, too, I was pretty mad at the Germans. I had been under fire . . . for two months and this seemed to be a good time to get back at them." With Hall's unit pinned to the ground, the sergeant from Boston crawled forward across 60 yards of flat, open terrain with the only shelter being the plowed furrow into which he had flopped. Spotting the nearest of the machine-gun nests, he hurled four grenades and demolished the position. As he crawled into it, he noticed two Germans were dead and four others were stunned and wounded. "I took them prisoner," he said, "and ordered them to crawl back to our line, which they did without any trouble."

There were still other machine-gun nests in action, preventing his platoon from moving forward, but Hall was out of grenades. Luckily, he spotted some "potato-masher" grenades in the position he had just captured and began priming them and flinging them at the next-closest nest. "I threw them quick," he said. "Every time I lifted my arm to throw, they'd fire a burst of machine-gun bullets back at me. I don't know why I didn't get hit."

The deadly duel finally ended when the machine-gun crew, probably out of ammunition, surrendered. When Hall slid into the position, he found five dead Germans and five live ones. As before, he sent the survivors back to his company. Hall then began making his way toward the third machine gun, which opened up on him. As he was crawling toward the position, an artillery shell screamed in and exploded near him, ripping his right leg to shreds. In great pain he looked down and saw that the leg was nearly severed. Without hesitation, he pulled out his combat knife and sliced through the few tendons and muscles that still attached one part of his leg to the rest and applied a tourniquet.

Angry that he would be unable to wipe out the third machine-gun nest, Hall, dragging his bloody stump behind him across the muddy ground, returned to his company's position, where a medic, Technician Nick Dana, applied first aid. Hall said, "I got fine treatment. They put a tourniquet on to stop the bleeding and gave me a sedative. I am eternally grateful to [Dana]. He really did a good job for me. Sure, I wanted to go on. I told the aid man to fix me up so that I could continue the fight, but he said it was impossible."

With two of the three machine-gun positions neutralized, the men of Company B went forward and wiped out the third gun. As they moved out, they could hear their sergeant complaining that he had not finished the job he had started. Hall would receive the Medal of Honor in April 1945.*[19]

NAMED FOR THE OLDEST STONE bridge in Rome, the little village of Ponte Rotto became, on May 23, one of the hottest spots in the line. On that day, Private first class Patrick L. Kessler (Company K, 30th Regiment, 3rd Division) also displayed extraordinary courage when his unit attacked German positions near Ponte Rotto. German machine-gun fire had killed five of his comrades and halted the advance of his company. Acting without orders, Kessler was determined to destroy the enemy gun. Ordering three soldiers to lay down fire, he left the cover of a ditch and crawled to within 50 yards of the enemy machine gun before he was discovered, whereupon he charged the emplacement and killed both the gunner and his assistant and, after a short struggle, captured a third German.

A fourth member of the crew escaped, but Kessler wounded him as he ran. While taking his prisoner to the rear, Kessler saw two of his

---

* George Hall died on February 16, 1946, of complications related to the wounds he had suffered at Anzio. "The Bravery of SSgt George J. Hall," *Stoneham (MA) Independent*, November 18, 2015.

buddies killed as they assaulted an enemy strong point, fire from which had already killed ten men in the company. Turning his prisoner over to another man, Kessler crawled 35 yards to the side of one of the casualties, relieved him of his BAR and ammunition, and continued on toward the strong point, more than 100 yards distant.

Although two machine guns concentrated their fire directly on him and shells exploded within 10 yards, knocking him over, Kessler crawled through a minefield to a point within 50 yards of the enemy and engaged the machine guns in a duel. When a shell burst close to him, he left the cover of a ditch and advanced upon the position in a slow walk, firing his BAR from the hip. Although the enemy poured heavy machine-gun and small-arms fire at him, Kessler succeeded in reaching the edge of their position, killed the gunners, and captured thirteen others.

Then, despite continuous shelling, he started to the rear. After going a short distance with his prisoners, Kessler was fired upon by two snipers only 100 yards away. Several of his prisoners attempted to escape; however, Kessler hit the ground, fired on either flank of his prisoners, forcing them to cover, and then engaged the two snipers in a firefight and captured them. With this last threat removed, Company K continued its advance, taking its objective without further opposition.

Two days later, May 25, at Terracina, VI Corps troops moving inland from Anzio met II Corps troops advancing up through Italy's middle. But the twenty-two-year-old Kessler would not be able to rejoice; he would be killed in the fighting that day. The family of Private first class Patrick L. Kessler, of Middletown, Ohio, was given his posthumous Medal of Honor on January 4, 1945.[20]

ALSO ON MAY 23, PENNSYLVANIA-BORN Private first class John W. Dutko (Company A, 30th Regiment, 3rd Division), a BAR man, had established his position in an abandoned German trench when the area was hit by a fierce artillery bombardment. Through the explosions and the smoke, Dutko spotted three German machine guns and a mobile 88mm field piece. Not waiting for assistance, he charged the machine-gun nests and 88mm gun as bullets and shells flew past him. He lobbed a grenade into the first nest he reached, killing the gunners, and then continued on to the second machine gun, whose bullets wounded but did not stop him. Undeterred, he pressed on to the 88mm gun and killed its five crew members with a long burst.

He then took out the crew of the machine gun that had wounded him and went for the third machine gun. Enemy bullets again tore into him as he advanced upon that gun, but he managed to fire a burst from his BAR before he fell. When the skirmish ended, his comrades came looking for Dutko and found his lifeless body on top of the machine-gun crew he had just killed. For his selfless courage, Dutko's family received his posthumous Medal of Honor.[21]

ANOTHER MEDAL OF HONOR WAS earned on May 23 by Technical Sergeant Ernest H. Dervishian (Company B, 133rd Regiment, 34th Division), who, while advancing in the face of enemy artillery and sniper fire near Cisterna with four members of his platoon, found themselves far ahead of their company. Approaching a railroad embankment, they saw a group of German soldiers hiding in holes dug into the side of the raised railroad bed. Dervishian directed his men to cover him as he boldly moved forward, firing his carbine and forcing ten Germans to give up. His men then advanced and captured fifteen more Germans occupying adjacent dugouts. The prisoners were returned to the rear to be picked up by advancing units.

From the railroad embankment, Dervishian and his men then observed nine Germans fleeing across a ridge and opened fire, wounding three of them. As his men were firing, Dervishian dashed forward alone and captured all of the fleeing enemy before his companions could join him on the ridge. At this point, four other men joined Dervishian's group. An attempt was made to send the four newly arrived men along the left flank of a large, dense vineyard that lay ahead, but murderous machine-gun fire forced them back. Redeploying his men, Dervishian led the advance into the vineyard, where they were suddenly pinned down by a machine gun firing at them from only 15 yards away. Feigning death while the weapon blazed away over him, Dervishian assaulted the position as the Germans were reloading. With nothing but a hand grenade and his carbine, he forced the gun crew to surrender.

Dervishian, a lawyer in civilian life, again directed the four men on the left flank to enter the vineyard but encountered another machine gun that killed one soldier and wounded another. At this moment, the nearby enemy intensified the fight by throwing potato-masher grenades at the American soldiers within the vineyard. Dervishian ordered his men to withdraw, but instead of following them, he jumped into the machine-gun position he had just captured and opened fire with the enemy's weapon in the direction of the second hostile nest. Observing movement in a dugout just ten feet away, Dervishian grabbed a machine pistol and, simultaneously blazing away at the entrance to the dugout to prevent its occupants from firing and firing his machine gun at the other German nest, he forced five Germans in both positions to surrender.

Determined to rid the area of all the enemy, Dervishian continued his advance alone. Noticing another machine-gun position beside a house, he picked up an abandoned enemy weapon and forced six more Germans to give up by spraying their position with bullets. Unable to locate additional targets in the vicinity, Dervishian conducted these prisoners to the rear. Soon thereafter, he was promoted to second lieutenant; he ultimately achieved the rank of colonel. The U.S. Army Reserve Center in North Chesterfield (Richmond), Virginia, is named in his honor.[22]

TANKERS WERE NO LESS BRAVE than the infantrymen. Second Lieutenant Thomas W. Fowler, a 1943 graduate of Texas A&M University and a member of the 191st Tank Battalion (Independent), distinguished himself in action on May 23. Assigned as a liaison officer to an infantry unit, Fowler watched as two infantry platoons moving into the attack found themselves completely stymied and disorganized when they stumbled into an unmarked German minefield during the armor-infantry attack on Carano.

Disregarding his own safety, Fowler made a personal reconnaissance through the minefield while under fire, clearing a seventy-five-yard path by lifting the antipersonnel mines out of the ground with his hands. After he had crawled through the belt of deadly explosives, he returned to the infantry and led them through the cleared path, one squad at a time. As they deployed, Fowler, despite the constant danger from small-arms fire directed at him and the profusion of mines, made a reconnaissance into enemy territory in search of a route to continue the advance. He then returned through the minefield and, on foot, led the tanks through the mines into a position from which they could best support the infantry. Scouting 300 yards in front of the infantry, Fowler continued to lead the two platoons forward until he had gained his objective, where he came upon several dug-in German soldiers. Having taken them by surprise, Fowler dragged them out of their foxholes and sent them to the rear.

Fowler was not yet finished. Realizing that a dangerous gap existed between his tank company and the unit to his right, Fowler decided to continue his advance until the gap was filled. He reconnoitered to his front, brought the infantry into position where they dug in, and, under heavy mortar and small-arms fire, brought his tanks forward. A few minutes later, the enemy began an armored counterattack. Several Mark VI tanks fired their cannons directly at Fowler's position, setting one of his tanks aflame. With shells bursting near him, and with utter disregard for his own life, he ran directly through the enemy tank fire to reach the burning vehicle.

Although all other elements had been forced to withdraw under intense fire from the advancing panzers, Fowler, for a solid half hour, remained in his forward position and attempted to rescue the wounded tank crew. Only when the enemy tanks had almost overrun him did he withdraw a short distance, where he personally rendered first aid to nine wounded infantrymen in the midst of the relentless incoming fire. He was awarded the Medal of Honor but did not live to receive it; he was killed eleven days later by a German sniper while performing a reconnaissance mission for his tank platoon near Rome.[*][23]

PRIVATE FIRST CLASS HENRY SCHAUER, an Oklahoma-born, Montana-raised member of Company E, 15th Regiment, 3rd Infantry Division, also distinguished himself on May 23. Although he had been wounded in Sicily and spent 151 days recuperating, he was not shy about wanting to get back into battle. During the fight for Cisterna, he and his buddies, on a patrol to reach and cut Highway 7, southeast of the town,

---

[*] Fowler Hall, a campus dormitory at Texas A&M University, was named in his honor; his Medal of Honor is on display at the school. https://tshaonline.org /handbook/online/articles/ffodp.

were pinned down in a ditch by five snipers. Having had quite enough of that, the expert marksman leaped up and moved forward, picking off the snipers one by one with his BAR.

His patrol moved forward, only to be stopped again by artillery and machine-gun fire. Schauer once more exposed himself to danger, ignoring the exploding shells and the bullets cracking by.[24] Company E's Second Lieutenant James M. Dorsey Jr. witnessed with awe Schauer's display of bravery:

> The man acted as though nothing could kill him. He assumed the kneeling position on the bank of a ditch. Bullets from both machine guns swept about him, miraculously missing him by inches. Fragments from enemy shells, which burst no more than fifteen yards from him, hit the ground all around him. He permitted none of this fire to ruffle his composure. Schauer engaged the first machine gun, the one sixty yards away, opening up on it with a full clip of ammunition. In one long burst of fire he killed the gunner and the man alongside him. He put a new magazine in his BAR, fired two short bursts, and killed the two remaining Germans who ran to man the weapon.[25]

The following day, Schauer was still on his personal quest to rid the area of Germans. While on the move, Schauer and his patrol came under tank and machine-gun fire. Although his .30-caliber bullets could do nothing about the tank, he went after the machine-gun crew with a vengeance and, in a brief but fierce duel, killed all four of them. For his two-day effort, he was awarded the Medal of Honor on October 17, 1944, by Lieutenant General Alexander Patch, head of the Seventh U.S. Army. And, because he had killed seventeen Germans in seventeen hours, a war correspondent dubbed him "Kraut-an-Hour Schauer."[26]

When asked how much ammunition he had used to kill seventeen Germans, he replied that he had ten magazines that each held twenty rounds. "I used them all before I was through." Like most Medal of Honor recipients, after the war Schauer played down his heroics, saying, "The ones who really deserved it are already buried, and nobody knows what they did."[27]

IN THE CENTER OF THE beachhead area, William Willis Eagles's 45th Infantry Division also contributed to the breakout, and courageous acts
too numerous to recount were performed by individuals, squads, platoons, and companies. In one, Second Lieutenant Charles A. Brandt
(Company G, 2nd Battalion, 180th Infantry Regiment), accompanied by
Technical Sergeant John Sessions, headed out through a minefield to
attack their objective: a cluster of German machine-gun nests and mortar pits. Advancing single file with Brandt and Sessions in the lead, the
3rd Platoon swiftly killed or wounded sixty-five Germans and captured
another eighty-five; Sessions single-handedly killed fifteen of the enemy.
A mortar shell exploded nearby, wounding Brandt in the elbow, but despite his wounds, he picked up a BAR and continued leading his men to
knock out more enemy installations. It is estimated that he personally
killed or wounded twenty-five of the enemy before he was evacuated to
an aid station. Sessions, too, accounted for a large number of Germans
and was instrumental in the platoon's neutralizing six mortar positions
and five machine-gun emplacements. For their undaunted leadership,
Brandt was awarded the Distinguished Service Cross and Sessions the
Silver Star.[28]

Lieutenant Colonel Chester G. Cruikshank, from the small farming
town of Ault, Colorado, had been an outstanding athlete (playing on
his college football team and having been the U.S. national champion
in the hammer throw in 1939 and 1942); he obtained a Reserve Officers' Training Corps commission at Colorado State University in 1940.
After the previous three commanders of the 2nd Battalion, 180th Regiment, 45th Division, had all been wounded and evacuated, he was promoted from major to lieutenant colonel, transferred from his position
of regimental executive officer, and given command of the battalion.
During the breakout, Cruikshank moved his companies around like
chess pieces, filling a gap here, stopping a German attack there, exposing
himself constantly to enemy fire, and administering first aid to seven of
his wounded men while continuing to direct the troops under intense
enemy fire. For his leadership, Cruikshank would be awarded the Distinguished Service Cross.[29]

The 157th Infantry Regiment, battered though it was, exhibited inci-
dents of courage that were just as numerous. Technical Sergeant Van T.

Barfoot's unit, Company L, had been in defensive positions in the town of Carano when Buffalo kicked off. On the morning of May 23, Barfoot, a Choctaw Indian from Mississippi, requested permission to lead a squad. Because of his previous patrols, he knew the terrain and the minefield that guarded the German positions ahead of him. Barfoot and his patrol set out low across the open ground until he told his men to take cover while he advanced alone through the minefield. Coming within a few yards of a machine-gun nest on the German flank, he lobbed a grenade and destroyed the position. He then advanced toward a second machine gun, killing two soldiers with his Thompson sub-machine gun and capturing three others. When he reached a third gun, the entire crew surrendered to him. During his foray, Barfoot had captured a total of seventeen German soldiers and killed eight. But he was not yet done.

When the Germans launched a three-tank armored counterattack directly at his platoon's position later in the day, Barfoot used a bazooka to knock out one panzer at a range of 75 yards; the other two quickly changed direction and departed the field. As the crew of the disabled tank crawled out, Barfoot opened up with his Tommy gun and killed three. He then advanced deeper into enemy-held territory and destroyed an abandoned German artillery piece with a demolition charge placed in the gun's breech. He returned to his own lines and helped guide two wounded soldiers from his squad nearly a mile to the rear. For his display of skill and courage, he was given a battlefield commission and awarded the Medal of Honor.[30]

To cite these few examples is to ignore the hundreds, perhaps thousands, of other equally courageous acts that were performed on May 23 and the many days that followed—acts that will never be known.

ACCOMPANYING THE INFANTRY WERE, OF course, the medics. "Doc Joe" Franklin (Company I, 157th Infantry Regiment, 45th Division) recalled:

During the breakout, Tech Sergeant Youtsey was with my buddy Tech Sergeant Wilkerson when a German killed him. Wilkerson saw the German run from one hole to another. He told me that he grabbed Youtsey's tommy gun and put it on full automatic as he ran to the hole he saw the German disappear into. As he stood over the hole, six Germans came out with their hands up, trying to surrender. "I emptied the whole thirty-shot magazine into them," Wilkerson told me.

Later that morning, I cared for a staff sergeant with only half a face. His whole jaw had been blown away. The sergeant was heroically calm and showed no fear. There was no bleeding, and all I could do was sprinkle on some sulfa powder and tie on a Carlisle bandage. Such wounds were heart-wrenching.[31]

Franklin added:

When a GI was wounded and in severe pain, I would inject a whole syrette of morphine. We had a tube of lipstick in our medical pouches with which we were supposed to print a large "M" on a wounded man's forehead to warn the aid station and field hospital that morphine had already been administered. However, if the man was fully conscious, he might think this was effeminate (I had some like this) and would wipe his arm across his forehead and smear out the "M." Frequently, when the man arrived at the forward aid station and was asked if he had morphine, he was in such pain that he either didn't remember or couldn't talk, so he was given another syrette which was noted on his evacuation tag as the "first shot."

In the field hospital, he was still in great pain and was usually administered another syrette. Until now, he had been in partial shock. Warmed under blankets, his blood began flowing freely and three syrettes of morphine hit his brain at once and the man died from morphine poisoning. It took several months to figure this out, and I know that it wasn't until Anzio that we were warned to squeeze out half the syrette before administering it. We also learned to make a secure pin from the sharp needle of the syrette and its aluminum container. This was pinned onto the man's shirt collar so that it could be easily seen.[32]

LATE IN THE AFTERNOON OF May 23, Paul Brown (Graves Registration Section, 179th) recorded in his diary: "Made big push . . . early this morning. Our [45th] Div. gained their objective without too much trouble. Took 300 or so captives so far or so as reported. 180th led 157th beachhead out and 179th reserved them for first time. They went around 'Factory' and cut Appian Highway. We picked up three KIAs also that night. We lost several tanks but so did Nazis. Sure am getting nervous over this going home."[33]

BY THE TIME THE SMOKE of battle cleared at the conclusion of the first day of Operation Buffalo, the Germans had, in most places, held firm but suffered horrendous losses. The 362nd Infantry Division had lost half of its manpower, while two regiments of the 715th Infantry Division had nearly ceased to exist.

On the Allied side, there was reason to be optimistic. Although the 65th German Division was still in control of the Albano Highway in the Aprilia-Carroceto area, Eagles's 45th Division was making slow but steady progress in pushing the 3rd Panzer-Grenadier Division back, while O'Daniel's 3rd Division was encircling Cisterna and Harmon's 1st Armored Division had crossed the railroad line at Femmina Morta Creek. The only note of concern was that Frederick's 1st Special Service Force, protecting the 3rd Division's right flank, had made a lunge at Highway 7 but was then driven back by a panzer attack. But more than 1,500 German prisoners had been taken on the first day, and Truscott noted with satisfaction, "The attack was going well."[34]

THE SECOND DAY OF THE breakout from the beachhead was as bloody, violent, and courage filled as the first. Second Lieutenant Francis E. Liggett (Battery C, 158th Field Artillery Battalion, 45th Division) recalled:

After the artillery pulverized the German positions awhile, we moved out in the attack. The first thing we encountered was a German minefield. I was following one of the platoon leaders and was close behind him when he stepped on a mine, which blew off one of his feet. I took his platoon on through. We had just gotten past the minefield when the platoon leader of the following platoon stepped on a mine, so I went back and led his platoon through. Luckily I didn't step on one.

Most of the Germans were still in their holes and either too scared to come out or too shocked from all the artillery fired on them to offer much resistance. We hollered at them to come out and if they didn't immediately comply, we threw hand grenades in and went on to the next holes. As we advanced, we radioed back and lifted the artillery barrage so that it stayed ahead of us—a rolling barrage. By about noon we had gotten ahead of the units on either side of us, so we stopped just over the top of a long hill and occupied some of the shallow German trenches while we waited for them to catch up.

Liggett was then struck in the head with a shell fragment that penetrated his helmet and fractured his skull, but he refused to be evacuated. Continuing to lead two platoons, he recalled that six German Mark VI tanks started up the hill toward him.

When the closest one was about a block-and-a-half away, he spotted us. In my mind's eye I can still see him lowering his 88mm gun down. The first three shells he fired missed me by about a foot or so directly above me; I could feel the heat from them as they went by. Then he lowered it down a little more and nearly buried us with the next three shots fired.

All the time the tanks were advancing and shooting at us, I had been trying to get some phosphorous artillery shells on them. Finally it came. I got two tanks and I think the others pulled back, but we didn't stick around there any longer to find out. I didn't know what the next move for the Germans would be, but it was clear that we were in an exposed position well ahead of our flanking units, and just staying there didn't appear to be a good option. Also, I wasn't in very good condition from the head injury and all the recent excitement, and we were in a hurry to get back over the hill and away from them.[35]

PRIVATE JAMES H. MILLS (COMPANY F, 15th Infantry Regiment, 3rd Division) was a new replacement fresh from the States who was about to be thrown into his first battle. The slightly built twenty-one-year-old Floridian, who had been an avid hunter in civilian life, was acting as point man for his platoon as it advanced down a draw to reach a position near Cisterna from which an attack could be launched against a heavily fortified strongpoint.

After the platoon had gone about 300 yards, Private Mills was fired on by a machine gun a short distance away. Instead of going to ground, he rushed the position, killed the gunner, and forced the assistant gunner to surrender. Mills then saw a German soldier behind a large bush with a potato-masher grenade. Aiming his rifle at the German, Mills forced him to drop the grenade and captured him. While the American was taking his two prisoners to the rear, another enemy soldier attempted to throw a grenade at him; Mills blew him away with one shot.

Then it seemed that every German within range began firing at Mills and his prisoners. A machine gun, two machine pistols, and three rifles opened up on him at a range of only fifty feet. Instead of diving for cover and cowering like an ordinary person would do, he charged headlong toward the sources of the gunfire, firing his M-1 Garand from the hip. Completely demoralized by Mills's daring charge, all six Germans in that position surrendered. As he neared the end of the draw with his eight prisoners, Mills was brought under fire by a machine gunner 20 yards away. Although he had absolutely no cover, Mills again used only one shot to kill the gunner. Two enemy soldiers in the position then began firing wildly at Mills before they fled; Mills fired twice, killing one of them. During his advance to the objective, he captured another soldier.

But Mills's platoon leader decided that the enemy position was too strong to be taken by the platoon's frontal assault and that to continue the attack would result in heavy casualties. The platoon leader asked for someone to create a diversion while the rest of the unit approached by the flank; Private Mills immediately volunteered to do just that. Standing up in full view of the enemy less than 100 yards away, he shouted and fired his rifle at the Germans. His Medal of Honor citation said, "His ruse worked exactly as planned. The enemy centered his fire on Private Mills. Tracers passed within inches of his body, rifle and machine-pistol bullets ricocheted off the rocks at his feet. Yet he stood there firing until his rifle was empty."

Intent on covering the flanking movement of his platoon, Mills jumped into the draw, reloaded, climbed out again, and continued to lay down a base of fire. After repeating this action four times, his platoon was able to reach the designated spot undiscovered, from which position it assaulted and overwhelmed the enemy, capturing twenty-two Germans and taking the objective without casualties. Besides killing at least four of the enemy, he had taken thirty-one Germans prisoner.[*][36]

TO ADD THEIR FIREPOWER TO the Allied breakout at Anzio, U.S. Navy and British Royal Navy warships took targets under fire. Near Cisterna, 3rd Panzer-Grenadier Division mortarman August Schlag recalled the heavy shelling his unit received:

> At 4 PM, one of my friends, Robert Raab, was killed by naval gunfire that landed close to my hole. He was covered with blood. I was horrified and shocked. I bent close to him and called his name but he didn't answer. I wasn't able to hold back the tears. Robert had been my schoolmate and neighbor. We were drafted into the army together when we were both eighteen years of age and we had been in the same platoon during training. The Allies continued to attack our position until we had to withdraw in a ditch. Only five men remained of our platoon.

Schlag's unit, or what remained of it, was pushed all the way back to the north of Rome, where it built a new defensive line. (Schlag was later transferred from Anzio to France, where, while fighting in the Eifel Mountains, he was captured by the Americans on February 7, 1945. He would spend a year as a POW before being repatriated to his homeland.)[37]

STAFF SERGEANT AUDIE MURPHY (COMPANY B, 15th Infantry Regiment, 3rd Division) said that his unit's task on May 24 was to cut the railroad line that ran south of Cisterna. "The Germans have dug in along its sides; and the track bed is protected by a lashing stream of automatic fire." Moving into position to silence the enemy weapons, Murphy directed his men into the assault, but the attack did not go well. "I have the

---

* After leaving the army, Mills went to work for the Veterans Administration in Florida. On November 8, 1973, while driving home outside of Gainesville, he stopped to help three men who appeared to be having car trouble. The three men attacked and beat him unconscious and stole his car; he died of his injuries on November 11, 1973 (Veterans Day), at age fifty. Bill Rufty, "James Henry Mills Won a Medal of Honor in WWII," *Lakeland* (FL) *Ledger*, May 24, 2004.

sudden, sickening feeling that we are being lured into a trap, but I cannot hesitate," Murphy wrote. Eight of his men were hit by machine-gun fire, leaving Murphy the last man standing in his group. He carefully began maneuvering to where he could get a clear shot at the enemy, but the gunners saw him and unleashed a torrent of bullets in his direction. Around him, other units were moving up, keeping low, making their advances in short, fast rushes. A tank pulled up to aid the infantrymen. The Germans took off running. One small skirmish in a day full of them.[38]

AMERICAN SOLDIERS CONTINUED TO DISTINGUISH themselves during the breakout. While his unit—the same as Murphy's—was assaulting Cisterna, Sergeant Sylvester Antolak of St. Clairsville, Ohio, took it upon himself to charge 200 yards over flat, coverless terrain to destroy an enemy machine gun that was harassing his squad. Fully 30 yards in advance of his squad, he ran into a fusillade of German fire and was hit three times but, each time, regained his feet and continued his advance. With one shoulder deeply gashed and his right arm shattered, he continued to rush directly into the enemy fire with his sub-machine gun wedged under his uninjured arm until he got within 15 yards of the enemy strongpoint and opened fire, killing two Germans and forcing the remaining ten to surrender. Although badly wounded, he refused to seek medical attention, choosing instead to lead an attack on another strongpoint 100 yards away. Utterly disregarding the hail of bullets concentrated upon him, Antolak stormed ahead before being instantly killed by enemy fire. Inspired by his example, his squad went on to overwhelm the enemy troops. Antolak was credited with killing twenty Germans, capturing a machine gun, and clearing the path for his company to take its objective.[39] Antolak was awarded the Medal of Honor, posthumously.

PAUL BROWN WROTE IN HIS diary on May 24: "Artillery has been continuous for two days now. None are reaching too close around here, probably ½ mile away. Sometimes they go over our heads hitting hospital area. We are still improving positions. News of Cassino front is very good also. Beachheads should only be about 25 miles apart now. Oh happy day when they meet. 3rd Div. is taking Littoria [sic—Cisterna]. Weather is sure fine."[40]

THE GERMANS TRIED EVERYTHING THEY could to hold back the fast-rising Allied tide of battle. Strong counterattacks were thrown against the 45th Division, but the Thunderbirds held firm. The 1st Armored Division tanks had punched their way to the outskirts of Velletri. But the holdouts in Cisterna were refusing to budge, and O'Daniel was preparing to use the 3rd Division's 7th Infantry Regiment to drive them out.

Later that day, Truscott and Clark met. The Fifth Army commander asked the VI Corps commander if he had given more thought to the plan to change the axis of attack from the north to the northwest—a direct line toward Rome—a move called Operation Turtle. Truscott said he had but wondered if such a move might not cause the Germans to concentrate their strength at the Valmontone Gap and slow down, if not entirely stop, Operation Buffalo. "Any such concentration might delay us at Valmontone long enough to permit the German main forces to escape," Truscott told Clark. If German resistance against the British and 45th Division's half of the beachhead began to crumble, "I thought that an attack to the northwest might be the best way to cut off the enemy withdrawal north of the Alban Hills." Clark agreed; such a move would hasten Fifth Army's entry into Rome while stymieing the British and being a sharp poke in Alexander's eye.[41]

IN THE UNITED STATES AND in Great Britain, the newspapers were filled with stories about the breakout. On May 24, under a six-column front-page headline that read, "Allies Start Drive at Anzio Beachhead," the *New York Times* reported, "The long pent-up power of the Allies' beach-head forces was hurled into the battle of Italy early today. . . . The British and American troops on the beachhead lunged into the savage offensive four months and one day after the original landings."[42]

THE 7TH INFANTRY REGIMENT, 3RD Infantry Division, was determined to grab Cisterna, the prize that had eluded them ever since the first disastrous attempt to seize the town on January 28; Thursday, May 25, became the day that it would finally happen.

Rousting the last vestiges of the Hermann Göring Parachute-Panzer Division from Cisterna on that Thursday, the 7th Infantry laid claim to the pile of rubble that used to be a town, while the division's 30th

Infantry Regiment pressed on to Cori, less than six miles to the north-east, and then a further seven miles north to Artena, where the enemy was crushed in a ferocious battle. Later that day, Highway 6 at the once-picturesque hilltop town of Valmontone, just two miles away, was reached, thereby ostensibly cutting the Tenth Army's escape route from the south.[43]

But Vietinghoff was too clever to be caught in such a trap and so avoided Highway 6—the Via Casilina—altogether, choosing instead to swing north of the Alban Hills on secondary roads and reach Rome, where he would join forces with Mackensen's Fourteenth Army that was pulling back from the Anzio area.[44]

Shortly after 10:00 A.M. on May 25, a special group of the Allied VI Corps beachhead forces—American and British—finally made contact at Borgo Grappa with members coming up from the Gustav Line. The first men to shake hands were Captain Benjamin H. Souza of the 36th Engineers and Lieutenant Francis X. Buckley of II Corps' 91st Cavalry Reconnaissance Squadron. Clark was there to observe the linkup—and to have his picture taken by army photographers.[45]

The day, however, was marred when American P-40 fighter-bombers, who were supposed to pounce on the Germans fleeing Cisterna, wrongly targeted the 15th Infantry Regiment racing in pursuit of the enemy. Swooping in, the P-40s bombed and strafed the Americans, killing or wounding a hundred of them. Several trucks loaded with ammunition exploded, adding to the carnage. American pilots also hit the town of Cori, which, by that time, was full of American infantrymen. More deaths and injuries by friendly fire resulted.[46]

On that evening, Paul Brown recorded in his diary: "Real news, our beachhead is now connected with south. All of us are very happy over such. We are taking many prisoners, and still gaining ground. Our Artillery is continuously raising hell, we now have Highway #7 & ready to cut Highway 6. They have many Germans cut off. Am still sweating the date I am to leave. We'd probably go to Naples by truck, that would be something to remember."[47]

It appeared that nothing now could prevent Clark and his Fifth Army from being the first Allied unit into Rome. Unless it was the Eighth British Army.

CHAPTER 19

"Even a soldier must cry sometimes"
MAY 26–31

TWO GERMAN DIVISIONS STILL BLOCKED the left shoulder of the An-zio breakout: Gräser's 3rd Panzer-Grenadier and Pfeiffer's 65th In-fantry, north and northwest of Campoleone. Although both had taken tremendous casualties during months of combat, they still offered stiff resistance, and the subsequent fighting was some of the most difficult of the entire Italian campaign.

Assigned to force that shoulder were the 1st and 5th British Divisions; to their right were the 34th and 45th Infantry Divisions and Combat Command A of the 1st Armored Division making a push for Cam-poleone, Velletri, and the Alban Hills. To their right was the other VI Corps' spearhead: O'Daniel's 3rd and Ryder's 34th "Red Bull" Infantry Divisions and other elements of Harmon's tanks (Combat Command B) heading toward Valmontone. To the right of this thrust, along the Mus-solini Canal, were the 1st Special Service Force and the 36th Engineers.

The general breakout was making slow but deliberate progress. The town of Lanuvio was the 34th's objective, while the 3rd concentrated once more on breaking the stubborn defense of Cisterna. To cut off any retreat by the German Tenth Army coming up from the broken Gustav Line, elements of the 3rd Infantry Division and the 1st SSF were or-dered transferred to II Corps to block Highway 6. The II Corps' 36th

THE BREAKOUT

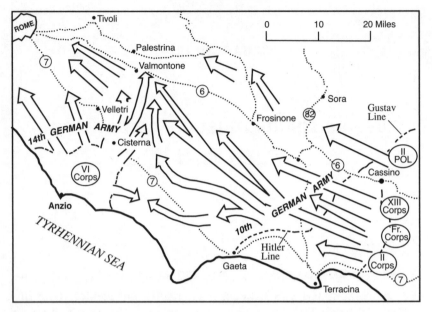

After Allied troops on the Gustav Line launched Operation Diadem on May 11, 1944, VI Corps at the Anzio beachhead began Operation Buffalo, which touched off the breakneck race to Rome. (Positions approximate)

U.S. Infantry Division, under Major General Fred Walker, would also take part in the action.[*][1]

But Harmon's boys were having problems. "I was ordered to turn the noses of the tanks . . . and scramble through the rugged hills of the Colli Laziali," he said. "It turned out to be, in terms of destruction of tanks and all-important tank crews, our most expensive operation in the Anzio theater."[2] With both Combat Commands A and B now reunited for the push to the Alban Hills, the division absorbed heavy losses; on May 26 eighteen tanks were knocked out. The next day an additional twenty-one Shermans and sixteen Stuarts were disabled or destroyed.[3]

---

[*] The 36th, which had been badly mauled in its attempt to cross the Rapido River west of Cassino on January 20–22, 1944, was a National Guard division from Texas that had several nicknames: the Texas Division, Panther Division, Lone Star Division, Arrowhead Division, and the T-Patchers. www.custermen.com.

KARL MULLER (3RD PANZER-GRENADIERS) RECALLED that, on the battlefield at 4:00 in the morning of May 26, with shells crashing all around,
a medic persuaded him to help carry a dead comrade back to friendly
lines. Muller said:

> It was not his personal companion, but he did not want to leave him
> here. Although I realized of the futility of our enterprise, I carried with
> him the dead soldier on a makeshift stretcher. We had to pause several
> times but the medic did not want to give up his plans. Again we pulled
> our load but I could not do it any longer. After a few steps I dropped the
> stretcher and, with a "Do what you want," I turned around and went in
> the opposite direction. I fell asleep in my sleep-hole but was awakened
> by the bombardment of our hole. The Americans were there and shot
> me in the left thigh. Later I thought of the medic with the dead man and
> whether he had succeeded in escaping.[4]

The Germans were in trouble, and Mackensen knew it. The 362nd
Division that had been clinging to Cisterna had been reduced to half
strength, and the 715th wasn't in much better shape. Realizing that disaster was looming, he requested that Kesselring allow him to pull his
left flank back to the Lepini Mountains, closer to Valmontone; Kesselring said no. Send in the Hermann Göring Parachute-Panzer Division,
he told Mackensen, and attack the American 3rd Division that was approaching Valmontone; it was vital that Valmontone and the highway
that ran through it not fall to the Allies.[5]

Valmontone now became the most important piece of real estate to
both sides. The Hermann Göring Division and other units of the LXXVI
Panzer Corps had rushed to the town and were under orders to attack
American forces and recapture nearby Artena. Elements of the 29th
Panzer-Grenadier Division, along with the Hermann Göring—both of
which had just returned from Civitavecchia—were also ordered to bolster the Velletri sector. But Kesselring also needed Mackensen to use the
29th to block the II Corps' advance up Route 7 between Fondi and Terracina and prevent the two U.S. corps from linking up (Kesselring was
late getting the news that the linkup had already been achieved). Mackensen did not agree, telling his superior that he thought the 29th should

be kept closer to the beachhead in order to block VI Corps' expected northward push. Their feud would soon lead to Mackensen's dismissal.[6]

That evening, just as Schmalz prepared to throw his Hermann Göring Division into the attack, he was taken by surprise by John O'Daniel's 3rd Division and Robert Frederick's 1st SSF moving into the Valmontone Gap. Before the two sides could clash, however, tragedy struck. Hamilton Howzes's 1st Battalion, 6th Armored Infantry Regiment, 1st Armored Division, was accidentally bombarded by a battery of 155mm American howitzers, causing heavy losses. Then American warplanes swooped in and added to the carnage. A furious Ernie Harmon sent an appropriately furious message to Truscott: "Friendly planes have strafed our troops three times in the last two hours. Tell the Air Corps to get the hell out of the air, as we can get along better without the SOB's. If they don't stop strafing our troops, we are going to shoot the hell out of them."[7]

MARK CLARK WAS CERTAIN THAT the thrust toward Valmontone by the 3rd Division, augmented by Harmon's tanks, would be enough to satisfy Alexander, thus allowing him to realize his true objective: Fifth Army's capture of Rome. Truscott received a secondhand order—passed through Don Brann, the Fifth Army G-3 (Operations) officer—that Clark wanted him to keep the 3rd Division and 1st SSF in the attack at Valmontone while sending the rest of VI Corps around the west side of the Alban Hills and on to Rome. Truscott protested, saying that conditions were not right, that the Germans were still too strong to the northwest of the beachhead, and that now was not the time to engage in an unnecessary and unusually complicated shuffling of VI Corps forces. "Such was the order that turned the main effort of the beachhead forces from the Valmontone Gap and prevented the destruction of the German Tenth Army," he wrote bitterly. But an order was an order, and Truscott was duty bound to carry it out. He began juggling his forces around, no mean feat.

He later wrote:

Our plan was to concentrate the 34th Infantry Division southwest of Velletri, and then move northwest with the 34th and 45th Infantry Divisions abreast to seize the line Lanuvio-Campoleone. While this was under way, we could relieve the 1st Armored Division with the 36th Infantry Division opposite Velletri, then move the 1st Armored across the rear of the 34th and 45th Infantry Divisions to the Carano-Padiglione area in readiness to join with the 45th Infantry Division in the drive from Campoleone. Meanwhile, the 3rd Infantry Division, with the 1st Special Service Force and Task Force Howze attached, would block Highway 6 in the vicinity of Valmontone.

Truscott also realized that such a maneuver would also necessitate major disruptions to the supply operations and displacement of all the corps and division artillery units, not to mention all command posts and communications. "A more complicated plan would be difficult to conceive," he grumbled. Somehow, some way, the reshuffling of a majority of the beachhead forces was accomplished without any major disasters occurring.[8]

ON THE TWENTY-SIXTH, THE THIRD day of the breakout, the Americans were making decent progress. Although Harmon's 1st Armored Division had lost dozens of tanks and TDs on the first day of the operation, his tankers and Ryder's 34th Division were closing in on Velletri, while advance elements of the 3rd Division were nearing Artena—only three miles from the objective: Valmontone and Highway 6. In addition, Eagles's 45th Division was preparing to make a final assault on Campoleone; simultaneously, Penney's 1st British Division would push to drive the last of the defenders out of Aprilia.[9]

Near Cisterna on May 26, thirty-three-year-old First Lieutenant Beryl R. "Dick" Newman (Company F, 133rd Infantry Regiment, 34th Infantry Division) displayed courage and valor above and beyond the call of duty. While scouting with four enlisted men ahead of his platoon, he was fired on by two German machine guns located on the crest of a hill about 100 yards to his front. The four scouts with him immediately hit the ground, but Lieutenant Newman, trying to see exactly what his unit was facing, remained standing, despite the enemy fire, to ascertain the positions of the emplacements. Newman called back to his platoon and ordered one squad to advance to him and another to flank the enemy to the right.

Then, still standing despite enemy machine-gun fire, Newman opened up with his Thompson sub-machine gun on the gunners, but he was too far away for his fire to be effective. With his squad unable to advance, Newman, in full view of the German gunners and in the face of their continuous fire, advanced alone against the enemy, firing his Tommy gun as he closed with them. He succeeded in wounding a German in each of the nests and forcing the remaining two Germans to flee from their positions into a nearby house. Three more enemy soldiers then came out of the house and ran toward a third machine gun. Newman, still relentlessly advancing toward them, killed one German before he could reach the gun and the second before he could fire it; the third German fled back into the house. Although he had no idea how many Germans were in the house, Newman boldly attacked alone, yelling for the occupants to surrender. Hearing no positive response, he kicked in the door. Inside he found eleven heavily armed and apparently intimidated Germans who meekly surrendered to him. Single-handedly, Newman had silenced three enemy machine guns, wounded two Germans, killed two more, and had taken eleven prisoners. President Roosevelt personally later awarded the Medal of Honor to him in a White House ceremony.[10]

That evening, Paul Brown wrote in his diary, "May 26: We have Cisterna now, very good news. Our Regt. CP is on Highway No. 7. No KIA last night. No air raids, some Artillery. Things are sure moving on beachhead. Prisoners admit it has been hell—much ruffer than Russian Front."[11]

ANOTHER MEDAL OF HONOR WAS earned the next day when acting squad leader Private first class Salvador J. Lara and his unit (Company L, 180th Infantry Regiment, 45th Division) were attacking enemy positions west of Aprilia. Lara's squad knocked out several German machine guns that lay in the company's zone of advance. After the initial objective had been taken, Lara's squad came to the assistance of other squads that his platoon leader noticed were heavily engaged. Moving far out to the front and left flank of his company were Lara and his squad. He took three men with him and, on his own initiative, cleared out a wide section of the ditch along which the Germans were entrenched. Although he was wounded, there he killed four Germans and captured fifteen. When the German crews of a couple of nearby 50mm mortars saw what was happening to their comrades, they fled in haste, abandoning their weapons in usable condition.[12]

Initially awarded the Distinguished Service Cross, Lara died due to still-unknown circumstances on September 1, 1945—less than three months after the war in Europe ended—while then serving with the 602nd Ordnance Armament Maintenance Battalion. His DSC was upgraded to the Medal of Honor, and on March 18, 2014, the medal was presented to family members by President Barack Obama at the White House.[13]

"ON 28 MAY, WE ABANDONED Aprilia," recounted Ernst Kehrer, an information officer in Mackensen's command whose position was in the town, "which was almost razed to the ground, and we directed toward the north."[14] Moving into the ruins of Mussolini's once-pristine model farm settlement were beat-up but happy elements of Penney's 1st British Division. It had been a long and hard-won victory for a pile of rubble that barely resembled a town.[15]

Meanwhile, in the 45th Division's sector, the 157th and 180th Regiments were fighting their way forward, but it was slow going. To the 157th's right, across the fields north of Aprilia, the 135th Infantry Regiment of the 34th Division had run into defiant, almost fanatical, opposition by the Germans. This caused the 157th to push farther up the railroad line toward Campoleone Station, leaving the 135th behind and creating an exposed flank that the Germans quickly exploited. Operating on a front nearly a half mile wide, waves of German infantry hit the 157th's 3rd Battalion from behind. So intense was the attack that at least two platoons from Company I were captured, and the company commander, Captain James Evans, radioed to the battalion command post, "This looks like the end. I'm signing off," just before he was also taken prisoner.[16]

The 133rd and 168th Regiments of the 34th Division were having difficulties of their own in taking Lanuvio, northeast of Campoleone Station. Truscott decided that VI Corps "would continue the attack the following day, but would have the 34th Division pass around to the west of Lanuvio. Meanwhile, we would leave the Corps engineers opposite Velletri, and move the 36th Infantry Division up behind the 34th Division to climb Monte Artemisio in the Alban Hills and encircle Lanuvio from the east." General Walker, the Texas Division's commander, liked the plan and prepared his men for the next day's battle. Walker's engineers had found a gap in the German lines that would allow his men to reach the heights above the town. "With some engineer work on the trail," Truscott said, "even tanks would be able to accompany the infantry. . . . This was our turning point in our drive to the northwest."[17]

Things were not going Ernie Harmon's way, however; his 1st Armored Division's progress had been stymied by attacks by the 4th Parachute Division. "I have always believed," he wrote, "that, at this point in the battle, the 1st Armored could—and should—have rolled onto Highway 6 and been in Rome in an hour and a half. The Germans had not recovered from their confusion, the valley road was ideal for tanks, and there wasn't then much in the way of military strength between us and the outskirts of the city."

NEAR ARTENA ON MAY 28, Staff Sergeant Rudolph B. Davila (Company H, 7th Infantry Regiment, 3rd Division) of Vista, California, risked certain death to provide heavy-weapons support for a beleaguered rifle company. Leading a twenty-four-man patrol advancing along an exposed hillside against a well-entrenched German force that had his company pinned down, his machine gunners were sent to ground, unable to advance farther. Undeterred, Davila crawled 50 yards to the nearest machine gun and opened fire on the enemy. In order to observe the effect of his fire, Sergeant Davila fired from the kneeling position, ignoring the enemy bullets that clanged off the tripod and passed between his legs. Ordering a gunner to take over, he crawled forward to a better vantage point and directed the firefight with hand and arm signals until both hostile guns were silenced.

Davila then directed his three remaining machine guns to begin firing and drove the enemy back about 200 yards. Although wounded in the leg, he limped to a burned-out tank and engaged a second enemy force from the tank's turret. Dismounting, he advanced 130 yards in short rushes, crawled 20 more yards, running inside an enemy-held house to eliminate the five defenders with his rifle and a hand grenade. Climbing to the attic, he opened fire on the enemy below. Although the walls of the house were crumbling, he continued to fire until he had destroyed two more enemy machine guns. His intrepid actions brought desperately needed heavy-weapons support to a hard-pressed rifle company and silenced four machine gunners, which forced the enemy to abandon their prepared positions.[18]

Afterward, Davila, who was later promoted to second lieutenant, said, "I don't remember being afraid or timid. It just happened. I wasn't that kind of person. I wasn't violent. In fact, I was kind of a passive kind of guy. I just wanted to be a good soldier." Davila, an Asian American (Filipino mother, Spanish father), received the Distinguished Service Cross, which was upgraded to the Medal of Honor in 2000—fifty-six years after the deed.[19]

PAUL BROWN SUMMARIZED HIS VIEW of the day's events in his diary: "Bombers sure got close again last night. . . . Our troops are very close to Highway 6 from this side, British are close to it on another front. Germans are going to be cut off. Our Artillery is very busy all afternoon. Am going to Cisterna later this afternoon, have 7 KIAs to pick up."[20]

ANOTHER MEDAL OF HONOR—THE TWENTY-FIRST—WAS earned on May 29 during the sixth day of the breakout. Twenty-four-year-old Captain William W. Galt (1st Battalion, 168th Infantry Regiment, 34th Division) had seen much combat in his sixteen months overseas—Kasserine Pass, the drive across Algeria and Tunisia, the push from Salerno, the river assault on the Volturno (where he earned the Silver Star), the battle for Monte Cassino, and now Anzio. Along the way, he collected three Purple Hearts, but his luck was about to run out.

After being hospitalized again (this time for exhaustion), Galt rejoined his unit just before the breakout but was reassigned to be S-3 (operations officer) of the 1st Battalion. As a staff officer, he did not have to participate in combat again, but, true to his nature, he volunteered to lead an attack against stubborn defenders holding Villa Crocetta, a town that Robert Wallworth (Company A, 168th Infantry Regiment) described as being "the strongest point in the whole German line before

Rome. The Villa was on top of a hill and was surrounded with trenches and strong points. . . . It was manned by a paratroop regiment of the German 4th Parachute Division." During the assault, Wallworth said a sniper's round just missed his head. "We hit the ground and just at that time one of our M-10 Tank Destroyers opened up on the sniper with his 76mm gun. I can tell you that being in front of a high-velocity tank gun when it fires is not the place to be. The shock wave from that shell just over our heads lifted us off the ground and temporarily deafened us. We got away from there but the sniper was still firing at us."[21]

With Company G pinned down by heavy enemy fire, Captain Galt ordered another tank destroyer to move up and help the company. The driver refused until Galt jumped onto the M-10, pointed his pistol into the open turret, and said, "You are either going to die here or die up there." With that persuasive incentive, the driver began moving forward with infantrymen following in the vehicle's wake. Despite a flurry of bullets ricocheting off the TD's armored hull, Galt manned the M-10's machine gun, killing forty of the enemy and was flinging grenades at Germans when the tank destroyer was hit by an 88mm shell, killing Galt instantly.

Without Galt, Company G's thrust lost its momentum and had to pull back; Galt's body was found by the Germans and buried at Villa Crocetta. It was recovered in September by the Americans, reburied at Nettuno, and returned to his hometown of Great Falls, Montana, in 1947. His posthumous Medal of Honor was presented to his family.[*22]

FARTHER TO THE EAST, AS O'Daniel's 3rd Division reached the high ground near Valmontone, one officer, Lieutenant Robert Tubb (15th Infantry Regiment), looked back toward the shoreline with amazement. "I didn't appreciate the terrible position that the 3rd Division occupied at Anzio until after the breakout . . . when I could look back from the high ground and see how the German artillery could cover every inch of the terrain from there to the sea."[23]

---

* The Captain John E. Moran and Captain William Wylie Galt Armed Forces Reserve Center in Great Falls is named in his honor.

Early on the morning of May 29, near Campoleone, the 1st Armored Division was moving northward, the huge engines of the Shermans roaring and growling like enraged dinosaurs, when the armored formation came under unusually heavy and accurate artillery fire. Taking shelter in the deep gulches and draws of the area, the tankers and accompanying infantrymen thought they were safe for the moment, but a shell exploded on the reverse slope of a deep gully, toppling tons of dirt and rocks onto the men below, burying many alive.

Wearily, the men of the 45th Division's 157th Regiment, who had spent six days in almost constant combat, trudged into Campoleone, found it deserted, and collapsed onto whatever bed or sofa, no matter how dirty, they came across. Their places on the front lines were taken, for the time being, by the 6th Armored Infantry Regiment and the British troops who had overrun and passed through Aprilia.[24]

IT IS BY NO MEANS unheard of for higher-ranking officers to be killed or wounded while leading their troops in combat. Such a fate befell Lieutenant Colonel Edward "Eddie" Weber, West Point class of 1934 and commanding officer of the 3rd Battalion, 179th Infantry Regiment, 45th Division, who was leading his men in the battle for the small town of Casalpozzo, southwest of Velletri.

An account of the battle, which began on May 29, reads, "The battle for Casalpozzo was one of the most terrific actions of the entire Italian Campaign the 179th Infantry Regiment had experienced. Both sides threw in everything they had and the losses were the heaviest ever experienced." Battalion headquarters had lost communication with Company L, which was under heavy fire, so Weber went forward to see what help he could render. While calling in an artillery strike on suspected enemy positions, Weber's forward command post was obliterated by enemy shells; his mangled body was not found until June 3. He received the Silver Star, posthumously.

Two days before he was killed, Weber had written home:

Reconnoitered forward yesterday and looked back on the positions we held for four months, boy oh boy! Jerry sure had the advantage of roads and fields of fire, thousands of yards of level ground we had to come over and dig them out of the hills, they just hang on until the last moment; the boys did a swell job. This will really amount to a great victory for our forces. It is almost inconceivable how they were entrenched and what beautiful positions they had. Day after tomorrow I ought to be where we can see Rome.

He never got to see Rome. Weber's commanding officer, Colonel Harold A. Meyer, wrote to Weber's parents:

I have in front of me the official award of the Silver Star (Posthumously) for Gallantry and Leadership in action, of Eddie. I was with him several hours of the morning before he moved out personally to insure the success of a mission that had to succeed. Need I say more, for one of my sweetest friends, one of West Point's grandest soldiers, put his life on the line for Duty, Honor, Country. . . .

The first person I saw at Anzio was Eddie. My last act at Anzio was to pay homage at his grave. I'll write Tammy [Weber's widow] now, but as you know even a soldier must cry sometimes. I loved your son, too.[25]

PAUL BROWN, WHOSE PLANS FOR going home were put on temporary hold because of Buffalo, wrote in his diary on May 29: "All the towns are sure knocked down. The dead are all along the highway. I counted at least 30 enemy tanks, that many or more trucks, several were in good condition. Sure got dusty. Will probably go up again. Yet I have no business taking such chances."

The next day, Brown wrote, "Bombers came over last night again. No damage. Our Regt. has several dead. Sgt. Harbferson finally got it after being wounded 3 times. Velletri is a tough place. 180th lost most of their 3rd Bn. Just heard I will be leaving next Monday."[26]

MAY 31 WAS ANOTHER DAY of savage, unrelenting combat as the Allied beachhead forces made their final lunge toward Rome through the crumbling line of German resistance. The 135th Regiment of the 34th Division had been given orders to take Lanuvio—known as Lanuvium in Roman times, and surrounded by an ancient wall—on a hilltop four and a half miles west of Velletri and nineteen miles southeast of Rome.

The assault ran into trouble almost immediately after it was launched. The 135th's 3rd Battalion managed to advance 800 yards before being forced to halt by intense artillery, mortar, and machine-gun fire. At 7:00 P.M., while the battalion was pulling back from its untenable position, it was attacked by waves of infantry and panzers. The Americans, backed by thirteen artillery battalions, yielded not a foot of ground. More than 400 Germans were killed at a cost to the 3rd Battalion of 264 killed and wounded.[27]

Hundreds, even thousands, of individual acts of astounding heroism—deeds that will go forever unknown—were performed that day. In just one, Private Furman L. Smith (Company L, 135th Infantry Regiment, 34th Division) acted "above and beyond the call of duty"—but at the cost of his life.

Smith, who had just turned nineteen, and his unit were attacking a German strongpoint at Lanuvio that was holding up their advance toward Rome. Suddenly, a force of about 80 Germans counterattacked and inflicted numerous casualties on the Americans. Disregarding his own safety, Private Smith refused to pull back when ordered to do so, choosing instead to remain at his post and defend two wounded men lying at his feet. Dragging them to the shelter of a shell crater, Smith alone then held off several attempts by the enemy to overrun his position.

Having grown up as a hunter in rural South Carolina, he was a crack shot with an M-1, once having remarked, "If I had a gun like this at home, there wouldn't be a rabbit alive in Pickens County." With considerable proficiency, Furman continued to pick off the enemy each time one of them showed himself. His battalion commander, Fillmore Means, later recalled, "[The Germans] seemed stunned, bewildered, unable to comprehend that a man from a nation they had been taught to believe soft and decadent could be so tough."

Inspired by Smith's heroics, Company L was able to reorganize and ready itself to come to his aid and regain the lost ground. But as his nephew Charles Taylor later noted, "For several glorious moments, Private Smith, a lone American doughboy, held these much vaunted members of the mighty Wehrmacht at bay. . . . The scene was incredible. In defiance of what should have been a hopeless defeat, the area in front of Furman's shell hole became littered with dead and writhing wounded. The determined Private Smith killed ten of the enemy outright and injured many more."

But a burst at point-blank range from a machine pistol put an end to Smith's valorous efforts. When his comrades retook the lost ground, they found Smith dead, his M-1 Garand rifle still in his hand, the stock pressed to his shoulder, as if ready to fire another shot. His nephew wrote, "The company, energized by his furious stand, was able to withstand the German attack."

"His courage was a tremendous inspiration to our company and enabled us to throw back the counterattack," said First Lieutenant William Pulliam. "His valor had rejuvenated the battle-weary soldiers. The men of the company told themselves that 'his death would not be in vain.' The end was inevitable, we all knew that, including Private Smith. But when those that were left of the Germans rushed our position, we beat them back. Next morning we attacked and destroyed the entire unit." For his courageous, and ultimately fatal, stand, Smith was awarded the Medal of Honor, posthumously.

The fight for Lanuvio proved to be the costliest for the 135th Infantry Regiment in terms of casualties; in the battle that would last four days, the 135th lost 476 men killed, wounded, or missing.[28]

THE DRIVE OUT OF THE beachhead was gaining steam, plunging forward, propelled by its own momentum. Besides enemy action, the heat of late May was also taking its toll. Medic "Doc Joe" Franklin (Company I, 157th) recalled, "A lot of guys were passing out from heat exhaustion, dead on their feet. War always seems to be one extreme or another— you're always either too hot or too cold, too wet or too dry, and you're always either too bored or too scared."[29]

ON MAY 31, CLARK HELD a briefing for the war correspondents. The five divisions in Truscott's VI Corps, he pointed out, were heading directly for Rome in a northwesterly direction, while the two and a half divisions of Keyes's II Corps were driving for Valmontone with the mission of cutting Highway 6 and trapping Vietinghoff's Tenth Army that was abandoning the Cassino front. He would note in his diary, "There is much pressure upon me, although it is not being applied directly, to have the Eighth Army in on the battle for Rome." He wanted the Americans to reach Rome first—before Operation Overlord was launched and overshadowed him and his Fifth Army.[30]

But Clark was running out of time if he wanted to capture Rome— and the headlines.

CHAPTER 20

"We entered Rome . . . amid cheers"
JUNE 1-8

A FTER THE ALLIES CRACKED THE Gustav Line on May 11, Major
General Geoffrey Keyes and his II US Corps, along with Oliver
Leese's Eighth British Army, began pouring into the Liri Valley, chasing
Vietinghoff's Tenth Army toward Rome. But while the success of Oper-
ation Diadem had made possible the success of Buffalo, Mark Clark was
of no mind to allow the British a share of the spoils.

To prevent the British from getting to Rome first, Clark ordered
Truscott to direct Walker's 36th Infantry Division to skirt the fighting
at Lanuvio, attacking instead Velletri—situated in a saddle between the
Alban Hills and the Lepini Mountains. Walker told Truscott that a reconnaissance patrol had found a way to attack Velletri and catch the
Germans holding the town by surprise. It entailed sending two regiments around the west end of Velletri, making a night climb up Monte
Artemisio (a four-mile ridge that loomed 3,000 feet above the town),
and then coming down and attacking from the eastern side. Truscott
liked the plan and gave Walker permission to implement it.[1]

The division's historian wrote that Velletri was the "key bastion in
the German line defending Rome, another cork in another bottle. The
36th pulled the cork." While the 141st Regiment took the town's defenders under fire, the 142nd and the 143rd Regiments took to the densely
wooded hills on the left flank and climbed the mountain. Caught by

surprise from the troops on the mountain above and behind them, the Germans abandoned Velletri.[2]

Colonel Herbert E. MacCombie, the 36th's head chaplain, recalled, "We all had great confidence in General Walker. Whatever he planned and wherever he led, we would be glad to follow. Velletri was not easy, but it held a real chance for victory." MacCombie noted that, during the fight for the town, he was targeted by a sniper. "He missed me, and two of our men went after him. They brought him in minus his rifle and his helmet. He called out, '*Kamerad*.' I did not feel very much like a comrade just then." The chaplain then survived a German artillery barrage. "Four shells landed in the adjacent ravine. . . . Evidently the Germans were so sure of themselves, they didn't adjust their fire to make allowance for any errors. Thanks to their assurance, none of our men were injured."[3]

Walker had personally led the 36th's attack on Velletri and nearly paid for his leadership with his life. On June 1, an American M-10 tank destroyer was chasing a German self-propelled 88mm gun up a mountain road when the German vehicle turned and fired. The shell missed the M-10 but killed Colonel Harold Reese, a member of the 36th's headquarters staff, and narrowly missed Walker.

It was shortly after 7:00 P.M. on June 1 when the Germans—two battalions from the Hermann Göring Parachute-Panzer Division—pulled out of Velletri and fled toward Rome, leaving the ruined town to the Texans. General Truscott pulled up in his jeep, and Walker greeted him with a smile. "You can go in now, General," he said. "The town is yours."[4]

WHILE THE 36TH DIVISION WAS battling for Velletri, farther to the west the 45th Infantry and 1st Armored Divisions were having difficulty near Campoleone. A number of American tanks—sixty-one Shermans and thirty-six Stuarts—had been knocked out since Operation Buffalo began, forcing Truscott to halt the attack in order to give Harmon the chance to pull back briefly to repair some of his tanks and bring up replacements before continuing the assault.[5]

With VI Corps struggling, Keyes and his II Corps were also running into resistance attacking toward Valmontone on Highway 6. A few elements of the Hermann Göring Parachute-Panzer Division were holding the town under strict orders from Kesselring to deny it to the Allies. If the Allies could be stopped at Valmontone, he believed, then perhaps Army Group C had a chance to be able to escape to Rome and form a new defensive line.

On June 2, while II Corps and Leese's Eighth Army were approaching Valmontone, the French Expeditionary Force slipped in front of the British—a clever bit of subterfuge concocted by Clark and the commander of the 112,000-man FEF, General Alphonse-Pierre Juin (who had opposed the American invasion of Algeria in November 1942) to deny the British an unfettered access to Rome. When a British advance unit approached a French column and demanded they get off they road, the French commander told them that his men would fire on the Brits if they attempted to pass![6]

Naturally, the situation did not please Alexander, who politely requested that Clark explain himself. Clark later wrote that he felt, "There is some inclination on the part of Alexander to commence alibiing for his Eighth Army. . . . Alexander is worried that I have sabotaged his directive to attack Valmontone. I have not done so. I am throwing everything I have into this battle, hoping to crack this key position which will make it necessary for Kesselring to withdraw both of his armies to the north of Rome."[7]

Meanwhile, Kesselring was battling with Mackensen, his Fourteenth Army commander, for the latter's failure to prevent VI Corps from breaking out of the beachhead area. Kesselring noted, "After many disagreeable interviews, the inability of the Fourteenth Army to close the gap led to a change of command. In fact, the gap, which at the beginning could have been closed by a single battalion, kept widening until 31 May, with the result that our flank was turned and the road to Rome finally opened to the enemy. It was a catastrophe that the divisions which fought with such exemplary bravery on the right flank and in the centre had no equal partner on the left."

The "disagreeable interviews" to which Kesselring alluded resulted in Mackensen being relieved of his command; he would be replaced on June 4 by General of Armored Troops Joachim Lemelsen, who, with his long face and prominent nose, bore a striking resemblance to Mark Clark.[8]

ON JUNE 2 ANOTHER AMERICAN performed acts that would eventually earn for him the Medal of Honor. Near Lanuvio, the 100th Infantry Battalion, made up mostly of Japanese Americans from Hawaii and attached to the 34th Division, came under fire from several German machine-gun nests. Sergeant Yeiki Kobashigawa (Company B) was determined to eliminate the danger, so, along with one of his men, he advanced and destroyed one of the guns with a grenade, but the others turned their fire on him. Kobashigawa continued on, ignoring both crisscrossing enemy and friendly fire, until he had destroyed a second position. With his men now behind him, he managed to wipe out two other nests and capture a number of prisoners. He earned the Distinguished Service Cross for his actions, which was upgraded fifty-six years later to the Medal of Honor and awarded to him by President Bill Clinton.

Nearby, on that same day, Private Shinyei Nakamine, also of the 100th Battalion, performed a similar feat, single-handedly advancing toward three enemy machine-gun nests at nearby La Torreto and destroying two of them. As he crawled toward the third, then stood up to charge the gun, he was cut down in midstride. His posthumous DSC was also upgraded to the Medal of Honor in 2000.[9]

TRUSCOTT LEARNED THAT THE 85TH and 88th U.S. Infantry Divisions, part of Keyes's II Corps, were rapidly advancing up Highway 6 from Cassino. While this might ordinarily have been good news, Truscott heard a rumor that Clark planned to join II Corps as it became the first Allied unit to enter Rome—a rumor that rankled the VI Corps commander. His corps had not suffered and bled for the past four months to allow another corps, even if it was American, the honor of being first into Rome. He put the spurs to his men.

"Our assault in the morning encountered stubborn German rearguard action protecting their flight north," said Truscott. "While the 34th and 45th Infantry Divisions cleared out the last resistance around Lanuvio, Genzano, and Albano . . . Harmon's tanks were driving down Highway 7 and a parallel road to the south, all headed for Rome."[10]

Harmon, too, was incensed when he learned that one of Colonel Hamilton Howze's tank battalions from the 1st Armored Division had been transferred by Keyes to the II Corps' 88th Infantry Division. Having none of it, Harmon appealed to Howze's friendship and sense of loyalty to disregard the order and keep his task force within 1st Armored for the dash to the finish line. Howze agreed. Even though ambushes knocked out an occasional M-4 Sherman or M-5 Stuart, Task Force Howze continued barreling ahead, determined to allow nothing to stop it.

The race to Rome now became a contest between two VI Corps units—Walker's infantrymen and Harmon's tankers—until they ran into an unexpected obstacle moving along a parallel road: the 85th Infantry Division that Keyes had rushed forward in an effort to cut off the VI Corps' advance.

For his part, Keyes was just as determined that Truscott's VI Corps would not beat him to Rome. He organized a sixty-man patrol in eighteen jeeps, under the command of Captain Taylor Radcliffe, a member of the 1st SSF who had earlier been taken prisoner but escaped German captivity, and told them to go flat out for Rome. Keyes also sent a newspaper correspondent, a movie cameraman, and two still photographers with the patrol to record for posterity II Corps' triumphant arrival. The night of June 3 would find Radcliffe's exhausted patrol taking a brief rest within the Cinecittà movie studio's lot on Rome's southern fringes.[11]

From II Corps came a dark-horse entry in the race for Rome: the 88th Infantry Division. The 88th, which had first seen combat in March 1944 along the Gustav Line, was now galloping full speed for the Eternal City.[12] The gallop, however, almost ended the lives of Clark and Harmon. On June 3, while the men were poring over a map on the outskirts of Rome, a German machine gunner inside a stone outhouse opened up, barely missing both generals. "We threw ourselves flat on the ground," said Harmon. As the two generals lay there in the dust, a Sherman tank rumbled up the highway, and Harmon shouted and pointed to the outhouse. "The Sherman tank didn't bother with its guns. It just turned at right angles and charged across the field and butted squarely into the building. When the tank had finished, there was neither machine gun, outhouse, nor German. This was the ultimate anticlimax. The two of us, who had gone through so much together, were to be killed by fire from an Italian privy."[13]

IT WAS ALSO ON JUNE 3 that twenty-five-year-old Serjeant (British spelling) Maurice Albert Windham Rogers of the 2nd Battalion, Wiltshire Regiment (Duke of Edinburgh's), on VI Corps' left flank, became only the second British soldier during the Anzio campaign to earn the Victoria Cross. During the breakout, Rogers's battalion was ordered to attack a position held by the well-dug-in enemy but was quickly sent to ground. The Carrier Platoon of the leading company was then ordered to dismount from their tracked vehicles and advance on foot to knock out the resistance and capture the final objective. Moving forward under intense fire, the platoon sustained a number of casualties and, checked by the enemy's barbed-wire entanglements and the fire of seven machine guns firing at ranges of 50 to 100 yards, was forced to take cover some 70 yards short of their objective.

But Rogers refused to take cover. Advancing alone, he penetrated 30 yards inside the German defenses, drawing their fire and throwing the enemy into confusion. Inspired by his example, the platoon began to follow his assault. Although Serjeant Rogers was blown off his feet by a grenade and wounded in the leg, he refused to halt or even slow down his attack, running toward an enemy machine-gun position in an attempt to silence it with his Thompson sub-machine gun. The Germans opened up on him, killing him at point-blank range. But his undaunted determination, fearless devotion to duty, and superb courage helped his platoon seize their objective.[14]

Serjeant Rogers's heroics were certainly worthy of the Victoria Cross, but so were the actions of countless numbers of British soldiers who risked—and sometimes gave—their lives to save their mates, their units, and the beachhead itself.

THE GERMAN DEFENSES ALONG WHAT was called the Caesar Line, which ran from Ostia on the west coast through Valmontone to Pescara on the Adriatic, began buckling and cracking, tottering like a dam about to burst, unable to withstand the immense pressure being hurled against it. Rome was not yet in American hands, nor had the Germans abandoned hope that they still might stop the Allies, but it would take considerable effort on the part of the Americans—and the British, too—to reach Rome. Sadly, many of the troops who had striven so mightily to march triumphantly through the ancient gates and down the timeworn marble streets like a conquering legion would not live to take part in that parade. Some 4,000 American casualties had already been incurred during the breakout.[15]

Two of them, Private Herbert F. Christian and Private Elden H. Johnson (both of Company H, 15th Infantry Regiment, 3rd Division) would earn Medals of Honor but would lose their lives in the process. While on a night patrol near Valmontone at 1:00 A.M. on June 3, the thirty-one-year-old Christian, from Steubenville, Ohio, and Johnson, twenty-three, from East Weymouth, Massachusetts, were hit when the patrol was ambushed and their patrol leader was killed. Christian had his left leg torn off by a 20mm antitank round, while Johnson went down with machine-gun bullets in his stomach. Both Christian and Johnson, although in great pain and probably realizing they were mortally wounded, remained at their positions and kept up a continuous fire to beat back the enemy and allow eleven survivors of the patrol to withdraw.[16]

ON JUNE 3, HITLER DID something completely out of character; the man who became apoplectic whenever a field commander intentionally gave up ground reluctantly allowed Kesselring to withdraw his troops from Rome and retreat to the north. Although Rome was now declared an "open city"—meaning that it would not be defended—it did not mean the Germans would roll out the red carpet and retire quietly. Every road into the capital was manned by a rear guard whose mission it was to slow the Allies' entry into the city for as long as possible in order to allow the rest of the German units to fall back and establish new blocking positions.[17]

To prepare the citizens of Rome for the imminent liberation of their city, Field Marshal Alexander broadcast the following radio message, translated into Italian: "The Allied armies are approaching Rome. The liberation of the Eternal City is at hand." He then cautioned the citizens to be watchful and to do everything possible to speed the Allies' entry into the city while also doing whatever they could to hinder any German plans for destruction, specifically advising them to hide food from the Germans; protect bridges, telephone and telegraph lines, railways, trains, and buses; and notify Allied forces of any suspected demolition devices or booby traps. "Citizens of Rome, this is not the time for demonstrations. Do what we tell you and continue with your work. Rome is yours. Your job is to save the city. Ours is the destruction of the enemy."[18]

FROM THE SOUTH, DASHING UP Highways 6 and 7, the phalanx of American II and VI Corps units charged onward, rolling past burned German vehicles and sprawled German corpses and long lines of Italian refugees carrying bundles or pulling carts filled with their belongings. One historian wrote, "War had become a macabre game, the more exciting for the lack of rules, control, or firm opposition. A refugee child kicked viciously at a German corpse while his mother pulled off the dead man's boots. A reporter, Eric Sevareid, of the Columbia Broadcasting system, ran blindly down the road, his eyes watering, his nostrils inflamed, his throat clogged with vomit from the terrible stench of human flesh decomposing under the hot summer sun." In a very odd way, it smelled like victory.

Rushing toward Rome—practically elbowing each other out of the way—were a number of units: Captain Taylor Radcliffe's sixty-man patrol, 1st Armored's Task Force Howze, elements of O'Daniel's 3rd Division, parts of the 1st Special Service Force, and the 88th Infantry Division. Hard on their heels were the 34th, 36th, 45th, and 85th U.S. Infantry Divisions. Eating the dust of the Americans were the British, whom Clark had deliberately not invited to the party and was doing everything within his power to obstruct.

Before dawn on June 4, Radcliffe and his patrol that had spent the night at the Cinecittà film studio located along the Via Tuscolana, just six miles from the center of Rome, was awakened by the news that another American column was roaring up the road; Radcliffe ordered his men to mount up and ride. Correctly assuming that the departing Germans had placed demolition charges on an overpass his patrol needed to use to get into the city, Radcliffe had combat engineers with his group disable the munitions; the patrol roared ahead toward the Porta San Giovanni, one of Rome's ancient gates through the Aurelian Wall, near the Church of Saint John in Chains. At 6:00 A.M., just before entering, the patrol was hit by a blast of small-arms fire; so heavy was the fire that the patrol was pinned down for much of the day.

Twenty-five minutes later, another patrol, this one part of Task Force Howze, reached the railroad yards inside Rome, but it, too, was forced to halt due to enemy fire. This was followed by more probes by recon units from the 3rd and 88th Infantry Divisions.[19] The Germans were still doing their best to slow down the advance, but it was futile; a bazooka-wielding 88th Division private, Asa Farmer, knocked out seven German vehicles—a light tank, two halftracks, and four *Kubelwagen* (Germany's answer to the jeep)—at a hastily built roadblock and took sixty prisoners. Others from the 88th also accounted for their share of dead, wounded, and captured enemy soldiers.[20]

AT 8:00 A.M. ON JUNE 4, the culmination of nine months of savage combat that had been raging ever since the British and Americans had landed in southern Italy was finally realized. There has always been contention about exactly which person or unit was first into the city and deserves the title of "the Liberator of Rome." There were five candidates—Captain Radcliffe of the 1st SSF; an element of Task Force Howze; a recon patrol led by First Lieutenant Frank Greenlee of the 3rd Recon Troop, 3rd Infantry Division; the 88th Recon Troop of the 88th Infantry Division; and a Frenchman from the French Expeditionary Force, Captain Pierre Planès.[21]

In his memoirs, Churchill gave credit to the 88th, writing that "at 7:15 PM [*sic*] [A.M.] on June 4 the head of their 88th Division entered the Piazza Venezia, in the heart of the capital."[22] The historian of the 88th Division concurred, "At 0715 on 4 June, transmissions from the 3rd Platoon of the 88th Reconnaissance Troop crackled with the news: the 88th Infantry Division was into Rome—and first!"[23]

Brigadier General Robert T. Frederick, commanding the 1st Special Service Force, was making his way through Rome's maze of streets when shots rang out. One of his men fell dead, and Frederick was grazed by a bullet—his ninth wound of the war. Just before a full-scale firefight broke out, the men doing the shooting showed themselves—they were members of the 88th Infantry Division who had mistaken Frederick's party for Germans. "Look what you did to us," Frederick angrily yelled at the officer in charge of the 88th party. "Aren't there enough Krauts around here to shoot at?"[24]

As morning turned to afternoon, the roads leading into Rome from the south were clogged with a monumental olive-drab traffic jam—tanks, jeeps, trucks, antitank vehicles, towed artillery pieces, ambulances, weapons carriers, the full gamut of American military vehicles. But no British vehicles. The Romans, weary of war, of being under German occupation, and grateful that the liberation had finally come, were out in such force as had not been seen since the triumphs of the Roman legions returning to the capital two millennia earlier—waving, cheering, applauding, throwing flowers, offering bottles of vino to the troops marching through.

All across the city church bells were ringing in a cacophony of joy. The GIs riding in and on the vehicles responded with waves, big smiles, and "V for Victory" hand gestures; Alexander's entreaties to not obstruct the passage of Allied troops had gone unheeded. Fred Walker, the 36th Infantry Division's commander, was furious; he was trying to pursue the Germans as they fled the city, but the enthusiastic Romans kept getting in his division's way. They swarmed over, around, and on top of his vehicles, offering gifts and kisses, completely halting their progress.[25]

"We found the streets filled with people in holiday mood," Lucian Truscott wrote, "and flags were breaking out of windows all along the streets. Our jeep, with siren screaming, was slowed to a snail's pace but, with an Italian boy riding the hood to show us the way, we managed to press through crowds tossing flowers, offering glasses and bottles of wine, fruit, bread, and embraces, to arrive at Capitoline Hill." Truscott was soon joined by Clark, and the two men stood on the same balcony above the Piazza Venezia, in front of the huge white-marble monument to King Victor Emmanuel, where Mussolini used to posture before adoring crowds. The crowds now rushed into the square and cheered two of the Americans who had helped to defeat Mussolini.[26]

Corporal John E. Gallagher (Company A, 84th Chemical Mortar Battalion) never forgot his unit's entry into Rome: "What a reception; people throwing flowers and offering drinks, and young girls in light-colored dresses. Though they weren't American beauties, they were indeed a welcome change from farm girls and no girls at all. A soldier without flowers stuck all over him, or a jeep without two or three excited civilians, looked out of place."[27]

Few of the units lingered long in Rome; the fleeing enemy needed to be chased down. "We didn't get a chance to stop in Rome," lamented Robert Wallworth (34th Division). His division's mission was to stay hot on the heels of the retreating Germans to prevent them from establishing any major defensive positions. Unfortunately, the Germans already had prepared positions to fall back to. The 34th continued through Rome until the Red Bulls ran into a well-established roadblock, manned by determined German soldiers, some four miles north of the city, that took quite some time to destroy.

As Wallworth's unit reached the roadblock, they received a new man—from the U.S. Army Air Force. Wallworth said, "The Army was exchanging a few men on a temporary basis between the Army ground forces and those in the Air Force. This was so the different outfits would have a feeling how the other organizations operated. These men were not supposed to be put into combat positions. Unfortunately, this airman got on the wrong truck and ended up with our company, which was trying to catch up with the retreating German divisions."

Then all hell broke loose. Snipers, machine-gun fire, and heavy artillery hit the unit and stalled the advance for several hours before the rearguard troops could be eliminated by American artillery. "When it was all over," Wallworth said, "the airman, who had been right in the middle of it, told us this was much worse than anything that he experienced on bombing raids. He was quite shook up after seeing a dead German with his head blown off. Just as soon as he could catch a ride, he left for a location more to the rear. That night we took the ridge that dominated the area."[28]

Although the enemy had put up some resistance, had destroyed a few bridges, laid mines, set up roadblocks, and sniped at the Americans, most of the Germans retreating to the north had obeyed Kesselring's order declaring Rome an "open city," thus sparing it from the hard fighting and destruction that had left so many other beautiful European cities—such as Leningrad, Stalingrad, and Warsaw—totally in ruins.

In his memoirs, General Siegfried Westphal, somewhat disingenuously, said that Kesselring did much to refrain from imposing onerous conditions upon the Romans as his armies abandoned the city: "Each day he spent hours in seeing how the needs of the civilians could be satisfied. . . . Moreover, Kesselring made it a point of pride that the Eternal City should be spared. . . . This concern for the city was why the Field-Marshal omitted to prepare any obstruction to the enemy along the Tiber when Rome was relinquished in June 1944, and forbade the destruction of any bridges in Rome because the gas and water mains were suspended from them. Such consideration in the heat of war may well be accounted a rarity. Kesselring helped the Italians whenever he could."[29]

Be that as it may, the retreating Germans decided to do everything possible to slow the Allies' pursuit of them north of Rome, but it was like trying to stop an onrushing train with one's bare hands; the pursuit came to a halt when the exhausted Allies wore themselves out in the heat of mid-June near Chiusi, 110 miles north of Rome. With German lines on the Russian Front crumbling, the Hermann Göring Division was extracted from Italy and, along with other units from other theaters, rushed to the Eastern Front in a desperate attempt to bolster the line against the Soviets.[30]

MARK CLARK SAW HIMSELF AS the liberator of Rome, the conquering hero. Despite the British vying for the honor, it was the American divisions of his Fifth Army that had entered the city first. The next day, after the last of the snipers had been cleared out, Clark, accompanied by Truscott, Keyes, and Frederick, returned to the teeming streets of the ancient city to bask in the sunlight and the warm applause of the throngs who packed the sidewalks. Clark and his entourage made their way through the still surging, cheering crowds to Rome's city hall on Capitoline Hill, where he, Keyes, and Truscott met with the leaders of the Resistance, who officially turned over the city to him.

Later that day, June 5, the first British elements—a flying column of South African tanks from Leese's Eighth Army, accompanied by a battalion of Grenadier Guards—reached the city, understandably dismayed at having come in second in the race for Rome. After all, they had suffered equally with their American cousins for the past eight months, but Clark had done everything except bomb and strafe the British to keep them from sharing in the glory.[31] These also included some of Truscott's VI

Corps British units. For example, although Penney's 1st British Infantry Division, along with Gregson-Ellis's 5th, had taken part in the breakout, they were ordered to bypass Rome and continue on to Italy's northern Apennine Mountains without being able to enjoy the liberation of Rome for which they had striven so many months.[32]

Fred Mason (2nd North Staffs) said, "The 2nd North Staffs took part in the breakout, but unfortunately I had contracted malaria and finished the war in hospital. Didn't get to Rome. I never caught up with my unit again."[33]

Medic Robert "Doc Joe" Franklin recalled that his division, the 45th,

didn't parade through Rome; we chased the Germans north around it. They were backtracking so fast we couldn't catch them; we bivouacked in a field not too far north of the city. From this bivouac area we were allowed to visit Rome. A truck from the regiment took a load of us in one day. Because of the lingering effects of trench foot, I spent most of the day hobbling around the city—Hadrian's Tomb, an ancient temple, the Coliseum, the Forum, and the Catacombs—everything was open to us. . . . At noon Scottish Highlanders, their kilts swaying, marched around the huge plaza in front of Saint Peter's Basilica playing bagpipes. Never before had I enjoyed bagpipe music, but I've loved it ever since.[34]

James Bird (160th Field Artillery Battalion, 45th Division) recalled:

I hitched a ride on a donkey cart into Rome and was left off at the Italian War Memorial and gawked at it for a few minutes. It was a happy moment, totally unreal. The sun was shining, the people were cheering. Forgotten for the moment were all the months of hardship leading up to this moment. Of course, we had many more months of hard fighting ahead of us, but it was a moment to savor. Then I headed off to St. Peter's Cathedral. As I was walking around St. Peter's, a priest beckoned to me and several other GIs and we went into a small alcove. A few minutes later a jeep stopped nearby and we were herded over to it and an old man stood up. It was Pope Pius XII, who spoke to us. I don't remember a word he said or if it was even in English.

Bird reflected, "Mark Clark's vanity was costly. Instead of shutting off all avenues of retreat for the Germans, he wanted to be regarded and photographed as the 'liberator' of Rome. Consequently, many German soldiers escaped north to fight us again. A short time later, MPs [military police] were gathering all 45th Infantry Division people and sending us back to our units because we were moving south [to Naples] to prepare for the invasion of southern France [Operation Dragoon]."[35]

Sergeant Milton Orshefsky (Company C, 84th Chemical Mortar Battalion) recalled the relief the men in his unit felt: "Rome, the men soon discovered, was worth the fighting for. This was the first real rest they had had since landing in Italy, and it was a good one. Garrison duties were kept to a minimum; passes to Rome given regularly and freely, including a nightly movie truck to the Red Cross theater, Sunday church services, and separate trips to St. Peter's. Two company supper dances went off happily without incident."[36]

Another member of the battalion, Corporal Philip W. Smith, recounted, "Civilization was a strange, almost forgotten sight after coming off the dusty, battle-raked roads and fields that made up our environment for the past four months."[37]

Lieutenant Al Kincer (Company B, 48th Battalion, 1108th Engineer Combat Regiment) recalled:

We entered Rome . . . amid cheers, kisses, and a shower of flowers. We were bivouacked in a schoolyard that was surrounded by a tile fence. My CP was in a downstairs room. A balcony jutted out over the schoolyard from an upstairs room. The men were gathered below and were waiting with baited breath for a speech from their "beloved leader." I told them of the beautiful women of Rome, how good they smelled and what nice clothes they wore but that the risk of disease was there, just as with the urchins of Naples. I reiterated that anyone that got VD would be broken to private.[38]

The soldiers had also been warned by chaplains and unit doctors about the dangers of venereal disease, but their lectures went mostly disregarded. "We were there to have a good time and to celebrate our capture of Rome," said one liberator. "We let our hair down and went all out. The Italian girls were happy to ease our 'battle fatigue.' Hell, we might get killed the next day, so why worry about the clap?"[39]

FOLLOWING THE TROOPS INTO ROME a few days later was a contingent of medical personnel, nurse Avis Dagit (56th Evac Hospital) and fellow nurse Mary DeLaHunt among them. "Pope Pius XII scheduled an audience for the troops almost daily," Dagit said.

> The prospect of seeing the Pope thrilled me as much as it did Mary. I found a uniform without too many wrinkles and buffed the dust from my shoes. Gathering all our rosaries and souvenir religious articles, we set out for the city. The doors to the Sistine Chapel were not open when we arrived and hundreds of soldiers pressed against the doors.
>
> "There are two nurses here. Let them through," someone shouted. The crowd pushed us to the head of the line. The doors opened and the crush of the people continued to propel us forward. I found myself on the stage with Mary and five high-ranking officers. My heart raced, and I thought, *What am I doing here? I'm not Catholic. Will the Pope be able to tell?* The door near the back of the chapel opened and the Pope appeared.

Borne in a white canopy-covered carriage on the shoulders of the Vatican's Swiss Guards, the pontiff was brought forward and stopped in front of Dagit and her friend. In three languages he spoke: "'Please raise your articles for blessing.' He gave the blessing while everyone raised hands full of rosaries, medals, and crucifixes. Mary knelt and kissed his ring while I stood a few feet away." When the audience ended after five or six minutes, the pope left the chapel. "I felt equally blessed with everyone else present," Dagit said.[40]

On June 8, three days after he had entered Rome, Clark would also have a brief audience with Pope Pius XII. By that time, however, Italy was already old news; what the world wanted to hear about was the new operation—Overlord—that was sweeping inland from the northern coast of France, a region called Normandy, carrying with it the promise of early victory over Nazi Germany.[41]

ALTHOUGH ROME WAS AT LAST in Allied hands, the war in Italy was far from over (in fact, it would go on for another eleven months), but what had once been one of the three major Axis capitals had finally fallen.

On June 5, beneath a headline that stretched across all eight columns of the front page, the *New York Times* proclaimed, "Rome Captured Intact by the 5th Army After Fierce Battle Through Suburbs; Nazis Move Northwest; Air War Rages." The unnamed reporter wrote, "The Fifth Army captured Rome tonight, liberating for the first time a German-enslaved European capital. German rear guards were fleeing in disorganized retreat to the northwest. . . . A force from the old Anzio beachhead completed the mopping up of German forces at 9:15 PM by knocking out an enemy scout car in front of the Bank of Italy in the shadow of Trajan's Column."[42]

Another article in the same issue noted, "What Hannibal did not dare to do, the Allies' generals accomplished, but at such a cost in blood, matériel and time that it will probably never again be attempted."[43]

The British Broadcasting Corporation also hailed the event:

Early this morning it was announced the German troops had been ordered to withdraw. Rome is the first of the three Axis powers' capitals to be taken and its recapture will be seen as a significant victory for the Allies and the American commanding officer who led the final offensive, Lieutenant General Mark Clark.

In Rome itself, the people have been celebrating. Shops have closed and huge crowds have taken to the streets, cheering, waving, and hurling bunches of flowers at the passing army vehicles. First reports from the city say it has been left largely undamaged by the occupying German forces.

The Pope appeared on the balcony of St. Peter's this evening and addressed the thousands of Italians who had gathered in the square. He said, "In recent days we trembled for the fate of the city. Today we rejoiced because, thanks to the joint goodwill of both sides, Rome has been saved from the horrors of war."[44]

President Franklin Roosevelt, too, happily told reporters, "Rome fell to American and Allied troops. The first of the Axis capitals is now in our hands. One up and two to go!" And *Life* magazine reported: "In twenty-three days US, British, Dominion, and French troops had smashed seventy-five miles from the Gustav Line to the Tiber. They broke eighteen or nineteen German divisions, drove them out of Rome before they could seriously damage the city, were still driving them north this week as Rome's citizens kissed startled US soldiers and pelted their tanks with roses. Pope Pius gave thanks that Rome was spared destruction. The king turned over his authority to son Umberto. Partisans scrawled 'Death to Traitors' on the walls."[45]

THE NUTI FAMILY RETURNED FROM Naples to what was left of Aprilia on June 7. Pasqualino had vivid memories of seeing his shattered town for the first time since evacuating it in January:

> Papa accompanied us to where was our house was, or rather what was left. "See, that was our home," said my father. In fact, the adjacent building had been hit by a bomb, which had opened a hole right in our apartment, leaving standing only the wall of the room with about half of the floor, on which a toilet was suspended. . . . The only area that could be considered a living area was the cellar, which was all that was left. The cellar became the room of my parents and Franco, while I was placed in the adjacent corridor, separated from the "room" with a partition made from a pile of firewood."

As boys often are, Pasqualino was fascinated by the detritus of war. He dug through the rubble of his home in search of anything that might bring back memories. "By dint of digging, my hands were skinned, but my effort was rewarded: I retrieved various documents, old photos, books, some pieces of tattered washing, and objects of all kinds, all in poor condition but certainly useful for our recovery." He also began exploring the neighborhood—the church that was in ruins and the two towers at the Piazza Roma that had been reduced to stumps; a German Tiger tank lay buried in the rubble. "Everything was completely destroyed," he recalled. He also climbed over the piles of broken timbers and masonry at the market and saw some wooden boxes. When he went to investigate, a man stopped him. "*Non toccare quella*

roba—sono mine!" ("Do not touch that stuff—they are mines!") Pasqualino backed off.

One day Pasqualino and his friends paid a visit to a battery of
small-caliber German artillery pieces that sat abandoned in a field on the
outskirts of town and saw some unfired shells stacked nearby. "Seeing
the guns with their ammunition," he said, "I took a shell and inserted it
into the cannon." After closing the gun's breech, he decided not to fire it;
it was time to go home. After returning to his basement room, he heard a
loud explosion; the gun had been fired by a friend, the shell exploding in
the center of a crossroads along the Via Nettunese. "Fortunately, no one
was passing at that moment," Pasqualino said. "Evidently my friend had
been curious and had completed the work I had started."

The youngster also discovered the gruesome side of war. One day,
while playing soccer in the rubble-strewn street with a ball made of rags,
the ball fell into an open manhole. "There was a dispute over who should
go down to retrieve the ball; I then said I would go first. There were some
steps of iron, but the first step gave way and I fell about three meters and
found myself almost in the arms of a dead American soldier; the smell
was terrible. With this vision in mind, I catapulted out of the manhole."

On another occasion, Pasqualino wandered the now-silent battlefields ringing the town—a very dangerous thing to do because the extensive minefields had not yet been cleared. Dead bodies also still littered
the landscape—bodies which possessed a morbid fascination for him.
He wanted to dig into the backpacks strapped to many of the bodies but
was dissuaded from doing so when he was told that the backpacks were
full of hand grenades that might explode at any moment. Another sight
he never forgot was seeing a German helmet with the severed head of a
soldier placed in plain view on top of a pile of debris.

> Several times I worked hard to move it, but someone always put it back
> there. It was a horrible scene that still accompanies my memories of those
> difficult days. Another shocking image destined to remain indelible in
> my memory was that of, when walking through the rubble of the slaugh-
> terhouse, I saw some dismembered bodies of German soldiers. My eye
> dwelt in particular on one of these, almost completely covered by rubble

and in a state of decomposition. Under his half-open jacket I could see emerging from the stomach a seedling of tomatoes with some ripe fruits.[46]

FOLLOWING THE LOSS OF ROME, Kesselring flew back to Germany and met personally with Hitler to explain the Italian situation and request that he be allowed a free hand to conduct the campaign as he saw fit. Hitler, taking the other tack, said that no more ground should be given up, that every soldier in Italy must be ordered to fight to the last bullet. "The point is not whether my armies are fighting or running away," Kesselring brazenly told his Führer. "I can assure you that they will fight and die if I ask it of them. We are talking about something entirely different, a question much more vital: whether, after Stalingrad and Tunis, you can afford the loss of two more armies."

Kesselring went on to guarantee that, unless his hands were tied by Hitler or OKW to follow some self-destructive strategy, he could, through a skillful fighting withdrawal into the northern Apennines, appreciably delay the advance of the Allies up the peninsula and, by so doing, buy time that would allow the Führer to devise plans that might hold back the Americans, British, and Russians on the other war fronts. Hitler, evidently seeing the wisdom in that argument, relented and gave Kesselring the free hand he had requested.*[47]

---

* After Rome fell to the Allies, Kesselring continued to skillfully use his dwindling resources to frustrate Allied attempts to reach the Alps. On October 23, 1944, Kesselring's staff car collided with a towed artillery piece, and he was severely injured; he recovered and returned to command a much-depleted Army Group C in Italy that was scrambling to contain the surging Allied drive toward the Po River Valley. In March 1945 Hitler summoned him home and placed him in command of OB West, after Gerd von Rundstedt had been removed. Hitler regarded Kesselring so highly that on March 8, 1945, with his Third Reich on the verge of defeat, he named Kesselring commander in chief of all troops in the East and South and of the air force; Grand Admiral Karl Dönitz would be commander in chief of the North and of the navy. Despite his best efforts, Kesselring was unable to hold back the British and American forces that had penetrated Germany's western borders and were making mincemeat of the Wehrmacht; in early May 1945 he surrendered to the 101st Airborne Division near Salzburg, Austria. After Germany's defeat, the Allies charged him as a war criminal—specifically for his orders to ruthlessly put down partisan operations in Italy and for his alleged

THERE IS A FREQUENTLY TOLD story about the 1945 Memorial Day (it was still called Decoration Day then) ceremony held at the Sicily-Rome American Cemetery on May 30, 1945. The final resting place for thousands of soldiers still looked like an unfinished park, with little grass, few trees, and no permanent structures. Instead of marble headstones, there was a sea of white wooden crosses and Stars of David. Giving the main address was Lieutenant General Lucian K. Truscott, who had been promoted to Fifth Army commander, standing on a wooden podium.

In addition to the usual assemblage of dignitaries, honor guard, and military band, Bill Mauldin was in attendance, representing the *Stars and Stripes* newspaper. He wrote movingly of Truscott's speech, probably the most unusual ever given during a memorial ceremony:

> When Truscott spoke, he turned away from the visitors and addressed himself to the corpses he had commanded there. It was the most moving gesture I ever saw. It came from a hard-boiled old man who was incapable of planned dramatics. The general's remarks were brief and extemporaneous. He apologized to the dead men for their presence here. He said everybody tells leaders it is not their fault that men get killed in war, but that every leader knows in his heart this is not altogether true. He said he hoped that anybody here through any mistake of his would forgive him, but he realized that was asking a hell of a lot under the circumstances. . . .
>
> Truscott said he would not speak of the glorious dead because he didn't see much glory in getting killed in your late teens or early twenties. He promised that if in the future he ran into anybody, especially old men, who thought that death in battle was glorious, he would straighten them out. He said he thought it was the least he could do.[48]

---

involvement in the Ardeatine Caves massacre in March 1944. He was found guilty and sentenced to death but, upon Churchill's surprising request for clemency, had his sentence changed to life in prison. Based on secret notes he had made while in prison, his autobiography, *The Memoirs of Field-Marshal Kesselring*, was published in 1953. He was released in 1952, ostensibly due to poor health resulting from his October 1944 automobile accident, and died in Bad Nauheim on July 16, 1960. Richard Raiber, *Anatomy of Perjury: Field Marshal Albert Kesselring, Via Rasella, and the Ginny Mission*.

IN HIS MEMOIRS, BRITISH PRIME Minister Winston Churchill reflected on the titanic battles that took place at Anzio: "Such is the story of the struggle at Anzio; a story of high opportunity and shattered hopes, of skillful inception on our part and swift recovery by the enemy, of valour shared by both." He also conceded that "the Anzio stroke made its full contribution towards the success of 'Overlord.'"[49]

Churchill, who was probably the most responsible for the launch of Operation Shingle, provided a fitting tribute to the combatants, both living and dead: "But fortune, hitherto baffling, rewarded the desperate valour of the British and American armies. . . . The fighting was intense, losses on both sides were heavy, but the deadly battle was won."[50]

Although Churchill was a master of the English language, perhaps a simple soldier, Private first class Robert Lynch (Company K, 15th Infantry Regiment, 3rd Infantry Division), summed up Anzio best. In a letter home after the battle, he wrote:

> It's funny—the Germans had so much going for them and we had so little, but still they couldn't conquer us. They sent tanks at us, and we had nothing to throw at them except artillery and guts. They fired point-blank at our foxholes, but it wasn't enough. They sent their men right into our ranks, but it still wasn't enough. They tossed their finest and best soldiers at us . . . but it wasn't enough. They couldn't lick us no matter how hard they tried because the American soldier is made of something down deep inside that can take anything the others throw at him and still come back for more.[51]

Epilogue

THE CAPTURE OF ROME, WHILE a glorious moment for all those who took part, was not the end of the war in Italy. The war moved northward, and the survivors of the battles moved with it, doomed to a Sisyphean existence until either the war was finished or they were, actors in a drama that seemed to have no final scene. The Germans in Italy honed their skills as masters of the fighting withdrawal and continued to stymie Allied efforts to reach the Alps. There would be fighting for nearly every mountain peak and mountain pass in the 340 miles between Rome and Lake Garda, fighting for the Gothic Line, fighting for the Po River, fighting for the cities of Bologna, Rimini, Verona, and many more.

Oddly, the taking of Rome on June 4, 1944, seemed anticlimactic—more like a prelude than a meaningful conclusion that should have been better savored, appreciated, and celebrated. The previous nine months of bloodletting, and the thousands of human beings left dead and wounded along the march to Rome, were quickly forgotten two days later as the bigger story—the long-awaited Normandy invasion—swept the Italian campaign from the news. It was now the turn of Operation Overlord and the battles across northern Europe to dominate the world's attention and give hope of final victory in Europe. From now on, the war grinding on in Italy would be a sideshow, a postscript, a footnote to history. It was as though someone had said to the Allied troops, who had suffered and struggled so long at Anzio and along the Gustav Line, "Thanks, but you've had your moment in the spotlight. Now get off the stage." Rarely would Italy make the front pages of the American and British newspapers again.

This diminished interest in the Italian campaign was a curious, if understandable, reaction—Italy had been too long, too difficult, too bloody. The Allies' bold drives across France, Belgium, and Holland were much more inspiring, much more exciting. Just as curious, the staunch defenses of Stalingrad and Leningrad are celebrated in Russia even today as great national victories, whereas the successful defense of Anzio and the ultimate breakout are still viewed by many as an Allied failure.

IN AUGUST 1944, OPERATION DRAGOON, the invasion of southern France, took place—and involved many of the same divisions that had spilled their blood in Italy. Transferred from Fifth Army (now under Truscott) to Alexander Patch's Seventh Army in France were the 3rd, 36th, and 45th U.S. Infantry Divisions, along with the 1st Special Service Force and the 442nd Regimental Combat Team. Remaining in Italy to slug it out for the duration of the war would be the 34th, 85th, and 88th U.S. Infantry Divisions, along with the 1st U.S. Armored Division. Three new American divisions—the 91st and all-black 92nd Infantry Divisions and the 10th Mountain Division—would arrive in Italy in June and August 1944 and January 1945, respectively. They would keep German forces tied down there, far from the other battlefields of the war, until the war in Italy ended with the capitulation of German forces on May 2, 1945. Six days later, with Hitler dead and the Third Reich in ruins, Nazi Germany would formally surrender to the Allies.[1]

Statistics vary, but official U.S. Army figures say that, during the battle of Anzio—from January 22 until the breakout that began on May 23, 1944—approximately 4,400 VI Corps soldiers (British and American) died, 18,000 were wounded, and 6,800 were taken prisoner (4,400 British and 2,400 Americans). In addition to the combat losses must be added more than 37,000 noncombat casualties (illness, accidents, self-inflicted wounds, and so on), of which some 26,000 were Americans. The Germans had similar numbers: Mackensen's Fourteenth Army lost approximately 5,500 killed and 17,500 wounded in action, with some 4,500 men taken prisoner.[2]

But whether they were German, British, or American, each casualty was someone's son, husband, father, brother, or nephew and was deeply mourned by his family. The nurses, too, killed during the attacks on the hospitals, had left loved ones behind who would forever treasure their memory and mourn their loss. Participants on both sides of this terrible war rewrote the definition of what *courage* and *valour* mean.

It is safe to say that everyone who survived Anzio came away scarred—either physically or emotionally or both; to not be affected in profound ways by the fighting, the fear, and the horror would be to deny one's humanness. After the war, many veterans refused to share their experiences with their families, keeping their experiences and emotions bottled up, as though they still felt the need to protect them from the war, just as they had gone off to war to protect the homeland. Only when they got together with other veterans would they dare to crack open the wall that they had built around themselves and speak of what they had gone through.

THE TWO MAIN ALLIED COMMANDERS—Alexander and Clark—escaped the stain of failure. Field Marshal Viscount Sir Harold Alexander, First Earl of Tunis, was promoted to commander in chief of all Allied forces in Italy in November 1944. After the war, he was appointed governor-general of Canada, a post he held for six years. Then, from 1952 to 1954, he was Britain's minister of defense in Winston Churchill's cabinet. He authored *The Alexander Memoirs, 1940–1945* and died on June 16, 1969, at age seventy-seven. His funeral was held at St. Georges Chapel, Windsor Castle, and he was buried on the grounds of his family's Hertfordshire estate.[3]

Lieutenant General Mark Clark, following Fifth Army's capture of Rome, was elevated to command Fifteenth Army Group in Italy upon Alexander's promotion in November 1944. Under Clark's leadership, the coalition forces pushed the Germans northward to the base of the Alps, where, on May 2, 1945, they surrendered. Clark then became commander of U.S. Occupation Forces and high commissioner in Austria.

Clark was sent to Tokyo in April 1952 to succeed Matthew B. Ridgway as UN commander in Korea and commander in chief of the U.S. Far East Command. He signed the Korean armistice on July 27, 1953, and retired

in October after thirty-six years in the army. The following spring he became president of the Citadel, the military college at Charleston, South
Carolina—a position he held until 1965. His memoir, *Calculated Risk*,
was published in 1950. He died on April 17, 1984, at age eighty-seven.[4]

ANZIO, NETTUNO, CISTERNA, APRILIA, AND all the other towns that had
occupied the world's attention for so long quickly faded from view—
except by the men who had fought there and the civilians who returned
to their shattered homes. It would take many years, but eventually
Pasqualino Nuti's hometown of Aprilia—as well as Anzio, Nettuno, Cisterna, Campoleone, Velletri, Valmontone, Lanuvio, and scores of other
Italian towns and villages over which the armies engaged in a death
struggle—would be rebuilt and most of the scars of war erased.

The cities that were flattened by the war have all undergone a rebirth. Anzio is thriving once again, and, except for a few small plaques
on buildings at the harbor, there is no sign of the battles that once swept
through there. Nettuno, too, has come back to life and appears to be
a bright, happy town. Even Aprilia, which had a prewar population of
2,000 before being completely destroyed, has more than 73,000 residents
today and a booming economy.

Unfortunately, this rebirth came at the expense of history. There is
apparently no battlefield preservation society in Italy, and many of the
places where—as the small vine-covered sign on the Overpass/Flyover
says—"thousands of men fought and died near here" have been allowed
to be overrun by shops, stores, housing developments, car dealerships,
and factories. The hallowed ground that was once soaked with the blood
of the fallen has been desecrated, and there are virtually no signs, memorials, or monuments to commemorate or recall the momentous events
that took place there from January to May 1944.[5]

SO WHAT IS THE LEGACY of Operation Shingle?

As a landing on a hostile shore, Shingle was a success. The invasion
completely surprised the Germans and was not defeated at the water's
edge, where amphibious invasions must be defeated. However, as far
as either swiftly capturing Rome or causing the Tenth German Army

holding the Gustav Line to panic and abandon its positions, it fell short of expectations.

Major General John Lucas was, in this author's view, unfairly blamed for the "failure" of Shingle. On paper, the plan sounded workable, a "school solution" that undoubtedly would have earned at least a B+ in a West Point or Sandhurst class on tactics. But assuming in advance how much ground one's own troops would seize—and how the enemy would react—and then actually seeing those assumptions work as envisioned are two very different things.

To be clear, Shingle was not Lucas's plan, but he was Shingle's sacrificial lamb. He had been excluded from top-level meetings where the operation had been discussed. His input and advice were not solicited. He was given ambiguous objectives. He exercised his right to "one last bleat," but no one paid any attention to his concerns. So he achieved Shingle's one unambiguous objective: he secured a beachhead.

John Lucas may have been cautious, but he was not exactly spurred on to greater aggressive action by his immediate superior, Mark Clark. "Don't stick your neck out, Johnny, as I did at Salerno" and "You can forget this goddam Rome business" were not exactly inspiring words designed to create a bull rush to Rome.

Could he have done more? Certainly. He could have probed farther and struck out for the Alban Hills, but without a clear-cut objective—and the sufficient resources with which to achieve the objective—Shingle was doomed to failure as an offensive operation. As General Ben Harrell, the former VI Corps Operations Officer (G-3), later reflected, "Had we gone into the Alban Hills, we could have gotten there, yes, but I think we would have been cut off. I think we would have lost the force. I don't see why people don't understand that."[6]

Shingle failed to live up to the hopes of its creators for one main reason: Albert Kesselring refused to follow the script that Clark, Alexander, and Churchill had written for him. Had the end run panicked him and caused him to abandon the Gustav Line, the Allies could have strolled leisurely into Rome with minimal casualties. As it was, Kesselring expertly set about constructing an iron wall around the beachhead and trapping the invasion force there for four months.

But Kesselring was also forced into making one big mistake: he tried to be aggressive and obey Hitler's order to drive the Allied invaders back into the sea. Had he chosen to disobey that directive (or gotten Hitler to rescind it), he could have acted as prudently as Lucas and simply kept the beachhead sealed off and used his artillery and limited air resources to pound the Allies and keep them locked in place. Such a defensive tactic would have spared the lives of thousands of German soldiers who were needlessly wasted by their commanders in futile, suicidal charges across open fields.

In the end, the Allies triumphed at Anzio because of the bravery and steadfastness the individual soldiers displayed over four months of being subjected to everything the Germans could throw at them: endless waves of infantry and panzer charges, artillery and aerial bombardment, flame-thrower attacks, unmanned glide bombs, miniature Goliath attacks—plus the atrocious weather conditions.

In several trips to the Anzio area, beginning in 1997, I never fail to come away with conflicting emotions. On the one hand, I am filled with awe when I contemplate the courage that was demonstrated by the nearly a quarter million men who fought here. On the other, especially when visiting the American, British, and German war cemeteries, I am overcome with waves of sadness at the terrible human loss that war brings.

But it is becoming harder and harder to visualize (and thus appreciate) what went on there from January 22 until the end of May 1944. A visitor must look long and hard to find any traces of the war. A few museums stand, and a few plaques are mounted on walls. The cemeteries, of course, are their own memorials. But too many of war's footprints have been erased forever. To be forgotten is the greatest tragedy.

It can truly be said that the courage of the British and American soldiers defending their perimeter was the supreme factor in the eventual triumph at Anzio. No matter what historians may say about Operation Shingle, the battle of Anzio represented desperate men fighting with desperate valour.

NOTES

Prologue

1. Martin Blumenson, *United States Army in World War II: The Mediterranean Theater of Operations—Salerno to Cassino*, 3–57; Basil Liddell Hart, *History of the Second World War*, 433–475.

2. Winston S. Churchill, *Closing the Ring*, 378.

3. Lucian K. Truscott Jr., *Command Missions: A Personal Story*, 291–292.

4. Martin Blumenson, *Mark Clark: The Last of the Great World War II Commanders*, 159.

5. Stephen E. Ambrose, *Eisenhower: Soldier, General of the Army, President-Elect—1890–1952*, 237.

6. Truscott, *Command Missions*, 547.

7. Tony Heathcote, *The British Field Marshals, 1736–1997*, 13–14; Rudyard Kipling, *The Irish Guards in the Great War*, vol. 2, webcache.google usercontent.com/search?q=cache; Irish Guards, www.di2.nu/files/kipling /IrishGuardsv2; *London Gazette*, September 22, 1911, and February 7, 1913.

8. Heathcote, *British Field Marshals*, 16; *London Gazette*, March 31, 1942.

9. Field Marshal Earl (Harold R. L. G.) Alexander, *The Alexander Memoirs, 1940–1945*, dust jacket.

10. "After the Auk," 32.

11. Richard Mead, *Churchill's Lions: A Biographical Guide to the Key British Generals of World War II*, 44.

12. Truscott, *Command Missions*, 546–547.

13. Alexander, *Alexander Memoirs*, 120.

14. Blumenson, *Mark Clark*, 163.

Chapter 1. "We have every confidence in you"

1. Harold Alexander, interview by George F. Howe, n.d., Sydney Matthews Collection, U.S. Army Military History Institute, Carlisle, PA; Blumenson, *Mark Clark*, 163.

2. John P. Lucas, "From Algiers to Anzio" (unpublished manuscript), Lucas Papers, U.S. Army Military History Institute, Carlisle, PA, 295–296.

3. Carlo D'Este, *Fatal Decision: Anzio and the Battle for Rome*, 113, 133.

4. Milan N. Vego, "The Allied Landing at Anzio-Nettuno, 22 January–4 March 1944."

5. John P. Lucas, diary, January 10, 1944, Lucas Papers.

6. Lucas, "From Algiers to Anzio," 307.

7. Samuel Eliot Morison, *Sicily-Salerno-Anzio, January 1943–June 1944*, 332.

8. Truscott, *Command Missions*, 302–303.

9. Blumenson, *Salerno to Cassino*, 355.

10. "Memories: Diary of Peter Geoffrey Bate," www.bbc.co.uk/history/ww2peopleswar/article2759123.

11. Truscott, *Command Missions*, 304.

12. Lucas, diary, January 19, 1944.

13. D'Este, *Fatal Decision*, 108.

14. Morison, *Sicily-Salerno-Anzio*, 332; Blumenson, *Salerno to Cassino*, 355.

15. Lucas, "From Algiers to Anzio," 305–306.

16. Blumenson, *Mark Clark*, 163; Albert Kesselring, *The Memoirs of Field-Marshal Kesselring*, 191.

17. Kesselring, *Memoirs of Kesselring*, 193.

18. *Fifth Army History, 16 January 1944–31 March 1944*, pt. 4, *Cassino and Anzio*, 17.

19. George Avery, "I Remember Anzio," http://4point2.org/hist-84A.htm.

20. Lucas, "From Algiers to Anzio," 314.

21. Avery, "I Remember Anzio."

22. Lucas, diary, January 21, 1944.

23. Blumenson, *Salerno to Cassino*, 357–360.

24. Churchill, *Closing the Ring*, 425.

25. Blumenson, *Salerno to Cassino*, 357–358.

Chapter 2. "One of the most complete surprises in history"

1. John Bowditch, ed., *Anzio Beachhead*, 13–14.

2. William R. C. Penney, www.unithistories.com/officers/Army_officers _P01.html#Penney_WRC.

3. 1st British Infantry Division, www.revolvy.com/main/index.php?s=1st InfantryDivision&stype=topics&cmd=list.

4. Patrizio Colantuono, *Anzio e i suoi lidi: Cartoline illustrate dal 1900 al 1960*, 93.

5. Eric Alley, "The Landings at Anzio: A View from the Sea," www.bbc.co .uk/history/ww2peopleswar/article4015243.

6. Robert Katz, *The Battle for Rome*, 149.

7. Basil H. Liddell Hart, *History of the Second World War*, 528.

8. Robley D. Evans et al., "American Armor at Anzio: A Research Report Prepared by Committee 2," 7.

9. Trevor Bray, "A Gordon's Story," submitted on behalf of Trevor Bray, www.bbc.co.uk/history/ww2peopleswar/article4178801.

10. Peter Geoffrey Bate, "Memories: Diary of Peter Geoffrey Bate."

11. William Woodruff, *Vessel of Sadness*, 44–51.

12. "The Landing at Anzio," ww2talk.com/index.php?threads/anzio -another-day.13110.

13. Woodruff, *Vessel of Sadness*.

14. Lucas, diary, January 22, 1944, Lucas Papers.

15. Stanley R. Smith (3rd Infantry Division), memoir, U.S. Army Military History Institute, Carlisle, PA.

16. James Arness with James E. Wise Jr., *James Arness: An Autobiography*, 39–40.

17. Smith, memoir.

18. Frank Pistone, memoir, www.anziobeachheadveterans.com/frank-s -pistone.html.

19. William O. Darby and William H. Baumer, *Darby's Rangers: We Led the Way*, 143–155.

20. T. R. Fehrenbach, *The Battle of Anzio*, 5.

21. Darby and Baumer, *Darby's Rangers*, 149–151.

22. Pier Paolo Battistelli, *Albert Kesselring: Leadership—Strategy— Conflict*, 38–40.

23. "World Battlefronts—Italy," 30.

24. Kesselring, *Memoirs of Kesselring*, 191; *German Order of Battle, 1944: The Directory, Prepared by Allied Intelligence, of Regiments, Formations and Units of the German Armed Forces*, D42.

25. Georg Tessin, *Verbände und Truppen der deutschen Wehrmacht und der Waffen-SS im Zweiten Weltkrieg, 1939–1945*, 251.

26. Siegfried Westphal, *The German Army in the West*, 158.

27. *German Order of Battle*, D62–D63.

28. D'Este, *Fatal Decision*, 130.

29. *German Order of Battle*, D38; D'Este, *Fatal Decision*, 130; Lloyd Clark, *Anzio: Italy and the Battle for Rome—1944*, 113.

30. D'Este, *Fatal Decision*, 130–133.

31. Kesselring, *Memoirs of Kesselring*, 194.

32. *German Order of Battle*, D36.

33. L. Clark, *Anzio*, 113.

34. Timothy D. Saxon, "The German Side of the Hill: Nazi Conquest and Exploitation of Italy, 1943–45," 236.

35. Shelford Bidwell, "Kesselring," 265–285.

36. Vego, "Allied Landing at Anzio-Nettuno," 110.

37. L. Clark, *Anzio*, 113; Philip R. O'Connor, "A Loyola Rome Student's Guide to World War II in Rome and Italy," 2015, https://luc.edu/media /lucedu/rome/fall2015/Formatted%20Rome%20Guide%20--Eleventh%20 Edition%20(1).pdf, 18.

38. Richard Raiber, *Anatomy of Perjury: Field Marshal Albert Kesselring, Via Rasella, and the Ginny Mission*, 216.

39. Kesselring, *Memoirs of Kesselring*, 194.

40. Wolfram Freiherr von Richthofen, forum.12oclockhigh.net; Steven J. Zaloga, *Anzio, 1944: The Beleaguered Beachhead*, 15–17.

41. Kesselring, *Memoirs of Kesselring*, 193–194.

42. Richard Lamb, *War in Italy, 1943–1945: A Brutal Story*, 94.

43. Frank Joseph, *Mussolini's War: Fascist Italy's Military Struggles from Africa and Western Europe to the Mediterranean and Soviet Union, 1935–45*, 190.

44. Kesselring, *Memoirs of Kesselring*, 191; Walther-Peer Fellgiebel, *Die Träger Ritterkreuzes des Eisernen Kreuzes, 1939–1945*.

45. Kesselring, *Memoirs of Kesselring*, 193–194.

46. Westphal, *German Army in the West*, 158.

47. James Chubbuck and George W. Gardes, interview by Dr. John S. G. Shotwell, December 9, 1950, www.6thcorpscombatengineers.com.

48. Avery, "I Remember Anzio."

49. William Dugdale, *Settling the Bill: The Memoirs of Bill Dugdale*, 105; John M. Hargreaves, www.ancientfaces.com/person/john-michael -hargreaves/164162948.

50. Lucas, diary, January 22, 1944.

51. Blumenson, *Mark Clark*, 172.

52. Irish Guards War Diary, www.ww2guards.com.

53. John Kenneally, *The Honour and the Shame*, 157.

Chapter 3. "I hope to have good news for you"

1. Phil Nordyke, *More than Courage: The Combat History of the 504th Parachute Infantry Regiment in World War II*, 127.
2. Ibid., 130.
3. William Yarborough, letter to Silvano Casaldi, 1991, no date.
4. Edward Reuter, memoir, www.509thgeronimo.org.
5. Sal Chiefari, memoir, www.anziobeachheadveterans.com.
6. Joe F. Dickerson, C Company, 53rd DUKW Battalion, "The Men of the Landing—Anzio Beachhead Veterans of WWII," memoir, http://anzio beachheadveterans.com/men-of-the-landing.html.
7. Diego Cancelli, *Aprilia, 1944: Immagini quotidiane di una guerra, Gennaio–Maggio 1944*.
8. D'Este, *Fatal Decision*, 138.
9. Ernie Pyle, *Brave Men*, 234.
10. Pasqualino Nuti, *Aprilia: I giorni della guerra—e gli occhi di un bambino*, 51–52.
11. Smith, memoir.
12. Churchill, *Closing the Ring*, 426.
13. Kesselring, forum.12oclockhigh.net; Zaloga, *Anzio, 1944*, 24–25.
14. Kesselring, *Memoirs of Kesselring*, 193–194.
15. Wolfgang Schneider, *Tigers in Combat*, 321–327.
16. Wilhelm Ernst Terheggen, letter to Silvano Casaldi, August 10, 1990.
17. Churchill, *Closing the Ring*, 425.

Chapter 4. "A whale wallowing on the beaches!"

1. R. H. Bull, "A Quiet Landing," ww2talk.com/index.php?threads /anzio-another-day.13110.
2. Edward Grace, *The Perilous Road to Rome and Beyond*, 89–90.
3. Flint Whitlock, *The Rock of Anzio: From Sicily to Dachau—a History of the U.S. 45th Infantry Division*.
4. James R. Bird, interview by the author, May 1, 1995.
5. Whitlock, *Rock of Anzio*, 6.
6. Martin Blumenson, *Anzio: The Gamble That Failed*, 145.
7. "William Eagles, Retired Army General, Dies," *Washington Post*, February 21, 1988.
8. Warren P. Munsell Jr., *The Story of a Regiment: A History of the 179th Regimental Combat Team*, 48.
9. Nuti, *Aprilia*, 52–54.

10. Wilhelm Ernst Terheggen, letter to Silvano Casaldi, August 10, 1990.

11. Kesselring, *Memoirs of Kesselring*, 193–196.

12. Munsell, *Story of a Regiment*, 48.

13. James Safrit, memoir, provided to the author by his son, Michael Safrit.

14. Lee Anderson, interview by the author, November 3, 2016.

15. Churchill, *Closing the Ring*, 432; Grace, *Perilous Road to Rome and Beyond*, 90.

16. Blumenson, *Mark Clark*, 173; Darby and Baumer, *Darby's Rangers*, 157.

17. Alexander quoted in Grace, *Perilous Road to Rome and Beyond*, 90.

18. Lucas, diary, January 23, 1944, Lucas Papers.

19. "Allied Units Land Behind Nazis in Italy," *New York Times*, January 23, 1944.

20. Dugdale, *Settling the Bill*, 105.

21. Peter Verney, *Anzio, 1944: An Unexpected Fury*, 56–57.

22. Horst Heinrich, letter to Silvano Casaldi, June 1, 1990.

23. James Luzzi, letter to Silvano Casaldi, 1999, n.d.

24. George F. Howe, *The Battle History of the 1st Armored Division*.

25. Carlo D'Este, *World War II in the Mediterranean*, 24–26.

26. Stanley P. Hirshson, *General Patton: A Soldier's Life*, 271–272, 310, 324, 256–357; Carlo D'Este, *Patton: A Genius for War*, 460; Shelby Stanton, *World War II Order of Battle*, 47–48.

27. Ernest N. Harmon, "8 NU's Maj. Gen. Ernest Harmon: 'The Second Patton," http://bicentennial.norwich.edu/8-ernest-harmon/.

28. Hirshson, *General Patton*, 271–272, 310, 324, 256–357; D'Este, *Patton*, 460; Stanton, *World War II Order of Battle*, 47–48.

29. William R. Buster, *Time on Target: The World War II Memoir of William R. Buster*, 57.

30. Hirshson, *General Patton*, 333.

31. Harmon, "8 NU's Maj. Gen. Ernest Harmon"; Rick Atkinson, *The Day of Battle: The War in Sicily and Italy, 1943–1944*, 427.

32. Ernest N. Harmon, memoir, Harmon Papers, U.S. Army Military History Institute, Carlisle, PA.

33. Ernest N. Harmon and Milton MacKaye, "Our Bitter Days at Anzio," 150.

34. Blumenson, *Salerno to Cassino*, 366–374.

35. Ray Sherman, "Ray Sherman's Recollections and Diary," www.45th division.org/Veterans/179thHistories.

36. Lucas, diary, January 24, 1944.

37. Carlo D'Este, "No Fear," 32.

38. Lucas, diary, January 24, 1944.

39. Smith, memoir.

40. Bowditch, *Anzio Beachhead*, 23–24; Blumenson, *Salerno to Cassino*, 387.

41. Bowditch, *Anzio Beachhead*, 23–24.

42. Verney, *Anzio, 1944*, 56.

43. E. O. Bowles, "Italy 2: Garigliano, Anzio, and Winter on the Adriatic (14 January to 1 April 1944)," www.ourstory.info/library/Rock/R11.html.

44. Verney, *Anzio, 1944*, 56.

45. Ross Glennon, "From Norway to Anzio: Sergeant Joe Dunne, DCM," 11.

46. Verney, *Anzio, 1944*, 58–59.

47. Grace, *Perilous Road to Rome and Beyond*, 93–94.

48. Verney, *Anzio, 1944*, 58–59.

49. Bowditch, *Anzio Beachhead*, 23–24.

50. Sydney Arthur Wright, www.bbc.co.uk/history/ww2peopleswar /article3763389.

51. Verney, *Anzio, 1944*, 58–59.

52. Lucas, diary, January 25, 1944.

53. Alexander, interview.

54. Grace, *Perilous Road to Rome and Beyond*, 95–98.

55. "The Angels of Anzio," www.darbysrangers.tripod.com/id76; www.med -dept.com/veterans-testimonies/veterans-testimony-arthur-b-degrandpre/.

56. Grace, *Perilous Road to Rome and Beyond*, 98.

57. Nuti, *Aprilia*, 53–56.

Chapter 5. "That one night has haunted me ever since"

1. Grace, *Perilous Road to Rome and Beyond*, 99.

2. Dugdale, *Settling the Bill*, 106.

3. Heinrich, letter to Casaldi, June 1, 1990.

4. Sidney Arthur Wright, www.bbc.co.uk/history/ww2peopleswar /article3763389.

5. BBC People's War, www.bbc.co.uk/history/ww2peopleswar/stories /69/a2429769.

6. Unnamed British soldier, www.bbc.co.uk/history/ww2peopleswar /article2429769.

7. Verney, *Anzio, 1944*, 58–61; L. Clark, *Anzio*, 126; British National Archives, WO 373/6; Thomas Hohler, www.ww2talk.com/index.php? threads/help-for-info-grandfather-served-with-grenadier-guards.43085 /page-2#post-512246.

8. Verney, *Anzio, 1944,* 61.

9. Kenneally, *Honour and the Shame,* 159–160.

10. J. H. Green, "Anzio," 52.

11. Bert Reed, www.battlefieldsww2.50megs.com/dad.

12. Joe D. Craver, www.anziobeachheadveterans.com/craver.

13. Churchill, *Closing the Ring,* 428.

14. Munsell, *Story of a Regiment,* 50.

15. L. Clark, *Anzio,* 125–127.

16. Lucas, diary, January 26, 1944, Lucas Papers; Green, "Anzio," 28; *A Fifth Army Report from the Beachhead,* U.S. Army Signal Corps film no. misc. 1039.

17. Munsell, *Story of a Regiment,* 50–51.

18. Henry L. S. Young, www.ww2guards.com/ww2guards/AWARDS_T_-_Z/Pages/YOUNG,_H.S.L._D.S.O.,_1BN.

19. Munsell, *Story of a Regiment,* 50–51.

20. Robert LaDu, interview by the author, April 3, 1995.

21. Ray McAllister, www.45thdivision.org/Veterans/McAllister.htm.

22. Paul Brown, diary, www.custermen.com/AtTheFront/ListKIA.

23. L. Clark, *Anzio,* 128.

24. Verney, *Anzio, 1944,* 61.

25. London Irish Rifles Association, "The London Irish at War, 1939–45," www.londonirishrifles.com/index.php/second-world-war/the-london-irish-at-war-1939-45/; unnamed British soldier, www.bbc.co.uk/history/ww2peopleswar/article2429769.

26. Fred Mason, e-mails to the author, September 4 and 29, 2015.

27. Lucas, diary, January 26, 1944.

28. Silvano Casaldi, *Gli uomini della sbarco: Anzio/Nettuno, 1944,* 205.

29. Avis Dagit Schorer, *A Half Acre of Hell: A Combat Nurse in WWII,* 128–140.

30. Casaldi, *Gli uomini della sbarco,* 262.

31. Brown, diary, January 27, 1944.

32. Darby and Baumer, *Darby's Rangers,* 154.

33. Mark W. Clark, *Calculated Risk,* 290–292.

34. Lucas, diary, January 25, 1944.

35. M. Clark, *Calculated Risk,* 290–292.

36. Heinrich, letter to Casaldi.

37. Truscott, *Command Missions,* 547.

38. Smith, memoir.

39. Gerald F. Linderman, *The World Within War: America's Combat Experience in World War II,* 283–299.

40. Munsell, *Story of a Regiment*, 50–51.

41. Dr. Peter C. Graffagnino, www.45thdivision.org/Veterans/Graffagnino 2.htm.

42. Louis V. "Cody" Wims, www.45thdivision.org/Veterans/Wims157_2 .htm.

43. Murray Levine, www.45thdivision.org/Veterans/Levine.htm.

44. Eric G. Gibson, www.qmfound.com.

45. M. Clark, *Calculated Risk*, 292–294.

46. Michael Burt, "Remembering the Loss of HMS *Spartan*," *Plymouth Herald* (UK), January 31, 2015.

47. Derek Evans, "The Loss of HMS *Spartan*," www.world-war.co.uk /spartan_loss.php3.

48. Milton Briggs, "The Anzio Beachhead," www.tankbooks.com.

49. Bowditch, *Anzio Beachhead*, 22.

50. *German Fourteenth Army Journal*, January 29, 1944, found in Peter Tompkins, *A Spy in Rome*, 133.

51. Katz, *The Battle for Rome*, 166.

52. Fred Sheehan, *Anzio: Epic of Bravery*, 70; *Fifth Army Antiaircraft Artillery: Salerno to Florence, 9 September 1943–8 September 1944*, 16.

53. Lucas, diary, January 29, 1944.

54. Ibid., January 30, 1944.

55. Smith, memoir.

56. Arness with Wise, *An Autobiography*, 43–44.

57. Howe, *Battle History of the 1st Armored Division*, 284–285.

58. Blumenson, *Anzio*, 113; Alfred Otte, *The HG Panzer Division*, 113.

59. Harmon, memoir; Harmon and MacKaye, "Our Bitter Days at Anzio," 48.

60. Young, www.ww2guards.com/ww2guards/AWARDS_T_-_Z/Pages /YOUNG,_H.S.L._D.S.O.,_1BN.

61. Lucas, diary, January 29, 1944.

62. Howe, *Battle History of the 1st Armored Division*, 284–285.

63. Heinrich, letter to Casaldi.

64. Avery, "I Remember Anzio."

65. Darby and Baumer, *Darby's Rangers*, 160–161.

66. William L. Newnan, *Escape in Italy: The Narrative of Lieutenant William L. Newnan, United States Rangers*, 1; Ennio Silvestri, *The Long Road to Rome*, 145.

67. Fehrenbach, *The Battle of Anzio*, 51.

68. Darby and Baumer, *Darby's Rangers*, 161–162.

Chapter 6. "They had . . . fought to the limit of human endurance"

1. Robert W. Black, *The Ranger Force: Darby's Rangers in World War II*, 265.

2. Carl H. Lehman, www.flashman.com.

3. Black, *Ranger Force*, 265.

4. D'Este, *Fatal Decision*, 165; Black, *Ranger Force*, 261–269.

5. L. Clark, *Anzio*, 150.

6. Black, *Ranger Force*, 266.

7. D'Este, *Fatal Decision*, 165; Black, *Ranger Force*, 261–269.

8. Roy A. Murray, After Action Report, January 1944, U.S. Army Military History Institute, Carlisle, PA.

9. Newnan, *Escape in Italy*, 1.

10. Milton Lehman quoted in Mack Morriss, "Rangers Come Home," *Stars and Stripes*, in *The Best from "Yank," the Army Weekly*, 128.

11. Victor Failmezger, *American Knights: The Untold Story of the Men of the Legendary 601st Tank Destroyer Battalion*, 124.

12. Newnan, *Escape in Italy*, 1–2, 3–48.

13. Lehman, www.flashman.com.

14. Darby and Baumer, *Darby's Rangers*, 165.

15. Ibid., 179.

16. Ibid., 170.

17. George A. Fisher, *The Story of the 180th Infantry Regiment*, 134.

18. Darby and Baumer, *Darby's Rangers*, 173.

19. Avery, "I Remember Anzio."

20. Heinrich, letter to Casaldi.

21. M. Clark, *Calculated Risk*, 296.

22. London Irish Rifles Association, "London Irish at War."

23. "History of the 36th Engineers," www.6thcorpscombatengineers .com/docs/36th/36th%20History%20WDRB.pdf.

24. Lloyd C. Hawks, Medal of Honor Recipients, World War II, Recipients G–L, U.S. Army Center of Military History, www.history.army.mil.

25. Truman O. Olson, Medal of Honor Recipients, World War II, Recipients M–S, U.S. Army Center of Military History, www.history.army .mil.

26. Heinrich, letter to Casaldi.

27. "Tom Gould Survived the Hell of the Anzio Landing," *Nottingham Post* (UK), August 21, 2010; A. McDougall, "History of the Sherwood Foresters," www.bbc.co.uk/history/ww2peopleswar/stories/66/a5298366.shtml.

28. Fred Vann, letter to Silvano Casaldi, no date, 1992.

29. "Tom Gould"; *Fifth Army History*, pt. 4, 104.

30. M. Clark, *Calculated Risk*, 297.

31. Lucas, diary, January 31, 1944.

Chapter 7. "This is one hell of a place"

1. Vere Williams, interview by the author, August 30, 1994.

2. Earl A. Reitan, memoir, U.S. Army Military History Institute, Carlisle, PA.

3. James Tolby Anderson, anziobeachheadveterans.com/james-tolby-anderson.html.

4. Michael E. Haskew, *Encyclopedia of Elite Forces in the Second World War*, 165–167.

5. Ibid., 165–167; "History of the First Special Service Force," www.firstspecialserviceforce.net/history.

6. Bill Mauldin, *The Brass Ring: A Sort of a Memoir*, 218.

7. Arness with Wise, *An Autobiography*, 44–47.

8. Pyle, *Brave Men*, 226.

9. Audie Murphy, *To Hell and Back*, 83; "Audie Murphy," 28–33.

10. Brown, diary, February 1, 1944.

11. "Alton W. Knappenberger, 84; Won Medal of Honor," *Washington Post*, June 28, 2008; Alton W. Knappenberger, Medal of Honor Recipients, World War II, Recipients G–L, U.S. Army Center of Military History, www.history.army.mil.

12. Murphy, *To Hell and Back*, 96.

13. John Batten, "9 Commando, Overseas," www.commandoveterans.org/9_Commando_overseas.

14. Anderson, interview.

15. George Courlas, www.45thdivision.org/Veterans/Courlas_157.htm.

16. "British Veterans to Commemorate 70th Anniversary of Anzio Landings in Italy," *Daily Telegraph* (UK), January 22, 2014.

17. Pyle, *Brave Men*, 159, 169.

18. Munsell, *Story of a Regiment*, 50–51.

19. Lucas, diary, February 1, 1944, Lucas Papers.

20. Darby and Baumer, *Darby's Rangers*, 172.

21. Robert E. Dodge, *Memories of the Anzio Beachhead and the War in Europe*, 4.

22. Jim T. Broumley, *The Boldest Plan Is the Best: The Combat History of the 509th Parachute Infantry Battalion During WWII*, 152.

23. Levine, www.45thdivision.org/Veterans/Levine.htm.

24. Lucas, diary, February 2, 1944.

25. Truscott, *Command Missions*, 315.

26. Jack Hallowell, *History of the 157th Infantry Regiment (Rifle), 4 June '43–8 May '45*, 52.

27. Pyle, *Brave Men*, 160.

28. D'Este, *Fatal Decision*, 199–201.

29. London Irish Rifles Association, "London Irish at War."

30. Richard Dougherty, *The British Reconnaissance Corps in World War II*, 21–22.

31. "London Irish Rifles into Anzio," www.royal-irish.com/events/london -irish-rifles-arrive-anzio; London Irish Rifles Association, "London Irish at War."

32. Munsell, *Story of a Regiment*, 33–34.

33. Safrit, memoir.

34. *Fifth Army History*, pt. 4, 103.

35. Bowditch, *Anzio Beachhead*, 43.

36. Ibid.; *Fifth Army History*, pt. 4, 103.

37. Fritz Hubert Gräser, www.lexikon-der-wehrmacht.de/Personen register/G/GraeserFH.

38. Bowditch, *Anzio Beachhead*, 45–46.

39. *Fifth Army History*, pt. 4, 103.

40. George Oliver Jeffs, www.bbc.co.uk/history/ww2peopleswar/article A900019.

41. General Sir David Fraser, *And We Shall Shock Them: The British Army in the Second World War*, 284.

42. David M. L. Gordon-Watson, www.telegraph.co.uk/news/obituaries /.../Brigadier-Michael-Gordon-Watson.html.

43. Glennon, "From Norway to Anzio," 12–13.

44. Safrit, memoir.

45. Lucas, diary, February 3, 1944; www.rogerwaters.org/34/royalf1.

46. Reuter, memoir.

Chapter 8. "The British are in serious trouble"

1. Bowditch, *Anzio Beachhead*, 44–46; *Fifth Army History*, pt. 4, 103–104.

2. "Addendum to 2nd German Counter Attack," www.bbc.co.uk /history/ww2peopleswar/stories/50/a3608750.shtml.

3. Bowditch, *Anzio Beachhead*, 44–46; *Fifth Army History*, pt. 4, 103–104.

4. *Fifth Army History*, pt. 4, 103–104.

5. Bowditch, *Anzio Beachhead*, 44–46.

6. Murphy, *To Hell and Back*, 115.

7. Bird, interview.

8. Mauldin, *Brass Ring*, 220.

9. Bird, interview.

10. Smith, memoir.

11. Lucas, diary, February 4, 1944, Lucas Papers.

12. London Irish Rifles Association, "London Irish at War."

13. Bowditch, *Anzio Beachhead*, 46.

14. *Fifth Army History*, pt. 4, 108–110.

15. Bernie L. Stokes, www.45thinfantrydivision.com.

16. Chester Powell, interview by the author, March 13, 1995.

17. *Fifth Army History*, pt. 4, 110; Bowditch, *Anzio Beachhead*, 51.

18. Bowditch, *Anzio Beachhead*, 46–49.

19. *Fifth Army History*, pt. 4, 110–111.

20. Truscott, *Command Missions*, 316; *Fifth Army History*, pt. 4, 108–109.

21. Murphy, *To Hell and Back*, 109.

22. John McManus, *The Deadly Brotherhood: The American Combat Soldier in World War II*, 164–165.

23. Mason, e-mail to the author, August 17, 2015.

24. Charles B. MacDonald, *The Mighty Endeavor: American Armed Forces in the European Theater in World War II*, 208.

25. Smith, memoir.

26. "Trench Foot," emergency.cdc.gov/disasters/trenchfoot.asp.

27. Lyn MacDonald, *To the Last Man: Spring 1918*, 9.

28. "Dubbin," en.wikipedia.org/wiki/Dubbin.

29. Bird, interview.

30. M. Clark, *Calculated Risk*, 303.

31. Safrit, memoir.

32. Bowditch, *Anzio Beachhead*, 51.

33. Edgar F. Raines Jr., *Eyes of Artillery: The Origins of Modern US Army Aviation in World War II*, 171, 181.

34. Dodge, *Memories of the Anzio Beachhead and the War*, 17.

35. Lucas, diary, February 6, 1944.

36. Bowditch, *Anzio Beachhead*, 53–54; Katz, *The Battle for Rome*, 166–167; Lucas, diary, February 7, 1944.

37. Milton Bracker, "Allies Give Ground; Fall Back," *New York Times*, February 6, 1944.

38. *Fifth Army History*, pt. 4, 107.

39. Hallowell, *History of the 157th Infantry Regiment*, 54.

Chapter 9. "Do a Dunkirk while you still have time!"

1. London Irish Rifles Association, "London Irish at War."

2. Ivor Jones, "Pte. Ivor Jones," www.wartimememoriesproject.com/ww2/view.php?uid=218519.

3. Bowditch, *Anzio Beachhead*, 54.

4. Ibid., 48, 52.

5. Ibid., 110–111.

6. Ibid., 52–53.

7. Kenny Franks, *Citizen Soldiers: Oklahoma's National Guard*, 88.

8. Robert J. Franklin, interview by the author, April 21, 1996.

9. Dodge, *Memories of the Anzio Beachhead and the War*, 10–11.

10. Von Hardesty, *Black Wings: Courageous Stories of African Americans in Aviation and Space History*, 89–90.

11. "Tale of a Red-Tailed Angel," *Buckeye Guard*, 10–14.

12. "Negro Fliers Praised," *New York Times*, February 6, 1944.

13. Bowditch, *Anzio Beachhead*, 52–53; *Fifth Army History*, pt. 4, 110–111.

14. Mary T. Sarnecky, *A History of the US Army Nurse Corps*, 226.

15. Schorer, *Half Acre of Hell*, 142–146.

16. Kathi Jackson, *They Called Them Angels: American Military Nurses of World War II*, 59.

17. Nordyke, *More than Courage*, 141.

18. Arness with Wise, *An Autobiography*, 47–48.

19. London Irish Rifles Association, "London Irish at War."

20. Bowditch, *Anzio Beachhead*, 57; D'Este, *Fatal Decision*, 211–212.

21. Safrit, memoir.

22. Hallowell, *History of the 157th Infantry Regiment*, 54–56.

23. Bowditch, *Anzio Beachhead*, 56–58.

24. Sheehan, *Anzio: Epic of Bravery*, 104–105.

25. William P. Sidney, Victoria Cross citation, www.britishempire.co.uk/forces/armyunits/britishinfantry/grenadierwilliamsidney.htm; "Victoria Cross for Tommygun Stand at Anzio," *London Gazette*, March 28, 1944; Sydney Arthur Wright, www.bbc.co.uk/history/ww2peopleswar/stories/89/a3763389.shtml.

26. John R. Large, www.wartimememoriesproject.com.

27. "Lt.-Col. Dick Evans," obituary, *Telegraph* (UK), February 20, 2013.

28. Jones, "Pte. Ivor Jones."

29. North Staffordshire Regiment Living History Association, www.northstaffordshirelha.org.

30. London Irish Rifles Association, "London Irish at War."

31. Bowditch, *Anzio Beachhead*, 55–57.

Chapter 10. "What a sight a mortar barrage is"

1. London Irish Rifles Association, "London Irish at War."

2. Bowditch, *Anzio Beachhead*, 57.

3. London Irish Rifles Association, "London Irish at War."

4. Bowditch, *Anzio Beachhead*, 57.

5. London Irish Rifles Association, "London Irish at War."

6. Franks, *Citizen Soldiers*, 89.

7. Glen Hanson, interview by the author, April 28, 1996.

8. Bowditch, *Anzio Beachhead*, 55.

9. Franks, *Citizen Soldiers*, 89; Whitlock, *Rock of Anzio*, 165.

10. Hallowell, *History of the 157th Infantry Regiment*, 54–57.

11. Failmezger, *American Knights*, 131.

12. Hallowell, *History of the 157th Infantry Regiment*, 54–57.

13. Bowditch, *Anzio Beachhead*, 52–57.

14. Roy Parker Jr., "Anzio Landing Was a Time of Valor for US Paratroopers," *Fayetteville (NC) Observer*, January 20, 1994; Paul B. Huff, Medal of Honor Recipients, World War II, Recipients G–L, U.S. Army Center of Military History, www.history.army.mil.

15. Oliver North and Joe Musser, *War Stories: Heroism in the Pacific*, 371.

16. Hallowell, *History of the 157th Infantry Regiment*, 57.

17. Bowditch, *Anzio Beachhead*, 57.

18. Ibid., 58–60.

19. London Irish Rifles Association, "London Irish at War."

20. John Ellis, *The Sharp End: The Fighting Man in World War II*, 62–63.

21. Mason, e-mail to the author, October 28, 2015.

22. Williams, interview.

23. Anthony Stefanelli, "Veteran Recounts His Winter of '43 to '44 Experiences," *Nutley (NJ) Sun*, June 9, 1994.

24. Bill Mauldin quoted in Douglas Brinkley, ed., *World War II: The Allied Counteroffensive, 1942–1945*, 158.

25. L. Clark, *Anzio*, 45–46; Blumenson, *Salerno to Cassino*, 386.

26. Green, "Anzio," 28–29.

27. Cesare Puccillo, "Anzio delle delizie: Le dimore nobiliari," Centro Studi Neptunia, August 1997, www.comune.nettuno.roma.it.

28. Murphy, *To Hell and Back*, 116–117.

29. Silvestri, *Long Road to Rome*, 171.

30. London Irish Rifles Association, "London Irish at War."

31. Bowditch, *Anzio Beachhead*, 60.

32. Harmon, memoir.

33. Bowditch, *Anzio Beachhead*, 60–61.

34. Friedrich Hummel, letter to Silvano Casaldi, January 29, 1991.

35. Safrit, memoir.

36. Bowditch, *Anzio Beachhead*, 62.

37. McManus, *Deadly Brotherhood*, 118.

38. Bowditch, *Anzio Beachhead*, 62.

39. L. Clark, *Anzio*, 170–171.

40. Bowditch, *Anzio Beachhead*, 60–61.

41. Ted Lees, www.bbc.co.uk/history/ww2peopleswar/stories/91/a20638 91.shtml.

42. Christopher Hibbert, *Benito Mussolini: The Rise and Fall of Il Duce*, 103.

43. Blumenson, *Anzio*, 114–115.

44. Munsell, *Story of a Regiment*, 53–54; 179th After Action Report, February 1944, U.S. Army Military History Institute, Carlisle, PA; Bowditch, *Anzio Beachhead*, 64–65.

Chapter 11. "Battle is kind of a nightmare"

1. Guardsman McIntosh, www.bbc.co.uk/history/ww2peopleswar /article1164124; Bowditch, *Anzio Beachhead*, 62.

2. Peter H. Mornement, "Letters of P. H. Mornement," www.surrey cc.gov.uk/heritage-culture-and-recreation/archives-and-history/surrey -history-centre/marvels-of-the-month/letters-of-major-p-h-mornement.

3. M. Clark, *Calculated Risk*, 305.

4. London Irish Rifles Association, "London Irish at War."

5. Bowditch, *Anzio Beachhead*, 61–62.

6. "Report of German Operations at Anzio Beachhead, 22 January–3 May 1944," Military Intelligence Division, War Department, Camp Ritchie, MD, 42.

7. Munsell, *Story of a Regiment*, 53–54.

8. Lucas, diary, February 10, 1944, Lucas Papers.

9. Chubbuck and Gardes, interview by Shotwell; Bowditch, *Anzio Beachhead*, 62.

10. 33rd Field Hospital, http://history.amedd.army.mil.

11. McAllister, www.45thdivision.org/Veterans/McAllister.htm.

12. Brown, diary, February 10, 1944.

13. Munsell, *Story of a Regiment*, 54.

14. Brummett Echohawk, "Drawing Fire," manuscript, 228.

15. Munsell, *Story of a Regiment*, 54; Bowditch, *Anzio Beachhead*, 62–64; Sheehan, *Anzio: Epic of Bravery*, 111.

16. Munsell, *Story of a Regiment*, 54; Sheehan, *Anzio: Epic of Bravery*, 111.

17. Munsell, *Story of a Regiment*, 54; Bowditch, *Anzio Beachhead*, 62–64.

18. Echohawk, "Drawing Fire," 228.

19. Munsell, *Story of a Regiment*, 54; Bowditch, *Anzio Beachhead*, 62–64; Nuti, *Aprilia*, 24–25, 27.

20. Echohawk, "Drawing Fire," 228.

21. Munsell, *Story of a Regiment*, 54; Bowditch, *Anzio Beachhead*, 62–64; 179th After Action Report, February 1944.

22. Lucas, diary, February 11, 1944.

23. Bowditch, *Anzio Beachhead*, 62–64; 179th After Action Report, February 1944.

24. Munsell, *Story of a Regiment*, 53–54; Bowditch, *Anzio Beachhead*, 61–64.

25. Echohawk, "Drawing Fire," 234.

26. Munsell, *Story of a Regiment*, 54; Bowditch, *Anzio Beachhead*, 64–65.

27. Munsell, *Story of a Regiment*, 54; Sheehan, *Anzio: Epic of Bravery*, 111.

28. Echohawk, "Drawing Fire," 234.

29. Munsell, *Story of a Regiment*, 54.

30. Churchill, *Closing the Ring*, 431–432.

31. Alexander, *Alexander Memoirs*, 126.

32. D'Este, *Patton*, 580.

33. Ibid.; Hirshson, *General Patton*, 438; Blumenson, *Mark Clark*, 187.

34. Sheehan, *Anzio: Epic of Bravery*, 111; Munsell, *Story of a Regiment*, 54.

35. Bowditch, *Anzio Beachhead*, 64–65; Munsell, *Story of a Regiment*, 54.

36. Anderson, interview by the author.

37. Safrit, memoir.

38. Harmon, memoir.

39. Bowditch, *Anzio Beachhead*, 61–62.

Chapter 12. "Do not kill any cows!"

1. Lucas, diary, February 12, 1944, Lucas Papers.

2. M. Clark, *Calculated Risk*, 304.

3. Lucas, diary, February 12, 1944.

4. Bowditch, *Anzio Beachhead*, 64–65; Munsell, *Story of a Regiment*, 54.

5. Bowditch, *Anzio Beachhead*, 65–66; D'Este, *Fatal Decision*, 238.

6. C. Northcote Parkinson, *Always a Fusilier: The War History of the Royal Fusiliers (City of London Regiment)*, 102.

7. D'Este, *Fatal Decision*, 82.

8. Eric Waters, www.rogerwaters.com.

9. Oxfordshire and Buckinghamshire Light Infantry Regiment, 7th Battalion (7th Ox and Bucks), www.lightbobs.com/7th-bn-oxf—bucks-li -january-1944-june-1944.

10. Bernard L. Kahn, *Fight On: A GI's Odyssey Back to Nazi Germany*, 177.

11. McManus, *Deadly Brotherhood*, 48–49.

12. Bill Mauldin, *Up Front*, 35.

13. Theodore Draper, *The 84th Infantry Division in the Battle of Germany, November 1944–May 1945*, 34–35.

14. Murphy, *To Hell and Back*, 115.

15. Kahn, *Fight On*, 180–181.

16. Lees, "Before Anzio."

17. Raleigh Trevelyan, *The Fortress: A Diary of Anzio and After*, 32–33.

18. Bill Whitman, *Scouts Out!*, 86.

19. Harmon, memoir.

20. Russell Cloer (3rd U.S. Infantry Division), memoir, U.S. Army Military History Institute, Carlisle, PA.

21. Charles F. Marshall, *A Ramble Through My War: Anzio and Other Joys*, 52.

22. Trevelyan, *Fortress*, 28.

23. Avery, "I Remember Anzio."

24. Trevelyan, *Fortress*, 127.

25. Whitman, *Scouts Out!*, 83.

26. Trevelyan, *Fortress*, 25.

27. Avery, "I Remember Anzio."

28. "Psychiatric Disorder Report," October 4, 1944, quoted in Munsell, *Story of a Regiment*, 46.

29. Munsell, *Story of a Regiment*, 37.

30. Brown, diary, various dates.

31. Francis E. Liggett, memoir, 45thinfantrydivision.com/index18.htm.

32. Mason, e-mail to the author, July 28, 2016.

33. Marshall, *Ramble Through My War*, 45–46.

34. Bowles, "Italy 2."

35. Kesselring, *Memoirs of Kesselring*, 195.

36. Lucas, diary, February 13, 1944.

37. 157th Infantry Regiment After Action Report, February 14, 1944, U.S. Army Military History Institute, Carlisle, PA.

38. Bowditch, *Anzio Beachhead*, 70.

39. Williams, interview.

40. Al Bedard, interview by the author, August 30, 1994.

41. Mason, e-mail to the author, September 4, 2015.

42. G. Fisher, *Story of the 180th Infantry Regiment*, 134.

43. Saxon, "German Side of the Hill," 242.

44. 36th Combat Engineers, www.6thcorpscombatengineers.com/36th .htm.

45. London Irish Rifles Association, "London Irish at War."

46. "Alexander Sees Second Round Won," *New York Times*, February 17, 1944.

47. William Heard, "7th Ox and Bucks Wiped Out Holding the Line at Anzio," http://ww2today.com/15-february-1944-7th-ox-and-bucks-wiped -out-holding-the-line-at-anzio.

48. Liddell Hart, *History of the Second World War*, 529–530; Blumenson, *Salerno to Cassino*, 403–417.

49. Churchill, *Closing the Ring*, 433.

50. London Irish Rifles Association, "London Irish at War."

51. Nettuno airstrip, www.iwm.org.uk/history/anzio-the-invasion-that -almost-failed.

52. *Fifth Army History*, pt. 4, 135–136; Katz, *The Battle for Rome*, 175–178.

53. Ibid.

54. Katz, *The Battle for Rome*, 175–178.

55. Adrian Greaves, *Rorke's Drift*; Stephen L. Hardin, "Battle of the Alamo," in *The Handbook of Texas Online*, published by the Texas State Historical Association, tshaonline.org/handbook/online/articles/qea02.

Chapter 13. "The shrill, demented choirs of wailing shells"

1. Eduard Mark, *Aerial Interdiction: Air Power and the Land Battle in Three American Wars*, 136.

2. Kesselring, *Memoirs of Kesselring*, 196.

3. Grace, *Perilous Road to Rome and Beyond*, 143.

4. Whitman, *Scouts Out!*, 90.

5. Ralph Krieger, interview by the author, March 20, 1995.

6. Munsell, *Story of a Regiment*, 54.

7. Gotthold Schwegler, letter to Silvano Casaldi, May 20, 1990.

8. Hans Schuhle, letter to Silvano Casaldi, September 2, 1990.

9. Kesselring, *Memoirs of Kesselring*, 196.

10. Westphal, *German Army in the West*, 159.

11. Bowditch, *Anzio Beachhead*, 70–72.

12. Liddell Hart, *History of the Second World War*, 157–198, 241–342, 397–432, 477–497.

13. Churchill, *Closing the Ring*, 433.

14. Harmon and MacKaye, "Our Bitter Days at Anzio," 9, 18, 48.

15. Bowditch, *Anzio Beachhead*, 73–74.

16. Hallowell, *History of the 157th Infantry Regiment*, 57–58.

17. Felix Sparks, interview by the author, October 15, 1996; 157th Infantry Regiment After Action Report, February 16, 1944.

18. Alvin McMillan, interview by the author, October 30, 1994.

19. Daniel Ficco, interview by the author, April 19, 1995.

20. Kenneth Stemmons, interview by the author, March 21, 1995.

21. Munsell, *Story of a Regiment*, 54–55.

22. Merlon O. Tryon, interview by the author, March 31, 1996.

23. William H. Gordon, interview by the author, March 13, 1995.

24. Ian V. Hogg and John Weeks, *The Illustrated Encyclopedia of Military Vehicles*, 80–81.

25. LaDu, interview.

26. Charles Reiman, monograph, 45th Infantry Division Museum.

27. Bowditch, *Anzio Beachhead*, 75.

28. Donald E. Knowlton, valor.militarytimes.com/recipient.php?recipient id=22338; D'Este, *Fatal Decision*, 313.

29. Munsell, *Story of a Regiment*, 58.

Chapter 14. "This was the big attack"

1. Bowditch, *Anzio Beachhead*, 74–75.

2. Reynolds Packard, "Beachhead Piled with German Dead," *New York Times*, February 19, 1944.

3. William P. Yarborough, interview by John R. Meese and Houston P. Houser III, March 28, 1975, Senior Officer Debriefing Program, U.S. Army Military History Institute, Carlisle, PA.

4. Lawrence Butler, World War II Survey, U.S. Army Military History Institute, Carlisle, PA.

5. Yarborough, interview.

6. Phil Miller, letter to Silvano Casaldi, no date, 1998.

7. Bowditch, *Anzio Beachhead*, 68–75.

8. Hallowell, *History of the 157th Infantry Regiment*, 64.

9. Sparks, interview.

10. Hallowell, *History of the 157th Infantry Regiment*, 64.

11. Bowditch, *Anzio Beachhead*, 70–74.

12. Mason, e-mails to the author, September 4 and 29, 2015.

13. Everett W. Easley, interview by the author, January 18, 1995.

14. 157th Infantry Regiment After Action Report, February 16, 1944.

15. Munsell, *Story of a Regiment*, 60; Heard, "7th Ox and Bucks Wiped Out."

16. Cordino Longiotti, letter to Silvano Casaldi, 2001, no date.

17. Sherman, "Ray Sherman's Recollections and Diary."

18. Paula Ann Mitchell, "New Paltz Man Recalls Life as a WWII POW," *Kingston (NY) Daily Freeman*, June 12, 2014.

19. Bowditch, *Anzio Beachhead*, 75.

20. M. Clark, *Calculated Risk*, 308.

21. Alexander, interview.

22. Blumenson, *Mark Clark*, 188.

23. M. Clark, *Calculated Risk*, 306.

24. Lucas, diary, February 16, 1944, Lucas Papers.

25. Lucas, "From Algiers to Anzio," 386.

26. Westphal, *German Army in the West*, 159–160; Kesselring, *Memoirs of Kesselring*, 196.

Chapter 15. "I do not feel that I should have sacrificed my command"

1. Bowditch, *Anzio Beachhead*, 75–80.

2. *Fifth Army Report from the Beachhead*.

3. G. Fisher, *Story of the 180th Infantry Regiment*, 139–140.

4. 157th Infantry Regiment After Action Report, February 14, 1944.

5. Munsell, *Story of a Regiment*, 56; Atkinson, *Day of Battle*, 424.

6. Darby and Baumer, *Darby's Rangers*, 175.

7. Blumenson, *Anzio*, 135–136.

8. London Irish Rifles Association, "London Irish at War."

9. Charles M. Wiltse, the United States Army in World War II, the Technical Services, *Medical Service in the Mediterranean and Minor Areas*, 28.

10. Bowditch, *Anzio Beachhead*, 75.

11. Hallowell, *History of the 157th Infantry Regiment*, 66.

12. Henry Kaufman, *Vertrauensmann: Man of Confidence*, 21.

13. Hallowell, *History of the 157th Infantry Regiment*, 66.

14. D'Este, *Fatal Decision*, 236, 238.

15. Blumenson, *Anzio*, 145.

16. M. Clark, *Calculated Risk*, 308–309.

17. Lucas, diary, February 17, 1944, Lucas Papers.

18. M. Clark, *Calculated Risk*, 306.

19. Harmon, memoir.

20. Hallowell, *History of the 157th Infantry Regiment*, 63.

21. Lucas, diary, February 17, 1944.

22. Bowditch, *Anzio Beachhead*, 80.

23. William Donovan, OSS Papers, U.S. Army Military History Institute, Carlisle, PA, quoted in Tompkins, *A Spy in Rome*.

24. Heard, "7th Ox and Bucks Wiped Out."

25. Krieger, interview.

26. Munsell, *Story of a Regiment*, 56.

27. Echohawk, "Drawing Fire," 237–238.

28. Hallowell, *History of the 157th Infantry Regiment*, 61–65.

29. Bill Hemingway, "The Anguish of Anzio," *Denver Post*, November 19, 1978, Empire section.

30. Kaufman, *Vertrauensmann: Man of Confidence*, 21.

31. Bedard, interview.

32. Bowditch, *Anzio Beachhead*, 68.

33. Blumenson, *Anzio*, 130.

34. Safrit, memoir.

35. William J. Johnston, Medal of Honor Recipients, World War II, Recipients G–L, U.S. Army Center of Military History, www.history.army.mil.

36. Heard, "7th Ox and Bucks Wiped Out."

37. Nick Pisa, "Touching Moment: Pink Floyd Star Visits World War II Cemetery in Italy to Honour His Soldier Father Who Died in Heroic Final Stand," *Daily Mail* (UK), October 13, 2013.

38. HMS *Penelope*, www.wrecksite.eu/wreck.aspx?15428.

39. Harmon, memoir.

40. Truscott, *Command Missions*, 321–323.

41. Harmon, memoir.

42. Lucas, diary, February 18, 1944.

Chapter 16. "The stakes are very high"

1. Harmon, memoir.

2. Lees, "Before Anzio."

3. Duke of Lancaster's Regiment Lancashire Infantry Museum, www.lancashireinfantrymuseum.org.uk/world-war-ii-1/.

4. Green, "Anzio," 28.

5. Munsell, *Story of a Regiment*, 56.

6. Duke of Lancaster's Regiment Lancashire Infantry Museum, www.lancashireinfantrymuseum.org.uk/world-war-ii-1/.

7. Harmon, memoir; Howe, *Battle History of the 1st Armored Division*, 296–298.

8. Harmon, memoir.

9. Munsell, *Story of a Regiment*, 56.

10. Pisa, "Touching Moment."

11. Philip Burke, interview by the author, October 19, 1994.

12. Kaufman, *Vertrauensmann: Man of Confidence*, 23–24.

13. Sparks, interview.

14. Westphal, *German Army in the West*, 160.

15. Jack Montgomery, interview by the author, May 5, 1996.

16. Hallowell, *History of the 157th Infantry Regiment*, 70.

17. Sparks, interview.

18. Kaufman, *Vertrauensmann: Man of Confidence*, 25–27.

19. Edwin P. Hoyt, *The GI's War: American Soldiers in Europe During World War II*, 282.

20. Katz, *The Battle for Rome*, 180.

21. Alley, "Landings at Anzio"; Blumenson, *Anzio*, 27.

22. Bowditch, *Anzio Beachhead*, 96–98.

23. Broumley, *Boldest Plan Is the Best*, 186–191.

24. "Report of German Operations at Anzio Beachhead," 75.

25. Nettuno airstrip, www.iwm.org.uk/history/anzio-the-invasion-that -almost-failed.

26. Thomas M. Moriarty, www.2ndbombgroup.org.

27. Audie Murphy, valor.militarytimes.com/recipient.php?recipientid =209; Murphy, *To Hell and Back*, 124.

28. Bowditch, *Anzio Beachhead*, 104; Robin Neillands, *By Land and by Sea: The Story of the Royal Marine Commandos*, 105–107; www.combined ops.com; www.wikiwand.com/en/40_Commando.

29. Neillands, *By Land and by Sea*, 106–107.

30. Churchill, *Closing the Ring*, 434.

31. Burgess W. Scott, "Hot Spot in Italy."

32. Jon Clayton, letter, March 14, 1944, U.S. Army Military History Institute, Carlisle, PA.

33. Robert J. Franklin, *Medic: How I Fought WWII with Morphine, Sulfa, and Iodine Swabs*, 73.

34. "History of the 36th Engineers," March 4–5, 1944.

35. Westphal, *German Army in the West*, 160.

36. Bowditch, *Anzio Beachhead*, 102.

37. Kenneth D. Williamson, *Tales of a Thunderbird in World War II*, 103–106.

38. Darby and Baumer, *Darby's Rangers*, 146.

39. Alexander quoted in Fred Majdalany, *The Battle of Cassino*, 74.

40. 33rd Field Hospital, http://history.amedd.army.mil.

41. Bowditch, *Anzio Beachhead*, 105.

42. Westphal, *German Army in the West*, 160–161.

43. Brown, diary, March 4, 1944.

44. London Irish Rifles Association, "London Irish at War"; Ken Ford, *Cassino, 1944: Breaking the Gustav Line*, 76.

45. Sheehan, *Anzio: Epic of Bravery*, 226.

46. www.britishmilitaryhistory.co.uk.

47. Trevelyan, *Fortress*, 16–17.

48. Whitman, *Scouts Out*, 108, 113–114.

49. www.britishmilitaryhistory.co.uk.

50. London Irish Rifles Association, "London Irish at War."

51. Blumenson, *Salerno to Cassino*, 438–441.

52. Sara E. Pratt, "March 17, 1944: The Most Recent Eruption of Mount Vesuvius."

53. Nordyke, *More than Courage*, 165–167.

54. www.combinedops.com; www.commandoveterans.org/book/export /html/976.

55. Dodge, *Memories of the Anzio Beachhead and the War*, 18.

56. John Wukovits, *Soldiers of a Different Cloth: Notre Dame Chaplains in World War II*, 4, 144.

57. Schorer, *Half Acre of Hell*, 162–163.

Chapter 17. "They liked to send us out to stir things up"

1. Pratt, "March 17, 1944."

2. Vesuvius, www.warwingsart.com/12thAirForce/Vesuvius.html.

3. Katz, *The Battle for Rome*, 219–230; O'Connor, "Loyola Rome Student's Guide," 20.

4. Pyle, *Brave Men*, 294–295.

5. "Ernie Pyle Is Killed on Ie Island; Foe Fired When All Seemed Safe," *New York Times*, April 19, 1945.

6. Clyde Easter, www.everytownusa.com/everytown-usa/anzio-beach head-reunion.

7. Truscott, *Command Missions*, 364–365.

8. Westphal, *German Army in the West*, 162.

9. Ian Billingsley, "War Is Looming," www.bbc.co.uk/history/ww2 peopleswar/stories/87/a4001987.shtml.

10. Bowditch, *Anzio Beachhead*, 22.

11. Verney, *Anzio, 1944*, 223.

12. Truscott, *Command Missions*, 361–362.

13. Edgar Clark, "Anzio Papers Headline Men Who Make the News," *Stars and Stripes*, May 1, 1944.

14. Verney, *Anzio, 1944*, 227.

15. Truscott, *Command Missions*, 364.

16. Ibid., 361–362.

17. Courlas, www.45thdivision.org/Veterans/Courlas_157.htm.

18. Katz, *The Battle for Rome*, 180.

19. Karl Muller, letter to Silvano Casaldi, April 10, 1989.

20. "56th Evacuation Hospital Unit History," www.med-dept.com/unit-histories/56th-evacuation-hospital.

21. Schorer, *Half Acre of Hell*, 168–170.

22. "History of the 36th Engineers," April 1944.

23. Avery, "I Remember Anzio."

24. "History of the 36th Engineers," April 1944.

25. Brown, diary, April 18, 19, 23, 1944.

26. John C. Squires, Medal of Honor Recipients, World War II, Recipients M–S, U.S. Army Center of Military History, www.history.army.mil.

27. Muller, letter to Casaldi.

28. "History of the 36th Engineers," April 1944.

29. James R. Bird, unpublished memoir, 7.

30. Bowditch, *Anzio Beachhead*, 112.

31. Reed, www.battlefieldsww2.50megs.com/dad.

32. Brown, diary, May 3, 5, 1944.

33. Westphal, *German Army in the West*, 162–167; Otte, *The HG Panzer Division*, 113.

34. Blumenson, *Mark Clark*, 198–201.

35. D'Este, *Fatal Decision*, 334–338, 340–341; L. Clark, *Anzio*, 271–272; Bowditch, *Anzio Beachhead*, 116–117.

36. Blumenson, *Mark Clark*, 198–201.

37. Truscott, *Command Missions*, 368–369.

38. M. Clark, *Calculated Risk*, 201.

39. Truscott, *Command Missions*, 369.

40. Churchill, *Closing the Ring*, 538.

41. Brown, diary, May 6, 8, 1944.

42. Muller, letter to Casaldi.

43. Audie Murphy, www.arlingtoncemetery.net/audielmu; Audie Murphy, Medal of Honor Recipients, World War II, Recipients M–S, U.S. Army Center of Military History, www.history.army.mil.

44. Brown, diary, May 9, 1944.

45. Truscott, *Command Missions*, 366–367.

46. 100th Infantry Battalion Veterans Education Center, www.100th battalion.org.

47. Churchill, *Closing the Ring*, 538; Ernest F. Fisher Jr., *United States Army in World War II: The Mediterranean Theater of Operations, Cassino to the Alps*, 110–111.

48. E. Fisher, *United States Army in World War II*, 114–115.

49. Brown, diary, May 10, 11, 1944.

50. Truscott, *Command Missions*, 370.

51. Joseph Menditto quoted in Matthew Parker, *Monte Cassino: The Hardest Fought Battle of World War II*, 298–299.

52. E. Fisher, *United States Army in World War II*, 79–80.

53. Truscott, *Command Missions*, 370–371.

54. Harmon, memoir.

55. Steven J. Zaloga, *Armored Thunderbolt: The US Army Sherman in World War II*, 89.

56. John Shirley, anziobeachheadveterans.com/men-of-the-landing.html; Zaloga, *Armored Thunderbolt*, 89; John J. Toffey IV, *Jack Toffey's War: A Son's Memoir*, 193.

57. Brown, diary, May 12–15, 18, 19, 1944.

58. Daniel R. Champagne, *Dogface Soldiers: The Story of B Company, 15th Regiment, 3rd Infantry Division*, 99.

Chapter 18. "I told the aid man to fix me up"

1. Verney, *Anzio, 1944*, 230.

2. Bowditch, *Anzio Beachhead*, 121–122; Blumenson, *Mark Clark*, 208–210.

3. Harmon, memoir.

4. Howe, *Battle History of the 1st Armored Division*, 322.

5. "Battle of Italy: Nightmare's End," 27.

6. Truscott, *Command Missions*, 371.

7. A. C. Sedgwick, "Germans at Anzio Taken by Surprise," *New York Times*, May 24, 1944.

8. Truscott, *Command Missions*, 372.

9. Nathan N. Prefer, "Key to the Eternal City," 40–42.

10. Bowditch, *Anzio Beachhead*, 119; Battistelli, *Albert Kesselring*, 44.

11. Otte, *The HG Panzer Division*, 117.

12. Truscott, *Command Missions*, 372.

13. Edwin P. Hoyt, *Backwater War: The Allied Campaign in Italy, 1943–45*, 185.

14. Prefer, "Key to the Eternal City," 42.

15. Shirley, anziobeachheadveterans.com/men-of-the-landing.html.

16. Howe, *Battle History of the 1st Armored Division*, 322–326.

17. Franklin, interview.

18. Stemmons, interview.

19. "The Bravery of SSgt. George J. Hall," *Stoneham* (MA) *Independent*, November 18, 2015; George J. Hall, Medal of Honor Recipients, World War II, Recipients G–L, U.S. Army Center of Military History, www .history.army.mil.

20. Patrick L. Kessler, Medal of Honor Recipients, World War II, Recipients G–L, U.S. Army Center of Military History, www.history.army.mil.

21. John W. Dutko, Medal of Honor Recipients, World War II, Recipients A–F, U.S. Army Center of Military History, www.history.army.mil.

22. Ernest H. Dervishian, Medal of Honor Recipients, World War II, Recipients A–F, U.S. Army Center of Military History, www.history.army.mil.

23. Thomas W. Fowler, Medal of Honor Recipients, World War II, Recipients A–F, U.S. Army Center of Military History, www.history.army.mil.

24. Jim Morrison, *Letters from Joe*, 299; Duane Vachon, "'Kraut-an-Hour Schauer': T/Sgt. Henry Schauer, U.S. Army, WW II Medal of Honor (1918-1997)," *Hawaii Reporter*, November 20, 2011, www.hawaiireporter.com /kraut-an-hour-schauer-tsgt-henry-schauer-u-s-army-ww-ii-medal-of -honor-1918-1997/123.

25. Prefer, "Key to the Eternal City," 42.

26. Henry Schauer, Medal of Honor Recipients, World War II, Recipients M–S, U.S. Army Center of Military History, www.history.army.mil; Morrison, *Letters from Joe*, 299; "'Kraut-an-Hour Schauer.'"

27. Dorothy Rustebakke, "Scobey's One-Man Army—Henry Schauer," ww2aa.proboards.com/thread/7087/kraut-hour-schauer.

28. G. Fisher, *Story of the 180th Infantry Regiment*, 176–177.

29. Chester G. Cruikshank, www.findagrave.com; valor.militarytimes .com/recipient.php?recipientid=22018.

30. Van Barfoot, interview by the author, August 11, 1996; Nick Del Calzo and Peter Collier, *Medal of Honor: Portraits of Valor Beyond the Call of Duty*, 16.

31. Franklin, interview.

32. Robert Franklin, e-mail to the author, November 4, 2003.

33. Brown, diary, May 23, 1944.

34. Truscott, *Command Missions*, 373–374.

35. Liggett, memoir.

36. James H. Mills, Medal of Honor Recipients, World War II, Recipients M–S, U.S. Army Center of Military History, www.history.army.mil.

37. August Schlag, letter to Silvano Casaldi, July 15, 1990.

38. Murphy, *To Hell and Back*, 150–151.

39. Sylvester Antolak, Medal of Honor Recipients, World War II, Recipients A–F, U.S. Army Center of Military History, www.history.army.mil; Champagne, *Dogface Soldiers*, 102.

40. Brown, diary, May 24, 1944.

41. Truscott, *Command Missions*, 374.

42. Milton Bracker, "Allies Start Drive at Anzio Beachhead," *New York Times*, May 24, 1944.

43. Truscott, *Command Missions*, 375–377.

44. Blumenson, *Mark Clark*, 212; Bowditch, *Anzio Beachhead*, 122.

45. Howe, *Battle History of the 1st Armored Division*, 316; "Battle of Italy: Nightmare's End," 27.

46. Morrison, *Letters from Joe*, 299.

47. Brown, diary, May 25, 1944.

Chapter 19. "Even a soldier must cry sometimes"

1. E. Fisher, *United States Army in World War II*, 172; Truscott, *Command Missions*, 375–377.

2. Harmon, memoir.

3. Howe, *Battle History of the 1st Armored Division*, 322–323.

4. Muller, letter to Casaldi.

5. Bowditch, *Anzio Beachhead*, 119.

6. Katz, *The Battle for Rome*, 308; W. G. F. Jackson, *The Battle for Italy*, 239.

7. Katz, *The Battle for Rome*, 308.

8. Truscott, *Command Missions*, 375–376.

9. Bowditch, *Anzio Beachhead*, 119.

10. Beryl R. Newman, Medal of Honor Recipients, World War II, Recipients M–S, U.S. Army Center of Military History, www.history.army.mil.

11. Brown, diary, May 26, 1944.

12. G. Fisher, *Story of the 180th Infantry Regiment*, 193.

13. "World War II SSgt. Salvador Lara Receives Posthumous Medal of Honor Nearly 70 Years Later," www.abmc.gov/news-events/news/world-war-ii-ssgt-salvador-lara-receives-posthumous-medal-honor-nearly-70-years.

14. Ernst Kehrer, letter to Silvano Casaldi, May 22, 1990.

15. Bowditch, *Anzio Beachhead*, 120.

16. Hallowell, *History of the 157th Infantry Regiment*, 93–94.

17. Truscott, *Command Missions*, 377.

18. Del Calzo and Collier, *Medal of Honor*, 51.

19. Rudolph B. Davila, www.arlingtoncemetery.net.

20. Brown, diary, May 28, 1944.

21. Robert N. Wallworth, www.deadfamilies.com/Wallworth.

22. William W. Galt, Medal of Honor Recipients, World War II, Recipients G–L, U.S. Army Center of Military History, www.history.army .mil; biography of William W. Galt, theirfinesthour.net/2014/05/captain -william-w-galt-usa-may-29-1944.

23. Champagne, *Dogface Soldiers*, 83.

24. Hallowell, *History of the 157th Infantry Regiment*, 94.

25. Edward Weber, www.westpointaog.org/memorial-article?id=e82a20 43-f9ab-457e-90c3-70392c0b284f.

26. Brown, diary, May 29 and 30, 1944.

27. 34th Infantry Division history, www.34infdiv.org/history/135inf.

28. Furman L. Smith, Medal of Honor Recipients, World War II, Recipients M–S, U.S. Army Center of Military History, www.history.army.mil; Charles D. Taylor, "Twenty Miles to Rome: The Story of South Carolina's First Medal of Honor Winner in World War II," 79–86.

29. Franklin, interview.

30. Blumenson, *Mark Clark*, 211–212.

Chapter 20. "We entered Rome . . . amid cheers"

1. Truscott, *Command Missions*, 377.

2. *The Story of the 36th Infantry Division*, 10–11; E. Fisher, *United States Army in World War II*, 186.

3. Herbert E. MacCombie, "Chaplains of the 36th Infantry Division," www.texasmilitaryforcesmuseum.org/36division/archives/chaplain/030.

4. Dan Kurzman, *The Race for Rome*, 346–347.

5. Truscott, *Command Missions*, 377; Howe, *Battle History of the 1st Armored Division*, 335.

6. Kurzman, *The Race for Rome*, 347–348.

7. Blumenson, *Mark Clark*, 211.

8. Kesselring, *Memoirs of Kesselring*, 203.

9. Yeiki Kobashigawa and Shinyei Nakamine, www.homeofheroes.com.

10. Truscott, *Command Missions*, 378.

11. Kurzman, *The Race for Rome*, 370–375.

12. John Sloan Brown, *Draftee Division: The 88th Infantry Division in World War II*, 137–138.

13. Harmon, memoir.

14. Maurice A. Rogers, supplement to the *London Gazette*, August 8, 1944.

15. Harmon, memoir.

16. *Blue and White Devils*, n.d., 25; Herbert F. Christian, Medal of Honor Recipients, World War II, Recipients A–F, U.S. Army Center of Military History, www.history.army.mil; Elden H. Johnson, Medal of Honor Recipients, World War II, Recipients G–L, U.S. Army Center of Military History, www.history.army.mil.

17. Blumenson, *Mark Clark*, 213.

18. "Alexander's Statement," *New York Times*, June 5, 1944; L. Clark, *Anzio*, 311–312.

19. Kurzman, *The Race for Rome*, 369, 375–376.

20. J. Brown, *Draftee Division*, 137.

21. Ibid., 138; Kurzman, *The Race for Rome*, 395.

22. Churchill, *Closing the Ring*, 539.

23. J. Brown, *Draftee Division*, 138.

24. Kurzman, *The Race for Rome*, 398; L. Clark, *Anzio*, 316.

25. Kurzman, *The Race for Rome*, 401.

26. Truscott, *Command Missions*, 379–380.

27. John E. Gallagher, http://4point2.org/hist-84A.

28. Wallworth, www.deadfamilies.com/Wallworth.

29. Westphal, *German Army in the West*, 168–169.

30. Otte, *The HG Panzer Division*, 117.

31. Kurzman, *The Race for Rome*, 402–403.

32. Ibid., 402; D'Este, *Fatal Decision*, 356; Green, "Anzio," 38.

33. Mason, e-mail to the author, January 27, 2017.

34. Franklin, interview.

35. Bird, interview; Bird, unpublished memoir, 8.

36. Milton Orshefsky, http://4point2.org/hist-84A.

37. Philip W. Smith, http://4point2.org/hist-84A.

38. Al Kincer, www.6thcorpscombatengineers.com/AlKincer.htm.

39. 45th U.S. Infantry Division veteran who requested anonymity.

40. Schorer, *Half Acre of Hell*, 189–191.

41. Kurzman, *The Race for Rome*, 417, 421–423.

42. "Rome Captured Intact by the 5th Army," *New York Times*, June 5, 1944.

43. Herbert L. Matthews, "Conquerors' Goal Reached by Allies," *New York Times*, June 5, 1944.

44. news.bbc.co.uk/onthisday/hi/dates/stories/june/5/newsid_3547000/3547329.

45. "Rome Falls; Liberators Get a Wild Welcome," *Life*, June 12, 1944, 38.
46. Nuti, *Aprilia*, 92–96.
47. Kesselring, *Memoirs of Kesselring*, 207.
48. Mauldin, *Brass Ring*, 272.
49. Churchill, *Closing the Ring*, 437.
50. Ibid., 433.
51. Robert Lynch, *A Letter Marked Free*, 81–82.

Epilogue

1. Liddell Hart, *History of the Second World War*, 523–542; Stanton, *World War II Order of Battle*.
2. Bowditch, *Anzio Beachhead*, 116.
3. "Field Marshal Harold Alexander, First Earl of Tunis, Dies at 77," *Times* (UK), June 17, 1969.
4. "Gen. Mark Clark Dies at 87; Last of World War II Chiefs, Conqueror of Rome," *New York Times*, April 17, 1984.
5. Author's observations after visits to the region.
6. Ben Harrell, interview by Robert T. Hayden, December 17, 1971, 36, typescript in U.S. Army Military History Institute, Carlisle, PA.

BIBLIOGRAPHY

Interviews, Letters, and Unpublished Memoirs

157th Infantry Regiment After Action Report, February 14, 1944. U.S. Army Military History Institute, Carlisle, PA.

Alexander, Sir Harold. Interview by George Howe. Sydney Matthews Collection, U.S. Army Military History Institute, Carlisle, PA.

Anderson, Lee (45th U.S. Infantry Division). Interview by the author, November 3, 2016.

Barfoot, Van. Interview by the author, August 11, 1996.

Bird, James R. (45th U.S. Infantry Division). Interview by the author, May 1, 1995.

———. Unpublished memoir.

Burke, Philip. Interview by the author, October 19, 1994.

Butler, Lawrence (1st Armored Division). World War II Veterans Survey. U.S. Army Military History Institute, Carlisle, PA.

Clayton, Jon. (3rd U.S. Infantry Division). Memoir. U.S. Army Military History Institute, Carlisle, PA.

Cloer, Russell (3rd U.S. Infantry Division). Memoir. U.S. Army Military History Institute, Carlisle, PA.

Easley, Everett W. Interview by the author, January 18, 1995.

Echohawk, Brummett. "Drawing Fire." Edited by Mark Ellenbarger and Trent Riley. Manuscript.

Ficco, Daniel. Interview by the author, April 19, 1995.

Franklin, Robert J. Interview by the author, April 21, 1996.

Gordon, William H. Interview by the author, March 13, 1995.

Hanson, Glen. Interview by the author, April 28, 1996.

Harmon, Ernest (1st U.S. Armored Division). Memoir. Harmon Papers. U.S. Army Military History Institute, Carlisle, PA.

Harrell, Ben (G-3, 3rd U.S. Infantry Division). Interview by Robert T. Hayden, December 17, 1971. U.S. Army Military History Institute, Carlisle, PA.

Heinrich, Horst. Letter to Silvano Casaldi, June 1, 1990.

Hummel, Friedrich. Letter to Silvano Casaldi, January 29, 1991.

Krieger, Ralph. Interview by the author, March 20, 1995.

LaDu, Robert. Interview by the author, April 3, 1995.

Longiotti, Cordino. Letter to Silvano Casaldi, n.d. 2001.

Lucas, John P. Diary. "From Algiers to Anzio" (unpublished autobiography). Lucas Papers. U.S. Army Military History Institute, Carlisle, PA.

———. Papers. U.S. Army Military History Institute, Carlisle, PA.

Luzzi, James. Letter to Silvano Casaldi, 1999, n.d.

Mason, Fred. E-mail correspondence with author. Various dates.

McMillan, Alvin. Interview by the author, October 30, 1994.

Miller, Phil. Letter to Silvano Casaldi, 1998, no date.

Montgomery, Jack. Interview by the author, May 5, 1996.

Muller, Karl. Letter dated April 10, 1989. Provided to the author by Silvano Casaldi. Nettuno, Italy.

Murray, Roy A. After Action Report. U.S. Army Military History Institute, Carlisle, PA.

Powell, Chester. Interview by the author, March 13, 1995.

Reitan, Earl A. Memoir. U.S. Army Military History Institute, Carlisle, PA.

Safrit, James. Memoir. Provided to author by his son, Michael Safrit.

Schlag, August. Letter to Silvano Casaldi, July 15, 1990.

Schuhle, Hans. Letter to Silvano Casaldi, September 2, 1990.

Schwegler, Gotthold. Letter to Silvano Casaldi, May 20, 1990.

Smith, Stanley R. (3rd U.S. Infantry Division). Memoir. U.S. Army Military History Institute, Carlisle, PA.

Sparks, Felix. Interview by the author, October 15, 1996.

Stemmons, Kenneth. Interview by the author, March 21, 1995.

Terheggen, Wilhelm Ernst. Letter to Silvano Casaldi, August 10, 1990.

Tryon, Merlon O. Interview by the author, March 31, 1996.

Vann, Fred. Letter to Silvano Casaldi, 1992, no date.

Williams, Vere. Interview by the author, August 30, 1994.

Wukovitz, John. *Soldiers of a Different Cloth*. Manuscript, 2017.

Yarborough, William P. (509th Parachute Infantry Battalion). Interview by John R. Meese and Houston P. Houser III, March 28, 1975. Senior Officer Debriefing Program, U.S. Army Military History Institute, Carlisle, PA.

Yarborough, William. Letter to Silvano Casaldi, 1991, no date.

Books

Alexander, Field Marshal Earl (Harold R. L. G.). *The Alexander Memoirs, 1940–1945.* Edited by John North. New York: McGraw-Hill, 1962.

Ambrose, Stephen E. *Eisenhower: Soldier, General of the Army, President-Elect—1890–1952.* Vol. 1. New York: Touchstone/Simon & Schuster, 1983.

Anders, Władysław. *An Army in Exile: The Story of the Second Polish Corps.* Nashville: Battery Press, 1981.

Anzio Beachhead. Washington, DC: U.S. Army Center of Military History, 1990.

Arness, James, with James E. Wise Jr. *James Arness: An Autobiography.* Jefferson, NC: McFarland, 2001.

Atkinson, Rick. *The Day of Battle: The War in Sicily and Italy, 1943–1944.* New York: Henry Holt, 2007.

Battistelli, Pier Paolo. *Albert Kesselring: Leadership—Strategy—Conflict.* Oxford: Osprey, 2012.

The Battle for Anzio. Paducah, KY: Turner, 1995.

Beard, Mary. *S.P.Q.R.: A History of Ancient Rome.* New York: Liveright, 2015.

Berlin, Robert H. *US Army World War II Corps Commanders: A Composite Biography.* Fort Leavenworth, KS: Combat Studies Institute, U.S. Army Staff and Command College, 1989.

The Best from "Yank," the Army Weekly. Cleveland: World, 1945.

Bidwell, Shelford. "Kesselring." In *Hitler's Generals,* edited by Corelli Barnett. New York: Grove Weidenfeld, 1989.

Black, Robert W. *The Ranger Force: Darby's Rangers in World War II.* Mechanicsburg, PA: Stackpole, 2009.

Blue and White Devils. N.p., n.d.

Blumenson, Martin. *Anzio: The Gamble That Failed.* Philadelphia: J. B. Lippincott, 1963.

———. *Mark Clark: The Last of the Great World War II Commanders.* New York: Congdon & Weed, 1984.

———. *United States Army in World War II: The Mediterranean Theater of Operations—Salerno to Cassino.* Washington, DC: Office of the Chief of Military History, U.S. Army, 1969.

Borsato, Felice. *Shingle: Cinquant'anni dopo Anzio Cassino.* Rome: Europe '92 Edizioni Internazionali, 1993.

Bowditch, John, ed. *Anzio Beachhead.* American Forces in Action, vol. 14. Washington, DC: Historical Division, Department of the Army, 1947.

Brinkley, Douglas, ed. *World War II: The Allied Counteroffensive, 1942–1945.* New York: Henry Holt, 2003.

Broumley, Jim T. *The Boldest Plan Is the Best: The Combat History of the 509th Parachute Infantry Battalion During WWII*. Sequim, WA: Rocky Marsh, 2011.

Brown, John Sloan. *Draftee Division: The 88th Infantry Division in World War II*. Novato, CA: Presidio Press, 1998.

Burns, James, Jr. *Friends at Anzio: Stories of Bacon and Burns, 180th Infantry, 45th Division*. Fayetteville, NC: Old Mountain Press, 2001.

Buster, William R. *Time on Target: The World War II Memoir of William R. Buster*. Lexington: University Press of Kentucky, 2001.

Cancelli, Diego. *Aprilia, 1944: Immagini quotidiane di una guerra, Gennaio–Maggio 1944*. Aprilia, Italy: Poligraf, 1994.

Carter, Field Marshal Lord. *The Imperial War Museum Book of the War in Italy, 1943–1945*. London: Sedgwick & Jackson, 2001.

Casaldi, Silvano. *Gli uomini della sbarco: Anzio/Nettuno, 1944*. Rome: Herald Editore, 2006.

Chalou, George C., ed. *The Secrets War: The Office of Strategic Services in World War II*. Washington, DC: National Archives and Records Administration, 1992.

Champagne, Daniel R. *Dogface Soldiers: The Story of B Company, 15th Regiment, 3rd Infantry Division*. Bennington, VT: Merriam Press, 2003.

Christopher, John. *The Race for Hitler's X-Planes*. The Mill, Gloucestershire: History Press, 2013.

Churchill, Winston S. *Closing the Ring*. Vol. 5 of *The Second World War*. Boston: Houghton Mifflin, 1985.

Clark, Lloyd. *Anzio: Italy and the Battle for Rome—1944*. New York: Atlantic Monthly Press, 2006.

Clark, Mark W. *Calculated Risk*. New York: Harper & Brothers, 1950.

Colantuono, Patrizio. *Anzio e i suoi lidi: Cartoline illustrate dal 1900 al 1960*. Anzio: Tipografia Marina, n.d.

Compagno, Gianfranco. "Aprilia: 60 anni, storia e cronaca." In *L'impresa—Civiltà e memorie storiche: Cura comitato Apriliana*. Aprilia, Italy: Tipolitografia Grafica, 2000.

Darby, William O., and William H. Baumer. *Darby's Rangers: We Led the Way*. San Rafael, CA: Presidio Press, 1980.

Del Calzo, Nick, and Peter Collier. *Medal of Honor: Portraits of Valor Beyond the Call of Duty*. New York: Workman/Artisan, 2003.

D'Este, Carlo. *Fatal Decision: Anzio and the Battle for Rome*. New York: HarperCollins, 1991.

———. *Patton: A Genius for War*. New York: HarperCollins, 1995.

———. *World War II in the Mediterranean*. Chapel Hill, NC: Algonquin, 1990.

Dodge, Robert E. *Memories of the Anzio Beachhead and the War in Europe.* New York: Vantage Press, 2004.

Dougherty, Richard. *The British Reconnaissance Corps in World War II.* Oxford: Osprey, 2007.

Draper, Theodore. *The 84th Infantry Division in the Battle of Germany, November 1944–May 1945.* New York: Viking Press, 1946.

Dugdale, William. *Settling the Bill: The Memoirs of Bill Dugdale.* London: Endeavour, 2011.

Eisenhower, Dwight D. *Crusade in Europe.* Garden City, NY: Doubleday, 1948.

Ellis, John. *The Sharp End: The Fighting Man in World War II.* New York: Charles Scribner's Sons, 1980.

Failmezger, Victor. *American Knights: The Untold Story of the Men of the Legendary 601st Tank Destroyer Battalion.* Oxford: Osprey, 2015.

Fehrenbach, T. R. *The Battle of Anzio.* New York: Open Road, 1962.

Fellgiebel, Walther-Peer. *Die Träger Ritterkreuzes des Eisernen Kreuzes, 1939–1945.* Friedberg, Germany: Podzun-Pallas, 2000.

Fifth Army Antiaircraft Artillery: Salerno to Florence, 9 September 1943–8 September 1944. N.p.: Antiaircraft Artillery Section, HQ, Fifth Army, n.d.

Fifth Army History, 16 January 1944–31 March 1944. Pt. 4, *Cassino and Anzio.* Florence, Italy: L'Impronta Press, 1944.

Fifth Army History. Pt. 5, *The Drive to Rome.* Milan: Pizzi & Pizio, 1944.

Fisher, Ernest F., Jr. *United States Army in World War II: The Mediterranean Theater of Operations, Cassino to the Alps.* Washington, DC: Office of the Chief of Military History, United States Army, 1984.

Fisher, George A. *The Story of the 180th Infantry Regiment.* San Angelo, TX: Newsfoto, 1947.

Fitzsimons, Bernard, ed. *The Illustrated Encyclopedia of 20th Century Weapons and Warfare.* New York: Columbia House/BPC, 1978.

Ford, Ken. *Cassino, 1944: Breaking the Gustav Line.* Oxford: Osprey, 2004.

Forty, George. *Fifth Army at War.* New York: Charles Scribner's Sons, 1980.

———. *Tiger Tank Battalions in World War II.* Minneapolis: Zenith Press, 2008.

Forty-Fifth Infantry Division. Baton Rouge: Army & Navy, 1945.

Franklin, Robert J. *Medic: How I Fought WWII with Morphine, Sulfa, and Iodine Swabs.* Lincoln: University of Nebraska Press, 2006.

Franks, Kenny. *Citizen Soldiers: Oklahoma's National Guard.* Norman: University of Oklahoma Press, 1983.

Fraser, General Sir David. *And We Shall Shock Them: The British Army in the Second World War.* London: Hodder and Stoughton, 1983.

German Order of Battle, 1944: The Directory, Prepared by Allied Intelligence, of Regiments, Formations and Units of the German Armed Forces. Mechanicsburg, PA: Stackpole, 1994.

Grace, Edward. *The Perilous Road to Rome and Beyond.* Barnsley, UK: Pen & Sword, 1993.

Greaves, Adrian. *Rorke's Drift.* London: Cassell, 2002.

Hallowell, Jack. *History of the 157th Infantry Regiment (Rifle), 4 June '43–8 May '45.* N.p., n.d.

Hardesty, Von. *Black Wings: Courageous Stories of African Americans in Aviation and Space History.* New York: HarperCollins/Smithsonian, 2008.

Haskew, Michael E. *Encyclopedia of Elite Forces in the Second World War.* London: Amber Books, 2007.

Heathcote, Tony. *The British Field Marshals, 1736–1997.* London: Pen & Sword, 1999.

Hibbert, Christopher. *Anzio: The Bid for Rome.* New York: Ballantine, 1970.

———. *Benito Mussolini: The Rise and Fall of Il Duce.* New York: Penguin, 1965.

Hirshson, Stanley P. *General Patton: A Soldier's Life.* New York: HarperCollins, 2002.

Hogg, Ian V., and John Weeks. *The Illustrated Encyclopedia of Military Vehicles.* London: New Burlington Books, 1980.

Howe, George F. *The Battle History of the 1st Armored Division.* Nashville: Battery Press, 1979.

Hoyt, Edwin P. *Backwater War: The Allied Campaign in Italy, 1943–45.* Westport, CT: Praeger, 2002.

———. *The GI's War: American Soldiers in Europe During World War II.* New York: McGraw-Hill, 1988.

Jackson, Kathi. *They Called Them Angels: American Military Nurses of World War II.* Lincoln: University of Nebraska Press, 2006.

Jackson, W. G. F. *The Battle for Italy.* New York: Harper & Row, 1967.

Jeffers, H. Paul. *Onward We Charge: The Heroic Story of Darby's Rangers in World War II.* New York: NAL Caliber, 2007.

Joseph, Frank. *Mussolini's War: Fascist Italy's Military Struggles from Africa and Western Europe to the Mediterranean and Soviet Union, 1935–45.* Havertown, PA: Casemate, 2010.

Kahn, Bernard L. *Fight On: A GI's Odyssey Back to Nazi Germany.* Brule, WI: Cable, 2013.

Katz, Robert. *The Battle for Rome.* New York: Simon & Schuster, 2003.

Kaufman, Henry. *Vertrauensmann: Man of Confidence.* New York: Rivercross, 1994.

Keegan, John. *Churchill's Generals*. London: Cassell Military, 2005.

Kenneally, John. *The Honour and the Shame*. London: Headline Review, 1991.

Kesselring, Albert. *The Memoirs of Field-Marshal Kesselring*. 1954. Reprint, New York: Skyhorse, 2016.

Kurzman, Dan. *The Race for Rome*. Garden City, NY: Doubleday, 1975.

Lamb, Richard. *War in Italy, 1943–1945: A Brutal Story*. New York: St. Martin's Press, 1993.

Liddell Hart, Basil H. *History of the Second World War*. New York: G. P. Putnam's Sons, 1970.

Linderman, Gerald F. *The World Within War: America's Combat Experience in World War II*. Cambridge, MA: Harvard University Press, 1999.

Lynch, Robert. *A Letter Marked Free*. Indianapolis: Dog Ear, 2007.

MacDonald, Charles B. *The Mighty Endeavor: American Armed Forces in the European Theater in World War II*. New York: Oxford University Press, 1969.

MacDonald, Lyn. *Somme*. London: Michael Joseph, 1983.

———. *To the Last Man: Spring 1918*. New York: Carroll & Graf, 1999.

Majdalany, Fred. *The Battle of Cassino*. New York: Ballantine, 1957.

Mark, Eduard. *Aerial Interdiction: Air Power and the Land Battle in Three American Wars*. Washington, DC: Center for Air Force History, 1994.

Marshall, Charles F. *A Ramble Through My War: Anzio and Other Joys*. Baton Rouge: Louisiana State University Press, 1998.

Mauldin, Bill. *The Brass Ring: A Sort of a Memoir*. New York: W. W. Norton, 1971.

———. *Up Front*. New York: Henry Holt, 1945.

McManus, John. *The Deadly Brotherhood: The American Combat Soldier in World War II*. Novato, CA: Presidio Press, 1998.

Mead, Richard. *Churchill's Lions: A Biographical Guide to the Key British Generals of World War II*. Stroud, UK: Spellmount, 2007.

Mitcham, Samuel W. *Rommel's Desert Commanders: The Men Who Served the Desert Fox, North Africa, 1941–42*. Mechanicsburg, PA: Stackpole, 2008.

Morison, Samuel Eliot. *Sicily-Salerno-Anzio, January 1943–June 1944*. Vol. 9 of *History of United States Naval Operations in World War II*. Boston: Little, Brown, 1984.

Morrison, Jim. *Letters from Joe*. Victoria, Canada: Trafford 2004.

Munsell, Warren P., Jr. *The Story of a Regiment: A History of the 179th Regimental Combat Team*. Privately printed, 1946.

Murphy, Audie. *To Hell and Back*. New York: Henry Holt, 1949.

Neillands, Robin. *By Land and by Sea: The Story of the Royal Marine Commandos*. Barnsley, UK: Pen and Sword, 2004.

Newnan, William L. *Escape in Italy: The Narrative of Lieutenant William L. Newnan, United States Rangers*. Ann Arbor: University of Michigan Press, 1945.

Nordyke, Phil. *More than Courage: The Combat History of the 504th Parachute Infantry Regiment in World War II*. Minneapolis: Zenith Press, 2008.

North, Oliver, and Joe Musser, *War Stories: Heroism in the Pacific*. Washington, DC: Regnery, 2004.

Nuti, Pasqualino. *Aprilia: I giorni della guerra—e gli occhi di un bambino*. Privately printed, 2014.

Otte, Alfred. *The HG Panzer Division*. West Chester, PA: Schiffer, 1989.

Parker, Matthew. *Monte Cassino: The Hardest Fought Battle of World War II*. London: Headline Press, 2003.

Parkinson, C. Northcote. *Always a Fusilier: The War History of the Royal Fusiliers (City of London Regiment)*. London: Sampson Low, 1949.

Pyle, Ernie. *Brave Men*. New York: Henry Holt, 1944.

Quick, John. *Dictionary of Weapons and Military Terms*. New York: McGraw-Hill, 1973.

Raiber, Richard. *Anatomy of Perjury: Field Marshal Albert Kesselring, Via Rasella, and the Ginny Mission*. Plainsboro Township, NJ: Associated University Presses, 2008.

Raines, Edgar F., Jr. *Eyes of Artillery: The Origins of Modern US Army Aviation in World War II*. Army Historical Series. Washington, DC: Center of Military History, U.S. Army, 2000.

Reiman, Charles. Monograph. 45th Infantry Division Museum.

Sarnecky, Mary T. *A History of the US Army Nurse Corps*. Philadelphia: University of Pennsylvania Press, 1999.

Schneider, Wolfgang. *Tigers in Combat*. Vol. 1. London: Stackpole, 2004.

Schorer, Avis Dagit. *A Half Acre of Hell: A Combat Nurse in WWII*. Lakeville, MN: Galde Press, 2002.

Sheehan, Fred. *Anzio: Epic of Bravery*. Norman: University of Oklahoma Press, 1994.

Shirer, William L. *The Rise and Fall of the Third Reich*. New York: Crest, 1960.

Silvestri, Ennio. *The Long Road to Rome*. Privately printed, 1994.

Stanton, Shelby. *World War II Order of Battle*. New York: Galahad Books, 1984.

The Story of the 36th Infantry Division. Paris: Desfosse-Neogravure, 1945.

Tessin, Georg. *Verbände und Truppen der deutschen Wehrmacht und der Waffen-SS im Zweiten Weltkrieg, 1939–1945.* Osnabruck: Biblio-Verlag, 2011.

Toffey, John J., IV. *Jack Toffey's War: A Son's Memoir.* New York: Fordham University Press, 2008.

Tompkins, Peter. *A Spy in Rome.* New York: Avon Books/HarperCollins, 1962.

Trevelyan, Raleigh. *The Fortress: A Diary of Anzio and After.* London: Faber & Faber, 2010.

Truscott, Lucian K., Jr. *Command Missions: A Personal Story.* Novato, CA: Presidio Press, 1990.

Vaughn-Thomas, Wynford. *Anzio.* London: Longmans, 1961.

Verney, Peter. *Anzio, 1944: An Unexpected Fury.* London: B. T. Batsford, 1978.

Westphal, Siegfried. *The German Army in the West.* London: Cassell, 1951.

Whitlock, Flint. *The Rock of Anzio: From Sicily to Dachau—a History of the U.S. 45th Infantry Division.* Boulder, CO: Westview Press, 1998.

Whitlock, Flint, and Bob Bishop. *Soldiers on Skis: A Pictorial Memoir of the 10th Mountain Division.* Boulder, CO: Paladin Press, 1992.

Whitman, Bill. *Scouts Out!* Los Angeles: Authors Unlimited, 1990.

Williamson, Kenneth D. *Tales of a Thunderbird in World War II.* Privately printed, 1994.

Wiltse, Charles M., the United States Army in World War II, the Technical Services. *Medical Service in the Mediterranean and Minor Areas.* Army Historical Series. Washington, DC: Center of Military History, U.S. Army, 1987.

Woodruff, William. *Vessel of Sadness.* New York: Harper & Row, 1978.

Wukovits, John. *Soldiers of a Different Cloth: Notre Dame Chaplains in World War II.* Notre Dame, IN: Notre Dame Press, 2018.

Zaloga, Steven J. *Anzio, 1944: The Beleaguered Beachhead.* Oxford: Osprey, 2005.

———. *Armored Thunderbolt: The US Army Sherman in World War II.* Mechanicsburg, PA: Stackpole, 2008.

MAGAZINES, NEWSPAPERS, AND OTHER PERIODICALS

"After the Auk." *Time,* August 31, 1942.

Alexander, Field Marshal. Obituary. *Times,* June 17, 1969.

"Alexander Sees Second Round Won." *New York Times,* February 17, 1944.

"Alexander's Statement." *New York Times,* June 5, 1944.

"Allied Beachheads: One in the Pacific Is a Success; One in Italy Is in Trouble." *Life*, February 21, 1944.

"Allied Units Land Behind Nazis in Italy." *New York Times*, January 23, 1944.

"Alton W. Knappenberger, 84; Won Medal of Honor." *Washington Post*, June 28, 2008.

"Audie Murphy." *After the Battle*, no. 3 (1973).

Baldwin, Hanson. "The Situation in Italy." *New York Times*, January 27, 1944.

"Battle of Italy: Nightmare's End." *Time*, June 5, 1944.

"Battle of Italy: Out of the Storm." *Time*, February 21, 1944.

"Battle of Italy: Third Landing." *Time*, January 31, 1944.

Bracker, Milton. "Allies Give Ground; Fall Back." *New York Times*, February 6, 1944.

———. "Allies Start Drive at Anzio Beachhead." *New York Times*, May 24, 1944.

———. "Harbor Captured." *New York Times*, January 23, 1944.

———. "Nazis Retake Aprilia Near Rome." *New York Times*, February 17, 1944.

"British Veterans to Commemorate 70th Anniversary of Anzio Landings in Italy." *Telegraph* (UK), January 22, 2014.

Citino, Robert M. "Last Ride at Anzio." *Military History Quarterly* (Summer 2016).

Clark, Edgar. "Anzio Papers Headline Men Who Make the News." *Stars and Stripes*, May 1, 1944.

Clark, Mark W. Obituary. *New York Times*, April 17, 1984.

D'Este, Carlo. "No Fear." *World War II* (January–February 2016).

"Ernie Pyle Is Killed on Ie Island; Foe Fired When All Seemed Safe." Obituary. *New York Times*, April 19, 1945.

Glennon, Ross. "From Norway to Anzio: Sergeant Joe Dunne, DCM." *Reveille* (Winter 2014).

Green, J. H. "Anzio." *After the Battle*, no. 52 (1986).

Harmon, Ernest N., and Milton MacKaye. "Our Bitter Days at Anzio." *Saturday Evening Post*, September 9 and 18, 1948.

———. "We Break Out at Anzio." *Saturday Evening Post*, September 25, 1948.

Hemingway, Bill. "The Anguish of Anzio." *Denver Post*, November 19, 1978, Empire section.

"Lt.-Col. Dick Evans." Obituary. *Telegraph* (UK), February 20, 2013.

Mitchell, Paula Ann. "New Paltz Man Recalls Life as a WWII POW." *Kingston (NY) Daily Freeman*, June 12, 2014.

"Negro Fliers Praised." *New York Times*, February 6, 1944.

Packard, Reynolds. "Beachhead Piled with German Dead." *New York Times*, February 19, 1944.

Parker, Roy, Jr. "Anzio Landing Was a Time of Valor for US Paratroopers." *Fayetteville* (NC) *Observer*, January 20, 1994.

Pisa, Nick. "Touching Moment: Pink Floyd Star Visits World War II Cemetery in Italy to Honour His Soldier Father Who Died in Heroic Final Stand." *Daily Mail* (UK), October 13, 2013.

Pratt, Sara E. "March 17, 1944: The Most Recent Eruption of Mount Vesuvius." *Earth* (March 2016). www.earthmagazine.org.

Prefer, Nathan N. "Key to the Eternal City." *WWII History* (April 2016).

Puccillo, Cesare. "Anzio delle delizie: Le dimore nobiliari." Centro Studi Neptunia, August 1997. www.comune.nettuno.roma.it.

"Rome Captured Intact by the 5th Army After Fierce Battle Through Suburbs; Nazis Move Northwest; Air War Rages." *New York Times*, June 5, 1944.

"Rome Falls; Liberators Get a Wild Welcome." *Life*, June 12, 1944.

Rufty, Bill. "James Henry Mills Won a Medal of Honor in WWII." *Lakeland* (FL) *Ledger*, May 24, 2004.

Scott, Burgess, W. "Hot Spot in Italy." *Yank*, March 3, 1944.

Sedgwick, A. C. "Germans at Anzio Taken by Surprise." *New York Times*, May 24, 1944.

Sidney, William P. "Victoria Cross for Tommygun Stand at Anzio." *London Gazette*, March 28, 1944.

"Silver Stars Pinned on Nurses at Anzio." *New York Times*, February 23, 1944.

Stefanelli, Anthony. "Veteran Recounts His Winter of '43 to '44 Experiences." *Nutley* (NJ) *Sun*, June 9, 1994.

"Stimson Urges US to End Pessimism; Calls Anzio Status 'Good.'" *New York Times*, February 18, 1945.

"Tale of a Red-Tailed Angel." *Buckeye Guard* (Spring 1999).

"Tom Gould Survived the Hell of the Anzio Landing." *Nottingham Post* (UK), August 21, 2010.

Vego, Milan N. "The Allied Landing at Anzio-Nettuno, 22 January–4 March 1944." *Naval War College Review* 67, no. 4 (2014).

"Veteran Recounts His Winter of '43 to '44 Experiences." *Nutley* (NJ) *Sun*, June 9, 1994.

"War News Summarized." *New York Times*, February 18, 1944.

"William Eagles, Retired Army General, Dies." Obituary, *Washington Post*, February 21, 1988.

"World Battlefronts—Italy." *Time*, February 28, 1944, 30.

WEBSITES

1st British Infantry Division. www.revolvy.com/main/index.php?s=1st InfantryDivision&stype=topics&cmd=list.

1st Special Service Force. www.firstspecialserviceforce.net/history.

33rd Field Hospital. http://history.amedd.army.mil.

34th Infantry Division history. www.34infdiv.org/history/135inf.

36th Combat Engineers. www.6thcorpscombatengineers.com/docs/36th /36th%20History%20WDRB.

"56th Evacuation Hospital Unit History." www.med-dept.com/unit-histories /56th-evacuation-hospital.

100th Infantry Battalion Veterans Education Center. www.100thbattalion .org.

179th Infantry Regiment War Journal, February 1944. www.lsu.edu/faculty /fanselm/Journal/February.

"Addendum to 2nd German Counter Attack." www.bbc.co.uk/history/ww2 peopleswar/stories/50/a3608750.shtml.

Alley, Eric. "The Landings at Anzio: A View from the Sea." www.bbc.co.uk /history/ww2peopleswar/article4015243.

Anderson, James Tolby. anziobeachheadveterans.com/james-tolby-ander son.html.

"The Angels of Anzio." www.darbysrangers.tripod.com/id76; med-dept .com/veterans-testimonies/veterans-testimony-arthur-b-degrandpre.

Antolak, Sylvester. Medal of Honor Recipients, World War II, Recipients A–F, U.S. Army Center of Military History. www.history.army.mil.

"Anzio Annie." www.army.mil/article/48580/169609.

Avery, George. "I Remember Anzio." http://4point2.org/hist-84A.htm.

Bate, Peter Geoffrey. "Memories: Diary of Peter Geoffrey Bate." www.bbc .co.uk/history/ww2peopleswar/article2759123.

Batten, John. "9 Commando, Overseas." www.commandoveterans.org /9_Commando_overseas.

BBC People's War. www.bbc.co.uk/history/ww2peopleswar/stories/69/a24 29769.

Billingsley, Ian. www.bbc.co.uk/history/ww2peopleswar/stories/87/a4001 987.shtml.

Bowles, E. O. "Italy 2: Garigliano, Anzio, and Winter on the Adriatic (14 January to 1 April 1944)." www.ourstory.info/library/Rock/R11.html.

Bray, Trevor. "A Gordon's Story." www.bbc.co.uk/history/ww2peopleswar /article4178801.

Briggs, Milton. "The Anzio Beachhead." www.tankbooks.com.

Brown, Paul. Diary. www.custermen.com/AtTheFront/ListKIA.

Bull, R. H. "A Quiet Landing." ww2talk.com/index.php?threads/anzio-another-day13110.

Burt, Michael. "Remembering the Loss of HMS *Spartan*." *Plymouth Herald* (UK), January 31, 2015. naval-history.net.

Chiefari, Sal. Memoir. www.anziobeachheadveterans.com.

Christian, Herbert F. Medal of Honor Recipients, World War II, Recipients A–F, U.S. Army Center of Military History. www.history.army.mil.

Chubbuck, James, and George W. Gardes. Interview by Dr. John S. G. Shotwell, December 9, 1950. www.6thcorpscombatengineers.com.

Courlas, George. www.45thdivision.org/Veterans/Courlas_157.htm.

Craver, Joe D. www.anziobeachheadveterans.com/craver.

Cruikshank, Chester G. www.findagrave.com; valor.militarytimes.com/recipient.php?recipientid=22018.

Davila, Rudolph B. www.arlingtoncemetery.net.

Dervishian, Ernest H. Medal of Honor Recipients, World War II, Recipients A–F, U.S. Army Center of Military History. www.history.army.mil.

Dickerson, Joe F. (C Company, 53rd DUKW Battalion). "The Men of the Landing—Anzio Beachhead Veterans of WWII." Memoir. www.anziobeachheadveterans.com/men-of-the-landing.html.

Dubbin. en.wikipedia.org/wiki/Dubbin.

Duke of Lancaster's Regiment Lancashire Infantry Museum. www.lancashireinfantrymuseum.org.uk/world-war-ii-1/.

Dutko, John W. Medal of Honor Recipients, World War II, Recipients A–F, U.S. Army Center of Military History. www.history.army.mil.

Easter, Clyde. www.everytownusa.com/everytown-usa/anzio-beachhead-reunion.

Evans, Derek. "The Loss of HMS *Spartan*." www.world-war.co.uk/spartan_loss.php3.

Fowler, Thomas W. Medal of Honor Recipients, World War II, Recipients A–F, U.S. Army Center of Military History. www.history.army.mil.

Gallagher, John E. http://4point2.org/hist-84A.

Galt, William W. Medal of Honor Recipients, World War II, Recipients G–L, U.S. Army Center of Military History. www.history.army.mil.

———. theirfinesthour.net/2014/05/captain-william-w-galt-usa-may-29-1944.

Gibson, Eric G. www.qmfound.com.

Gordon-Watson, David M. L. www.telegraph.co.uk/news/obituaries/.../Brigadier-Michael-Gordon-Watson.html.

Graffagnino, Peter C. www.45thdivision.org/Veterans/Graffagnino2.htm.

Gräser, Fritz Hubert. www.lexikon-der-wehrmacht.de/Personenregister/G/GraeserFH.

Hall, George J. Medal of Honor Recipients, World War II, Recipients G–L, U.S. Army Center of Military History. www.history.army.mil.

Hardin, Stephen L. "Battle of the Alamo." In *Handbook of Texas Online*, published by the Texas State Historical Association. tshaonline.org /handbook/online/articles/qea02.

Hargreaves, John M. www.ancientfaces.com/person/john-michael -hargreaves/164162948.

Harmon, Ernest N. "8 NU's Maj. Gen. Ernest Harmon: 'The Second Patton." www.bicentennial.norwich.edu/8-ernest-harmon/.

Hawks, Lloyd C. Medal of Honor Recipients, World War II, Recipients G–L, U.S. Army Center of Military History. www.history.army.mil.

Heard, William. "7th Ox and Bucks Wiped Out Holding the Line at Anzio." ww2today.com/15-february-1944-7th-ox-and-bucks-wiped-out -holding-the-line-at-anzio.

"History of the 36th Engineers." www.6thcorpscombatengineers.com /docs/36th/36th%20History%20WDRB.pdf.

"History of the First Special Service Force." www.firstspecialserviceforce .net/history.

HMS *Penelope*. www.wrecksite.eu/wreck.aspx?15428.

Hohler, Thomas. www.ww2talk.com/index.php?threads/help-for-info-grand father-served-with-grenadier-guards.43085/page-2#post-512246.

Huff, Paul B. Medal of Honor Recipients, World War II, Recipients G–L, U.S. Army Center of Military History. www.history.army.mil.

Irish Guards. www.di2.nu/files/kipling/IrishGuardsv2.

The Irish Guards in the Great War. Vol. 2. webcache.googleusercontent. com/search?q=cache.

Irish Guards War Diary. www.ww2guards.com.

Jeffs, George Oliver. www.bbc.co.uk/history/ww2peopleswar/articleA90 0019.

Johnson, Elden H. Medal of Honor Recipients, World War II, Recipients G–L, U.S. Army Center of Military History. www.history.army.mil.

Johnston, William J. Medal of Honor Recipients, World War II, Recipients G–L, U.S. Army Center of Military History. www.history.army.mil.

Jones, Ivor. "Pte. Ivor Jones." www.wartimememoriesproject.com/ww2 /view.php?uid=218519.

Jupp, Captain. www.bbc.co.uk/history/ww2peopleswar/article3608750.

Kesselring, Albert. forum.12oclockhigh.net.

Kessler, Patrick L. Medal of Honor Recipients, World War II, Recipients G–L, U.S. Army Center of Military History. www.history.army.mil.

Kincer, Al. www.6thcorpscombatengineers.com/AlKincer.htm.

Knappenberger, Alton W. Medal of Honor Recipients, World War II, Recipients G–L, U.S. Army Center of Military History. www.history.army.mil.

Knowlton, Donald E. www.valor.militarytimes.com/recipient.php?recipient id=22338n.

Kobashigawa, Yeiki, and Shinyei Nakamine. www.homeofheroes.com.

Lancashire Infantry Regiment. www.lancashireinfantrymuseum.org.uk/world-war-ii-1.

"The Landing at Anzio." ww2talk.com/index.php?threads/anzio-another-day.13110.

Lara, Salvador J. www.abmc.gov/news-events/news/world-war-ii-ssgt-salvador-lara-receives-posthumous-medal-honor-nearly-70-years.

Large, John R. www.wartimememoriesproject.com.

Lees, Ted. www.bbc.co.uk/history/ww2peopleswar/stories/91/a2063891.shtml.

Lehman, Carl H. www.flashman.com.

Levine, Murray. www.45thdivision.org/Veterans/Levine.htm.

Liggett, Francis E. Memoir. 45thinfantrydivision.com/index18.htm.

London Irish Rifles Association. "The London Irish at War, 1939–45." www.londonirishrifles.com/index.php/second-world-war/the-london-irish-at-war-1939-45/.

"London Irish Rifles into Anzio." www.royal-irish.com/events/london-irish-rifles-arrive-anzio.

MacCombie, Herbert E. www.texasmilitaryforcesmuseum.org/36division/archives/chaplain/030.

McAllister, Ray. www.45thdivision.org/Veterans/McAllister.htm.

McDougall, A. "History of the Sherwood Foresters." www.bbc.co.uk/history/ww2peopleswar/stories/66/a5298366.shtml.

McIntosh, Guardsman. www.bbc.co.uk/history/ww2peopleswar/article1164124.

Mills, James H. Medal of Honor Recipients, World War II, Recipients M–S, U.S. Army Center of Military History. www.history.army.mil.

Moriarty, Thomas M. www.2ndbombgroup.org.

Mornement, Peter H. www.surreycc.gov.uk/heritage-culture-and-recreation/archives-and-history/surrey-history-centre/marvels-of-the-month/letters-of-major-p-h-mornement.

Murphy, Audie. valor.militarytimes.com/recipient.php?recipientid=209.

Murray, A. S. P. ww2talk.com/index.php?threads/anzio-another-day.13110.

Nettuno airstrip. www.iwm.org.uk/history/anzio-the-invasion-that-almost-failed.

Newman, Beryl R. Medal of Honor Recipients, World War II, Recipients M–S, U.S. Army Center of Military History. www.history.army.mil.

North Staffordshire Regiment Living History Association. www.north staffordshirelha.org.

O'Connor, Philip R. "A Loyola Rome Student's Guide to World War II in Rome and Italy." 2015. https://luc.edu/media/lucedu/rome/fall2015 /Formatted%20Rome%20Guide%20--Eleventh%20Edition%20(1).pdf.

Olson, Truman O. Medal of Honor Recipients, World War II, Recipients M–S, U.S. Army Center of Military History. www.history.army.mil.

Orshefsky, Milton. http://4point2.org/hist-84A.

Oxfordshire and Buckinghamshire Light Infantry Regiment, 7th Battalion (7th Ox and Bucks). www.lightbobs.com/7th-bn-oxf--bucks-li -january-1944-june-1944.

Penney, William R. C. www.unithistories.com/officers/Army_officers_P01 .html#Penney_WRC.

Pfeiffer, Hans-Hellmuth. www.lexikon-der-wehrmacht.de/Personenregister /P/PfeiferH.htm.

Pistone, Frank. Memoir. www.anziobeachheadveterans.com/frank-s -pistone.html.

Puccillo, Cesare. "Anzio delle delizie: Le dimore nobiliari." Centro Studi Neptunia, August 1997. www.comune.nettuno.roma.it.

Reed, Bert. www.battlefieldsww2.50megs.com/dad.

Reuter, Edward. Memoir. www.509thgeronimo.org.

Richthofen, Wolfram Freiherr von. forum.12oclockhigh.net.

Rogers, Maurice A. Supplement to the London Gazette, August 8, 1944.

Rustebakke, Dorothy. "Scobey's One-Man Army—Henry Schauer." ww2aa .proboards.com/thread/7087/kraut-hour-schauer.

Saxon, Timothy D. "The German Side of the Hill: Nazi Conquest and Exploitation of Italy, 1943–45." PhD diss., University of Virginia, 1999. http://digitalcommons.liberty.edu/cgi/viewcontent.cgi?article=1053 &context=fac_dis.

Schauer, Henry. Medal of Honor Recipients, World War II, Recipients M–S, U.S. Army Center of Military History. www.history.army.mil.

Sherman, Ray. "Ray Sherman's Recollections and Diary." www.45th division.org/Veterans/Sherman179K.htm.

Sherwood Foresters. www.bbc.co.uk/history/ww2peopleswar/article529 8366.

Shirley, John. anziobeachheadveterans.com/men-of-the-landing.html.

Sidney, William P. Victoria Cross citation. www.britishempire.co.uk /forces/armyunits/britishinfantry/grenadierwilliamsidney.

Smith, Furman L. Medal of Honor Recipients, World War II, Recipients M–S, U.S. Army Center of Military History. www.history.army.mil.

Smith, Philip W. http://4point2.org/hist-84A.

Squires, John C. Medal of Honor Recipients, World War II, Recipients M–S, U.S. Army Center of Military History. www.history.army.mil.

Stokes, Bernie L. www.45thinfantrydivision.com.

Taylor, Charles D. "Twenty Miles to Rome: The Story of South Carolina's First Medal of Honor Winner in World War II." Master's thesis, Clemson University, August 2009. http://tigerprints.clemson.edu/cgi/view content.cgi?article= 1756&context=all_theses.

"Trench Foot." emergency.cdc.gov/disasters/trenchfoot.asp.

Unnamed British soldier. www.bbc.co.uk/history/ww2peopleswar/article 2429769.

Vachon, Duane. "'Kraut-an-Hour Schauer': T/Sgt. Henry Schauer, U.S. Army, WW II Medal of Honor (1918-1997)." *Hawaii Reporter*, November 20, 2011. www.hawaiireporter.com/kraut-an-hour-schauer -tsgt-henry-schauer-u-s-army-ww-ii-medal-of-honor-1918-1997/123.

Vesuvius. www.warwingsart.com/12thAirForce/Vesuvius.

Wallworth, Robert N. www.deadfamilies.com/Wallworth.

Waters, Eric. www.rogerwaters.org.

Weber, Edward. www.westpointaog.org/memorial-article?id=e82a2043-f9a b-457e-90c3-70392c0b284f.

Wims, Cody. www.45thdivision.org/Veterans/Wims157_2.htm.

"World War II SSgt. Salvador Lara Receives Posthumous Medal of Honor Nearly 70 Years Later." www.abmc.gov/news-events/news/world-war-ii -ssgt-salvador-lara-receives-posthumous-medal-honor-nearly-70-years.

Wright, Sydney Arthur. www.bbc.co.uk/history/ww2peopleswar/stories /89/a3763389.shtml.

Young, Henry L. S. www.ww2guards.com/ww2guards/AWARDS_T_-_Z /Pages/YOUNG,_H.S.L._D.S.O.,_1BN.

MISCELLANEOUS

179th After Action Report, February 1944. U.S. Army Military History Institute, Carlisle, PA.

Barker, Arthur C., Jr. "Infantry in Defense on a Wide Front." Ft. Benning, GA: Student monograph, Advanced Infantry Officers Course, 1955–1956.

Evans, Robley D., Brock H. Faulkner, Alex J. Rankin, Grover C. Richards Jr., John S. Robinson, Alford P. Holbrecht, John J. Wessmiller, and

William T. Unger. "American Armor at Anzio: A Research Report
    Prepared by Committee 2." Fort Knox, KY: Armored School, Officers
    Advanced Course, 1948–1949.
A Fifth Army Report from the Beachhead. U.S. Army Signal Corps film no.
    misc. 1039. 1944.
"History of the 36th Engineer (Combat) Regiment." Washington, DC: Ad-
    jutant General's Office, War Department Records Branch, AGO, His-
    torical Records Section, n.d.
Morning Report, Company A, 4th Ranger Battalion, 1 February 1944. U.S.
    Army Military History Institute, Carlisle, PA.
"Report of the German Operations at Anzio Beachhead, 22 January–31 May
    1944." Military Intelligence Division, War Department, Camp Ritchie,
    MD. U.S. Army Military History Institute, Carlisle, PA.
Sassman, Roger W. "Operation Shingle and Major General John P. Lucas."
    Fort Leavenworth, KS: Strategy Research Project, U.S. Army War Col-
    lege, 1999.
Senior Officers Debriefing Program, USAMHI.
Yarbrorough, William P., 509th PIB. Interview by Colonel John R. Meese
    and Lieutenant Colonel Houston P. Houser III, March 28, 1975. U.S.
    Army Military History Institute, Carlisle, PA.

ACKNOWLEDGMENTS

I've said it before, but I'll say it again: Writing a book is not unlike conducting a military operation. There is mission to be accomplished, an objective to be taken, obstacles to overcome, casualties to be expected (in the form of discarded paragraphs and whole pages), and (one hopes) a victory celebration after it's all over.

There are also many people upon whom the success of the operation will hinge. For this project, my heartfelt thanks go out to the many veterans, both living and dead, who committed their memories of their experiences of the battle of Anzio to paper or tape; their firsthand accounts of their experiences are a testament to courage beyond belief. I am also extremely grateful to the veterans who allowed me to interview them—not only for this book but also for my previous book on the subject, *The Rock of Anzio*. They will never know how much the retelling of their experiences has done to bring recognition to one of the most savage battles in all history. Their names are included in the Bibliography.

Like every other chronicler of the Anzio campaign, I relied heavily on Martin Blumenson's seminal work, *Cassino to the Alps* (one of the volumes in the U.S. Army's Green Book series), and who was encouraging of my work; you will find it quoted often herein. His biography of Mark Clark is also essential in understanding the personality issues behind the campaign.

While doing research for *The Rock of Anzio*, I traveled to Italy in the late 1990s with a pair of fellow military historians from Colorado, Russ

Morgan and the late Bruce Ryan. Accompanying us were several issues of *After the Battle* magazine, a quarterly British publication that made a name for itself with articles that were illustrated by "then" (wartime) and "now" (current) photographs of World War II battle sites. The day we visited Aprilia, we had with us issue number 52, which is devoted to Anzio. As we stood in front of the San Michele Church trying to line up a comparison shot to match the one in the magazine, we were approached by a nattily attired gentleman.

Although he spoke not a word of English and my Italian vocabulary consisted of about three words (two of which were *grazie* and *prego*), I somehow managed to communicate that we were military tourists in search of Italian battlefields. It turned out that the gentleman, whose name was Gianfranco Compagno, owned a gentlemen's clothing store in downtown Aprilia and was the town's "unofficial" historian. He was fascinated by the fact that we were fascinated by Aprilia and spent the rest of his day shepherding us around the town and nearby environs. In 2015 he also greeted another group of which I was the guiding historian—Colonel Don Patton's World War II History Roundtable from Minneapolis–St. Paul, Minnesota. I count Gianfranco as one of my dear Italian friends—even though we still don't speak each other's language.

There are few accounts by and about German soldiers who served at (and survived) Anzio. But another good Italian friend, Silvano Casaldi of Nettuno, founder of the Nettuno War Museum, located in an old beachfront castle, allowed me access to a number of written accounts that were provided to him by German veterans of Anzio. Another Italian who needs to be thanked is Gregory Paolucci, who has valiantly spearheaded the effort to preserve Kesselring's underground headquarters at Monte Soratte, north of Rome, and Pasqualino Nuti, who allowed me to excerpt passages from his memoir (in Italian) that detailed the life of his family, caught up in the fighting for their hometown of Aprilia. And since my command of the Italian language is about one on a scale of one hundred, I also must thank Dr. Maury Kitzman here in Denver for his ability to translate.

In Britain I wish to express my appreciation to Major Peter Lough and Richard O'Sullivan of the London Irish Rifles Association for all the kindnesses and assistance shown to me (and their permission to quote extensively from the unit history), as well as Dominic Butler at the Lancashire Infantry Museum.

And, of course, my new good friend, ninety-two-year-old Fred Mason, a veteran of the 2nd North Staffs, answered my endless string of questions and provided many keen insights about the life of a British soldier on the front lines—and provided many humorous e-mails as well.

Others with a link to the 45th Division are John Kelly, president of the division veterans' association, and Rob Riley, vice president of the 45th Infantry Division Re-creation Association, who allowed me to share many of the veterans' stories contained on their website, www .45thdivision.org. At the outstanding 45th Infantry Division Museum in Oklahoma City, I value the long friendship and working relationship I have with the curator, Major (U.S. Army, retired) Mike Gonzales and his staff, who extended to me every courtesy. I also appreciate Aaron Elson allowing me to quote from his interview with the irrepressible Murray Levine, 45th Infantry Division.

My gratitude also goes out to Marion Chard, a most enthusiastic daughter of a 36th Engineer Combat Regiment veteran and webmaster (webmistress?) of an excellent website (www.6thcorpscombatengineer-scom) devoted to the unit. (My wife's late uncle was a member of that regiment at Anzio; unfortunately, he left no papers regarding his experiences there.)

I thank the family of James Safrit for allowing me to quote from his memoirs, and also Joseph Schorer for permission to quote from his mother's memoir, *A Half Acre of Hell.*

I must also thank Dr. Richard J. Sommers, recently retired as senior historian of the U.S. Army Heritage and Education Center (AHEC), U.S. Army Military History Institute, and a professor at the U.S. Army War College in Carlisle, Pennsylvania, for more than sixty years of friendship and a shared love of military history. He did much to guide me in my research at the MHI. I also greatly appreciate the assistance of many of the other staffers at AHEC. I thank Susan Strange for all her efforts to locate and scan photographs at the U.S. National Archives and Records Administration in College Park, Maryland. This list of deserving people would be incomplete without two big salutes to my agent, Jody Rein, and my incomparable editor Bob Pigeon, along with Amber Morris and Annette Wenda at Da Capo Press. Without their guidance and expertise, this tale would not have been told.

I would be remiss if I failed to thank editors Mark Ellenbarger and Trent Riley for allowing me to quote from 45th Division veteran Brummett Echohawk's *Drawing Fire*, which is being published by the Univesity of Kansas Press.

Finally, there are the many friends whose encouragement over the years has kept my nose to the military history grindstone and my fingers to the keyboard—Colonel Don Patton, Major Adam Morgan of the Colorado National Guard, Terry and Carlie Barnhart, Rick and Pam Rolph, Ken and Paula Carpenter, and, of course, my wife, Dr. Mary Ann Watson, without whose love and support my career as a historian would not have been possible.

INDEX

Note: Commands and forces are noted by order of battle; regiments and battalions are listed under the divisions to which they were assigned.